STUDENT TESTED, FACULTY A

THE SELL SOLUTION

Special Note To Students

It is important to begin reading this text with one thing in mind: *This business course does not have to be difficult*. We have done everything possible to eliminate the problems that students encounter in a typical class. All the features in each chapter have been evaluated and recommended by instructors with years of teaching experience. In addition, business students were asked to critique each chapter component. Based on this feedback, the text includes the following features:

- *Learning objectives* appear at the beginning of each chapter.
- *Inside Business* is a chapter-opening case that highlights how successful companies do business on a day-to-day basis.
- *Margin notes* are used throughout the text to reinforce both learning objectives and key terms.
- *Boxed features* highlight how both employees and entrepreneurs can be successful.
- *Spotlight* features highlight interesting facts about business and society and often provide a real-world example of an important concept within a chapter.

Visually Engaging Textbook + **Online Study Tools** + **Tear-Out Review Cards** + **Interactive Ebook**

STUDENT RESOURCES:

- Interactive Ebook
- Interactive Quizzing
- Flashcards
- Games
- Glossary
- PowerPoint Slides
- Role-play Videos
- Chapter Cases and Role-Plays
- Continuing Case

Students sign in at **www.nelson.com/student**

INSTRUCTOR RESOURCES:

- Test Bank
- PowerPoint Slides
- First-day-of-class Instructions
- Instructor's Manual
- Instructor Prep Cards

Instructors sign in at **www.nelson.com/instructor**

"The online learning is great and the review cards in the back make test review easy!"

– Kyle McConnell, Student

SELL, Second Canadian Edition

by Thomas N. Ingram; Raymond A. Avila; Charles H. Schwepker Jr; Michael R. Williams; and Kirby L. J. Shannahan

Vice President, Editorial Higher Education:
Anne Williams

Publisher:
Amie Plourde

Marketing Manager:
David Stratton

Developmental Editor:
Suzanne Simpson-Millar

Photo Researcher:
Carrie McGregor

Permissions Coordinator:
Carrie McGregor

Production Project Manager:
Jaime Smith

Production Service:
Integra Software Services Pvt. Ltd.

Copy Editor:
Kelli Howey

Proofreader:
Integra Software Services Pvt. Ltd.

Indexer:
Integra Software Services Pvt. Ltd.

Design Director:
Ken Phipps

Managing Designer:
Franca Amore

Interior Design:
Jennifer Leung

Cover Design:
Jennifer Leung

Cover Image:
Kathryn Hollinrake

Compositor:
Integra Software Services Pvt. Ltd.

Printed and bound in the United States of America
1 2 3 4 19 18 17 16 15

For more information contact Nelson Education Ltd., 1120 Birchmount Road, Toronto, Ontario, M1K 5G4. Or you can visit our Internet site at http://www.nelson.com

Library and Archives Canada Cataloguing in Publication

Ingram, Thomas N., author

Sell / Thomas N. Ingram, Raymond A. Avila, Charles H. Schwepker, Michael R. Williams, and Kirby Shannahan. — Second Canadian edition.

Includes index.

ISBN 978-0-17-653090-7 (pbk.)

1. Selling—Textbooks. 2. Sales management—Textbooks. I. Title.

HF5438.25.S44 2015

658.85 C2014-904588-3

ISBN-13: 978-0-17-653090-7
ISBN-10: 0-17-653090-8

DEDICATION

For Rachelle, Simon, and Adrienne.

—KS

ACKNOWLEDGMENTS

This project could not have been completed without the assistance, support, guidance, mentorship, and friendship of many people. First, I would like to thank Drs. Thomas Ingram and Raymond Laforge for their initial support and faith in me as I embarked on this project. I would also like to thank my research assistant, Brittany McLean. Your hard work and dedication allowed this project to succeed, and for that, I thank you. A big thank-you also goes to Suzanne Simpson Millar for keeping me on track every step of the way. Dawn Hunter also deserves a special note of thanks for her superb editing. A special note of appreciation is also extended to Nelson Education Inc., and especially to Amie Plourde and Imoinda Romain for their dedication to the project. And thank you to Dr. Alan Bush, whose ongoing support has guided me through my career. Finally, for her unwavering support and invaluable advice, I thank my wife, best friend, and research partner, Dr. Rachelle Shannahan.

BRIEF CONTENTS

CONTENTS

© Barry Rosenthal/Taxi/Getty

3 Understanding Buyers 55

© Finite Digital

4 Communication Skills 93

© khz/Shutterstock

© CJG - Technology/Alamy

6 Planning Sales Dialogues and Presentations 139

© Fuse/Jupiter Images

7 Sales Dialogue 163

8 Addressing Concerns and Earning Commitment 187

9 Expanding Customer Relationships 209

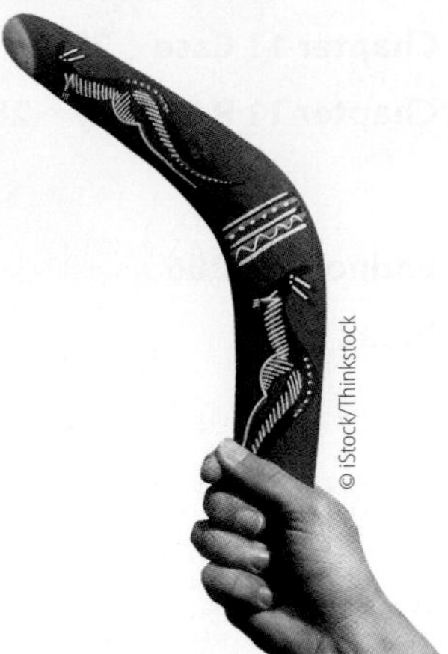
© iStock/Thinkstock

10 Adding Value 233

11 Sales Management and Sales 2.0 259

© Dmitriy Shironosov/Shutterstock

To succeed in sales,

talk *with* the customer, not *at* the customer

what do you think?

Successful salespeople must be very aggressive in their attempts to convince buyers to make purchases.

1 2 3 4 5 6 7

strongly disagree strongly agree

I

Overview of Personal Selling

After completing this chapter, you should be able to

1-1 Define personal selling and describe its unique characteristics as a marketing communications tool.

1-2 Distinguish between transaction-focused traditional selling and trust-based relationship selling, with the latter focusing on customer value and sales dialogue.

1-3 Describe the evolution of personal selling from ancient times to the modern era.

1-4 Explain the contributions of personal selling to society, business firms, and customers.

1-5 Discuss five alternative approaches to personal selling.

1-6 Understand the sales process as a series of interrelated steps.

Introduction

In recent years there has been a profound evolutionary shift in the way goods and services are sold. Today, customers are far more educated and sophisticated, with access to more information than ever before. And we all operate in an expanding global economy, facing intensified competition in almost every industry and sector. Therefore, historical approaches to sales are no longer effective.

Until recently, we all believed that the fundamental role of sales representatives was to get people to buy your product or service. But today, we finally realize that the single biggest key to sales success is to actually stop selling altogether. In today's marketplace, people (at home and in business) don't want to be "sold." In fact, they resist it strongly. Instead, customers want to "buy" independently, or work with business "partners." In order to succeed, we must break the historical push-pull dance that happens between salespeople and customers (sales tries to convince, and customers try to resist).

Today, professional selling requires a completely different approach than historically employed. It involves shifting focus away from what *you* want (the sale) and instead becoming entirely focused on the *customer*. Sales professionals must now adopt a truly value-based approach, whereby their mission is to add as much value as possible to the customer's bottom line.

The Canadian Professional Sales Association (CPSA) is one of the oldest associations in Canada. It was officially incorporated as a fraternal benefits society known as the Commercial Travellers Association by a special act of Parliament in 1874. In 1991 the association changed its name to the Canadian Professional Sales Association and updated its mission "to be the leader in developing and serving sales professionals."

Today the CPSA boasts a membership of 30,000 across Canada and has four key areas of focus: (1) developing salespeople through its comprehensive suite of offline and online sales training and coaching programs; (2) certifying salespeople through Canada's only government-endorsed designation: CSP, Certified Sales Professional; (3) providing extensive sales resources for members through its online Knowledge Centre; and (4) offering a comprehensive member benefit cost-saving program, the hallmark of which is its business travel cost-saving program for hotel stays, car rentals, and other related travel services.

—Harvey Copeman, President and CEO of CPSA

1-1 Personal Selling Defined

The successful professional salesperson is likely a better listener than a talker; is oriented more toward developing long-term relationships with customers than using high-pressure, short-term sales techniques; and has the skills and patience to endure lengthy, complex sales processes. Today's salesperson strives to deliver relevant presentations based on unique customer needs, and meeting those needs requires teamwork between salespeople and others in the organization.

Personal selling, an important part of marketing, relies heavily on interpersonal interactions between buyers and sellers to initiate, develop, and enhance customer relationships. The interpersonal communications dimension sets personal selling apart from other marketing communications such as advertising and sales promotion, which are directed at mass markets. Personal selling is also distinguished from direct marketing and electronic marketing in that salespeople are talking with buyers before, during, and after the sale. This contact allows for a high degree of immediate customer feedback, which becomes a strong advantage of personal selling over most other forms of marketing communications.

Although advertising is a far more visible activity, personal selling is the most important part of marketing communications for most businesses. This is particularly true in business-to-business marketing, in which more is spent on personal selling than on advertising, sales promotion, publicity, or public relations. In this book, we typically describe personal selling in this business-to-business context, in which a salesperson or sales team interacts with one or more individuals from another organization.

personal selling An important part of marketing that relies heavily on interpersonal interactions between buyers and sellers to initiate, develop, and enhance customer relationships.

trust-based relationship selling A form of personal selling that requires that salespeople earn customer trust and that their selling strategy meets customer needs and contributes to the creation, communication, and delivery of customer value.

customer value Customers' perception of what they get for what they have to give up; for example, benefits from buying a product in exchange for money paid.

1-2 Trust-Based Relationship Selling

Trust-based relationship selling (a form of personal selling) requires that salespeople earn customer trust and that their selling strategy meets customer needs and contributes to the creation, communication, and delivery of customer value. As illustrated in Exhibit 1.1, trust-based relationship selling is quite different from traditional selling. Rather than trying to maximize sales in the short run (also called a transaction focus), trust-based relationship selling focuses on solving customer problems, providing opportunities, and adding value to the customer's business over an extended period. Chapter 2 will provide detailed coverage of how salespeople can earn buyers' trust.

IMPORTANCE OF CUSTOMER VALUE

As personal selling continues to evolve, it is more important than ever that salespeople focus on delivering customer value while initiating, developing, and enhancing customer relationships. What constitutes value will likely vary from one customer to the next depending on the customer's situation, needs, and priorities, but **customer value** will always be determined by customers' perception of what they get in exchange for what they have to give up. In the simplest situations, customers buy a product in exchange for money. In most situations, however, customers define value in a more complex manner, by addressing such questions as these:

- Does the salesperson do a good job in helping me make or save money?
- Is this salesperson dependable?
- Does this salesperson help me achieve my strategic priorities?
- Is the salesperson's company easy to work with (i.e., hassle-free)?
- Does the salesperson enlist others in his or her organization when needed to create value for me?
- Does the sales representative understand my business and my industry?

Personal selling also recognizes that customers would like to be heard when expressing what they want suppliers and salespeople to provide for them. In days gone by, personal selling often consisted of

EXHIBIT 1.1

Comparison of Transaction-Focused Traditional Selling with Trust-Based Relationship Selling

	Transaction-Focused Traditional Selling	Trust-Based Relationship Selling
Typical skills required	Selling skills, e.g., finding prospects, making sales presentations	Selling skills Information gathering Listening and questioning Strategic problem solving Creating and demonstrating unique, value-added solutions Teambuilding and teamwork
Primary focus	The salesperson and the selling firm	The customer and the customer's customers
Desired outcomes	Closed sales, order volume	Trust, joint planning, mutual benefits, enhanced profits
Role of salesperson	Make calls and close sales	Business consultant and long-term ally Key player in the customer's business
Nature of communications with customers	One-way, from salesperson to customer Pushing products	Two-way and collaborative Strive for dialogue with the customer
Degree of salesperson's involvement in customer's decision-making process	Isolated from customer's decision-making process	Actively involved in customer's decision-making process
Knowledge required	Product knowledge Competitive knowledge Identifying opportunities Account strategies	Product knowledge Selling company resources Competitive knowledge Identifying opportunities General business and industry knowledge and insight Customer's products, competition, and customers Account strategies Costs
Postsale follow-up	Little or none: move on to conquer next customer	Continued follow-through to • ensure customer satisfaction • keep customer informed • add customer value • manage opportunities

sales dialogue Business conversations between buyers and sellers that occur as salespeople attempt to initiate, develop, and enhance customer relationships. Sales dialogue should be customer focused and have a clear purpose.

delivering a message or making a pitch. That approach was typically associated with a "product push" strategy in which customers were pressured to buy without much appreciation for their real needs. Today, sales organizations are far more interested in establishing a productive dialogue with customers than in simply pitching products that customers may or may not want or need. In our highly competitive world, professional buyers have little tolerance for aggressive, pushy salespeople.

Customers want to be heard loud and clear when expressing what they want from suppliers and salespeople.

© Janet Kimber/Getty Images

Successful salespeople must be able to make sales presentations, but they must also be able to engage customers in sales dialogue, or business conversations that build customer relationships.

IMPORTANCE OF SALES DIALOGUE

Sales dialogue refers to the series of conversations between buyers and sellers that take place over time in an attempt to build relationships. These conversations have several purposes:

- To determine whether a prospective customer should be targeted for further sales attention
- To clarify the prospective customer's situation and buying processes
- To discover the prospective customer's unique needs and requirements
- To determine the prospective customer's strategic priorities
- To communicate how the sales organization can create and deliver customer value
- To negotiate a business deal and earn a commitment from the customer
- To make the customer aware of additional opportunities to increase the value received
- To assess sales organization and salesperson performance so that customer value is continually improved

As you can see, sales dialogue is far more than idle chitchat. The business conversations that constitute the dialogue are customer-focused and have a clear purpose; otherwise, there would be a high probability of wasting both the customer's and the salesperson's time, which no one can afford in today's business environment. Whether the sales dialogue features a question-and-answer format, a conversation dominated by the buyer conveying information and requirements, or a formal sales presentation in which the salesperson responds to buyer feedback throughout, the key idea is that both parties participate in and benefit from the process.

Throughout this course, you will learn about new technologies and techniques that have contributed to the evolution of the practice of personal selling. This chapter provides an overview of personal selling, affording insight into the operating rationale of today's salespeople and sales managers. It also describes different approaches to personal selling and presents the sales process as a series of interrelated steps. The appendix at the end of the chapter discusses several important aspects of sales careers, including types of selling jobs and characteristics and skills needed for sales success. In the highly competitive, complex international business community, personal selling and sales management have never played more critical roles.

1-3 Evolution of Personal Selling

Ancient Greek history documents selling as an exchange activity, and the term *salesman* appears in the writings of Plato.[1] However, true salespeople—those who earned a living only by selling—did not exist in any sizable number until the Industrial Revolution in England, from the mid-eighteenth century to the mid-nineteenth century. Before this time, traders, merchants, and artisans filled the selling function. These predecessors of contemporary marketers were generally viewed with contempt because deception was often used in the sale of goods.[2]

In the later phase of the Middle Ages, the first door-to-door salesperson appeared in the form of the peddler. Peddlers collected produce from local farmers, sold it to townspeople, and, in turn, bought manufactured goods in town for subsequent sale in rural areas.[3] Like many other early salespeople, they performed other important marketing functions, too—in this case, purchasing, assembling, sorting, and redistributing goods.

INDUSTRIAL REVOLUTION ERA

With the onset of the Industrial Revolution in the middle of the eighteenth century, the economic justification for salespeople gained momentum. Local economies were no longer self-sufficient, and as intercity and international trade began to flourish, economies of scale in production spurred the growth of mass markets in geographically dispersed areas. The continual need to reach new customers in these dispersed markets called for an increasing number of salespeople.

POST–INDUSTRIAL REVOLUTION ERA

By the early nineteenth century, personal selling was well established in England but just beginning to develop in North America.[4] This situation changed noticeably after 1850, and by the later part of the century salespeople were a well-established part of business practice.

canned sales presentation Sales presentations that include scripted sales calls, memorized presentations, and automated presentations.

At the dawning of the twentieth century, an exciting time in the economic history of North America, it became apparent that marketing, especially advertising and personal selling, would play a crucial role in the rapid transition of the economy from an agrarian base to one of mass production and efficient transportation.

Glimpses of the lives of salespeople in the early 1900s, gained from the literature of that period, reveal an adventuresome, aggressive, and valuable group of employees often working on the frontier of new markets. Already, however, the independent maverick salespeople who had blazed the early trails to new markets were beginning to disappear. One clear indication that selling was becoming a more structured activity was the development of a **canned sales presentation** by John H. Patterson, of the National Cash Register Company (NCR). This presentation, a script to guide NCR salespeople on how to sell cash registers, was based on the premise that salespeople are not "born, but rather they are made."[5]

WAR AND DEPRESSION ERA

The 30 years from 1915 to 1945 were marked by three overwhelming events: two world wars and the Great Depression. Because economic activity concentrated on the war efforts, new sales methods did not develop quickly. During the Great Depression, however, business firms, starved for sales volume, often employed aggressive salespeople to produce badly needed revenue. Then, with renewed prosperity in the post–World War II era, salespeople emerged as important employees for an increasing number of firms that were beginning to realize the benefits of research-based integrated marketing programs.

PROFESSIONALISM: THE MODERN ERA

In the middle of the 1940s, personal selling became more professional. Buyers not only began to demand more, but also grew intolerant of high-pressure, fast-talking

Sales is becoming more professional as indicated by a growing knowledge base with publications and training material available from academics, corporate trainers and sales executives, and professional organizations.

salespeople, preferring instead a well-informed, customer-oriented salesperson.

An emphasis on **sales professionalism** is the keynote of the current era. The term has varied meanings, but in this context we use it to mean a customer-oriented approach that uses truthful, nonmanipulative tactics to satisfy the long-term needs of both the customer and the selling firm. The effective salesperson of today is no longer a mere presenter of information and now must stand equipped to respond to a variety of customer needs before, during, and after the sale. In addition, salespeople must be able to work effectively with others in their organizations to meet or exceed customer expectations.

sales professionalism
A customer-oriented approach that uses truthful, nonmanipulative tactics to satisfy the long-term needs of both the customer and the selling firm.

Although many business-to-business salespeople have considerable decision-making autonomy, others have very little. Public trust could be improved by a widely accepted certification program similar to the CA or CMA designations for accountants. At present, however, very few salespeople have professional certification credentials, and public trust in certification programs is modest. Thus, the results are mixed as to whether the sales profession meets this professional criterion.

The final area in which sales needs to improve is in adherence to a uniform ethical code. Although many companies have ethical codes and some professional organizations have ethical codes for salespeople, there is no universal code of ethics with a mechanism for dealing with violators. Until such a code is developed and widely accepted in business, some members of society will not view sales as a true profession.

Whether or not sales is viewed as a true profession, comparable to law and medicine, salespeople can benefit tremendously from embracing high ethical standards, participating in professional organizations, and working from a continually evolving knowledge base. In so doing, they not only will be more effective but also will help advance sales as a true profession.

Evolution is inevitable as tomorrow's professional salesperson responds to a more complex, dynamic environment. And the increased sophistication of buyers and of new technologies will demand more from the next generation of salespeople. Exhibit 1.2 summarizes some of the likely events of the future.*[6]

1-4 Contributions of Personal Selling

As mentioned earlier in this chapter, more money is spent on personal selling than on any other form of marketing communications. Salespeople are usually well compensated, and salesforces of major companies often number in the thousands. For example, Xerox has 15,000 salespeople, Johnson & Johnson has 8,500, and Coca-Cola has 9,000.[7]

We now take a look at how this investment is justified by reviewing the contributions of personal selling to society in general, to the employing firm, and to customers.

---

*Pages 7–8: From Ingram/Laforge/Avila/Schwepker. *Professional Selling*, 4E. © 2008 South-Western, a part of Cengage Learning, Inc. Reproduced by permission. www.cengage.com/permissions.

EXHIBIT 1.2

Continued Evolution of Personal Selling

Change	Salesforce Response
Intensified competition	More emphasis on developing and maintaining trust-based, long-term customer relationships More focus on creating and delivering customer value
More emphasis on improving sales productivity	Increased use of technology (e.g., laptop computers, electronic mail, databases, customer relationship management software) Increased use of lower-cost-per-contact methods (e.g., telemarketing for some customers) More emphasis on profitability (e.g., gross margin) objectives
Fragmentation of traditional customer bases	Sales specialists for specific customer types Multiple sales channels (e.g., major accounts programs, telemarketing, electronic networks) Globalization of sales efforts
Customers dictating quality standards and inventory/shipping procedures to be met by vendors	Team selling Salesforce compensation sometimes based on customer satisfaction and team performance More emphasis on sales dialogues rather than on sales pitches
Demand for in-depth, specialized knowledge as an input to purchase decisions	Team selling More emphasis on customer-oriented sales training

SALESPEOPLE AND SOCIETY

Salespeople contribute to their nation's economic growth in two basic ways: They act as stimuli for economic transactions, and they further the diffusion of innovation.

Salespeople as Economic Stimuli

Salespeople are expected to stimulate action in the business world—hence the term **economic stimuli**. In a fluctuating economy, salespeople make valuable contributions by assisting in recovery cycles and helping to sustain periods of relative prosperity. As the world economic system deals with such issues as increased globalization of business, more emphasis on customer satisfaction, and building competitiveness through quality improvement programs, it is expected that salespeople will be recognized as a key force in executing the appropriate strategies and tactics necessary for survival and growth.

Salespeople and Diffusion of Innovation

Salespeople play a critical role in the **diffusion of innovation**, the process whereby new products, services, and ideas are distributed to the members of society. Consumers who are likely to be early adopters of an innovation often rely on salespeople as a primary source of information. Frequently, well-informed, specialized salespeople provide useful information to potential consumers who then purchase from a lower-cost outlet. The role of salespeople in the diffusion of industrial products and services is particularly crucial. Imagine trying to purchase a companywide computer system without the assistance of a competent salesperson or sales team!

While acting as an agent of innovation, the salesperson invariably encounters a strong resistance to change in the later stages of the diffusion process. The status quo seems to be extremely satisfactory

economic stimuli
Something that stimulates or incites activity in the economy.

diffusion of innovation
The process whereby new products, services, and ideas are distributed to the members of society.

revenue producers A role fulfilled by salespeople that brings in revenue or income to a firm or company.

to many parties, even though, in the long run, change is necessary for continued progress or survival. By encouraging the adoption of innovative products and services, salespeople may indeed be making a positive contribution to society.

SALESPEOPLE AND THE EMPLOYING FIRM

Because salespeople are in direct contact with the all-important customer, they can make valuable contributions to their employers. Salespeople contribute to their firms as revenue producers, as sources of market research and feedback, and as candidates for management positions.

Salespeople as Revenue Producers

Salespeople occupy the somewhat unique role of **revenue producers** in their firms. Consequently, they usually feel the brunt of that pressure along with the managers in the firm. Although accountants and financial staff are concerned with profitability in bottom-line terms, salespeople are constantly reminded of their responsibility to achieve a healthy "top line" on the profit and loss statement. This should not suggest that salespeople are concerned only with sales revenue and not with overall profitability. Indeed, salespeople are increasingly responsible for improving profitability, not only by producing sales revenues but also by improving the productivity of their actions.

Along with the management of a firm, salespeople occupy the somewhat unique role of revenue producers in their firms.

© Mark Evans/E+/Getty

Market Research and Feedback

Because salespeople spend so much time in direct contact with their customers, it is only logical that they would play an important role in market research and in providing feedback to their firms. For example, entertainment and home products retailer Best Buy relies heavily on feedback from its sales associates in what it calls a customer-centricity initiative, which places the customer at the centre of its marketing strategy. Feedback from sales associates helps Best Buy offer tailored products to specific customer segments, design appealing in-store merchandising formats, increase sales volume for in-home services, and improve the effectiveness of customer-support call centres. Results of the customer-centricity program have been so positive that Best Buy is rapidly increasing the number of participating stores as it tries to fend off Walmart and other major competitors.[8]

The emergence of communications technologies gives salespeople and their organizations more opportunities to gather customer feedback. For example, retailers and service providers routinely use Facebook to solicit customer feedback. In the business-to-business sector, buyers are increasingly sharing their opinions, identifying problems, and asking for vendor recommendations via Twitter and LinkedIn. Customer relationship management programs such as Chatter by Salesforce.com are incorporating social media to improve collaboration between customers and the sales organization.

Some would argue that salespeople are not trained as market researchers, or that salespeople's time could be better used than in research and feedback activities. Many firms, however, refute this argument by finding numerous ways to capitalize on the salesforce as a reservoir of ideas. It is not an exaggeration to say that many firms have concluded they cannot afford to operate in the absence of salesforce feedback and research.

Salespeople as Future Managers

In recent years, marketing and sales personnel have been in strong demand for upper management positions. Recognizing the need for a top management trained in sales, many firms use the sales job as an entry-level position that provides a foundation for future assignments. As progressive firms continue to emphasize customer orientation as a basic operating concept, it is only natural that salespeople who have learned how to meet customer needs will be good candidates for management jobs.

SALESPEOPLE AND THE CUSTOMER

Given the increasing importance of building trust with customers and an emphasis on establishing and maintaining long-term relationships, it is imperative that salespeople are honest and candid with customers. Salespeople must also be able to demonstrate knowledge of their products and services, especially as they compare competitive offerings. Customers also expect salespeople to be knowledgeable about market opportunities and relevant business trends that may affect a customer's business. There has been a longstanding expectation that salespeople need to be the key contact for the buyer, who expects that they will coordinate activities within the selling firm to deliver maximum value to the customer.

The overall conclusion is that buyers expect salespeople to contribute to the success of the buyer's firm. Buyers value the information furnished by salespeople, and they expect salespeople to act in a highly professional manner.[9] (See "An Ethical Dilemma" for a scenario in which the salesperson must think about where to draw the line in sharing information with customers.)

An Ethical Dilemma

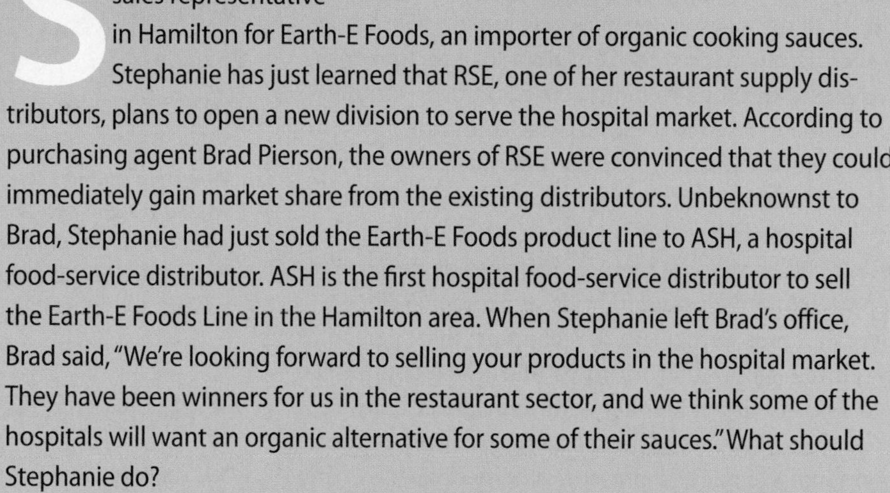
© OJO Images/Getty

Stephanie Miles is a sales representative in Hamilton for Earth-E Foods, an importer of organic cooking sauces. Stephanie has just learned that RSE, one of her restaurant supply distributors, plans to open a new division to serve the hospital market. According to purchasing agent Brad Pierson, the owners of RSE were convinced that they could immediately gain market share from the existing distributors. Unbeknownst to Brad, Stephanie had just sold the Earth-E Foods product line to ASH, a hospital food-service distributor. ASH is the first hospital food-service distributor to sell the Earth-E Foods Line in the Hamilton area. When Stephanie left Brad's office, Brad said, "We're looking forward to selling your products in the hospital market. They have been winners for us in the restaurant sector, and we think some of the hospitals will want an organic alternative for some of their sauces." What should Stephanie do?

a) Tell her contact at ASH about the RSE plan to enter the hospital market to build her reputation as a valued source of information.
b) Treat the news of RSE's expansion plan as confidential information and not share it with ASH or any other customers.
c) Avoid bringing up RSE's expansion plans in conversation, but discuss it with her contact at ASH and other customers who mention it.

As salespeople serve their customers, they simultaneously serve their employers and society. When the interests of these two groups conflict, the salesperson can be caught in the middle. By learning to resolve these conflicts as a routine part of their jobs, salespeople further contribute to developing a business system based on progress through problem solving. Sales ethics will be discussed in detail in Chapter 2.

As salespeople serve their customers, they simultaneously serve their employers and society.

1-5 Alternative Personal Selling Approaches

In this section, we take a closer look at alternative approaches to personal selling that professionals may choose from to best interact with their customers. Some of these approaches are simple; others are more sophisticated and require that the salesperson play a strategic role to use them successfully. More than four decades ago, four basic approaches to personal selling were identified: stimulus-response, mental states, need satisfaction, and problem solving.[10] Since that time, another approach to personal selling, termed consultative selling, has gained popularity. All five approaches to selling are practised today. Furthermore, many salespeople use elements of more than one approach in their own hybrids of personal selling.

Recall from earlier in the chapter that personal selling differs from other forms of marketing communications because it is personal communication delivered by employees or agents of the sales organization. Because the personal element is present, salespeople have the opportunity to alter their sales messages and behaviours during a sales presentation or as they encounter unique situations and customers. This method is referred to as **adaptive selling**. Because salespeople often encounter buyers with different personalities, communication styles, needs, and goals, adaptive selling is an important concept. Adaptive selling is prevalent with the need satisfaction, problem-solving, and consultative approaches. It is less prevalent with mental states selling and essentially nonexistent with stimulus-response selling.

© Barry Rosenthal/Taxi/Getty

Adaptive selling requires that salespeople alter their sales messages and behaviours during sales presentations or as they encounter unique sales situations or customers. Selling at a trade show is quite different from selling in a customer's office.

STIMULUS-RESPONSE SELLING

Of the five views of personal selling, **stimulus-response selling** is the simplest. The theoretical background for this approach originated in early experiments with animal behaviour. The key idea is that various stimuli can elicit predictable responses. Salespeople furnish the stimuli from a repertoire of words and actions designed to produce the desired response. This approach to selling is illustrated in Figure 1.1.

adaptive selling The ability of salespeople to alter their sales messages and behaviours during a sales presentation or as they encounter different sales situations and different customers.

stimulus-response selling An approach to selling in which the key idea is that various stimuli can elicit predictable responses from customers. Salespeople furnish the stimuli from a repertoire of words and actions designed to produce the desired response.

FIGURE 1.1
Stimulus-Response Approach to Selling

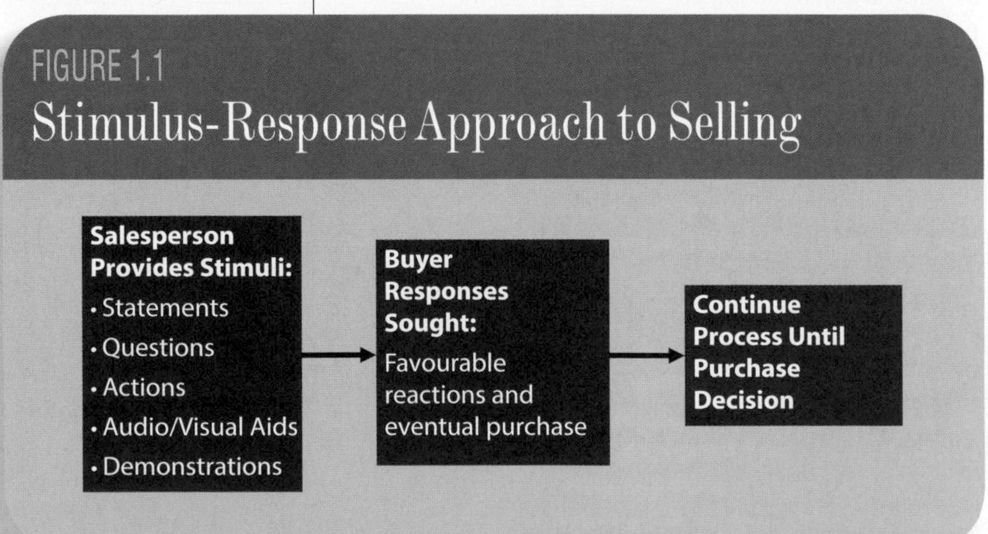

The salesperson attempts to gain favourable responses from the customer by providing stimuli, or cues, to influence the buyer. After the customer has been properly conditioned, the salesperson tries to secure a positive purchase decision.

An example of the stimulus-response view of selling would be **continued affirmation**, a method in which a series of questions or statements furnished by the salesperson is designed to condition the prospective buyer to answering "yes" time after time—until, it is hoped, he or she will be inclined to say "yes" to the entire sales proposition. This method is often used by telemarketing personnel, who rely on comprehensive sales scripts read or delivered from memory.

Stimulus-response sales strategies, particularly when implemented with a canned sales presentation, have some advantages for the seller. The sales message can be structured in a logical order. Questions and objections from the buyer can usually be anticipated and addressed before they are magnified during buyer–seller interaction. Inexperienced salespeople can rely on stimulus-response sales methods in some settings, and this may eventually contribute to sales expertise.

The limitations of stimulus-response methods, however, can be severe, especially if the salesperson is dealing with a professional buyer. Most buyers like to take an active role in sales dialogue, and the stimulus-response approach calls for the salesperson to dominate the flow of conversation. The lack of flexibility in this approach is also a disadvantage, as buyer responses and unforeseen interruptions may neutralize or damage the effectiveness of the stimuli.

Considering the net effects of this method's advantages and disadvantages, it appears most suitable for relatively unimportant purchase decisions, when time is severely constrained and when professional buyers are not the prospects. As consumers in general become more sophisticated, this approach will become more problematic.

EXHIBIT 1.3

Mental States View of Selling

Mental State	Sales Step	Critical Sales Task
Curiosity	Attention	Get prospects excited, and then you get them to like you
Interest	Interest	Interview: needs and wants
Conviction	Conviction	"What's in it for me?" Product—"Will it do what I want it to do?" Price—"Is it worth it?" "The hassle of change" "Cheaper elsewhere" Peers—"What will others think of it?" Priority—"Do I need it now?" (sense of urgency)
Desire	Desire	Overcome their stall
Action	Close	Alternative choice close: which, not if!

MENTAL STATES SELLING

Mental states selling, or the *formula approach* to personal selling, assumes that the buying process for most buyers is essentially identical and that buyers can be led through certain mental states, or steps, in the buying process. These mental states are typically referred to as **AIDA** (attention, interest, desire, and action). Appropriate sales messages provide a transition from one mental state to the next. The mental states method is illustrated in Exhibit 1.3.[11] Note that this version includes "conviction" as an intermediate stage between interest and desire. Such minor variations are commonplace in different renditions of this approach to selling.

As with stimulus-response selling, the mental states approach relies on a highly structured sales presentation. The salesperson does most of the talking, as feedback from the

continued affirmation An example of stimulus-response selling in which a series of questions or statements furnished by the salesperson is designed to condition the prospective buyer to answering "yes" time after time, until, it is hoped, he or she will be inclined to say "yes" to the entire sales proposition.

mental states selling An approach to personal selling that assumes that the buying process for most buyers is essentially identical and that buyers can be led through certain mental states, or steps, in the buying process; also called the formula approach.

AIDA An acronym for the various mental states salespeople must lead their customers through when using mental states selling: attention, interest, desire, and action.

prospect could be disruptive to the flow of the presentation.

A positive feature of this method is that it forces the salesperson to plan the sales presentation before calling on the customer. It also helps the salesperson recognize that timing is an important element in the purchase decision process and that careful listening is necessary to determine which stage the buyer is in at any given point.

A problem with the mental states method is that it is difficult to determine which state a prospect is in. Sometimes a prospect is spanning two mental states or moving back and forth between two states during the sales presentation. Consequently, the heavy guidance structure the salesperson implements may be inappropriate, confusing, and even counterproductive to sales effectiveness. We should also note that this method is not customer-oriented. Although the salesperson tailors the presentation to each customer somewhat, this is done by noting customer mental states rather than needs. (See "An Ethical Dilemma" for a situation in which the salesperson is contemplating the movement of the prospect into the "action" stage.)

An Ethical Dilemma

Kelly Toms sells corporate sponsorship packages for the Bellview Blasters, a minor league hockey team in New England. The packages include advertising in game programs throughout the season, signage in the arena, and a block of season tickets. The packages range in price from $5,000 to $10,000, depending on the size of the ads and signs and how many season tickets are included. Kelly's sales manager is pushing the salesforce to sell as many $10,000 packages as possible. Kelly tries to match the sponsorship package to the budget and needs of each potential customer rather than pushing the $10,000 packages. Her sales manager is not happy and told Kelly, "You need to get with the program and max your sales of the $10,000 packages. This is a good deal for sponsors. What's the matter—don't you believe in your product?" What should Kelly do?

a) Be a loyal employee and follow her manager's directive.
b) Try to convince her manager that a customer-oriented approach will be best over the long run.
c) Tell her manager that she will try to sell more $10,000 packages, but continue her current sales approach.

NEED SATISFACTION SELLING

Need satisfaction selling is based on the notion that the customer is buying to satisfy a particular need or set of needs. This approach is shown in Figure 1.2. It is the salesperson's task to identify the need to be met and

need satisfaction selling An approach to selling based on the notion that the customer is buying to satisfy a particular need or set of needs.

FIGURE 1.2
Need Satisfaction Approach to Selling

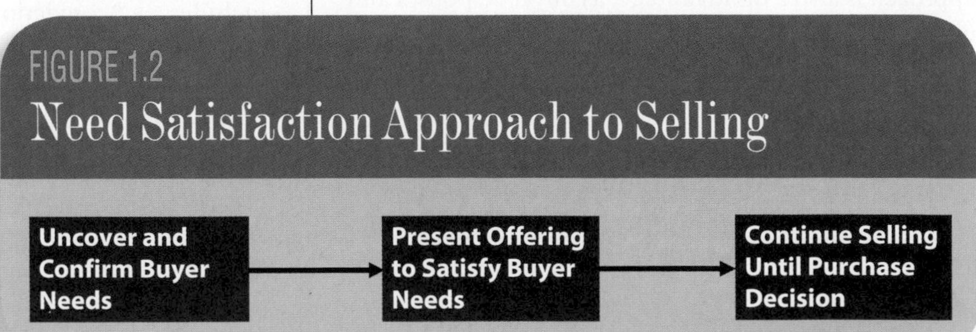

The salesperson attempts to uncover customer needs that are related to the product or service her or she is offering. This may require extensive questioning in the early stages of the sales process. After confirming the buyer's needs, the salesperson proceeds with a presentation based on how the offering can meet those needs.

then help the buyer meet that need. Unlike the mental states and stimulus-response methods, this method focuses on the customer rather than on the salesperson. The salesperson uses a questioning, probing tactic to uncover important buyer needs. Customer responses dominate the early portion of the sales interaction, and only after relevant needs have been established does the salesperson begin to relate how his or her offering can satisfy these needs.

Customers seem to appreciate this selling method and are often willing to spend considerable time in preliminary meetings to define needs before a sales presentation or written sales proposal. Also, this method avoids the defensiveness that arises in some prospects when a salesperson rushes to the persuasive part of the sales message without adequate attention to the buyer's needs.

PROBLEM-SOLVING SELLING

Problem-solving selling is an extension of need satisfaction selling. It goes beyond identifying needs to developing alternative solutions for satisfying these needs. The problem-solving approach to selling is depicted in Figure 1.3. Sometimes even competitors' offerings are included as alternatives in the purchase decision.

The problem-solving approach typically requires educating the customer about the full impact of the existing problem and clearly communicating how the solution delivers significant customer value. This is true in cases where the customer does not perceive a problem or even when the solution seems to be an obviously beneficial course of action for the buyer.

Jody Kinmon, a sales coach for Miami-based Carnival Cruise Lines, says, "Sometimes people feel safer not doing anything, especially if there is not an immediate need or crisis. As a salesperson, your job is to open their eyes. If customers knew what they wanted, they wouldn't need salespeople."[12] To be successful in problem-solution selling, salespeople must be able to get the buyer to agree that a problem exists and that solving it is worth the time and effort required.

problem-solving selling An extension of need satisfaction selling that goes beyond identifying needs to developing alternative solutions for satisfying these needs.

consultative selling The process of helping customers reach their strategic goals by using the products, services, and expertise of the sales organization.

The problem-solving approach to selling can take a lot of time. In some cases, the selling company cannot afford this much time with each prospective customer. In other cases, the customers may be unwilling to spend the time. Insurance salespeople, for example, report this customer response. The problem-solving approach appears to be most successful in technical industrial sales situations, in which the parties involved are usually oriented toward scientific reasoning and processes and thus find this approach to sales amenable.

CONSULTATIVE SELLING

Consultative selling is the process of helping customers reach their strategic goals by using the products, services, and expertise of the sales organization.[13] This approach is shown in Figure 1.4. Notice that this method focuses on achieving strategic goals of customers, not just meeting needs or solving problems. Salespeople confirm their customers' strategic goals, and then work collaboratively with customers to achieve those goals.

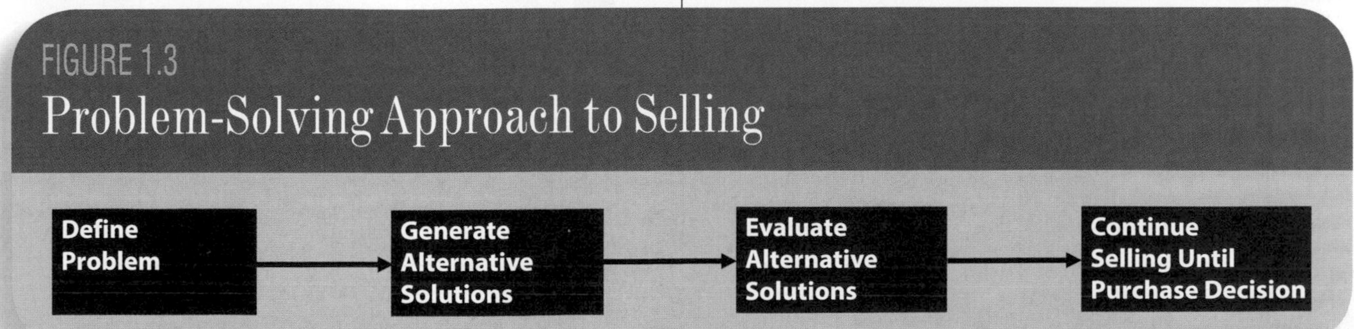

The salesperson defines a customer problem that may be solved by various alternatives. Then an offering is made that represents at least one of these alternatives. All alternatives are carefully evaluated before a purchase decision is made.

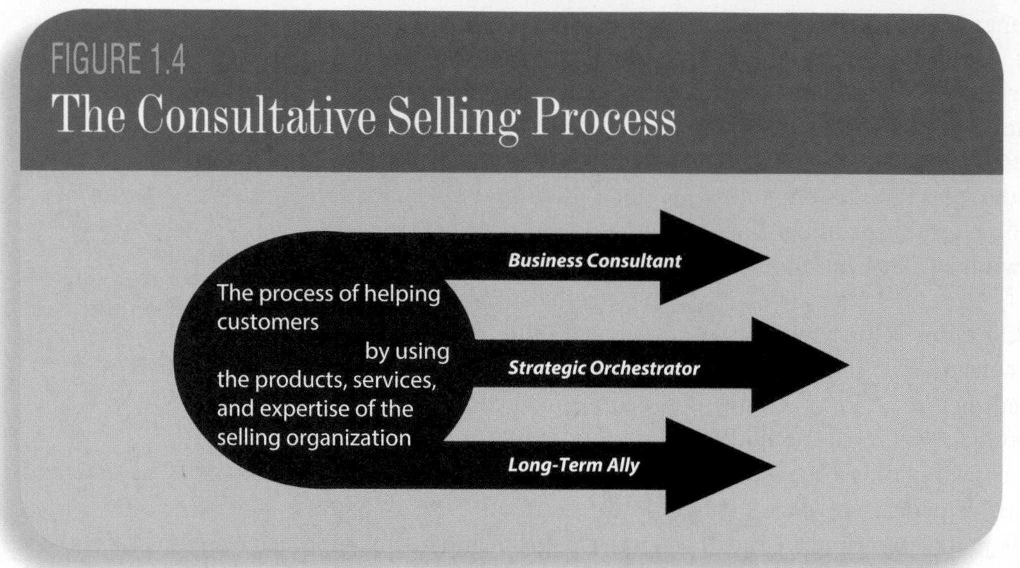

FIGURE 1.4
The Consultative Selling Process

The salesperson helps customers reach their strategic goals by fulfilling three roles with customers.

strategic orchestrator A role the salesperson plays in consultative selling in which he or she arranges the use of the sales organization's resources in an effort to satisfy the customer.

business consultant A role the salesperson plays in consultative selling in which he or she uses internal and external (outside the sales organization) sources to become an expert on the customer's business. This role also involves educating customers on the sales firm's products and how these products compare with competitive offerings.

long-term ally A role the salesperson plays in consultative selling in which he or she supports the customer, even when an immediate sale is not expected.

sales process A series of interrelated steps beginning with locating qualified prospective customers. From there, the salesperson plans the sales presentation, makes an appointment to see the customer, completes the sale, and performs postsale activities.

In consultative selling, salespeople fulfil three primary roles: strategic orchestrator, business consultant, and long-term ally. As a **strategic orchestrator**, the salesperson arranges the use of the sales organization's resources in an effort to satisfy the customer. This usually calls for involving other individuals in the sales organization. For example, the salesperson may need expert advice from production or logistics personnel to address a customer problem or opportunity fully. In the **business consultant** role, the salesperson uses internal and external (outside the sales organization) sources to become an expert on the customer's business. This role also includes an educational element—that is, salespeople educate their customers on products they offer and how these products compare with competitive offerings. As a **long-term ally**, the salesperson supports the customer, even when an immediate sale is not expected.

Yellow Pages Group (YPG), Canada's leading local commercial search provider and largest directory publisher, uses consultative selling to satisfy the needs of a wide variety of small businesses. Nearly all of YPG's revenues are derived from the sale of Yellow Pages directory advertising to businesses, mostly small- and medium-sized enterprises (SME). To be successful, YPG salespeople must be able to understand and explain the value of their products in the context of the customer's overall business strategy and be able to provide details of the expected and actual return on investment. Accordingly, YPG incorporates these topics into its sales training program.[14]

For more on consultative selling, see "Professional Selling in the 21st Century: Consultative Selling."

1-6 The Trust-Based Sales Process

The nonselling activities on which most salespeople spend a majority of their time are essential for the successful execution of the most important part of the salesperson's job: the **sales process**. The sales process has traditionally been described as a series of interrelated steps beginning with locating qualified prospective customers. From there, the salesperson plans the sales presentation, makes an appointment to see the customer, completes the sale, and performs postsale activities.

As you should recall from the earlier discussion of the continued evolution of personal selling (refer to Exhibit 1.2), the sales process is increasingly being viewed as a relationship management process, as depicted in Figure 1.5.

In this conceptualization of the sales process, salespeople strive to attain lasting relationships with their customers. The basis for such relationships may vary, but the element of trust between the customer and the salesperson is an essential part of enduring relationships. To earn the trust of customers, salespeople should be customer-oriented, honest, and dependable. They must also be competent and able to display an appropriate level of expertise to their customers. Finally, the trust-building process is facilitated if salespeople are compatible with their customers—that is, if they get along with and work well with each other.[15] These attributes are reflected by Blake Conrad, who sells medical supplies for Centurion Specialty Care. Conrad, based in Denver, says:

> *You simply cannot have productive relationships with your customers unless they trust you. I work really hard to show customers that I care about their bottom line, and I would never sell them something they don't really need. If I don't have an answer for them on the spot, I make every effort to get the answer and get back to them the same day. Customers appreciate the fact that I do what I say and follow up on all the details. To me, being customer oriented and dependable is just part of my job. It makes selling a lot more fun when your customers trust you, and—guess what—I sell more to customers who trust me.*[16]

Another important element of achieving sound relationships with customers is to recognize that individual customers and their particular needs must be addressed with the appropriate selling strategies and tactics. In selling, we discuss strategy at four levels: corporate, business unit, marketing department, and the overall sales function. An individual salesperson is strongly guided by strategy at these higher levels in the organization but must also develop selling strategies and tactics to fit the sales territory, each customer, and, ultimately, each sales call. Our coverage in this text focuses on developing sales strategies for individual customers and specific sales calls.

When studying the sales process, we should note that there are countless versions of the process in terms of number of and names of steps. If, however, you were to examine popular trade books on selling and training

PROFESSIONAL SELLING IN THE 21ST CENTURY

Consultative Selling

The lacklustre economic environment of recent years puts additional pressure on salespeople to produce sales growth. In many cases, salespeople feel they must push customers harder, which can actually make it more difficult to achieve sales goals. Bluntly put, hard-sell tactics can backfire. Consultative sellers who focus more on helping customers reach their strategic priorities report better sales results than sales organizations that push products through high-pressure sales techniques. According to Nick Bock, CEO of Nebraska-based Five Nines Technology Group, a slow economy " . . . hurts people who sell stuff. We never walk into customers saying that we think you should buy a bunch of these things. When we walk in we want to know what they want to accomplish as a business and as an information technology organization." Sales trainer and consultant Linda Richardson counters the notion that consultative selling can be a long, arduous process, pointing out that since customer needs are clear, the seller's recommendations are more likely to be more on target, which can actually accelerate the sales process. Consultative selling can help salespeople become the go-to person when clients have questions or tough challenges. In time, consultative selling builds trust and strengthens customer loyalty.

Sources: Jessica Davis, "How to Recession-Proof Sales with Consultative Selling," from the online version of Channel Insider at www.channelinsider.com/index2" (accessed May 31, 2012), and Linda Richardson, "Defining Consultative Selling," from the Richardson Web site at http://www.richardson.com/resource-center/sales-tips (accessed May 31, 2012).

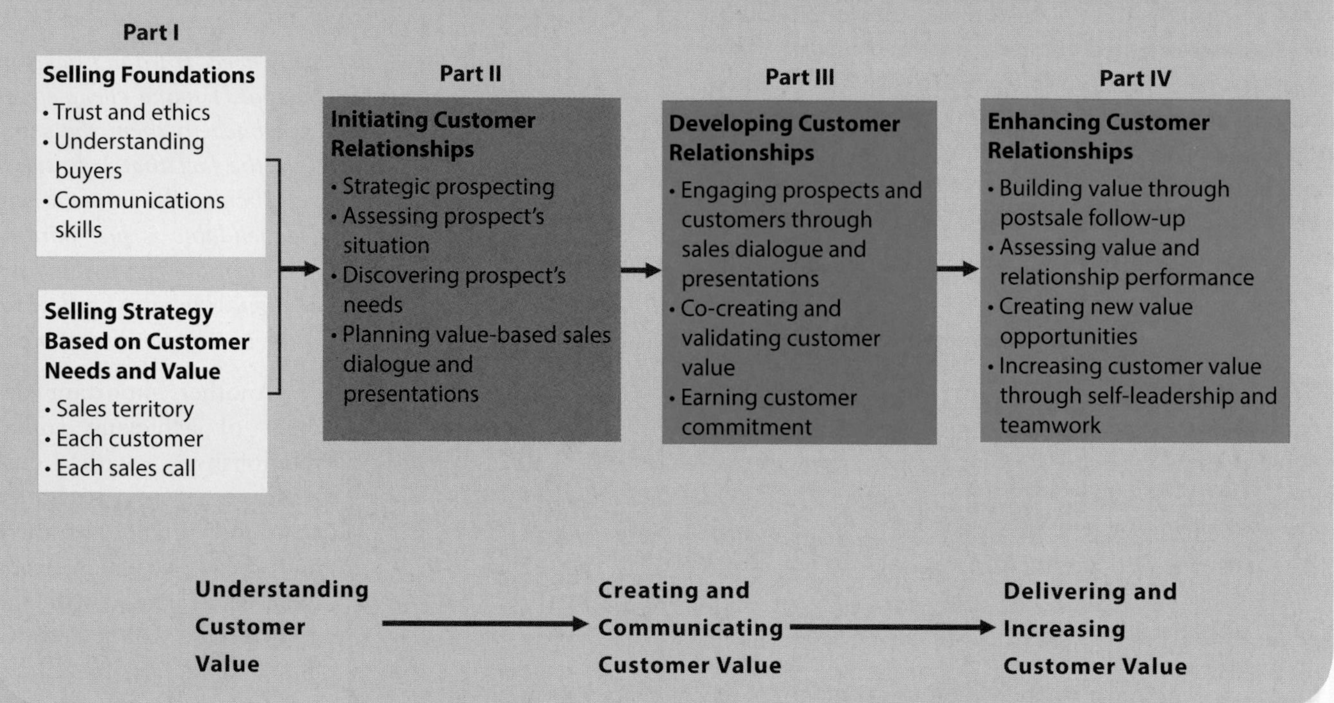

The three major phases of the sales process are initiating, developing, and enhancing customer relationships. Salespeople must possess certain attributes to earn the trust of their customers and be able to adapt their selling strategies to different situations. Throughout the sales process, salespeople should focus on customer value, first by understanding what it is and then by working with customers to create value, communicate value, and continually increase customer value.

manuals used by corporations, you would find that the various depictions of the sales process are actually more alike than different. The sales process shown in Figure 1.5 is comparable to most versions of the sales process, with the exception of those versions that advocate high-pressure methods focusing on getting the customer to "say yes" rather than focusing on meeting the customer's true needs. Our version of the sales process suggests that salespeople must have certain attributes to inspire trust in their customers and that salespeople should adapt their selling strategy to fit the situation.

Another point that should be stressed is that the sales process is broken into steps to facilitate discussion and sales training, not to suggest discrete lines between the steps. The steps are actually highly interrelated and, in some instances, may overlap. Further, the stepwise flow of Figure 1.5 does not imply a strict sequence of events. Salespeople may move back and forth in the process with a given customer, sometimes shifting from step to step several times in the same sales encounter. Finally, claiming a new customer typically will require multiple sales calls.

The remainder of this book explores the sales process shown in Figure 1.5. Chapters 2–4 comprise the foundations of personal selling. Chapter 2 discusses the important topics of building trust and sales ethics. Chapter 3 provides in-depth coverage of buyer behaviour, and Chapter 4 focuses on the communication skills necessary for sales success. Chapters 5 and 6 are about initiating customer relationships, starting with strategic prospecting in Chapter 5. Chapter 6 covers planning value-based sales dialogue and presentations as well as initiating contact with the customer. Developing customer relationships is next, with Chapter 7 discussing issues that arise during sales dialogues and presentations, and Chapter 8 discussing how salespeople can validate customer value and earn customer commitment. Enhancing customer relationships is presented in Chapters 9 and 10, and focuses on how salespeople add customer value through follow-up (Chapter 9) and through self-leadership and teamwork (Chapter 10). Chapter 11 concentrates on the techniques to develop and implement sales strategies, understanding and evaluating employees' performance while creating value to the customer through technology. To learn more about careers in professional selling, please see Appendix Chapter 1.

Visit **www.nelson.com/student** to find the resources you need today!

Located at the back of the textbook are rip-out Chapter Review cards. Make sure you also go online to check out other tools that SELL offers to help you successfully pass your course.

- Flashcards
- Glossary
- PowerPoint Notes
- Role-Play Videos
- Games
- Interactive Quizzing

APPENDIX CHAPTER 1

Sales Careers

This appendix is designed to give an in-depth look at sales careers. We first discuss characteristics of sales careers and then describe several different types of personal selling jobs. The appendix concludes with a discussion of the skills and qualifications necessary for success in sales careers.

Characteristics of Sales Careers

Although individual opinions will vary, the ideal career for most individuals offers a bright future, including good opportunities for financial rewards and job advancement. As you read the following sections on the characteristics of sales careers, you might think about what you expect from a career and whether your expectations could be met in a sales career. The following characteristics are discussed:

- Occupational outlook
- Advancement opportunities
- Immediate feedback
- Prestige
- Job variety
- Independence
- Compensation

OCCUPATIONAL OUTLOOK

Salespeople are revenue producers and thus enjoy relatively good job security compared with other occupational groups. Certainly, individual job security depends on individual performance, but in general salespeople are usually the last group to be negatively affected by personnel cutbacks.

Competent salespeople also have some degree of job security based on the universality of their basic sales skills. In many cases, salespeople are able to move successfully to another employer, maybe even change industries, because sales skills are largely transferable. For salespeople working in declining or stagnant industries, this is heartening news.

ADVANCEMENT OPPORTUNITIES

As the business world continues to become more competitive, the advancement opportunities for salespeople will continue to be an attractive dimension of sales careers. In highly competitive markets, individuals and companies that are successful in determining and meeting customer needs will be rewarded with opportunities for advancement. One reason that many successful salespeople ultimately find their way into top management is that they display some of the key attributes required for success in executive positions. Top executives must have highly developed personal skills, be able to communicate clearly and persuasively, and have high levels of self-confidence, motivation, business judgment, and determination.

IMMEDIATE FEEDBACK

Salespeople receive constant, immediate feedback on their job performance. Usually, the results of their efforts can be plainly observed by both salespeople and their sales managers—a source of motivation and job satisfaction. On a daily basis, salespeople receive direct feedback from their customers, and this can be stimulating, challenging, and productive. The opportunity to react immediately to customer feedback during sales presentations is a strong benefit of adaptive selling, and it distinguishes selling from other forms of marketing communications, such as advertising and public relations. The spontaneity and creativity involved in reacting to immediate feedback is one dimension of selling that makes it such an interesting job.

PRESTIGE

Traditionally, sales has not been a prestigious occupation in the eyes of the general public. There is some evidence that as the general public learns more about the activities and qualifications of professional salespeople, the image of salespeople, and thus the prestige of selling, is improving. An analysis of the popular press (excluding business publications) reveals that there are more positive than negative mentions of news-making salespeople. In a positive light, salespeople are frequently seen as knowledgeable, well-trained, educated, and capable of solving customer problems. The negative aspects of salespeople's image often centre on deception and high-pressure techniques.[1]

Another study indicates that salespeople historically have been depicted in movies and television programs more often than not in a negative light.[2] Even so, the struggling, down-and-out huckster as depicted by Willy Loman in Arthur Miller's 1949 classic *Death of a Salesman* is hardly typical of the professional salesperson of today and the future. Professional salespeople destroy such unfavourable stereotypes, and they would not jeopardize customer relationships by using high-pressure sales techniques to force a premature sale.[3] These perceptions are especially true in the business world, where encounters with professional salespeople are commonplace.

JOB VARIETY

Salespeople rarely suffer from boredom. Their jobs are multifaceted and dynamic. Multicultural diversity is increasing in most customer segments, and selling into global markets is on the rise. For a person seeking the comfort of a well-established routine, sales might not be a good career choice. For those who dislike office jobs, sales can be an especially good fit. In sales, day-to-day variation on the job is the norm. Customers change, new products and services are developed, and competition introduces new elements at a rapid pace. In addition to interacting with customers, many salespeople spend a considerable amount of time on such activities as training, attending trade shows, working with other salespeople at the distributor and retail levels to stimulate demand, and completing administrative tasks.

© Justin Lewis/Iconica/Getty

Salespeople work in a dynamic environment with a wide variety of job activities, including prospecting, planning and making sales calls, attending training sessions, participating in trade shows, and completing administrative tasks.

INDEPENDENCE

Sales jobs often allow independence of action. This independence is frequently a byproduct of decentralized sales operations in which salespeople live and work away from headquarters, therefore working from their homes and making their own plans for extensive travel.

Independence of action and freedom to make decisions are usually presented as advantages that sales positions have over tightly supervised jobs. Despite its appeal, however, independence does present some problems. New recruits working from their homes may find the lack of a company office somewhat disorienting. They may need an office environment to relate to, especially if their past work experience provided regular contact in an office environment.

The independence of action traditionally enjoyed by salespeople is being scrutinized by sales managers more heavily now than in the past. The emphasis on sales productivity, accomplished in part through cost containment, is encouraging sales managers to take a more active role in dictating travel plans and sales call schedules.

COMPENSATION

Compensation is generally thought to be a strong advantage of sales careers. Pay is closely tied to performance, especially if commissions and bonuses are part of the pay package.

Starting salaries for inexperienced salespeople with a university degree typically average $45,000, with opportunities to earn more through bonuses and commissions. Between the extremes of the highly experienced salesperson and the inexperienced recruit, an average salesperson earns approximately $60,000–$70,000 per year. More experienced salespeople, including those who deal with large customers, often earn in the $85,000–$135,000 range. Top salespeople can earn hundreds of thousands of dollars annually, with some exceeding a million dollars in annual earnings.

Classification of Personal Selling Jobs

Because there are so many unique sales jobs, the term *salesperson* is not by itself very descriptive. A salesperson could be a flower vendor at a busy downtown intersection or the sales executive negotiating the sale of Boeing aircraft to a major airline.

We briefly discuss six types of personal selling jobs:

- Sales support
- New business
- Existing business
- Inside sales (nonretail)
- Direct-to-consumer sales
- Combination sales jobs

sales support personnel A firm's personnel whose primary responsibility is dissemination of information and performance of other activities designed to stimulate sales.

missionary salespeople Salespeople who usually work for a manufacturer but may also be found working for brokers and manufacturing representatives. Sales missionaries are expected to "spread the word" to convert noncustomers to customers.

detailer A salesperson in the pharmaceutical industry working at the physician level to furnish valuable information regarding the capabilities and limitations of medications in an attempt to get the physician to prescribe their product.

technical support salespeople Technical specialists who may assist in design and specification processes, installation of equipment, training of the customer's employees, and follow-up service of a technical nature.

pioneers Salespeople who are constantly involved with either new products, new customers, or both. Their task requires creative selling and the ability to counter the resistance to change that will likely be present in prospective customers.

order-getters (hunters) Salespeople who actively seek orders, usually in a highly competitive environment.

SALES SUPPORT

Sales support personnel are not usually involved in the direct solicitation of purchase orders. Rather, their primary responsibility is dissemination of information and performance of other activities designed to stimulate sales. They might concentrate at the end-user level or another level in the channel of distribution to support the overall sales effort. They may report to another salesperson who is responsible for direct handling of purchase orders, or to the sales manager. There are two well-known categories of support salespeople: missionary or detail salespeople and technical support salespeople.

Missionary salespeople usually work for a manufacturer but may also work for brokers and manufacturing representatives, especially in the grocery industry. There are strong similarities between sales missionaries and religious missionaries. As with their counterparts, sales missionaries are expected to "spread the word" with the purpose of conversion—to customer status. Once converted, the customer receives reinforcing messages, new information, and the benefit of the missionary's activities to strengthen the relationship between buyer and seller.

In the pharmaceutical industry, the **detailer** is a fixture. Detailers working at the physician level furnish valuable information regarding the capabilities and limitations of medications in an attempt to get the physician to prescribe their product. Another sales representative from the same pharmaceutical company will sell the medication to the wholesaler or pharmacist, but it is the detailer's job to support the direct sales effort by calling on physicians.

Technical specialists are sometimes considered to be sales support personnel. These **technical support salespeople** may assist in design and specification processes, installation of equipment, training of the customer's employees, and follow-up service of a technical nature. They are sometimes part of a sales team that includes another salesperson who specializes in identifying and satisfying customer needs by recommending the appropriate product or service.

NEW BUSINESS

New business is generated for the selling firm by adding new customers or introducing new products to the marketplace. Two types of new-business salespeople are pioneers and order-getters.

Pioneers, as the term suggests, are constantly involved with new products, new customers, or both. Their task requires creative selling and the ability to counter the resistance to change that will likely be present in prospective customers.

Pioneers are well represented in the sale of business franchises, in which the sales representatives travel from city to city seeking new franchisees.

Order-getters, also called **hunters**, are salespeople who actively seek orders, usually in a highly competitive environment. Although all pioneers are also order-getters, the reverse is not true. An order-getter may serve existing customers on an ongoing basis, whereas the pioneer moves on to new customers as soon as possible. Order-getters may seek new business by selling an existing customer additional items from the product line. A well-known tactic is to establish a relationship with a customer by selling a single product from the line, then to follow up with subsequent sales calls for other items from the product line.

Most corporations emphasize sales growth, and salespeople operating as pioneers and order-getters are at the heart of sales growth objectives. The pressure to perform in these roles is fairly intense; the results are highly visible. For these reasons, the new-business salesperson is often among the elite in any company's salesforce.

EXISTING BUSINESS

In direct contrast to new-business salespeople, other salespeople's primary responsibility is to maintain and further cultivate relationships with existing customers. Salespeople who specialize in maintaining existing business include **order-takers** or **farmers**. These salespeople frequently work for wholesalers and, as the term *order-taker* implies, they are not too involved in creative selling. Route salespeople who work an established customer base, taking routine reorders of stock items, are order-takers. They sometimes follow a pioneer salesperson and take over the account after the pioneer has made the initial sale.

These salespeople are no less valuable to their firms than the new-business salespeople, but creative selling skills are less important to this category of sales personnel. Their strengths tend to be reliability and competence in ensuring customer convenience. Customers grow to depend on the services provided by this type of salesperson. As most markets are becoming more competitive, the role of existing-business salespeople is sometimes critical to prevent erosion of the customer base.

Many firms, believing that it is easier to protect and maintain profitable customers than it is to find replacement customers, are reinforcing sales efforts to existing customers. For example, Frito-Lay uses 18,000 route service salespeople to call on retail customers at least three times weekly. Larger customers see their Frito-Lay representative on a daily basis. These salespeople spend a lot of their time educating customers about the profitability of Frito-Lay's snack foods, which leads to increased sales both for the retailer and for Frito-Lay.

INSIDE SALES

In this text, **inside sales** refers to nonretail salespeople who remain in their employer's place of business while dealing with customers. The inside-sales operation has received considerable attention in recent years not only as a supplementary sales tactic but also as an alternative to field selling.

Inside sales can be conducted on an active or a passive sales basis. Active inside sales include the solicitation of entire orders, either as part of a telemarketing operation or when customers walk into the seller's facilities. Passive inside sales imply the acceptance, rather than solicitation, of customer orders, although it is common practice for these transactions to include add-on sales attempts. We should note that customer service personnel sometimes function as inside-sales personnel as an ongoing part of their jobs.

DIRECT-TO-CONSUMER SALES

Direct-to-consumer salespeople are the most numerous type of salespeople. There are approximately 1.6 million retail salespeople in Canada, with another 570,000 selling real estate, insurance, and securities. Not included in these numbers are the many sales representatives selling directly to the consumer for such companies as AVON, Mary Kay, and Tupperware.

This diverse category of salespeople ranges from the part-time, often temporary salesperson in a retail store to the highly educated, professionally trained stockbroker on Bay Street. As a general statement, the more challenging direct-to-consumer sales positions are those involving the sale of intangible services, such as insurance and financial services.

COMBINATION SALES JOBS

Now that we have reviewed some of the basic types of sales jobs, let us consider the salesperson who performs multiple types of sales jobs within the framework of a single position. We use the case of the territory manager's position with GlaxoSmithKline Consumer Healthcare (GSK) to illustrate the **combination sales job** concept. GSK, whose products include Aqua-Fresh toothpaste, markets a wide range of consumer healthcare goods to food, drug, variety, and mass merchandisers. The territory manager's job blends responsibilities for developing new business, maintaining and stimulating existing business, and performing sales support activities.

During a typical day in the field, the GSK territory manager is involved in sales support activities, such as merchandising and in-store promotion at the individual retail store level. Maintaining contact and goodwill with store personnel is another routine sales support activity. The territory manager also makes sales calls on chain headquarters personnel to handle existing business and to seek new business. And

order-takers (farmers) Salespeople who specialize in maintaining existing business.

inside sales Nonretail salespeople who remain in their employer's place of business while dealing with customers.

combination sales job A sales job in which the salesperson performs multiple types of sales jobs within the framework of a single position.

it is the territory manager who introduces new GSK products in the marketplace.

Qualifications and Skills Required for Success by Salespeople

Because there are so many different types of jobs in sales, it is rather difficult to generalize about the qualifications and skills needed for success. This list would have to vary according to the details of a given job. Even then, it is reasonable to believe that for any given job, different people with different skills could be successful. These conclusions have been reached after decades of research that has tried to correlate sales performance with physical traits, mental abilities, personality characteristics, and the experience and background of the salesperson.

Success in sales is increasingly being thought of in terms of a strategic team effort, rather than the characteristics of individual salespersons. For example, three studies of more than 200 companies that employ 25,000 salespeople found that being customer-oriented and cooperating as team players were critical to salespeople's success.[4]

Being careful not to suggest that sales success is solely a function of individual traits, let us consider some of the skills and qualifications that are thought to be especially critical for success in most sales jobs. Five factors that seem to be particularly important for success in sales are empathy, ego drive, ego strength, verbal communication skills, and enthusiasm. These factors have been selected after reviewing three primary sources of information:

- A study of more than 750,000 salespeople in 15,000 companies[5]
- Two reviews of four decades of research on factors related to sales success[6]
- Surveys of sales executives[7]

empathy The ability to see things as others would see them; salespeople with empathy are better able to adapt to various sales situations and adjust to customer feedback.

ego drive An indication of the degree of determination a person has to achieve goals and overcome obstacles in striving for success.

ego strength The degree to which a person is able to achieve an approximation of inner drives.

EMPATHY

In a sales context, **empathy** (the ability to see things as others would see them) includes being able to read cues furnished by the customer to better determine the customer's viewpoint. According to Spiro and Weitz, empathy is crucial for successful interaction between a buyer and a seller.[8] An empathetic salesperson is presumably in a better position to tailor the sales presentation to the customer during the planning stages. More important, empathetic salespeople can adjust to feedback during the presentation.

The research of Greenberg and Greenberg found empathy to be a significant predictor of sales success. This finding was partially supported in the review by Comer and Dubinsky, who found empathy to be an important factor in consumer and insurance sales but not in retail or industrial sales. Supporting the importance of empathy in sales success is a multi-industry study of 215 sales managers by Marshall, Goebel, and Moncrief.[9] These researchers found empathy to be among the top 25 percent of skills and personal attributes thought to be important determinants of sales success. Even though some studies do not find direct links between salesperson empathy and success, empathy is generally accepted as an important trait for successful salespeople. As relationship selling grows in importance, empathy logically will become even more important for sales success.

EGO DRIVE

In a sales context, **ego drive** (an indication of the degree of determination a person has to achieve goals and overcome obstacles in striving for success) is manifested as an inner need to persuade others in order to achieve personal gratification. Greenberg and Greenberg point out the complementary relationship between empathy and ego drive that is necessary for sales success. The salesperson who is extremely empathetic but lacks ego drive may have problems in taking active steps to confirm a sale. However, a salesperson with more ego drive than empathy may ignore the customer's viewpoint in an ill-advised, overly anxious attempt to gain commitment from the customer.

EGO STRENGTH

The degree to which a person is able to achieve an approximation of inner drives is **ego strength**. Salespeople with high levels of ego strength are likely to be self-assured and self-accepting. Salespeople with healthy egos are better equipped to deal with the possibility of rejection throughout the sales process. They are probably less likely to experience sales call reluctance and are resilient enough to overcome the disappointment of inevitable lost sales.

Salespeople with strong ego drives who are well-equipped to do their jobs will likely be high in **self-efficacy**; that is, they will strongly believe that they can be successful on the job. In situations in which their initial efforts meet resistance, rejection, or failure, salespeople high in self-efficacy are likely to persist in pursuing their goals. In complex sales involving large dollar amounts and a long sales cycle (the time from first customer contact to eventual sale), it is crucial to continue working toward a distant goal despite the very real possibility of setbacks along the way. For example, airplane manufacturers hoping to land contracts with the airlines typically pursue such contracts for several years before a buying decision is made. For those who persevere, however, the payoff can be well worth the extended effort.

INTERPERSONAL COMMUNICATION SKILLS

Interpersonal communication skills, including listening and questioning, are essential for sales success. An in-depth study of 300 sales executives, salespeople, and customers of 24 major sales companies in North America, Europe, and Japan found that effective salespeople are constantly seeking ways to improve communication skills that enable them to develop, explain, and implement customer solutions. The companies in the study are some of the best in the world at professional selling: Sony, Xerox, American Airlines, Fuji, and Scott paper.[10]

Another major study across several industries found that three communications skills in particular were among the top 10 percent of success factors for professional salespeople.[11] The highest-rated success factor in this study was listening skills, with ability to adapt presentations according to the situation and verbal communications skills following close behind.

To meet customer needs, salespeople must be able to solicit opinions, listen effectively, and confirm customer needs and concerns. They must be capable of probing customer expectations with open- and closed-ended questions and responding in a flexible manner to individual personalities and different business cultures in ways that demonstrate respect for differences.[12] This requires adaptable, socially intelligent salespeople, especially when dealing with multicultural customers.[13]

The importance of communication skills has been recognized by sales managers, recruiters, and sales researchers. These skills can be continually refined throughout a sales career, a positive factor from both a personal and a career development perspective.

ENTHUSIASM

When sales executives and recruiters discuss qualifications for sales positions, they invariably include **enthusiasm**. They are usually referring to dual dimensions of enthusiasm—an enthusiastic attitude in a general sense and a special enthusiasm for selling. On-campus recruiters have mentioned that they seek students who are well beyond "interested in sales" to the point of truly being enthusiastic about career opportunities in sales. Recruiters are somewhat weary of "selling sales" as a viable career, and they welcome the job applicant who displays genuine enthusiasm for the field.

self-efficacy The strong belief that success will occur on the job.

interpersonal communication skills Skills that include listening and questioning.

enthusiasm A strong feeling of excitement. Salespeople should have an enthusiastic attitude in a general sense and a specific enthusiasm for selling.

service motivation A strong desire to provide service to the customer. Service motivation comes from desiring the approval of others.

COMMENTS ON QUALIFICATIONS AND SKILLS

The qualifications and skills needed for sales success are different today from those required for success two decades ago. As the popularity of relationship selling grows, the skills necessary for sales success will evolve to meet the needs of the marketplace. For example, Greenberg and Greenberg's research has identified what they call an "emerging factor" for sales success, a strong motivation to provide service to the customer. They contrast this **service motivation** with ego drive by noting that although ego drive relates to persuading others, service motivation comes from desiring the approval of others. For example, a salesperson may be extremely gratified to please a customer through superior post-sale service. Greenberg and Greenberg conclude that most salespeople will need both service motivation and ego drive to succeed, although they note that extremely high levels of both attributes are not likely to exist in the same individual. Nonetheless, there is a growing interest in bringing service concepts and practices into the world of professional selling. Whereas it may be difficult to recruit salespeople who are high on the service dimension, it is certainly feasible to provide appropriate training and to reinforce the desired service behaviours through sales management practices. Without significant emphasis on servicing existing customers, a company is not truly practising relationship selling.[14]

Our discussion of factors related to sales success is necessarily brief, as a fully descriptive treatment of the topic must be tied to a given sales position. Veteran sales managers and recruiters can often specify with amazing precision what qualifications and skills are needed to succeed in a given sales job. These assessments are usually based on a mixture of objective and subjective judgments.

Professional selling offers virtually unlimited career opportunities for the right person. Many of the skills and qualifications necessary for success in selling are also important for success as an entrepreneur or as a leader in a corporate setting. For those interested in learning more about sales careers, consult these sources: *Sales & Marketing Management* magazine at http://salesandmarketing.com; *Selling Power* magazine at http://sellingpower.com; and Sales and Marketing Executives International, a professional organization, at http://www.smei.org.

CHAPTER 1 CASE

SLAVIK'S SPORTS INC.

Background

Slavik's Sports Inc. (SSI) is a Vancouver-based supplier of custom-made novelty sports items such as bobble-head figures, caps, sunglasses, and sweatshirts. Most of SSI's sales are to medium-sized businesses that use SSI products in employee motivation programs or as specialty advertising giveaways. SSI has been in business for 40 years, and has an excellent reputation as a reliable, competitive supplier. SSI has built a successful business across Canada. SSI sales representatives are knowledgeable and can advise their customers about how to use specialty advertising to build employee morale, introduce new products, and reinforce brand images.

Current Situation

Craig Robertson had recently been assigned to the western territory. Although this was his first sales job, he felt confident and was eager to begin. Craig had just completed SSI's training program and had a good understanding of SSI's products and the sales process. For most sales situations, SSI's sales trainers had recommended the use of an organized sales presentation in which the salesperson organizes the key points into a planned sequence that allows for adaptive behaviour by the salesperson as the sales call progresses.

Craig had been in his territory for 60 days, and he was enjoying his job. Days passed quickly, and he was never bored. He had landed some major customers, but was frustrated at how long it took some customers to make a buying decision. Overall, he thought he was doing a good job—and his sales manager, Felicia Jameson, had been consistently positive on the feedback form. Craig tried to be honest with himself as a way of improving his performance, and he was not happy as he reviewed today's last sales call.

Craig had called on H2G, a large manufacturer of garden tools. He intended to sell H2G several specialty advertising items to be used as giveaways at major trade shows in the coming year. After researching H2G on the Internet, he arranged a 4:00 p.m. meeting with Cam Evans, the director of marketing. Throughout the day, Craig was running late due to an unexpected snow storm and heavy traffic. He called to let Cam know that he would be late, but the best he could do was to leave a message. Craig arrived 15 minutes late, and was relieved to be shown into Cam's office without delay.

Craig apologized to Cam about running late, and was surprised to learn that Cam had not received his message. Craig was irritated that his message had not been passed along, but Cam did not seem to mind, indicating that he had plenty of time to meet with Craig. Given this signal, Craig decided to give Cam an overview of SSI's capabilities and success stories. Fifteen minutes later, Cam interrupted Craig and the following dialogue ensued.

> Cam: Thanks for the overview, Craig. I had a pretty good idea what SSI offers, but some of what you told me might be helpful. What have you learned about H2G that makes you think that SSI would be a good fit for our trade show programs?
>
> Craig: Well, I know that H2G participates in two national shows and several regional shows every year.
>
> Cam: That's right, and we work really hard to stand out at those shows.
>
> Craig: What works well for you in terms of standing out at the shows?
>
> Cam: Having a terrific, eye-catching product display is key. Doing a lot of pre-show communications to be sure key buyers visit our booths, and being sure we have enough people on hand to sustain a high-energy atmosphere during the show.
>
> Craig: How about specialty advertising to spice things up, maybe add to the fun element?
>
> Cam: I am not sure what you mean. We have wasted a lot of money on giveaways in the past and I don't believe that it differentiates us from our competitors.
>
> Craig: That's because you haven't worked with SSI. We're the best and I can fill you in on how we can add sizzle to your trade shows.
>
> Cam: O.K., but I just remembered that I need to pick my daughter up after her piano lesson. With the snow and traffic, that leaves us about 15 minutes.

Craig proceeded to describe how SSI works with most of their customers to supplement trade show communications. He felt rushed, as there were a lot of alternatives depending on the customer's budget and objectives for each trade show. About 10 minutes into his monologue, Cam told Craig: "Thanks for coming today. We will talk about this internally and I will get back with you if we decide to do more with specialty advertising this year. I really do have to run now. Sorry." As Craig drove home, he realized that he had never asked Cam about H2G's trade show objectives or their budget. With the abrupt end to the meeting, he also failed to try to get another appointment with Cam Evans. Craig realized that his call with H2G was not his best performance.

Questions

1. What problems do you see with Craig's H2G sales call?
2. If you were Craig's sales manager, what would you recommend he do to improve his chances of succeeding?

Role Play

Characters: Craig Robertson and four other SSI sales representatives; Felicia Jameson, SSI sales manager

Scene:

Location—SSI's Calgary office during a weekly sales meeting shortly after Robertson's sales call with H2G.

Action—Craig reviews his H2G sales call with other SSI sales representatives and their sales manager, Felicia Jameson. This is a regular feature of the weekly meetings, with the idea being that all sales representatives can learn from the experiences of others. Craig has decided to compare his call on H2G to some of the material from his sales training with SSI. This material, which contrasts transaction-focused selling with trust-based relationship selling, is shown in Exhibit 1.1 on page 5. His review will analyze whether he did or did not practise trust-based relationship selling during his call with Cam Evans at H2G.

Upon completion of the role play, address the following questions:

1. Is Craig's review of his sales call accurate?
2. What steps should Craig take to begin to develop a strong relationship with Cam Evans at H2G?

Role Play: Overview of Personal Selling, Specialty Sellers Inc.

Background

Specialty Sellers Inc. (SSI) was founded five years ago by Paul Cann and Danielle Nicholson as an employment agency specializing in the placement of professional sales representatives and sales trainees in a wide variety of industries. SSI is paid by the hiring companies, and job candidates are never charged fees for SSI's services. SSI represents college-educated individuals with sales experience levels ranging from zero (sales trainees) to several years of experience. For SSI to succeed, the company has to consistently do two things: (1) adapt to the hiring companies' needs and specific job descriptions in the sales area; and (2) save the hiring companies time and money in the hiring process by recommending only prescreened, highly qualified candidates. By focusing on these core competencies, SSI had grown to a company with 50 employees in five regional offices across the United States. SSI's revenues were increasing at an annual rate of 15 percent, which far outpaced revenue growth in the broadly defined employment agency sector.

Paul Cann and Danielle Nicholson have a good feel for how SSI can save hiring companies time and money by recommending only prescreened, highly qualified job candidates. Now that SSI was getting to be a larger company, Paul and Danielle needed to spread their knowledge to other SSI staff members who would also be involved in prescreening sales job candidates. In addition to their own experience over the years, Paul and Danielle had conducted research on the qualifications and skills needed for success in professional selling. Interestingly, there is a high correlation between their research findings and the research presented on pages 22–23 of this textbook. Paul and Danielle noted that some skills needed for sales success would be hard to assess until the salesperson had been on the job for a while. For example, being honest and ethical would probably take more time to assess. Even though a complete assessment of all of the attributes needed for sales success might extend past the job placement process, Paul and Danielle decided to identify key indicators for each of the 12 attributes shown on pages 22–23:

1. Active listening—to include asking appropriate questions and not interrupting at inappropriate times.
2. Service orientation—actively seeking ways to help customers.
3. Oral communications skills—including persuasive communications.
4. Coordination and problem solving—to include bringing others together and reconciling differences.
5. Written communications skills—including computer and other technologically facilitated communications.
6. Logical reasoning resulting in rational reasons to take action.
7. Strategic and organizational skills so that work can be planned and executed efficiently.
8. Dependability and attention to detail.
9. Motivation and persistence in the face of obstacles.
10. Integrity—honest and ethical.
11. Initiative—willing to take on responsibilities and challenges.
12. Adaptability—open to change and devoted to continual learning.

In the coming weeks, Paul and Danielle planned to work independently to identify a minimum of two to three indicators for each of the 12 qualifications and skills needed for sales success. They would then meet and select the best three indicators for each of the 12 success attributes and decide how and when each attribute would be assessed as they screened job candidates. For example, what could be assessed in personal interviews with job candidates? Alternatively, could some of these attributes be assessed from candidate résumés? Paul and Danielle were confident that if they could come up with the key indicators for each of the 12 success attributes, they would be able to train other SSI personnel to effectively prescreen job candidates and thus contribute to SSI's future growth.

Role Play

Situation: Review the above SSI case. Working in teams of two, select at least two success attributes from the list of 12.

Characters: Paul Cann and Danielle Nicholson, cofounders of SSI Inc.

Scene: After Paul and Danielle have independently developed two to three indicators for two of the 12 success factors, they meet to choose the best three indicators for each success factor and to determine how and when each indicator will be assessed. Both Paul and Danielle should distribute their written lists to each other and to others who will observe the role play.

Upon completion of the role play, address the following questions:

1. How would you rate Paul and Danielle in terms of preparedness? Can you identify any overlooked indicators for the chosen sales success attributes?
2. How well did Paul and Danielle work together to find the three best indicators for each success attribute?

© karen roach/Shutterstock

Trust reflects the extent

of the buyer's confidence in the salesperson's integrity.

2

Building Trust and Sales Ethics

Developing Trust and Mutual Respect with Clients

After completing this chapter, you should be able to

2-1 Explain what trust is, explain why it is important, and understand how to earn trust.

2-2 Know how knowledge bases help build trust and relationships.

2-3 Understand the importance of sales ethics and its legal implications.

Introduction

Megan Foley, vice president of A.S. Garden, an engineering firm, was looking to grow her company's business in the construction industry. Her team had identified a large commercial builder (Polar Edge Construction) in the Fort McMurray area as a good fit for their services. No one on Megan's team had done business with Polar Edge and only one member of her team had any connection with Polar Edge's people (i.e., one of Megan's team members belonged to the same country club as Don Edgett, the president).

Megan set out a strategy to develop relationships with the Polar Edge people over a six-month period. The initial contact would be to introduce A.S. Garden to Polar Edge Construction through their vice president of engineering, Ben Miller, and invite him to an upcoming seminar. Miller had attended past A.S. Garden seminars and seemed open to a meeting. Megan had her people meet once or twice a month strategizing the Polar Edge account.

After the seminar, the next three months were spent meeting with key players at Polar Edge (i.e., president, engineering VP, COO). Each member of Megan's team was assigned a person and asked to develop the relationship. The member of the country club arranged a round of golf with the president of both companies. A Stampeders football outing was planned as well as a Flames hockey game. The engineering department was courted as well as Miller. It was not until the end of the third month that a thorough needs assessment was started. The first three months were strictly getting to know Polar Edge. Several interesting things were uncovered during the first few months. First, Miller stated that he thought their present engineering firm was taking them for granted. New faces were coming and going, and he was not sure who was even in charge of their account. His engineering department was unhappy because they were supposed to get a copy of the specs on several projects to review ten days before their crews were to start work on the projects. Several times the specs were not available until the day before the project was to begin. And in one case, a mistake was found and the project could not be started on time. Mr. Edgett told Garden's president, Tim Proctor, that the time was probably right to look for another engineering firm. Late in the year, Polar Edge agreed to a full presentation. Megan and her team thought that they understood Polar Edge's needs and had a good relationship with all the key players. During the presentation, Megan introduced the team that would handle Polar Edge's account. Megan would lead the team, along with an experienced group in whom Megan had a great deal of confidence. Megan made it clear that she was only a phone call away if anyone at Polar Edge needed anything from A.S. Garden. Another part of their proposal included a date that Polar Edge would receive engineering specs before a project would begin (two weeks before they were due). This was backed with a penalty that A.S. Garden would pay if they missed this deadline. Soon after the presentation they received the order, and the Garden team were commended on their approach. Garden was also told that its competitors sold first and asked questions later. Polar Edge's people felt very comfortable with Megan and her team. Miller stated they were very impressed that all the promises made by Garden came true. He also thought that Garden demonstrated they really knew Polar Edge's business. Everyone was certain this was the start of a great relationship.

The extent of the buyer's confidence in the salesperson's integrity is known as **trust**. But trust can mean different things to different people. According to John Newman,[1] vice president of the Integrated Supply Chains Segment at A. T. Kearney, trust is defined in many ways. Buyers define trust with such terms as **openness**, dependability, candour, **honesty**, **confidentiality**, **security**, **reliability**, **fairness**, and predictability.[2] For example, in a Kearney study, one manufacturer related trust to credibility: "What trust boils down to, in a nutshell, is credibility, and when you say you are going to do something, you do it, and the whole organization has to be behind that decision."

trust The extent of the buyer's confidence that he or she can rely on the salesperson's integrity.

openness Completely free from concealment; exposed to general view or knowledge.

honesty Fairness and straightforward conduct.

confidentiality The state of being entrusted with information from a buyer that cannot be shared.

security The quality of being free from danger.

reliability Consistency of a salesperson over time to do what is right.

fairness Impartiality and honesty.

Another manufacturer related trust to confidentiality in that "they were afraid that the sales guys were going around and telling account B what account A is doing," which was identified as a violation of trust. Another company related trust to openness, claiming "we have to share information that traditionally is not shared." One president told how his engineers were sharing manufacturing secrets with their suppliers that five years earlier would have cost the engineers their jobs.[3]

FIGURE 2.1
Trust Builders

Expertise
Compatibility
Trust
Customer Orientation
Candour
Dependability

Trust means different things to different people. Trust can be developed by using any of the trust builders. It is the salesperson's job, through questioning, to determine what trust attributes are critical to relationship building for a specific buyer.

Research reveals that little is known about what ongoing behaviours (i.e., service behaviours) salespeople can employ to satisfy and build trust with customers.[4] A salesperson has to determine what trust means to each of his or her buyers, as shown in Figure 2.1. If it is confidentiality, then the salesperson must demonstrate how his or her company handles sensitive information. If credibility is the concern, then the salesperson must demonstrate that all promises will be kept. Therefore, the buyer defines trust; it is the salesperson's job through questioning to determine what trust attributes are critical to relationship building for a specific buyer.

In this chapter, we first discuss the meaning of trust in the sales context. Next, we explore the importance of trust to salespeople. This is followed by a discussion of how to earn trust and what knowledge bases a salesperson can use to build trust in buyer–seller relationships. Finally, we review the importance of sales ethics in building trust.

2-1 What Is Trust?

rust is earned when an industrial buyer believes and can rely on a salesperson's claims or promises when the buyer is dependent on the salesperson's honesty and reliability.[5] One of the keys to a long-term relationship with any client is to create a basis of trust between the sales representative and the client organization.[6]

Thus, gaining trust is essential to being seen as a reliable salesperson. Long-term sales success in any industry will generally be built on the concept of referral, in which trust plays an important role. Others argue that truthfulness is valuable for its own sake and instrumental to other goals, such as improved long-term relationships.[7] Clients obviously seek a salesperson they can trust. The problem is, depending on the industry and the situation, they may be influenced by previous bad experiences that make them wary of future partners. "An Ethical Dilemma" illustrates the challenges a salesperson faces on a daily basis. Consultative salespeople are in a unique position to capitalize on building credibility with customers who place a high value on trust. Customers are looking for trustworthy business partners but may have difficulty trusting most salespeople; the salesperson should recognize this as an opportunity.

An Ethical Dilemma

© Viorel Sima/Shutterstock

Jordan Fowler needed only one more order to win his company's "Rookie of the Year" award for the most sales for a first-year salesperson. He had one more week left in the year and one of his prospects had verbally committed to a rather large order that would definitely win him the award. The only catch was that his prospect wanted to wait until after the first of the year to sign the order. One of his company's older sales reps mentioned a technique he had used several times in his career in which he could tell the prospect that his discount would stand only until the end of the year and if the prospect waited he would have to pay full price. Jordan wanted to be Rookie of the Year, but was not sure if he was comfortable with this tactic. How would you handle this situation?

a) Go ahead and use the tactic and hope for the best.
b) Explain to the prospect his predicament and see if the client will sign early.
c) Attempt to find out why the prospect wants to wait until the next fiscal year to sign.

The "trust" described here is beyond the typical transaction-oriented trust schema. Many issues are only preliminary concerns—Will the product arrive as promised? Will the right product actually be in stock and be shipped on time? Will the invoice contain the agreed-on price? Can the salesperson be found if something goes wrong? In relationship selling, trust is based on a larger set of factors because of the expanded intimacy and long-term nature of the relationship. The intimacy of this relationship will result in both parties sharing information that could be damaging if leaked or used against the other partner.

Trust answers these questions:

1. Do you know what you are talking about? (competence, expertise)
2. Will you recommend what is best for me? (customer orientation)
3. Are you truthful? (honesty, candour)
4. Can you and your company back up your promises? (dependability)

Trust is an integral part of the relationship between customers and suppliers.

5. Will you safeguard confidential information that I share with you? (customer orientation, dependability)

Trust is an integral part of the relationship between customers and suppliers and results in increased long-term revenues and profits.[8]

WHY IS TRUST IMPORTANT?

In today's increasingly competitive marketplace, buyers typically find themselves inundated with choices regarding both products and suppliers. In this virtual buyers' market, traditional selling methods that focused on closing the sale have been inefficient and often counterproductive to the organization's larger, longer-term marketing strategy. In this new competitive environment, buyers are demanding unique solutions to their problems—product solutions that are customized on the basis of their particular problems and needs. Additionally, the adversarial, win-lose characteristics so customary in traditional selling are fading fast. In their place, long-term buyer–seller relationships are evolving as the preferred form of doing business. Although buyers are finding it more effective and efficient to do *more* business with *fewer* suppliers, sellers are finding it more effective to develop a continuing stream of business from the right customers. Such long-term relationships develop mutually beneficial outcomes and are characterized by trust, open communication, common goals, commitment to mutual gain, and organizational support.[9]

This shift toward relationship selling has altered both the roles salespeople play and the activities and skills they exercise in carrying out these roles—the selling process itself. Today's more contemporary selling process is embedded within the relationship marketing paradigm. As such, it emphasizes the initiation and nurturing of long-term buyer–seller relationships based on mutual trust and value-added benefits. As Megan Foley emphasized in the opening vignette, relationships take time—her firm spent more than three months learning about her prospect's business before the selling effort began. The level of problem-solving activity common to relationship selling requires deliberate and purposeful collaboration between both parties. These joint efforts are directed at creating unique solutions based on an enhanced knowledge and understanding of the customer's needs and the supplier's capabilities so that both parties derive mutual benefits. The nature of this integrative, win-win, and collaborative negotiation relies on augmented communication and interpersonal skills that nurture and sustain the reciprocal trust that allows all parties to share information fully and work together as a strategic problem-solving team.

A salesperson can build trust by demonstrating dependability through assisting in an order delivery.

expertise The ability, knowledge, and resources to meet customer expectations.

The skills and activities inherent to relationship selling can be classified according to their purpose as (1) initiation of the relationship (Chapters 5 and 6), (2) development of the relationship (Chapters 7 and 8), and (3) enhancement of the relationship (Chapters 9 and 10). As the activities comprising the selling process have changed, so too have the relative importance and degree of selling effort devoted to each stage of the process.

HOW TO EARN TRUST

Trust is important to any relationship. Several critical variables help salespeople earn a buyer's trust, such as **expertise**, dependability, candour, customer orientation, and compatibility. The importance of each is briefly discussed.

Expertise

Inexperience is a difficult thing for a young salesperson to overcome. Most recent university graduates will not have the expertise to be immediately successful, especially in industrial sales. Companies spend billions of dollars to train new recruits in the hope of speeding up the expertise variable. Training to gain knowledge on company products and programs, industry, competition, and general market conditions are typical subjects covered in most sales training programs. Young salespeople can shadow more experienced salespeople to learn what it takes to be successful. They must also go the extra distance to prove to their customers their dedication to service. For example, Missy Rust, of GlaxoSmithKline, had recently spent a

© PNC/Jupiter Images

few minutes with an anaesthesiologist discussing a new product, a neuromuscular blocker. A few days later, the physician called her at 1 a.m. to discuss a patient whom he thought was a good candidate for this drug. He was unsure of the correct dosage and needed Rust's expertise in this matter. Rust immediately drove to the hospital and was in the operating room for more than four hours observing the surgery and answering the doctor's questions about this new drug.[10]

Another factor to consider is that many organizations have recently been downsized, thus dramatically cutting the purchasing area in terms of both personnel and support resources. As a result, buyers have to do more with less and, as such, are thirsty for expertise, be it current insights into their own operations, financial situation, industry trends, or tactical skills in effectively identifying emerging cost-cutting and revenue opportunities in their business. Of course, expertise will be even more critical with certain buyers who are technical, detail-driven, and/or just uninformed in a certain area.

Salespeople should strive to help clients meet their goals. As an example, individuals or business owners can go online and trade stocks for themselves, but if they think a financial planner or securities company is more knowledgeable and brings more expertise to the table, then they will employ him or her.

Today's buyers will respond positively to any attempts to assist them in their efforts to reach bottom-line objectives, be it revenue growth, profitability, or financial or strategic objectives. Thus, "expertise" will take on an even more important role in the customer's assessment of the seller's credibility. For some buyers, especially those with economic or financial responsibilities (e.g., CFO, treasurer, owner-manager), a representative's ability to contribute to the bottom line will dominate the perception of a seller's credibility. This is a very important consideration for salespeople, given their pivotal strategy of penetrating accounts at the economic buyer level. Salespeople are seeking to convince clients that they are (1) actively dedicated to the task of positively influencing their bottom-line objectives and (2) capable of providing assistance, counsel, and advice that will positively affect the ability to reach objectives.[11] This is easier said than done because salespeople frequently do not understand the long-term financial objectives of their clients.[12]

Buyers today want recommendations and solutions, not just options. Salespeople must be prepared to help their clients meet their goals by adding value.

Buyers are continually asking themselves whether or not the salesperson has the ability, knowledge, and resources to meet his or her prospective customers' expectations. Salespeople are selling not only their knowledge, but also their entire organization and the support they bring to the buyer. Does the salesperson display a technical command of products and applications (i.e., is he or she accurate, complete, objective)? During one sales call, a buyer asked about a specific new product that the company was promoting in its advertising. The salesperson responded that the product was launched before he was trained on it. This response cast doubt not only on the salesperson's ability but also on the company for failing to train the salesperson.

Expertise also deals with the salesperson's skill, knowledge, time, and resources to do what is promised and what the buyer wants. Customers from small accounts must think that they are being treated as well as customers from large accounts and have access to the same resources.

Salespeople must exhibit knowledge generally exceeding that of their customer, not just in terms of the products and services they are selling but in terms of the full scope of the customer's financial and business operations (e.g., products, programs, competitors, customers, vendors). They must bring skills to the table, be it discovery, problem solving, program and systems development, financial management, or planning. These skills must complement those of the customer and offer insight into the best practices in the customer's industry. It is not enough to be an expert. This expertise must translate into observable results and **contributions** for the buyer.

Dependability

Dependability hinges on the **predictability** of the salesperson's actions. Buyers have been heard to say, "I can always depend on her. She always does what she says she is going to do." Salespeople must remember the promises they make to a customer or prospect. Once a promise is made, the buyer expects that promise to be honoured. The buyer should not have to call the salesperson to remind him or her of the promise. The salesperson should take notes during all sales calls for later review. It is harder to forget to do something if it is written down. A salesperson is trying to establish that his or her actions fit a pattern

contributions Something given to improve a situation or state for a buyer.

dependability Predictability of a person's actions.

predictability A salesperson's behaviour that can be foretold on the basis of observation or experience by a buyer.

candour Honesty of the spoken word.

customer orientation The act of salespeople placing as much emphasis on the customer's interests as their own.

of prior dependable behaviour. That is, the salesperson refuses to promise what he or she cannot deliver. The salesperson must also demonstrate an ability to handle confidential information. Buyers and sellers depend on each other to guard secrets carefully and keep confidential information confidential.

Candour

Candour deals with the honesty of the spoken word. A sales manager was overheard telling his salesforce to do "whatever it takes to get the order." One of the salespeople replied, "Are you telling us to stretch the truth if it helps us get the order?" The manager replied, "Of course!" The trustworthy salesperson understands doing "anything to get an order" will ultimately damage the buyer–seller relationship.

Salespeople have more than words to win over the support of the buyer; they have other sales aids, such as testimonials, third-party endorsements, trade publications, and consumer reports. The salesperson must be just as careful to guarantee that the proof is credible. It takes only one misleading event to lose all credibility. Jon Young, an independent sales consultant (see "Professional Selling in the 21st Century: The Importance of Fair and Balanced Presentations"), states, "I won't stretch the truth to get a contract signed … I feel I have my client's best interest at hand and they view me as a trusted advisor."

Customer Orientation

Customer orientation means placing as much emphasis on the customer's interests as you would on your own. An important facet of customer orientation is that salespeople work to satisfy the long-term needs of their customers rather than their own short-term goals.

A salesperson who has a customer orientation gives fair and balanced presentations. This includes covering both the pros and the cons of the recommended product. The pharmaceutical industry has done a good job understanding this principle, as many firms require their salespeople to describe at least one side effect of their drug for each benefit given. This is done not only because of the legal consideration but also to demonstrate expertise and trustworthiness to the physician. Traditional salespeople often ignored negative aspects of a product, which can turn off many buyers. A customer orientation should also include clear statements of benefits and not overpower the buyer with information overload.

Salespeople must truly care about the partnership, and they must be willing to "go to bat" for the client when the need arises. A warehouse fire left one company without any space to store inventory. The salesperson worked out same-day delivery until the warehouse was rebuilt. This left a lasting impression on the buyer, who

Professional Selling in the 21st Century

The Importance of Fair and Balanced Presentations

Jon Young, an independent sales consultant, talks about the importance of building long-term relationships. Jon knows it is critically important that he has the ability to build trust and transform this trust into long-term relationships.

I take a lot of pride in giving fair and balanced presentations. It is not unusual for me to point out a shortcoming of my product during a presentation. I don't want a customer asking me down the road why I was not forthcoming with my product. I truly feel my approach is the best as it cuts down on surprises. It only takes one misleading statement to lose my credibility. I won't stretch the truth to get a contract signed. I feel I do have my client's best interest at hand and they do view me as a trusted adviser.

knew that their salesperson would come through for them if they ever needed help.

Salespeople must be fully committed to representing the customer's interests. Although most salespeople are quick to "talk the talk" about their absolute allegiance to their customer's interests, when it comes to "walking the walk" for their customer on such issues as pricing, production flexibility, and design changes, many lack the commitment and/or skills necessary to support the interests of their clients.

To be an effective salesperson and gain access to a customer's business at a partnership level, the client must feel comfortable with the idea that the salesperson is motivated and capable of representing his or her interests. Exhibit 2.1 looks at some of the questions salespeople need to answer satisfactorily to gain the buyer's trust and confidence.

Compatibility/Likeability

Customers generally like to deal with sales representatives whom they know and like, and with whom they can feel a bond.

Some salespeople are too quick to minimize the importance of rapport building in this era of the economic buyer. It also may be true that today's buyers are not as prone to spending time discussing personal issues in sales calls as they might have been 10 or 15 years ago. Salespeople today have to be more creative and resourceful when attempting to build rapport. It is not unusual for a pharmaceutical salesperson to take a lunch for the entire staff into a physician's office. These lunches can be for as many as 20 to 40 people. The salesperson now has time to discuss his or her products over lunch with a captive audience.

Good salespeople are never in a hurry to earn commitment!

Salespeople have to be aware that their buyers are under considerable time pressure and that some will find it difficult to dedicate time to issues outside of the business. However, remember that buyers are human and do value compatibility—some more, some less.

Compatibility and likeability are important to establishing a relationship with key gatekeepers (e.g., receptionists and secretaries). First impressions are important, and a salesperson's ability to find commonalities with these individuals can go a long way in creating much-needed allies within the buying organization. Likeability is admittedly an emotional factor that is difficult to pin down, yet it is a powerful force in some buyer–seller relationships. "An Ethical

compatibility and likeability A salesperson's commonalities with other individuals.

EXHIBIT 2.1
Questions That Salespeople Need to Answer Satisfactorily to Gain a Buyer's Trust

Expertise: Does the salesperson know what he or she needs to know? Does the salesperson and his or her company have the ability and resources to get the job done right?

Dependability: Can I rely on the salesperson? Does the salesperson keep promises?

Candour: Is the salesperson honest in his or her spoken word? Is the salesperson's presentation fair and balanced?

Customer orientation: Does the salesperson truly care about the partnership? Will the salesperson go to bat for the customer (e.g., wrong order, late delivery)?

Compatibility: Will the buyer like doing business with the salesperson? Will the buyer like doing business with the salesperson's company?

competitor knowledge Knowledge of a competitor's strengths and weaknesses in the market.

Dilemma" demonstrates the challenges salespeople might face when trying to build key relationships with potential clients.

If a salesperson has done a good job of demonstrating the other trust-building characteristics, then compatibility can be used to enhance trust building. Buyers do not necessarily trust everyone they like; however, it is difficult for them to trust someone they do not like.

2-2 Knowledge Bases Help Build Trust and Relationships

The more the salesperson knows, the easier it is to build trust and gain the confidence of the buyer. Buyers have certain expectations of the salesperson and the knowledge that he or she brings to the table. As outlined in Figure 2.2, salespeople may draw from several knowledge bases. Most knowledge is gained from the sales training program and on-the-job training.

Sales training will generally concentrate on knowledge of the industry and company history, company policies, products, promotion, prices, market knowledge of customers, **competitor knowledge**, and basic selling techniques. Exhibit 2.2 summarizes topics generally covered during initial sales training programs.

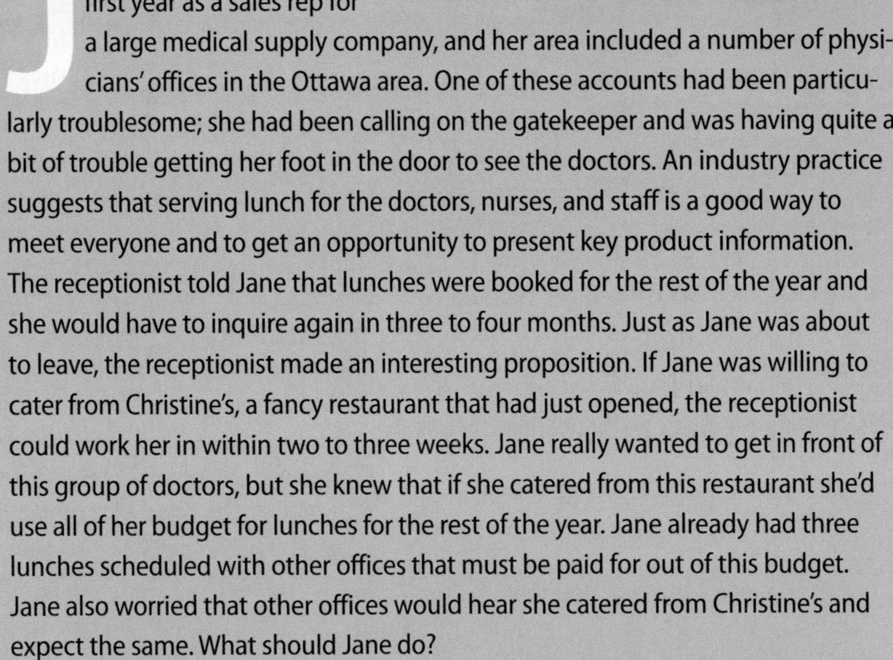

© Siri Stafford/Iconica/Getty

An Ethical Dilemma

Jane Staten was in her first year as a sales rep for a large medical supply company, and her area included a number of physicians' offices in the Ottawa area. One of these accounts had been particularly troublesome; she had been calling on the gatekeeper and was having quite a bit of trouble getting her foot in the door to see the doctors. An industry practice suggests that serving lunch for the doctors, nurses, and staff is a good way to meet everyone and to get an opportunity to present key product information. The receptionist told Jane that lunches were booked for the rest of the year and she would have to inquire again in three to four months. Just as Jane was about to leave, the receptionist made an interesting proposition. If Jane was willing to cater from Christine's, a fancy restaurant that had just opened, the receptionist could work her in within two to three weeks. Jane really wanted to get in front of this group of doctors, but she knew that if she catered from this restaurant she'd use all of her budget for lunches for the rest of the year. Jane already had three lunches scheduled with other offices that must be paid for out of this budget. Jane also worried that other offices would hear she catered from Christine's and expect the same. What should Jane do?

a) Go ahead and schedule the lunch. She needs to get in to see these doctors.
b) Politely tell the receptionist she'll be back in three months.
c) Talk to her boss about the situation and see if more money is available to pay for all the scheduled lunches.

INDUSTRY AND COMPANY KNOWLEDGE

Salespeople may be asked what they know about their company and industry. Every industry and company has a history. The personal computer industry has a short history of 30 years; fax technology, even shorter. Other industries have been around for centuries. Some industries change so quickly, such as the pharmaceutical

FIGURE 2.2
Knowledge Bases

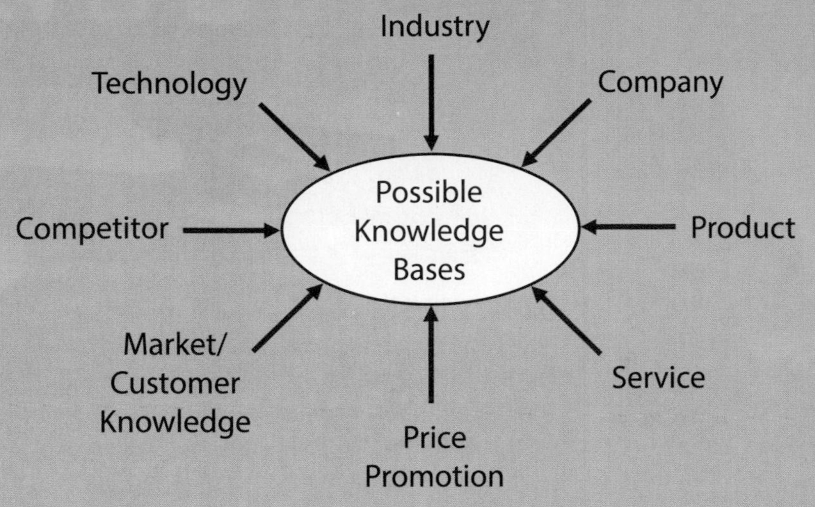

The more the salesperson knows, the easier it is to build trust and gain the confidence of the buyer. Buyers have certain expectations of the salesperson and the knowledge that he or she brings to the table. Most knowledge is gained from the sales training programs and on-the-job training.

industry through multiple mergers, that it is critical for the salesperson to know his or her industry to keep physicians informed on new companies, drugs, and procedures. Many buyers are too busy to stay informed and count on their salespeople to help them make sound decisions.

Salespeople should be familiar with their own company's operation and policies. Buyers may ask the salesperson such questions as: How long has your company been in the market? How many people does the company employ? Does the company have a local, a regional, a national, or an international customer base? Who started the company? Who is the president? the CEO? What is the company's market share? What is the market share on this particular product? Salespeople who could not answer such questions would not inspire the trust of the buyer.

Each company initiates policies to ensure consistent decisions are made throughout the organization. An organization implements policies to control such factors as price, guarantees, warranties, and how much to spend per week taking clients out to lunch. Knowing the company's policies prevents a misunderstanding.

For example, if a representative says a customer can return goods 60 days after receipt when company policy is 30 days, the shipping department might refuse to accept the returned merchandise. The salesperson looks incompetent to both sales management and the customer, and the angry customer who is not allowed to return goods to the factory probably will never buy from the salesperson again.

Salespeople must understand their company policies. This includes being familiar with the company's formal structure and key personnel. It is important to work as a team with all company personnel. This helps build team spirit and a willingness to cooperate when a salesperson needs help in meeting a customer's need. It is difficult to provide outstanding service when the sales department is not on good terms with shipping and delivery, for instance.

> Companies provide extensive training to be sure they send knowledgeable sales representatives into the field.

© Eric Audras/Jupiter Images

EXHIBIT 2.2

Topics Generally Covered During Initial Sales Training Programs

- Industry history
- Company history and policies
- Product
  —promotion —price
- Market
  —line of business (know your customer)
  —manufacturing
  —wholesaling
  —financial
  —government
  —medical, etc.
- Competitive knowledge
- Selling techniques
- Initiating customer relationship
  —prospecting —precall
  —approaching the customer
- Developing customer relationships
  —sales presentation delivery
  —handling sales resistance
- Enhancing customer relationships
  —follow-up —customer service

PRODUCT KNOWLEDGE

Product knowledge includes detailed information on the manufacture of a product and knowing whether the company has up-to-date production methods. What materials are used when making the products? What quality control procedures are involved? Who are the design engineers?

Salespeople representing their company are expected to be experts on the products they sell. The fastest way to win the respect of a buyer is to be perceived as an expert. If the buyer truly feels the salesperson knows what he or she is talking about, then the buyer will be more willing to discuss the salesperson's solution to the buyer's problems or opportunities.

Product knowledge
Detailed information on the manufacture of a product and knowing whether the company has up-to-date production methods.

© Steve Helber/AP Images

Buyers expect their salespeople to be experts on the products they sell.

The salesperson must know what his or her product can and cannot do. Just knowing product features is insufficient.

SERVICE

The effective salesperson must be ready to address **service issues** such as:

- Does the company service its products or does the company send them to a third party?
- Does the company service its products locally or send them off to another city for service?
- Does the price include service or will there be a service charge when service is needed?
- What does the service agreement include? Shipping? Labour? Or neither of these?
- How long does the service generally take? Same day? Within a week? Will a loaner be provided until the product is fixed?
- Are there any conditions that make service not available? After five years? Damage from flood? Fire?

Buyers need to be comfortable answering these questions, and a good salesperson will make sure they are answered appropriately.

Paul Gibbons from Rocket Systems in St. John's, Newfoundland, spends quite a bit of time discussing service with each of his prospects. His company sells collection software (i.e., receivables) that requires support from his field engineers. Rocket Systems also has a support group that takes calls 24 hours a day, seven days a week. Why is this important to Gibbons? One of his major competitors also has a support group, but only 8 a.m. to 5 p.m., Monday through Friday. Gibbons knows that he has service superiority. Salespeople who can offer the better service have an advantage for generating new business and taking away business from the competition. The salesperson's service mission is to provide added value for the customer. It is important for the salesperson to understand what service dimensions concern the buyer.

For instance, delivery, installation, training, field maintenance, and investing are all issues that a salesperson may be prepared to talk about. Buyers, however, may be concerned only with inventory, because their present supplier runs out of stock frequently.

Exhibit 2.3 reviews service dimensions in which a salesperson could demonstrate service superiority. Additions may be made depending on specific customer demands.

PROMOTION AND PRICE

Promotion knowledge and **price knowledge** are other knowledge tools that the salesperson must understand. The ability to use this knowledge often makes the difference between a well-informed buyer who is ready to make a decision and another buyer who is reluctant to move the sales process forward. Hershey Foods Corporation supports its retailers with heavy promotions during Halloween, Christmas, and Easter. The promotional programs must be explained properly so the buyer can place the correct order size during the promotion. How many dollars are to be spent? Is it a national program? Is this a co-op program? What will it cost the buyer? If these questions are answered properly, the buyer will be more at ease and ready to make a purchase.

Price can be another area that makes a buyer hesitant if not properly explained. Knowledge of pricing policies is important because the salesperson often is responsible for quoting price and offering discounts. As a representative of the selling firm, the salesperson's quotes legally bind a company to their completion.

Salespeople need complete understanding of their company's pricing policies. Does the company sell its products for a set price or can the salesperson negotiate? Can the salesperson give additional discounts to get a potential client whom the company has been after for years? Does the company allow trade-ins?

promotion knowledge
Knowledge tools salespeople must possess to explain their firms' promotional programs.

price knowledge
Knowledge tools salespeople must have about pricing policies in order to quote prices and offer discounts on products.

market knowledge
Information salespeople must have if larger companies break their customers into distinct markets; salespeople must be familiar with these markets to tailor their sales presentations.

customer knowledge
Information about customers that is gathered over time and from very different sources that helps the salesperson determine customer needs to better serve them.

EXHIBIT 2.3
Service Superiority

Dimension	Potential Superiority
1. Delivery	Can our company demonstrate speed? Deliver more often?
2. Inventory	Can we meet the demands of our customers at all times?
3. Training	Do we offer training? At our site? At our customer's?
4. Field maintenance	Do we go to the field to fix our products? Do our customers have to bring their equipment to us to fix?
5. Credit and financial consideration	Do we grant credit? Do we help finance?
6. Installation	Do we send a team to your site for start-up?
7. Guarantees and warranties	What are our guarantees? How long? What do we cover?
8. Others	Do we offer anything unique that our competition does not?

MARKET AND CUSTOMER KNOWLEDGE

Market knowledge and **customer knowledge** are critical to the success of today's salesperson.

Some companies today, because of their size, send their salesforce out to call on all customer types. Larger companies typically break their customers into distinct markets. Computer manufacturers may break out their customer types by markets (i.e., salespeople sell to a particular line of business). For instance, the salesperson may sell only to manufacturers, wholesalers, financial institutions, government, education, or medical companies. This allows the salesperson to become an expert in a line of business. For a salesperson to be effective, the salesperson must learn what the client needs, what benefits the client is seeking, and how the salesperson's products satisfy the buyer's specific needs. Buyers are not interested in factual knowledge unless it relates to fulfilling their specific needs. Having the salesforce learn one line of business well allows the salesperson to concentrate on the needs of a specific market. The salesperson can become an expert in one line of business more quickly than if he or she has to know how the entire marketplace uses the salesperson's products.

Information about customers is gathered over time and from very different sources. A salesperson can use trade associations, credit agencies, trade magazines, trade directories, newspapers, and the World Wide Web as valuable resources. Canada 411, owned by Yellow Pages Group, has directories on people, businesses, and Web sites. Using the Web to do an initial search on a company can tell a salesperson about what products a company makes, what markets they serve, and so on. A salesperson must use his or her time wisely when gathering information. Gabe Jones, COO, Ash & Company (see "Professional Selling in the 21st Century: Why Knowledge Is Important"), states, "I have to thoroughly know my industry and my customer's business. I must know where to find this information."

PROFESSIONAL SELLING IN THE 21ST CENTURY

© Lightspring/Shutterstock

Why Knowledge Is Important

Gabe Jones, COO, Ash & Company, understands why knowledge is important to a salesperson's success.

I've been in sales for over 20 years now and I know what my buyers want. They want KNOWLEDGE! I have seen large purchasing departments dwindle down to one and two people and they can't keep up with all the information that floats across their desks. I have to thoroughly know my industry and my customer's business. I must know where to find this information. I have to continually monitor my competition and know how my product stacks up against my competitor's offerings. One area I have seen many experienced (old) sales reps fall behind in is technological knowledge. I know several older reps that are afraid of using computers, the Web, and e-mail! I have to show my clients and prospects that I am on the cutting edge when it comes to any of the knowledge areas. I feel great when my clients come to me with questions about their industry and I know the answers or where to go to get the answers!

COMPETITOR KNOWLEDGE

Salespeople will probably be asked how their product stands up against the competition. The buyer may ask—Who are your competitors in our marketplace? How big are you compared with your competitors? How do your company's prices compare with others in your industry? How does your product quality compare with the industry norm? These are important questions that every salesperson must be prepared to answer. Salespeople must have knowledge of their competitors' strengths and weaknesses to better understand their own product's position when comparing. A good salesperson must adjust his or her selling strategy depending on the competition.

Salespeople must be able to deliver complete comparative product information in a sales presentation. Comparisons of competitors' products for a customer's

© michaeljung/Shutterstock

decision are critical, especially when your features and benefits are superior to those of the competition.

It is important that salespeople distinguish their products from the competition. The ultimate question a buyer asks is—Why should I use your product over the one I am currently using? A salesperson must have competitive knowledge to answer this question. What are the competitor's relative strengths and weaknesses? What weaknesses make this competitor vulnerable? Once the salesperson can determine the competitor's limitations, the salesperson can demonstrate the superiority of his or her product. A salesperson must answer these questions: How are you different from the competition? How are you better than the competition? A salesperson must be able to determine his or her differential competitive advantage.

Salespeople must be well versed in technology tools and how to use them effectively to build a bridge to the buyer.

TECHNOLOGY KNOWLEDGE

Salespeople must use **technology knowledge** to their advantage. Twenty years ago, salespeople had to know where a reliable pay phone was located in each city they visited. Many opportunities were missed because salespeople could not reach prospects while they were in the field. Today's salesperson has the luxury of smartphones, facsimile technology, the World Wide Web, voice mail, and e-mail.

technology knowledge Information salespeople must have about the latest technology.

Salespeople should communicate in the manner their prospects and clients prefer. Some clients use e-mail extensively and want to use e-mail over phone conversations. Some buyers like to fax in their orders and would rather not meet the salesperson face to face. A good salesperson must recognize these preferences and act accordingly. Each of these can either be a bridge to the customer or an obstacle. Salespeople should be building bridges to all their prospects and customers by using technology appropriately (see Exhibit 2.4). If a buyer likes to e-mail requests to a salesperson, then the salesperson must not use e-mail to screen buyers. Likewise, if a facsimile number is given to prospects, then the fax machine must be turned on at all times and working properly.

EXHIBIT 2.4
Using Technology to Build Bridges to Customers

Technology	Bridge
World Wide	Price updates can be placed on the Web for customers to access. New product information can be made available to customers and prospects.
E-mail	Buyer and salesperson can communicate 24 hours a day. Mass communications can be sent out to all customers and prospects.
Facsimile	Non-electronic documents can be transmitted 24 hours a day. Fax on demand.
Cell phones	Buyer and seller have immediate access to each other.
Voice mail	Salesperson and buyer can leave messages for each other and save time and effort.

Probably the most oversold form of technology is voice mail. Many companies have gone to this method of communication hoping to free up secretaries and make it easier to leave messages for the salesperson. The difficulty arises when a customer wants to talk to a salesperson and can only get a recording. Sometimes, the voice mailbox is full and it is impossible to leave a message. It is also possible to use voice mail to screen calls, and many buyers and salespeople complain that it is virtually impossible to make contact when their counterpart refuses to return their call.

Technology can be a friend or foe to a salesperson. If used properly, technology can build bridges to prospects and clients and develop relationships. If technology is *not* used properly, a salesperson can alienate customers and turn a potential resource into a reason for a prospect not to do business with the salesperson.

2-3 Sales Ethics and Legal Implications

Ethics refers to right and wrong conduct of individuals and the institutions of which they are a part. Personal ethics and formal codes of conduct provide a basis for deciding what is right or wrong in a given situation. Ethical standards for a profession are based on society's standards, and most industries have developed a code of behaviours that are compatible with society's standards. Many professions in North America owe much of their public regard to standards of conduct established by professional organizations. Reflecting this, the American Marketing Association has adopted a code of ethics, which is available in this book's companion website.[13]

ethics The right and wrong conduct of individuals and institutions of which they are a part.

Salespeople are constantly involved with ethical issues. In fact, salespeople are exposed to greater ethical pressures than individuals in many other occupations.[14] A sales manager might encourage his or her salesforce to pad their expense accounts in lieu of a raise, or ask a rep to withhold information from a prospect.[15] A salesperson might sell a product or service to a customer that the buyer does not need. A salesperson might exaggerate the benefits of a product to get a sale. The list can go on and on.

Recall that sales professionalism requires a truthful, customer-oriented approach. Customers are increasingly intolerant of nonprofessional, unethical practices. Sales ethics is closely related to trust. Deceptive practices, illegal activities, and noncustomer- oriented behaviour have to be attempted only once for a buyer to lose trust in his or her salesperson. Research has identified some of the sales practices deemed unethical, as shown in Exhibit 2.5.[16]

EXHIBIT 2.5
What Types of Sales Behaviours Are Unethical?

According to a survey of 327 customers, salespeople are acting unethically if they do any of the following:

1. Show concern for their own interest, not their clients'
2. Pass the blame for something they did wrong
3. Take advantage of poor or uneducated buyers
4. Accept favours from customers so the seller feels obliged to bend policies
5. Sell products/services that people do not need
6. Give answers when they do not really know answers
7. Pose as a market researcher when doing phone sales
8. Sell dangerous or hazardous products
9. Withhold information
10. Exaggerate benefits of product
11. Lie about product availability to make sale
12. Lie to competitors
13. Falsify product testimonials

IMAGE OF SALESPEOPLE AND SALES EXECUTIVES

Sales and Marketing Executives International (SMEI) has been concerned with the image of salespeople and has developed a code of ethics as a set of principles that outline the minimum requirements for professional conduct. SMEI has developed a 20- to 30-hour certification process that declares a salesperson shall support and preserve the highest standards of professional conduct in all areas of sales and in all relationships in the sales process. Exhibit 2.6[17] is the SMEI Code of Ethics that pledges a salesperson will adhere to these standards. Like SMEI, the Canadian Professional Sales Association (CPSA) has a professional development program that allows individuals to become a Certified Sales Professional. Once certified a salesperson must abide by the CPSA code of ethics as outlined in Exhibit 2.7.

A sales professional deserves and receives a high level of respect on the job. Buyers who do not interact with professional salespeople on a regular basis may believe in the negative stereotype of the salesperson as pushy, shifty, and untrustworthy. Where does this stereotype come from? Some salespeople are not professional in their approach and contribute to the negative stereotype. In the past, television programs, movies, and theatre productions have fostered the negative image of salespeople. During the 1960s and 1970s, the popular press also contributed to this negative image. A study of how salespeople are portrayed in the popular press found that salespeople are often associated with deceptive, illegal, and noncustomer-oriented behaviour.[18] Dilemmas exist also for sales executives implementing strategic account relationships regarding such issues as information sharing, trust, and hidden incentives for unethical behaviours.[19] Three of the more important areas of unethical behaviour—deceptive practices, illegal activities, and noncustomer-oriented behaviour—are discussed.

Today's professional salesperson is a trusted adviser to his or her buyers and receives a great level of respect for the services he or she provides to customers.

DECEPTIVE PRACTICES

Buyers have been turned off from dealing with all salespeople because of poor experiences with only a few unscrupulous salespeople. All salespeople (good and bad) pay the price for this behaviour. Unfortunately, some salespeople do use quota pressure as an excuse to be deceptive. The salesperson has the choice to either ignore the trust-building approach and persuade the customer to buy, or go to the next sales meeting and catch the wrath of his or her sales manager for being under quota. Salespeople giving unfounded answers, exaggerating product benefits, and withholding information might appear only to shade the truth, but when it causes harm to the buyers, such salespeople have jeopardized future dealings with the buyer.

NONCUSTOMER-ORIENTED BEHAVIOUR

Most of today's sales organizations emphasize trust-building behaviours and are customer-oriented. Unfortunately, a few salespeople and companies today concentrate on short-term goals and allow outmoded sales tactics to be practised. Most buyers will not buy from salespeople who are pushy and practise the hard sell. Too much is at stake to fall for the fast-talking, high-pressure salesperson. Buyers have been through their own training, and they understand the importance of developing a long-term relationship with their suppliers. Exhibit 2.8 summarizes these practices.

LEGAL IMPLICATIONS

When considering the legal implications involved in professional selling, it is important to consider the provincial, territorial, and federal legislation that is in place to regulate these activities.

The *Competition Act* is the major federal legislation in Canada that defines illegal practices, including

EXHIBIT 2.6

SMEI Certified Professional Salesperson Code of Ethics

The SMEI Certified Professional Salesperson (SCPS) Code of Ethics is a set of principles that outline minimum requirements for professional conduct. Those who attain SCPS status should consider these principles as more than just rules to follow. They are guiding standards above which the salesperson should rise.

An SCPS shall support and preserve the highest standards of professional conduct in all areas of sales and in all relationships in the sales process. Toward this end an SCPS pledges and commits to these standards in all activities under this code.

As an SCPS I pledge to the following individuals and parties:

I. With respect to **The Customer, I** will: Maintain honesty and integrity in my relationship with all customers and prospective customers.

Accurately represent my product or service in order to place the customer or prospective customer in a position to make a decision consistent with the principle of mutuality of benefit and profit to the buyer and seller. Continually keep abreast and increase the knowledge of my product(s), service(s), and industry in which I work. This is necessary to better serve those who place their trust in me.

II. With respect to **The Company** and other parties whom I represent, I will: Use their resources that are at my disposal and will be utilized only for legitimate business purposes.

Respect and protect proprietary and confidential information entrusted to me by my company.

Not engage in any activities that will either jeopardize or conflict with the interests of my company. Activities that may be or which may appear to be illegal or unethical will be strictly avoided. To this effect I will not participate in activities that are illegal or unethical.

III. With respect to **The Competition**, regarding those organizations and individuals that I compete with in the marketplace, I will:

Only obtain competitive information through legal and ethical methods.

Only portray my competitors, and their products and services in a manner which is honest, truthful, and based on accurate information that can or has been substantiated.

IV. With respect to **The Community** and society which provide me with my livelihood, I will: Engage in business and selling practices which contribute to a positive relationship with the communities in which I and my company have presence.

Support public policy objectives consistent with maintaining and protecting the environment and community.

Participate in community activities and associations which provide for the betterment of the community and society.

I AM COMMITTED to the letter and spirit of this code. The reputation of salespeople depends upon me as well as others who engage in the profession of selling. My adherence to these standards will strengthen the reputation and integrity for which we strive as professional salespeople.

I understand that failure to consistently act according to the above standards and principles could result in the forfeiture of the privilege of using the SCPS designation.

Candidate's Name (Please Print) ______________________________

Signature ______________________________

Date ______________________________

EXHIBIT 2.7

CPSA Sales Institute Code of Ethics

The CPSA Sales Institute Code of Ethics is the set of principles and standards that a certified sales professional will strive to adhere to with customers, organizations, competitors, communities, and colleagues.

The Certified Sales Professional pledges and commits to uphold these standards in all activities: I will:

1. Maintain honesty and integrity in all relationships with customers, prospective customers, and colleagues and continually work to earn their trust and respect.
2. Accurately represent my products or services to the best of my ability in a manner that places my customer or prospective customer and my company in a position that benefits both.
3. Respect and protect the proprietary and confidential information entrusted to me by my company and my customers and not engage in activities that may conflict with the best interest of my customers or my company.
4. Continually upgrade my knowledge of my products/services, skills, and my industry.
5. Use the time and resources available to me only for legitimate business purposes. I will only participate in activities that are ethical and legal, and when in doubt, I will seek counsel.
6. Respect my competitors and their products and services by representing them in a manner which is honest, truthful and based on accurate information that has been substantiated.
7. Endeavour to engage in business and selling practices which contribute to a positive relationship with the community.
8. Assist and counsel my fellow sales professionals where possible in the performance of their duties.
9. Abide by and encourage others to adhere to this Code of Ethics.

As a certified sales professional, I understand that the reputation and professionalism of all salespeople depends on me as well as others engaged in the sales profession, and I will adhere to these standards to strengthen the reputation and integrity for which we will strive. I understand that failure to consistently act according to this Code of Ethics may result in the loss of the privilege of using my professional sales designation.

EXHIBIT 2.8
Areas of Unethical Behaviour

Deceptive Practices	Illegal Activities	Noncustomer-Oriented Behaviour
Deceive	Defraud	Pushy
Hustle	Con	Hard sell
Scam	Misuse company assets	Fast talking
Exaggerate		High pressure
Withhold information/bluff		

price fixing Agreements between sellers to prevent or unduly lessen competition or to unreasonably enhance the price of a product by selling at a fixed price.

bid rigging An agreement in which competitors agree in advance who will win a bid based on the tenders submitted.

price discrimination Knwingly and systematically selling the same goods or services at different prices to different buyers.

predatory pricing A firm or an individual deliberately sets prices to incur losses for a long time to eliminate a competitor or to inhibit competition in the expectation that the firm or individual will later be able to recoup its losses by charging prices above competitive levels.

bait and switch selling Firms or individuals advertise products at bargain prices that they do not have available in reasonable quantities and try to sell more expensive products instead.

pyramid selling Fees or commissions paid not on the basis of product sales but on the recruitment of others to make sales.

price fixing, **bid rigging**, **price discrimination**, **predatory pricing**, **bait and switch selling**, and **pyramid selling**.

All Canadian provinces and territories have established a *cooling off* period during which the consumer may void a contract to purchase goods or services. These cooling off laws vary across jurisdictions, but their primary purpose is to give customers an opportunity to reconsider a buying decision made under a salesperson's persuasive influence. In most places, this legislation is referred to as the *Direct Sellers Act* or the *Consumer Protection Act*. For more information about the legislation involved with professional selling, please visit the Competition Bureau's website at www.competitionbureau.gc.ca.

It is also important to remember that sales representatives often have to engage in a contract with an individual or a firm to secure the sale. A *contract* is a promise or promises that the courts can enforce. Oral contracts are enforceable, but written contracts are preferable as they reduce the possibility of disagreement. Courts give written contracts greater weight in a lawsuit. A written contract may consist of a sales slip, a notation on a cheque, or any other writing that offers evidence of the promises the party made.

When a salesperson is hired, he or she may be asked to sign an employment contract. Most of these agreements include a *noncompete clause*. This prohibits salespeople from working for a competing firm for a set time (often a year) after they leave the position. Most clauses are legally binding even when an employee's position is cut.

Illegal Activities

Misuse of company assets has been a long-standing problem for many sales organizations. Using the company car for personal use, charging expenses that did not occur, and selling samples for income are examples of misusing company assets. Some of these violations of company property also constitute violations of Canada Revenue Agency (CRA) laws and are offences that could lead to jail or heavy fines.

Bribery is another area that causes some salespeople to run afoul of the law. A competitor may be offering bribes; this, in turn, puts pressure on the salesperson's company to respond with bribes of its own. It is difficult for a salesperson to see potential sales going to the competition. Salespeople offering bribes on their own can be punished. Companies that engage in bribery may find themselves being prosecuted and fined. In some cultures, giving bribes is perceived to be acceptable business practice. However, bribes or payoffs may violate federal government legislation. Canada has the *Corruption of Foreign Public Officials Act*, and for Canadian salespeople working with U.S. companies, the U.S. *Foreign Corrupt Practices Act (FCPA)* exists.

Another area of legal concern that involves the salesforce is product liability. Salespeople can create product liabilities for a company in three ways: **express warranty**, **misrepresentation**, and **negligence**. A salesperson can create a product warranty or guarantee that obligates the selling organization even if they do not intend to give the warranty. Express warranties are created by any affirmation of fact or promise, any description, or any sample or model that a salesperson uses, which is made part of the basis of the bargain.

Basis of the bargain is taken to mean that the buyer relied on the seller's statements in making the purchase decision. If a salesperson tells a prospect that a machine will turn out 50 units per hour, a legal obligation has been created for the firm to supply a machine that will accomplish this. A salesperson's misrepresentation can also lead to product liability even if the salesperson makes a false claim thinking it is true. The burden of accuracy is on the seller. Salespeople are required by law to exercise reasonable care in formulating claims. If a salesperson asserts that a given drug is safe without exercising reasonable care to see that this claim is accurate, the salesperson has been negligent. Negligence is a basis for product liability on the part of the seller.

Although these tactics may increase sales in the short run, salespeople ruin their trust relationship with their customer and company. Given the legal restrictions that relate to selling practices, a salesperson, as well as the selling organization, should exercise care in developing sales presentations.

HOW ARE COMPANIES DEALING WITH SALES ETHICS?

Many companies spend time covering ethics in their training programs. These programs should cover such topics as the appropriateness of gift giving, the use of expense accounts, and dealing with a prospect's unethical demands. Each company will have its own policies on gift giving. John Huff of Shering-Plough states, "Just a few years ago, I could spend my expense account on Indiana Pacers tickets or a golf outing with doctors. That is not the case today. There is a lot of grey area concerning gift giving by salespeople to their business clients and prospects. The pharmaceutical industry has policed itself so now gift giving has all but been eliminated. I must know the rules of my company and industry."[20] Some buyers are not allowed to accept gifts from salespeople.

Another important training area is the use of expense accounts. Salespeople should be trained in how to fill out the expense account form and what is acceptable for submission. Some companies allow personal kilometrage to be included; others do not. If guidelines are established, there is less chance for salesperson misunderstanding.

Sometimes unethical behaviour is not initiated by the salesperson but by the buyer. Salespeople must be trained in dealing with prospects who make unethical demands. Buyers can be under pressure from their company to stay within budget or to move up the timetable on an order. A buyer may ask a salesperson to move him or her up on the order list in exchange for more business down the road. One pharmacist set up a deal with a salesperson to buy samples illegally. The trust-based salesperson has to shut down any short-term gain for long-term success. A salesperson's career is over if the word circulates that he or she cannot be trusted.

A salesperson must also be concerned with our legal system and those of other countries. It cannot be an excuse for today's well-trained salesperson to say he or she did not know that a law was being broken. When in doubt, the salesperson must check out all provincial, territorial, and local laws. In addition, there are industry-specific rules and regulations to be considered. Exhibit 2.9 covers a number of legal reminders.

A salesperson has his or her reputation to tarnish only once. In this day and age of mass communication (phone, e-mail, Web sites), it is easy for a buyer to get the word out that a salesperson is acting unethically, possibly ending that salesperson's career.

express warranty A way a salesperson can create product liabilities by giving a product warranty or guarantee that obligates the selling organization even if the salesperson does not intend to give the warranty.

misrepresentation False claim(s) made by a salesperson.

negligence False claim(s) made by a salesperson about the product or service he or she is trying to sell.

basis of the bargain When a buyer relies on the seller's statements in making a purchase decision.

EXHIBIT 2.9

Legal Reminders

For salespeople

1. Use factual data rather than general statements of praise during the sales presentation. Avoid misrepresentation.
2. Thoroughly educate customers before the sale on the product's specifications, capabilities, and limitations.
3. Do not overstep your authority, as the salesperson's actions can be binding to the selling firm.
4. Avoid discussing these topics with competitors: prices, profit margins, discounts, terms of sale, bids or intent to bid, sales territories or markets to be served, rejection or termination of customers.
5. Do not use one product as bait for selling another product.
6. Do not try to force the customer to buy only from your organization.
7. Offer the same price and support to buyers who purchase under the same set of circumstances.
8. Do not tamper with a competitor's product.
9. Do not disparage a competitor's product without specific evidence of your contentions.
10. Avoid promises that will be difficult or impossible to honour.

For the sales organization

1. Review sales presentations and claims for possible legal problems.
2. Make the salesforce aware of potential conflicts with the law.
3. Carefully screen any independent sales agents the organization uses.
4. With technical products and services make sure the sales presentation fully explains the capabilities and dangers of products and service.

Visit **www.nelson.com/student** to find the resources you need today!

Located at the back of the textbook are rip-out Chapter Review cards. Make sure you also go online to check out other tools that SELL offers to help you successfully pass your course.

- Flashcards
- Glossary
- PowerPoint Notes
- Role-Play Videos
- Games
- Interactive Quizzing

KELLY MYERS' DILEMMA

Background

Kelly Myers has spent the past three months trying to gather all the information she needs to submit a bid on an order that is very important to her company. Bids are due tomorrow and the decision will be made within a week. She has made a great impression on the purchasing agent, Janet Williams, and she has just ended a conversation with her sales manager who believes Kelly needs to make one more call on Williams to see if she can find out any additional information that might help her prepare the bid. Kelly's boss specifically wants to know who the other bidders are.

Current Situation

Later that day, Kelly visited with Janet Williams. During the course of the conversation with Williams, Kelly asked who the other bidders were. Williams beat around the bush for a while, but she did not reveal the other bidders. She did mention the other bids were in and pulled the folder out of the filing cabinet where they were kept. Janet opened the file and looked over the bids in front of Kelly.

There was a knock on the door and Janet's boss asked if he could see her for a minute and she walked down the hall with her boss. Kelly realized all the bids were left out in front of her. There was a summary sheet of all of the bids on top and she could easily see all the bids. When Williams returned she returned the folder to the file and the two made some small talk and ended their conversation.

Kelly returned to her office and completed her bid and turned it in to Janet Williams the next morning. Kelly knew her bid would be the lowest by $500. One week later Kelly learned she won the bid.

Questions

1. What are the ethical issues involved in this situation?
2. If you were Kelly Myers, do you think Janet Williams intended for you to see the competitive bids? What would you have done, given this situation? Why?

CHAPTER 2

Role Play: Building Trust and Sales Ethics: Reef Uniform Company

Background

Reef Uniform Company (RUC) specializes in providing uniforms to hotels and restaurants. RUC is a new company from Australia trying to break into the Canadian market. They have had trouble breaking into larger accounts (Marriott, Delta, Sheraton) because as a new company they don't have the name recognition in Canada.

As the account exec in the area, you have been working on a new Sheraton hotel with over 5,000 rooms and 500 employees. You recently submitted a proposal and the buyer, Anthony Norman, has told you he is leaning your way with the order. He also told you that this order must come off without a hitch as his hide is on the line if things go wrong. You know there could be a problem down the road as one of your unions has been negotiating a contract that is about to expire. The last time this contract came up, there was a strike and orders were backlogged for weeks. The hotel has many customized uniforms and has to have these for their grand opening in three months. What is your obligation to the hotel having this information? This order will make your year and probably send you on a trip to Rome for exceeding quota.

Role Play

Location: Anthony Norman's office

Action: Role play a sales call with Anthony Norman, addressing the issues in the case.

© Rubberball Productions/Jupiter Images

what do you think?

Salespeople need to understand buyers so that they can manipulate them.

1 2 3 4 5 6 7

strongly disagree — strongly agree

Understanding buyers

provides a foundation for building customer value.

3 Understanding Buyers

After completing this chapter, you should be able to

3-1 Categorize the primary types of buyers, and discuss the distinguishing characteristics of business markets.

3-2 List the steps in the business-to-business buying process.

3-3 Discuss the different types of buyer needs.

3-4 Describe how buyers evaluate suppliers and alternative sales offerings by using the multiattribute model of evaluation.

3-5 Explain the two-factor model that buyers use to evaluate the performance of sales offerings and develop satisfaction.

3-6 Explain the different types of purchasing decisions.

3-7 Describe the four communication styles and how salespeople must adapt their own styles to maximize communication.

3-8 Explain the concept of buying teams and specify the different member roles.

3-9 Identify current developments in purchasing.

Introduction

Since 1898, International Paper (IP) has been one of the world's leading paper producers. As new media increasingly affected the demand and use for paper products, IP realized that it could no longer sell paper as a commodity, in which customers would check prices and make orders that IP would fulfill. It became ever apparent that the company needed salespeople who could add value to the customer interaction. Some customers, for example, might need advice about how various grades of paper could impact their brand image and subsequently affect their revenue. This prompted a need to change to a consultative selling approach, which required IP's salespeople to understand their customers' business and financial issues. "Business acumen is such an important part of our selling approach," says Calvin Carson, customer value manager of sales efficiency for International Paper. "If we don't understand how our customers make money and their financial situations, how can we provide tailored solutions? We need to understand their business strategies and how they go to market."

According to Carson, "International Paper's consultative sales approach requires sales representatives to look at and change many things. They listen to and identify a customer's needs, discover and validate those needs, create solutions, deliver those solutions and manage the customer's expectations. "This requires salespeople to understand what it takes for a customer to succeed. As such, salespeople must understand the financials of the customer's business and recognize how strategic concerns such as controlling capital expenditures, acquiring new equipment, cutting expenses, and improving accounts receivable can shape the bottom line. Thus, International Paper provided its salespeople with appropriate financial training so that they could fit the company's products and services within a customer's financial and strategic framework. Several signs suggest that the change in selling strategy is a success. First, their new selling approach helped customers to increase both the sale of their products and their margins. Second, salespeople did a better job of targeting customers, and improved the customer experience resulting in an increase in more cost-effective sales. Third, salespeople's greater knowledge of their customers resulted in more positive customer responses. Finally, training in the new process resulted in a more consultative sales approach. When salespeople began to discuss "summing up value and uncovering needs," Carson knew the new approach was a success. "I can say with confidence that as a result of this new sales approach, we've secured new business and we've renewed contracts," said Carson. "At the end of the day, we could quantify the value from a customer's perspective and from our perspective. It gave our sales organization more confidence to go in and talk to customers about what's on their minds and how we can help them succeed."

Source: "International Paper: Winning Business by Understanding Business," http://www.paradigmlearning.com/documents/ CS%20International%20Paper.pdf (accessed on May 11, 2011).

As the opening vignette illustrates, understanding customers is a key component in developing customer relationships. At International Paper, understanding the unique needs of each customer allows salespeople to tailor specific solutions for those needs. In doing so, salespeople are able to bring about value for these customers.

This chapter focuses on preparing you to better understand buyers. Following a discussion on different types of buyers, this chapter develops a model of the buying process and the corresponding roles of the salesperson. Buyer activities characteristic of each step of the purchase decision process are explained and related to salesperson activities for effectively interacting with buyers. This is followed by an explanation of different types of purchasing decisions to which salespeople must respond. The influence of individual communication styles on selling effectiveness is also discussed. The growing incidence of multiple buying influences and buying teams is then demonstrated, along with their impact on selling strategy. Finally, current developments such as the increasing use of information technology, buyers' access to and demand for relevant information, relationship strategies, supply-chain management, target pricing, and the increased importance of knowledge and creativity are discussed from the perspective of the salesperson.

consumer markets A market in which consumers purchase goods and services for their use or consumption.

business markets A market composed of firms, institutions, and governments that acquire goods and services to use as inputs into their own manufacturing process, for use in their day-to-day operations, or for resale to their own customers.

3-1 Types of Buyers

Salespeople work and interact with many different types of buyers. These buyer types range from heavy industry and manufacturing operations to consumers making a purchase for their own use. These variants of customer types arise out of the unique buying situations they occupy. As a result, one type of buyer will have needs, motivations, and buying behaviour that are very different from another type of buyer. Consider the different buying situations and the resulting needs of a corporate buyer for Foot Locker compared with the athletic equipment buyer for a major university or Joe Smith, attorney at law and weekend warrior in the local YMCA's basketball league. As illustrated in Exhibit 3.1, each of these buyers may be looking for athletic shoes, but their buying needs are very different. To maximize selling effectiveness, salespeople must understand the type of buyer with whom they are working and respond to their specific needs, wants, and expectations.

The most common categorization of buyers splits them into either (1) **consumer markets** or (2) **business markets**. Consumers purchase goods and services for their own use or consumption and are highly influenced by peer group behaviour, aesthetics, and personal taste. Business markets are composed of firms, institutions, and governments. These members of the business market acquire goods and services to use as inputs into their own manufacturing process (e.g., raw materials, component parts, and capital equipment), for use in their day-to-day operations (e.g., office supplies, professional services, insurance), or for resale to their own customers. Business customers tend to stress overall value as the cornerstone for purchase decisions.

Distinguishing Characteristics of Business Markets

Although there are similarities between consumer and business buying behaviours, business markets tend to be much more complex and possess several characteristics that are in sharp contrast to those of the consumer market. These distinguishing characteristics are described in the following sections.

CONCENTRATED DEMAND

Business markets typically exhibit high levels of concentration in which a small number of large buyers account for most of the purchases. The fact that business buyers tend to be larger in size but fewer in numbers can greatly affect a salesperson's selling plans and performance. For example, a salesperson selling grade

EXHIBIT 3.1
Different Needs of Different Athletic Shoe Buyers

	Buyer for Foot Locker Shoe Stores	University Athletic Equipment Buyer	Joe Smith—YMCA Weekend Warrior
Functional needs	• Has the features customers want • Well constructed—minimizes returns • Offers point-of-sale displays for store use • Competitive pricing	• Individualized sole texture for different player performance needs • Perfect fit and size for each team member • Custom match with university colours • Size of supplier's payment to coach and school for using their shoes	• Cutting-edge shoe features • Prominent brand logo • Highest-priced shoes in the store
Situational needs	• Can supply stores across North America • Ability to ship to individual stores on a just-in-time basis • Offers 90-day trade credit	• Ability to deliver on time • Provide supplier personnel for team fittings • Make contract payments to university and coach at beginning of season	• Right size in stock, ready to carry out • Takes Visa and MasterCard
Social needs	• Invitation for buying team to attend trade show and supplier-sponsored reception	• Sponsor and distribute shoes at annual team shoe night to build enthusiasm • Include team and athletes in supplier brand promotions	• Offers user-group newsletter to upscale customers • Periodic mailings for new products and incentives to purchase
Psychological needs	• Assurance that shoes will sell at retail • Brand name with strong market appeal • Option to return unsold goods for credit	• Brand name consistent with players' self-images • The entire team will accept and be enthusiastic toward product decision • Belief that the overall contract is best for the university, team, and coaches	• Reinforces customer's self-image as an innovator • Product will deliver the promised performance • Customer wants to be one of only a few people purchasing this style of shoe
Knowledge needs	• Level of quality—how the shoe is constructed • How the new features affect performance • What makes the shoe unique and superior to competitive offerings • Product training and materials for sales staff	• What makes the shoe unique and superior to competitive offerings • Supporting information and assurance that the contracted payments to university and coaches are superior to competitive offerings	• What makes the shoe unique and superior to competitive offerings • Assurance that everybody on the court will not be wearing the same shoe

industrial silicon for use in manufacturing computer chips will find that his or her fate rests on acquiring and nurturing the business of one or more of the four or five dominant chip makers around the world.

DERIVED DEMAND

Derived demand denotes that the demand in business markets is closely associated with the demand for consumer goods. When the consumer demand for new cars and trucks increases, the demand for rolled steel also goes up. Of course, when the demand for consumer products goes down, so goes the related demand in business markets. The most effective salespeople identify and monitor the consumer markets that are related to their business customers so they can better anticipate shifts in demand and assist their buyers in staying ahead of the demand shifts rather than being caught with too much, too little, or even the wrong inventory. Republic Gypsum's salespeople accurately forecasted a boom in residential construction and the pressure it would put on the supply of sheetrock wallboard. Working closely with their key customers, order quantities and shipping dates were revised to prevent those customers from being caught with inadequate inventories to supply the expanded demand. This gave those customers a significant advantage over their competitors, who were surprised and suddenly out of stock.

HIGHER LEVELS OF DEMAND FLUCTUATION

Closely related to the derived demand characteristic, the demand for goods and services in the business market is more volatile than that of the consumer market. In economics, this is referred to as the **acceleration principle**. As demand increases (or decreases) in the consumer market, the business market reacts by accelerating the buildup (or reduction) of inventories and increasing (or decreasing) plant capacity. A good example would be the rapidly growing demand for tri-mode wireless phones with advanced capabilities such as voice-activated dialling and vision-enabled access to the Internet and Web with enhanced full-colour screens. In response to higher consumer demand, wholesalers and retailers are increasing their inventories of these advanced phones while decreasing the number of single-mode voice-only devices they carry. In response, manufacturers have shifted their production away from the voice-only wireless phones to increase their production of the more advanced Internet-capable models. Salespeople are the source of valuable information and knowledge, enabling their customers to anticipate these fluctuations and assisting them in developing more effective marketing strategies. As a result, both the buying and selling organizations realize mutual positive benefits.

derived demand Demand in business markets that is closely associated with the demand for consumer goods.

acceleration principle When demand increases (or decreases) in the consumer market, the business market reacts by accelerating the buildup (or reduction) of inventories and increasing (or decreasing) plant capacity.

PURCHASING PROFESSIONALS

Buyers in the business markets are trained as purchasing agents. The process of identifying suppliers and sourcing goods and services is their job. This results in a more professional and rational approach to purchasing. As a result, salespeople must possess increased levels of knowledge and expertise to provide customers with a richer and more detailed assortment of application, performance, and technical data.

Salespeople in business markets work closely with buyers to satisfy various needs aimed at improving their business performance.

MULTIPLE BUYING INFLUENCES

Reflecting the increased complexity of many business purchases, groups of individuals within the buying firm often work together as a buying team or centre. As a result, salespeople often

© nyul/iStockphoto

work simultaneously with several individuals during a sales call and even different sets of buyers during different sales calls. Buying team members come from different areas of expertise and play different roles in the purchasing process. To be effective, the salesperson must first identify, and then understand and respond to, the role and key buying motives of each member.

Close Buyer–Seller Relationships

The smaller customer base and increased usage of supply chain management, characterized by buyers becoming highly involved in organizing and administering logistical processes and actively managing a reduced set of suppliers, has resulted in buyers and sellers becoming much more interdependent than ever before. This increased interdependence and desire to reduce risk of the unknown has led to an emphasis on developing long-term buyer–seller relationships characterized by increased levels of buyer–seller interaction and higher levels of service expectations by buyers. As demonstrated in "Professional Selling in the 21st Century: Achieving Sales Excellence,"[1] buyers are looking for concrete actions that demonstrate a salesperson's commitment to a relationship. Such actions show the salesperson's willingness to support the buyer and be a partner in his or her firm's success.

PROFESSIONAL SELLING IN THE 21ST CENTURY

Achieving Sales Excellence

Howard Stevens, chairman and CEO of the HR Chally Group, has spent more than a decade trying to understand what buyers expect from salespeople. The HR Chally Group spent 14 years interviewing 80,000 business customers and collecting data on 300,000 sales professionals representing 7,200 salesforces from over 15 major industries. The results provide several expectations that buyers have of salespeople, all of which demonstrate to buyers the seller's willingness to help the customer succeed. As such, salespeople are expected to:

- Personally manage the customer's desired results;
- Fully understand the customer's business;
- Act as an advocate on behalf of the customer by working with those within the seller's company to ensure customer value is delivered;
- Provide the customer with applications for how the offering will solve a problem and add value;
- Be easily accessible to respond to ongoing concerns;
- Solve customer problems after the sale, and;
- Provide innovative solutions to customer needs.

By fulfilling these expectations, salespeople can add value to the customer buying experience.

3-2 The Buying Process

Although not always the case in the consumer marketplace, buyers in the business marketplace typically undergo a conscious and logical process in making purchase decisions. As depicted in Figure 3.1, the sequential and interrelated phases of the business buyer's purchase process has eight phases: (1) recognition of the problem or need, (2) determination of the characteristics of the item and the quantity needed, (3) description of the characteristics of the item and quantity needed, (4) search for and qualification of potential sources, (5) acquisition and analysis of proposals, (6) evaluation of proposals and selection of suppliers, (7) selection of an order routine, and (8) performance feedback and evaluation.

Depending on the nature of the buying organization and the buying situation, the buying process may be highly formalized or simply a rough approximation of what actually occurs. The decision process General Motors employs for the acquisition of a new organization-wide computer system will be highly formalized and purposefully reflect each of the

FIGURE 3.1

Comparison of Buying Decision Process Phases and Corresponding Steps in the Selling Process

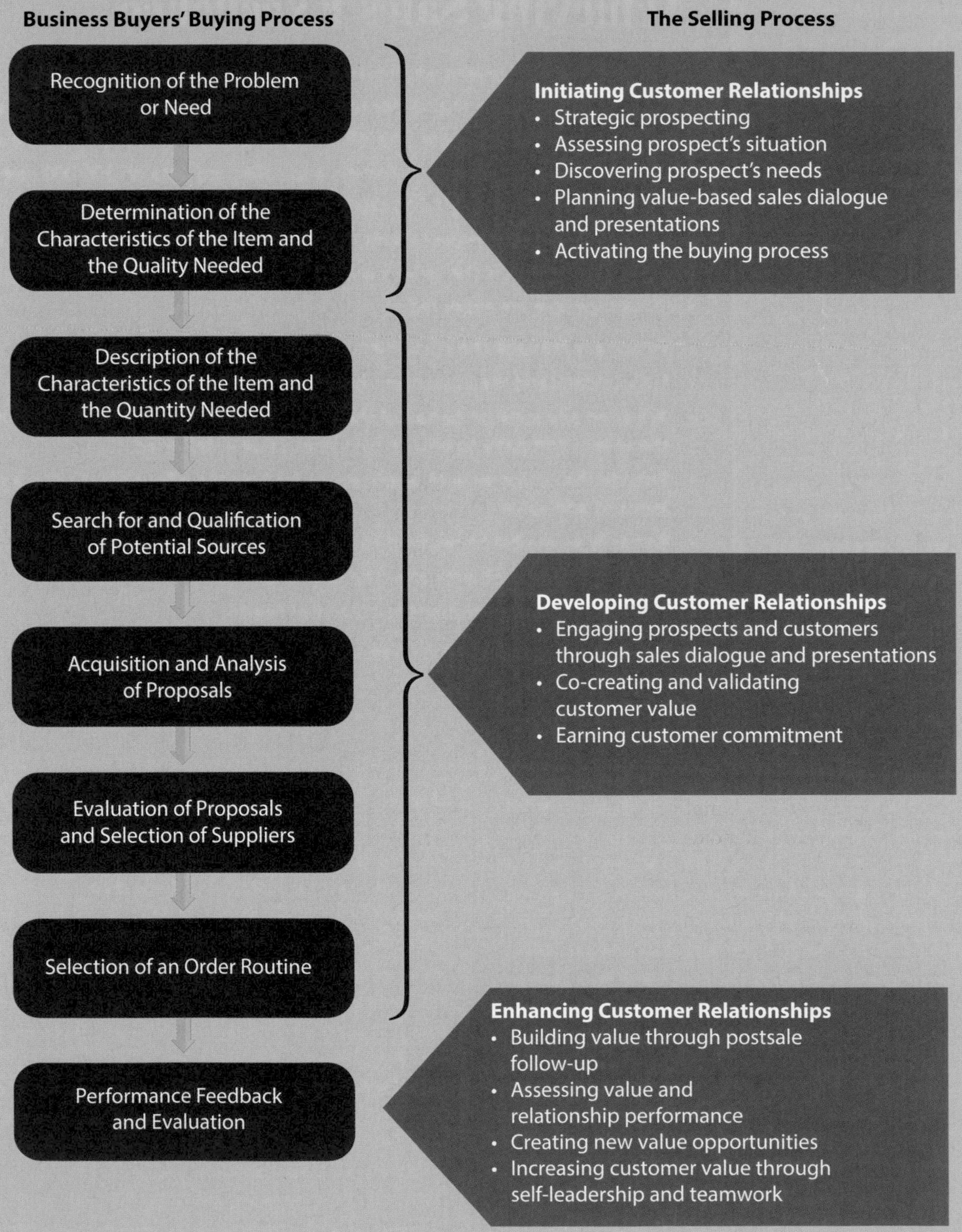

previously described decision phases. Compared with General Motors, the decision process of Bloomington Bookkeeping, a single office and four-person operation, could be expected to be less formalized. In the decision to replenish stock office supplies, both organizations are likely to use a much less formalized routine—but still, the routine will reflect the different decision phases.

As Figure 3.1 further illustrates, there is a close correspondence between the phases of the buyer's decision process and the selling activities of the salesperson. It is important that salespeople understand and make use of the interrelationships between the phases of the buying process and selling activities. Effective use of these interrelationships offers salespeople numerous opportunities to interact with buyers in a way that shapes product specifications and the selection of sources while facilitating the purchase decision.

Business buyers typically undergo a conscious and logical process in making purchase decisions.

PHASE ONE—RECOGNITION OF THE PROBLEM OR NEED: THE NEEDS GAP

Needs are the result of a gap between buyers' **desired states** and their **actual states**. Consequently, need recognition results from an individual cognitively and emotionally processing information relevant to his or her actual state of being and comparing it with the desired state of being. As illustrated in Figure 3.2, any perceived difference, or **needs gap**, between these two states activates the motivation or drive to fill the gap and reach the desired state. For example, the SnowRunner Company's daily production capacity is limited to 1,000 moulded skimobile body housings. Their research indicates that increasing capacity to 1,250 units per day would result in significant reductions in per-unit costs and allow them to enter additional geographic markets—both moves that would have significant and positive impacts on financial performance. The perceived need to expand production activates a corresponding motivation to search for information regarding alternative solutions and acquire the capability to increase production by 250 units.

However, if there is no gap, then there is no need and no active buying motive. It is common for salespeople to find themselves working with buyers who, for one reason or another, do not perceive a needs gap to be present. It is possible that they do not have the right information or lack a full understanding of the situation and the existence of options better than their current state. It is also possible that their understanding of the actual state might be incomplete or mistaken. For example, SnowRunner's buyers might not understand the cost-reduction possibilities and increased market potential that could result from increased capacity. As a result, they perceive no need to

desired states A state of being based on what the buyer desires.

actual states A buyer's actual state of being.

needs gap A perceived difference between a buyer's desired and actual state of being.

FIGURE 3.2
The Needs Gap

Desired State Produce 1,250 units per day	
	The Gap or Need 250 units per day
Actual State Produce 1,000 units per day	

The needs gap is the difference between the buyer's perceived desired state and the buyer's perceived actual state.

situational needs The needs that are contingent on, and often a result of, conditions related to the specific environment, time, and place.

functional needs The need for a specific core task or function to be performed.

social needs The need for acceptance from and association with others.

psychological needs The desire for feelings of assurance and risk reduction, as well as positive emotions and feelings, such as success, joy, excitement, and stimulation.

knowledge needs The desire for personal development, information, and knowledge to increase thought and understanding as to how and why things happen.

increase production—the desired state is the same as their actual state. Similarly, the buyers might be functioning with incomplete information regarding the company's actual state of reduced production capacity because of SnowRunner's existing moulding machines requiring increased downtime for maintenance. Properly realized, this lowering of the actual state would result in a needs gap. Successful salespeople position themselves to assist buyers in identifying and understanding needs as a result of their broader expertise and knowledge regarding product use and application. Salespeople can also use sales conversations to present buyers with information and opportunities that effectively raise the desired state, generate a need, and trigger the purchase decision process. Top-performing salespeople understand the importance of assisting their buyers in forming realistic perceptions of the actual state and the desired state. In this manner, the salesperson can continue to serve as a nonmanipulative consultant to the buyer while affecting buying motives that yield mutual benefits to all parties. However, it should be noted that the persuasive power of assisting the buyer in determining and comparing desired and actual states can also be misused and lead to unethical and manipulative selling behaviours, such as those exhibited in "An Ethical Dilemma."

3-3 Types of Buyer Needs

The total number of potential customer needs is infinite and sometimes difficult for salespeople to grasp and understand on a customer-by-customer basis. Consequently, many salespeople find it helpful to group customer needs into one of five basic types or categories that focus on the buying situation and the benefits to be provided by the product or service being chosen.[2] These five general types of buyer needs are described as follows:

- **Situational needs** are the specific needs that are contingent on, and often a result of, conditions related to the specific environment, time, and place (e.g., emergency car repair while travelling out of town, a piece of customized production equipment to fulfill a customer's specific situational requirements, or providing for quick initial shipment to meet a buyer's out-of-stock status).
- **Functional needs** represent the need for a specific core task or function to be performed—the functional purpose of a specific product or service. The need for a sales offering to do what it is supposed to do (e.g., alcohol disinfects, switches open and close to control some flow, the flow control valve is accurate and reliable).
- **Social needs** comprise the need for acceptance from and association with others—a desire to belong to some reference group. For example, a product or service might be associated with some specific and desired affinity group or segment (e.g., Polo clothing is associated with upper-income, successful people; ISO 9000 Certification is associated with high-quality vendors; leading e-commerce Web sites include discussion groups to build a sense of community).
- **Psychological needs** reflect the desire for feelings of assurance and risk reduction, as well as positive emotions and feelings such as success, joy, excitement, and stimulation (e.g., a Mont Blanc pen generates a feeling of success; effective training programs create a sense of self-control and determination; selection and use of well-known, high-quality brands provides assurance to buyers and organizations alike).
- **Knowledge needs** represent the desire for personal development, information, and knowledge to increase thought and understanding as to how and why things happen (e.g., product information, newsletters, brochures, along with training and user support group meetings or conferences, provide current information on products and topics of interest).

Categorizing buyer needs by type can assist the salesperson in bringing order to what could otherwise be a confusing and endless mix of needs and expectations. Organizing the buyer's different needs into their basic types can help salespeople in several ways. First, as Exhibit 3.1 and the example worksheet in Exhibit 3.2 illustrate, the basic types can serve as a checklist or worksheet to ensure that no significant problems or needs have been overlooked in the process of needs seeking should determine a salesperson's strategy for working with that buyer.

Consequently, it should be noted that the needs of business buyers tend to be more complex than consumers' needs. As with consumers, organizational buyers are influenced by the same functional, social, psychological, knowledge, and situational experiences and forces that affect and shape individual needs. However, in addition to those individual needs, organizational buyers must also satisfy the needs and requirements of the organization for which they work. As Figure 3.3 depicts, these organizational needs overlay and interact with the needs of the individual. To maximize selling effectiveness in the organizational or business-to-business market, salespeople must generate solutions addressing both the individual and organizational needs of business buyers.

An Ethical Dilemma

Jeff Hunt is a sales representative for a firm that manufactures and sells various packaging machines. Jeff is meeting with a prospect, Roger Halbot, who is a purchaser for a midsized beer manufacturer looking to expand its business. Thus, the company is in need of an additional bottle labeller. The bottle labeller currently used by the company was bought at auction several years ago. Having found Jeff's company on the Internet, Roger contacted Jeff and they set up a meeting at Roger's office. Upon assessing Roger's needs, Jeff determined that Roger was looking for a roll-fed bottle labeller capable of labelling up to 1,200 bottles per minute. This concerned Jeff because the fastest bottler he carried was capable of labelling only up to 1,000 bottles per minute. Currently, Roger's company was not running at full capacity, but he felt he would need this capability in the near future to meet expected demand. While Jeff knew his labeller would work fine for the near future, he also knew that given Roger's future needs, a faster bottler would actually be the most beneficial purchase. Jeff really wanted to make this sale as it would be instrumental in him achieving a bonus. The bonus would be particularly useful to help Jeff pay for the medications associated with his wife's cancer. Jeff believes he could work with Roger to get him to reassess his needs and convince him that the machine he has to offer will be quick enough to meet production needs now and in the future, particularly given that there is no guarantee of an expected growth in sales. Jeff surmises that if Roger's company outgrew this labeller, they could always purchase an additional labeller from him down the road. What should Jeff do?

a) Try to convince Roger he does not need a labeller that does 1,200 labels per minute.
b) Suggest an alternate label machine supplier and ask Roger to keep him in mind for additional packaging machinery needs.
c) Refer to his company's code of conduct and/or contact his sales manager and ask for advice.

discovery. Organizing what at first might appear to be different needs and problems into their common types also helps the salesperson to better understand the nature of the buyer's needs along with the interrelationships and commonalities between them. In turn, this enhanced understanding and the framework of basic types combine to serve as a guide for salespeople in generating and then demonstrating value-added solutions in response to the specific needs of the buyer.

As previously discussed, the specific circumstances or types of solution benefits that a buyer is

PHASE TWO—DETERMINATION OF THE CHARACTERISTICS OF THE ITEM AND THE QUANTITY NEEDED

Coincident to recognizing a need or problem is the motivation and drive to resolve it by undertaking a search for additional information leading to possible solutions. This particular phase of the buying process involves the consideration and study of the overall situation to understand what is required in the form of a preferred solution. This begins to establish the general characteristics and quantities necessary to resolve the need or

EXHIBIT 3.2

Example Worksheet for Organizing Buyer Needs and Benefit-Based Solutions

Primary Buyer: Buying Organization: Primary Industry:	**Bart Waits SouthWest Metal Stampings Stamped Metal Parts and Subcomponents**
Basic Type of Need	**Buyer's Specific Needs**
Buyer's situational needs	• Requires an 18 percent increase in production to meet increased sales • On-hand inventory will not meet production/delivery schedule • Tight cash flow pending initial deliveries and receipt of payment
Buyer's functional needs	• Equipment to provide effective and efficient increase in production • Expedited delivery and installation in six weeks or less • Equipment financing extending payments beyond initial receipts
Buyer's social needs	• Expansion in production transforms them into Top 10 in Industry • Belonging to user group of companies using this equipment • Feeling that they are an important customer of the supplier
Buyer's psychological needs	• Confidence that selected equipment will meet needs and do the job • Assurance that seller can complete installation in six weeks • Saving face—to believe borrowing for equipment is common
Buyer's knowledge needs	• Evidence that this is the right choice • Understanding new technology featured in the selected equipment • Training program for production employees and maintenance staff

problem. Through effective sales conversations, salespeople use their knowledge and expertise at this point to assist the buyer in analyzing and interpreting the problem situation and needs. Salespeople offer valuable knowledge of problem situations and solution options that buyers typically perceive as beneficial.

The ship-building company commissioned to build this ocean freightliner had specialized functional needs when it came to the boat's massive propeller.

© Dan Barnes/iStockphoto

PHASE THREE—DESCRIPTION OF THE CHARACTERISTICS OF THE ITEM AND THE QUANTITY NEEDED

Using the desired characteristics and quantities developed in the previous phase as a starting point, buyers translate that general information into detailed specifications

FIGURE 3.3

Complex Mix of Business Buyer Needs

Organizational Needs: Social, Psychological, Situational, Knowledge, Functional

Individual Needs: Social, Situational, Psychological, Knowledge, Functional

Business buyers' needs are a combination of the buyers' individual needs and the organization's needs.

describing exactly what is expected and required. The determination of detailed specifications serves several purposes. First, detailed specifications guide supplier firms in developing their proposals. Second, these specifications give the buyer a framework for evaluating, comparing, and choosing among the proposed solutions. Postpurchase specifications serve as a standard for evaluation to ensure that the buying firm receives the required product features and quantities. Trust-based buyer–seller relationships allow salespeople to work closely with buyers and collaboratively assist them in establishing the detailed specifications of the preferred solutions.

© Ethan Miller/Getty Images

PHASE FOUR—SEARCH FOR AND QUALIFICATION OF POTENTIAL SOURCES

Next, buyers must locate and qualify potential suppliers capable of providing the preferred solution. Although buyers certainly use information provided by salespeople to identify qualified suppliers, an abundance of information is available from other sources, such as trade associations, product source directories, trade shows, the Internet, advertising, and word of mouth. Once identified, potential suppliers are qualified on their ability to perform and deliver consistently at the level of quality and quantity required. Because of the large number of information sources available to buyers researching potential suppliers, one of the most important tasks in personal selling is to win the position of one of those information sources and keep buyers informed about the salesperson's company, its new products, and solution capabilities.

Buyers sometimes attend trade shows to find qualified suppliers.

requests for proposals (RFPs) A form created by firms and distributed to qualified potential suppliers that helps suppliers develop and submit proposals to provide products as specified by the firm.

PHASE FIVE—ACQUISITION AND ANALYSIS OF PROPOSALS

Based on the detailed specifications, **requests for proposals** (known in the trade as **RFPs**) are developed and distributed to the qualified potential suppliers. Based

multiattribute model A procedure for evaluating suppliers and products that incorporates weighted averages across desired characteristics.

on the RFP, qualified suppliers develop and submit proposals to provide the products as specified. Salespeople play a critical and influential role in this stage of the buying process by developing and presenting the proposed solution to the buyers. In this role, the salesperson is responsible for presenting the proposed features and benefits in such a manner that the proposed solution is evaluated as providing higher levels of benefits and value to the buyer than other competing proposals. Consequently, it is imperative that salespeople understand the basic evaluation procedures used by buyers in comparing alternative and competitive proposals so they can be more proficient in demonstrating the superiority of their solution over the competition.

3-4 Procedures for Evaluating Suppliers and Products

Purchase decisions are based on buyers' comparative evaluations of suppliers and the products and services they propose for satisfying buyers' needs. Some buyers may look for the sales offering that receives the highest rating on the one characteristic they perceive as being most important. Others may prefer the sales offering that achieves some acceptable assessment score across each and every attribute desired by the buyer. However, research into how purchase decisions are made suggests that most buyers use a compensatory, **multiattribute model** incorporating weighted averages across desired characteristics.[3] These weighted averages incorporate (1) assessments of how well the product or supplier performs in meeting each of the specified characteristics and (2) the relative importance of each specified characteristic.

ASSESSMENT OF PRODUCT OR SUPPLIER PERFORMANCE

The first step in applying the multiattribute model is to rate objectively how well each characteristic of the competing products or suppliers meets the buyers' needs. Let us use the example of General Motors (GM) evaluating adhesives for use in manufacturing. The buyers have narrowed the alternatives to products proposed by three suppliers: BondIt #302, AdCo #45, and StikFast #217. As illustrated in Exhibit 3.3, the GM buying team has assessed the competitive products according to how well they perform on certain important attributes. These assessments are converted to scores as depicted in Exhibit 3.4, with scores ranging from 1 (very poor performance) to 10 (excellent performance).

As illustrated, no single product is consistently outstanding across each of the eight identified

EXHIBIT 3.3
Important Product Information

Characteristics	BondIt #302	AdCo #45	StikFast #217
Ease of application	Excellent	Good	Very good
Bonding time	8 minutes	10 minutes	12 minutes
Durability	10 years	12 years	15 years
Reliability	Very good	Excellent	Good
Nontoxic	Very good	Excellent	Very good
Quoted price	$7 per L	$5.5 per L	$6.5 per L
Shelf-life in storage	6 months	4 months	4 months
Service factors	Good	Very good	Excellent

EXHIBIT 3.4

Product Performance Scores

Characteristics	BondIt #302	AdCo #45	StikFast #217
Ease of application	10	5	8
Bonding time	8	6	4
Durability	6	8	9
Reliability	8	10	5
Nontoxic	8	10	8
Quoted price	5	9	7
Shelf-life in storage	9	6	6
Service factors	5	8	10

characteristics. Although BondIt #302 is easy to apply and uses the buyer's current equipment, it is also more expensive and has the shortest durability time in the field. StikFast #217 also scores well for ease of application, and it has superior durability. However, it has the longest bonding time and could negatively influence production time.

ACCOUNTING FOR RELATIVE IMPORTANCE OF EACH CHARACTERISTIC

To compare these performance differences properly, each score must be weighted by the characteristic's perceived importance. In the adhesive example, importance weights are assigned on a scale of 1 (relatively unimportant) to 10 (very important). As illustrated in Exhibit 3.5, multiplying each performance score by the corresponding attribute's importance weight results in a weighted average that can be totalled to calculate an overall rating for each product. Keep in mind that each alternative product generally must meet a minimum specification on each desired product characteristic for it to be considered. The product or supplier having the highest comparative rating is typically the product selected for purchase. In this example, AdCo has the highest overall evaluation, totalling 468 points, compared with BondIt's 430 points and StikFast's 438 points.

EMPLOYING BUYER EVALUATION PROCEDURES TO ENHANCE SELLING STRATEGIES

Understanding evaluation procedures and gaining insight as to how a specific buyer or team of buyers is evaluating suppliers and proposals is vital for the salesperson to be effective and requires the integration of several bases of knowledge. First, information gathered before the sales call must be combined with an effective needs-discovery dialogue with the buyer(s) to delineate the buyers' needs and the nature of the desired solution. This establishes the most likely criteria for evaluation. Further discussion between the buyer and seller can begin to establish the importance the buyers place on each of the different performance criteria and often yields information as to what suppliers and products are being considered. Using this information and the salesperson's knowledge of how his or her products compare with competitors' offerings allows the salesperson to complete a likely facsimile of the buyers' evaluation. With this enhanced level of preparation and understanding, the salesperson can plan, create, and deliver a more effective presentation by using the five fundamental strategies that are inherent within the evaluation procedures buyers use.

- *Modify the Product Offering Being Proposed.* Often, in the course of preparing or delivering a presentation, it becomes apparent that the product offering will not maximize the buyer's evaluation score in comparison with a competitor's offering. In this case, the strategy would be to modify or change the product to one that better meets the buyer's overall needs and thus would receive a higher evaluation. For example, by developing a better understanding of the adhesive buyer's perceived importance of certain characteristics, the BondIt

EXHIBIT 3.5

Weighted Averages for Performance Times Importance (P × I) and Overall Evaluation Scores

	BondIt #302			AdCo #45			StikFast #217		
Characteristics	**P**	**I**	**P × I**	**P**	**I**	**P × I**	**P**	**I**	**P × I**
Ease of application	10	8	80	5	8	40	8	8	64
Bonding time	8	6	48	6	6	36	4	6	24
Durability	6	9	54	8	9	72	9	9	81
Reliability	8	7	56	10	7	70	5	7	35
Nontoxic	8	6	48	10	6	60	8	6	48
Quoted price	5	10	50	9	10	90	7	10	70
Shelf-life in storage	9	6	54	6	6	36	6	6	36
Service factors	5	8	40	8	8	64	10	8	80
Overall evaluation score			430			468			438

salesperson could offer a different adhesive formulation that is not as easy to apply (low perceived importance) but offers improved durability (high perceived importance) and more competitive price (high perceived importance).

- *Alter the Buyer's Beliefs about the Proposed Offering*. Provide information and support to alter the buyer's beliefs as to where the proposed product stands on certain attributes. This is a recommended strategy for cases in which the buyer underestimates the true qualities of the proposed product. However, if the buyer's perceptions are correct, this strategy would encourage the salesperson to exaggerate and overstate claims and, thus, should be avoided. In the instance of BondIt #302's low evaluation score, the salesperson could offer the buyer information and evidence that the product's durability and service factors actually perform much better than the buyer initially believed. By working with the buyer to develop a more realistic perception of the product's performance, BondIt #302 could become the buyer's preferred choice.

competitive depositioning Providing information to create a more accurate picture of a competitor's attributes or qualities.

- *Alter the Buyer's Beliefs about the Competitor's Offering*. For a variety of reasons, buyers often mistakenly believe that a competitor's offering has higher level attributes or qualities than it actually does. In such an instance, the salesperson can provide information to create a more accurate picture of the competitor's attributes. This has been referred to as **competitive depositioning** and is carried out by openly comparing (not simply degrading) the competing offering's attributes, advantages, and weaknesses. As an illustration, the BondIt salesperson might demonstrate the total cost for each of the three product alternatives, including a quoted price, ease of application, and bonding time. BondIt is much easier to apply and has a faster bonding time. Consequently, less of it needs to be applied for each application, which results in a significantly lower total cost and a much-improved evaluation score.
- *Alter the Importance Weights*. In this strategy, the salesperson uses information to emphasize and thus increase the importance of certain attributes on which the product offering is exceptionally strong. In the case of attributes on which the offering might be short, the strategy would be to deemphasize their importance. Continuing the adhesive purchase decision, BondIt's

salesperson might offer information to influence the buyer's importance rating for ease of application and storage shelf-life—two characteristics in which BondIt is much stronger than the two competitors.

- *Call Attention to Neglected Attributes.* If it becomes apparent that significant attributes may have been neglected or overlooked, the salesperson can increase the buyer's evaluation of the proposed offering by pointing out the attribute that was missed. For instance, the BondIt #302 adhesive dries to an invisible, transparent, and semiflexible adhesive compared with the two competitors, which cure to a light grey that could detract from the final product if the adhesive flowed out of the joint. The appearance of the final product is a significant concern, and this neglected attribute could substantially influence the comparative evaluations.

PHASE SIX—EVALUATION OF PROPOSALS AND SELECTION OF SUPPLIERS

The buying decision is the outcome of the buyer's evaluation of the various proposals acquired from potential suppliers. Typically, further negotiations will be conducted with the selected supplier(s) for the purpose of establishing the final terms regarding product characteristics, pricing, and delivery. Salespeople play a central role in gaining the buyer's commitment to the purchase decision and in the subsequent negotiations of the final terms.

PHASE SEVEN—SELECTION OF AN ORDER ROUTINE

Once the supplier(s) has been selected, details associated with the purchase decision must be settled. These details include delivery quantities, locations, and times along with return policies and the routine for reorders associated with the purchase. For cases in which the purchase requires multiple deliveries over time, the routine for placing subsequent orders and making deliveries must be set out and understood. Is the order routine standardized on the basis of a prearranged time schedule, or is the salesperson expected to monitor usage and inventories to place orders and schedule shipments? Will orders be placed automatically through the use of electronic data interchange or the Internet? Regardless of the nature of the order routine, the salesperson plays a critical role in facilitating communication, completing ordering procedures, and settling the final details.

As established in an order routine, a salesperson takes an order at the customer's site with a handheld device and then transmits the order via global system for mobile communications to the applicable warehouse.

PHASE EIGHT—PERFORMANCE FEEDBACK AND EVALUATION

The final phase in the buying process is the evaluation of performance and feedback shared among all parties for the purpose of improving future performance and enhancing buyer–seller relationships. Research supports that salespeople's customer interaction activities and communication at this stage of the buying process become the primary determinants of customer satisfaction and buyer loyalty. Consequently, it is critical that salespeople continue working with buyers after the sale. The salesperson's follow-up activities provide the critical points of contact between the buyer and seller to ensure consistent performance, respond to and take care of problems, maximize customer satisfaction, create new value opportunities, and further enhance buyer–seller relationships.

3-5 Understanding Postpurchase Evaluation and the Formation of Satisfaction

Research shows that buyers evaluate their experience with a product purchase on the basis of product characteristics that fall into a **two-factor model of evaluation** as depicted in Figure 3.4.[4] The first category, **functional attributes**, refers to the features and characteristics that are related to what the product actually does or is expected to do—its functional characteristics. These functional characteristics have also been referred to as **must-have attributes**, features of the core product that the customer takes for granted. These are the attributes that must be present for the supplier or product to even be included among those being considered for purchase. Consequently, they tend to be fairly common across the set of suppliers and products being considered for purchase by a buyer. Such characteristics as reliability, durability, conformance to specifications, competitive pricing, and performance are illustrative of functional attributes.

Psychological attributes make up the second general category. This category refers to how things are carried out and done between the buyer and seller. These supplier and market offering characteristics are described as the **delighter attributes**—the augmented features and characteristics included in the total market

two-factor model of evaluation A postpurchase evaluation process buyers use that evaluates a product purchase by using functional and psychological attributes.

functional attributes The features and characteristics that are related to what the product actually does or is expected to do.

must-have attributes Features of the core product that the customer takes for granted.

psychological attributes A category of product characteristics that refers to how things are carried out and done between the buyer and seller.

delighter attributes The augmented features included in the total market offering that go beyond the buyer's expectations and have a significant positive impact on customer satisfaction.

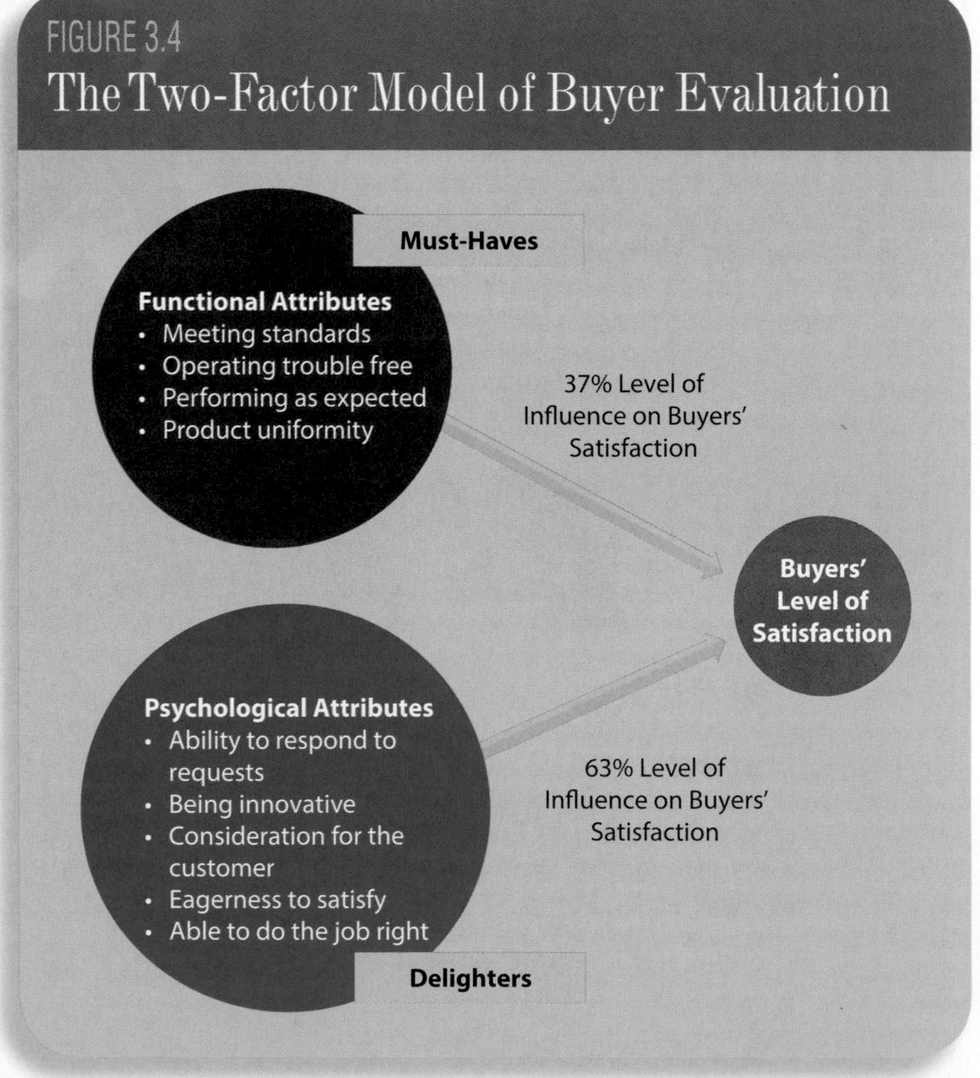

Buyers evaluate functional attributes and psychological attributes of a sales offering to assess overall performance and satisfaction.

offering that go beyond buyer expectations and have a significant positive impact on customer satisfaction. The psychological or delighter characteristics are not perceived as being universal features across the evoked set of suppliers and market offerings being considered. Rather, these are the differentiators between the competitors. The competence, attitudes, and behaviours of supplier personnel with whom the buyer has contact, as well as the salesperson's trustworthiness, consideration for the customer, responsiveness, ability to recover when there is a problem, and innovativeness in providing solutions, are exemplary psychological attributes.

THE GROWING IMPORTANCE OF SALESPEOPLE IN BUYERS' POSTPURCHASE EVALUATION

Understanding the differential impact of functional (*must-haves*) and psychological (*delighters*) attributes is important for salespeople. Functional attributes possess a close correspondence to the technical and more tangible product attributes whereas the psychological attributes are similar to the interpersonal communication and behaviours of salespeople and other personnel having contact with customers. Numerous research studies across a variety of industries evidence psychological attributes as having up to two times as much influence on buyer satisfaction and loyalty as functional attributes. This observation underscores special implications for salespeople, as it is their interpersonal communication and behaviours—what they do—that make up the psychological attributes. Although both categories of product characteristics are important and have significant influences on buyer satisfaction, the activities and behaviours of the salesperson as she or he interacts with the buyer have more impact on that buyer's evaluation than the features of the product or service itself.

3-6 Types of Purchasing Decisions

Buyers are learners in that purchase decisions are not isolated behaviours. Buyer behaviour and purchase decisions are based on the relevant knowledge that buyers have accumulated from multiple sources to assist them in making the proper choice. Internally, buyers reflect on past experiences as guides for making purchase decisions. When sufficient knowledge from past experiences is not available, buyers access external sources of information: secondary sources of information (e.g., trade journals, product test reports, advertising) and other individuals the buyer perceives as being trustworthy and knowledgeable in a given area.

The level of relevant experience and knowledge a buyer or buying organization possesses in relation to a given purchasing decision is a primary determinant of the time and resources the buyer will allocate to that purchasing decision. The level of a buyer's existing experience and knowledge has been used to categorize buyer behaviour into three types of purchasing decisions: straight rebuys, modified rebuys, and new tasks. As summarized in Exhibit 3.6, selling strategies should reflect the differences in buyer behaviours and decision making characteristic of each type of buying decision.

EXHIBIT 3.6

Three Types of Buying Decisions

	Decision Type		
	Straight Rebuy	**Modified Rebuy**	**New Task**
Newness of problem or need	Low	Medium	High
Information requirements	Minimal	Moderate	Maximum
Information search	Minimal	Limited	Extensive
Consideration of new alternatives	None	Limited	Extensive
Multiple buying influences	Very small	Moderate	Large
Financial risk	Low	Moderate	High

straight rebuy decision A purchase decision resulting from an ongoing purchasing relationship with a supplier.

electronic data interchange (EDI) Transfer of data electronically between two computer systems.

new task decision A purchase decision that occurs when a buyer is purchasing a product or service for the first time.

STRAIGHT REBUYS

If past experiences with a product resulted in high levels of satisfaction, buyers tend to purchase the same product from the same sources. Comparable with a routine repurchase in which nothing has changed, the **straight rebuy decision** is often the result of a long-term purchase agreement. Needs have been predetermined with the corresponding specifications, pricing, and shipping requirements already established by a blanket purchase order or an annual purchase agreement. Ordering is automatic and often computerized using **electronic data interchange (EDI)** and e-commerce (Internet, intranet, and extranet). Mitsubishi Motor Manufacturing of America uses a large number of straight rebuy decisions in its acquisition of component parts. Beginning as a primary supplier of automotive glass components, Vuteq has developed a strong relationship with Mitsubishi Motor Manufacturing of America over several years. As a result, Vuteq's business has steadily increased and now includes door trims, fuel tanks, and mirrors in addition to window glass. These components are purchased as straight rebuys using EDI, allowing Vuteq to deliver these components to Mitsubishi on a minute-to-minute basis, matching ongoing production.

Buyers allocate little, if any, time and resources to this form of purchase decision. The primary emphasis is on receipt of the products and their continued satisfactory performance. With most of the purchasing process automated, straight rebuy decisions are little more than recordkeeping that clerical staff in the purchasing office often handles.

For the in-supplier (a current supplier), straight rebuys offer the advantage of reduced levels of potential competition. Rather than becoming complacent, however, in-salespeople must continually monitor the competitive environment for advances in product capabilities or changes in price structures. They should also follow up on deliveries and interact with users as well as decision makers to make sure that product and performance continue to receive strong and positive evaluations.

Straight rebuy decisions present a major challenge to the out-salesperson. Buyers are satisfied with the products and services from current suppliers and see no need to change. This is a classic case in which the buyer perceives no difference or needs gap between their actual and desired state. Consequently, there is no active buying motive to which the out-salesperson can respond. In this case, out-salespeople are typically presented with two strategy choices. First, they can continue to make contact with the buyer so that when there is a change in the buying situation or if the current supplier makes a mistake, they are there to respond. Second, they can provide information and evidence relevant to either the desired or actual states so that the buyer will perceive a needs gap. For example, Vuteq's competitors will find it most difficult to gain this portion of Mitsubishi's business by offering similar or equal products and systems. However, a competitor might adopt future advances in technology that would enable them to offer significant added value beyond what Vuteq offers. Effectively communicating and demonstrating their advanced capabilities holds the potential for raising the desired state and thus producing a needs gap favouring their solution over Vuteq's existing sales offering.

NEW TASKS

The purchase decision characterized as a **new task decision** occurs when the buyer is purchasing a product or service for the first time. As illustrated in Figure 3.5, new task purchase decisions are located at the opposite

FIGURE 3.5
Continuum of Types of Buying Decisions

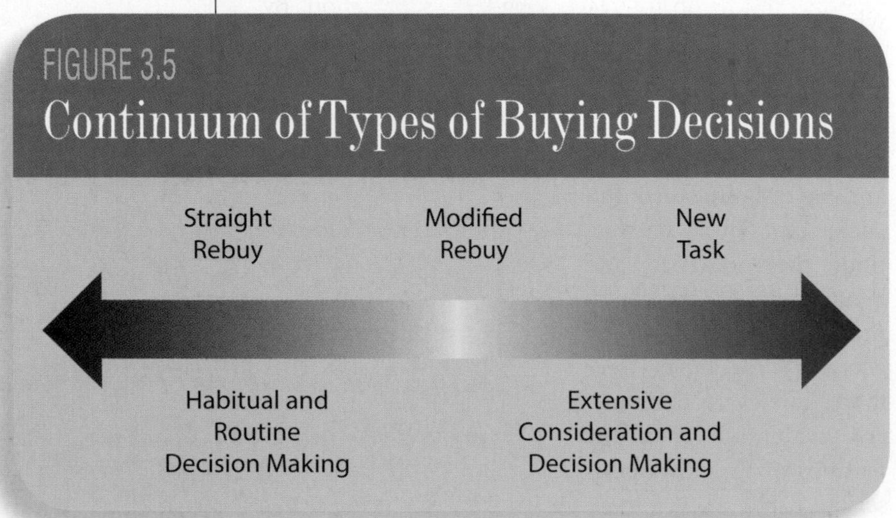

end of the continuum from the straight rebuy and typify situations in which buyers have no experience or knowledge on which to rely. Consequently, they undertake an extensive purchase decision and search for information designed to identify and compare alternative solutions. Reflecting the extensive nature of this type of purchase decision, multiple members of the buying team are usually involved. As a result, the salesperson will be working with several different individuals rather than a single buyer. Mitsubishi buyers and suppliers were presented with new task decisions when the new Mitsubishi four-wheel-drive sport utility vehicle was moving from design to production. Moving from their historical two-wheel-drive to four-wheel-drive power lines and transmissions presented a variety of new needs and problems.

Relevant to a new task purchasing decision, there is no in- or out-supplier. Further, the buyer is aware of the existing needs gap. With no prior experience in dealing with this particular need, buyers are often eager for information and expertise that will assist them in effectively resolving the perceived needs gap. Selling strategies for new task decisions should include collaborating with the buyer in a number of ways. First, the salesperson can provide expertise in fully developing and understanding the need. The salesperson's extensive experience and base of knowledge is also valuable to the buyer in terms of specifying and evaluating potential solutions. Finally, top salespeople will assist the buyer in making a purchase decision and provide extensive follow-up to ensure long-term satisfaction. By implementing this type of consultative strategy, the salesperson establishes a relationship with the buyer and gains considerable competitive advantage.

© Finite Digital

Sea World worked with St. Charles–based Craftsmen Industries to develop a pod of six Shamu cruisers to meet its new task decision on a means for conducting a special Shamu promotion.

MODIFIED REBUYS

Modified rebuy decisions occupy a middle position on the continuum between straight rebuys and new tasks. In these cases, the buyer has experience in purchasing the product in the past but is interested in acquiring additional information regarding alternative products and suppliers. As there is more familiarity with the decision, there is less uncertainty and perceived risk than for new task decisions. The modified rebuy typically occurs as the result of changing conditions or needs. Perhaps the buyer wants to consider new suppliers for current purchase needs or new products existing suppliers offer. Continuing the example of buyer–seller experiences at Mitsubishi, the company's recent decision to reexamine its methods and sources for training and education corresponds to the characteristics of a modified rebuy decision. Since its beginning, Mitsubishi Motor Manufacturing of America has used a mix of company trainers, community colleges, and universities to provide education and training to employees. Desiring more coordination across its training programs, the company has requested proposals for the development and continued management of a corporate university from a variety of suppliers, including several current and new sources.

modified rebuy decision A purchase decision that occurs when a buyer has experience in purchasing a product in the past but is interested in acquiring additional information regarding alternative products and suppliers.

Often a buyer enters into a modified rebuy type of purchase decision simply to check the competitiveness of existing suppliers in terms of the product offering and pricing levels. Consequently, in-salespeople will emphasize how well their product has performed in resolving the needs gap. Out-salespeople will use strategies similar to those undertaken in the straight rebuy. These strategies are designed to alter the relative positions of the desired and actual states in a way that creates a perceived gap and influences buyers to rethink and reevaluate their current buying patterns and suppliers.

3-7 Understanding Communication Styles

Verbal and nonverbal messages can also provide salespeople with important cues regarding buyers' personalities and communication styles. Experienced salespeople emphasize the importance of reading and responding to customer communication styles. Effectively sensing and interpreting customers' communication styles allows salespeople to adapt their own interaction behaviours in a way that facilitates buyer–seller communication and enhances relationship formation. Most sales training programs use a two-by-two matrix as a basis for categorizing communication styles into four primary types.[5] Figure 3.6 illustrates the characteristics based on two determinant dimensions: assertiveness and responsiveness.

assertiveness The degree to which a person holds opinions about issues and attempts to dominate or control situations by directing the thoughts and actions of others.

responsiveness The level of feelings and sociability an individual openly displays.

- *Assertiveness*—**Assertiveness** refers to the degree to which a person holds opinions about issues and attempts to dominate or control situations by directing the thoughts and actions of others. Highly assertive individuals tend to be fast-paced, opinionated, and quick to speak out and take confrontational positions. Low-assertive individuals tend to exhibit a slower pace. They typically hold back, let others take charge, and are slow and deliberate in their communication and actions.
- *Responsiveness*—**Responsiveness** points to the level of feelings and sociability an individual openly displays. Highly responsive individuals are relationship-oriented and openly emotional. They readily express their feelings and tend to be personable, friendly, and informal. However, low-responsive individuals tend to be task-oriented and very controlled in their display of emotions. They tend to be impersonal in dealing with others, with an emphasis on formality and self-discipline.

The actual levels of assertiveness and responsiveness will vary from one individual to another on a continuum ranging from high to low. An individual may be located anywhere along the particular continuum, and where the individual is located determines the degree to which he or she possesses and demonstrates the particular characteristics associated with that dimension (refer back to Figure 3.6).

Overlaying the assertiveness and responsiveness dimensions produces a four-quadrant matrix as illustrated in Figure 3.7. The four quadrants characterize an individual as exhibiting one of four different communication styles on the basis of his or her demonstrated levels of assertiveness and responsiveness. *Amiables* are high on responsiveness but low on assertiveness. *Expressives* are defined as high on both responsiveness

FIGURE 3.6

Comparison of the Principal Characteristics of Assertiveness and Responsiveness

Low Assertiveness		High Assertiveness
• Slow paced • Cooperative • Avoids taking risks • Supportive • Team player • Nondirective • Easygoing • Reserved in expressing opinions		• Fast paced • Competitive • Takes risks • Independent • Directive • Confrontational • Forcefully expresses opinions

Low Responsiveness		High Responsiveness
• Task oriented • Guarded and cool • Rational • Meticulous organizer • Inflexible regarding time • Controlled gesturing • Nondirective • Formal	⟷	• Relationship oriented • Open and warm • Emotional • Unorganized • Flexible regarding time • Highly animated • Spontaneous • Informal

Most sales training programs use a two-by-two matrix as a basis for categorizing communication styles into four primary types. The four styles are based on two dimensions: assertiveness and responsiveness.

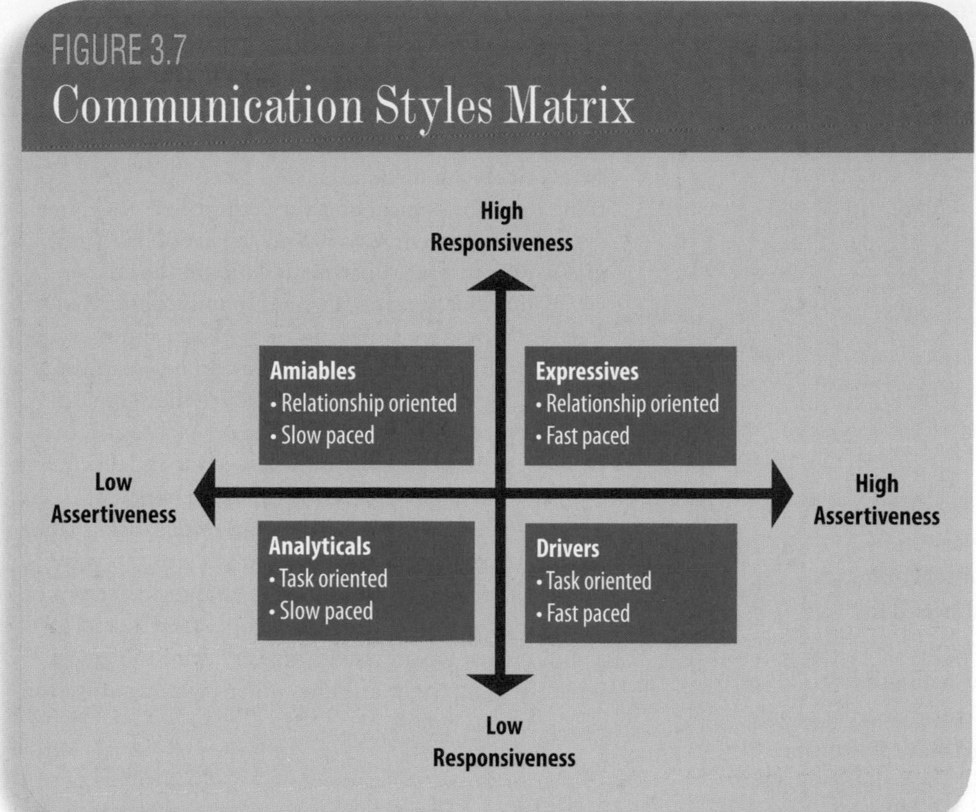

The four quadrants characterize an individual as having one of four different communication styles on the basis of his or her demonstrated levels of assertiveness and responsiveness. A salesperson's skill in properly classifying customers can provide valuable cues regarding customer attitudes and behaviours.

amiables Individuals who are high on responsiveness, low on assertiveness, prefer to belong to groups, and are interested in others.

expressives Individuals who are high on both responsiveness and assertiveness, are animated and communicative, and value building close relationships with others.

and assertiveness. *Drivers* are low on responsiveness but high on assertiveness. *Analyticals* are characterized as being low on assertiveness as well as responsiveness. A salesperson's skill in properly classifying customers can provide valuable cues regarding customer attitudes and behaviours. In turn, these cues allow the salesperson to be more effective by adapting his or her communication and responses to better fit the customer's style.

- *Amiables*—Developing and maintaining close personal relationships is important to **amiables**. Easygoing and cooperative, they are often characterized as friendly back-slappers because of their preference for belonging to groups and their sincere interest in other people—their hobbies, interests, families, and mutual friends. With a natural propensity for talking and socializing, they have little or no desire to control others but rather prefer building consensus. Amiables are not risk takers and need to feel safe in making a decision. Somewhat undisciplined with regard to time, amiables appear to be slow and deliberate in their actions. They avoid conflict and tend to be more concerned with opinions—what others think—than with details and facts. When confronted or attacked, amiables tend to submit. In working with an amiable customer, salespeople should remember that their "must-have" is to be liked and their fundamental "want" is for attention.
- *Expressives*—**Expressives** are animated and highly communicative. Although very competitive by nature, they also exhibit warm personalities and value building close relationships with others. In fact, they dislike being alone and readily seek out others. Expressives are extroverted and are highly uninhibited in their communication. When confronted or crossed, they will attack. Enthusiastic and stimulating, they seem to talk in terms of people rather than things and have a ready opinion on everything. Yet they remain open-minded and changeable. Expressives are fast paced in their decision making and behaviour and prefer the big

Verbal and nonverbal messages can provide salespeople with important cues regarding buyers' personalities and communication styles.

© JGI/Jupiter Images

picture rather than getting bogged down in details. As a result, they are very spontaneous, unconcerned with time schedules, and not especially organized in their daily lives. They are creative, comfortable operating on intuition, and demonstrate a willingness to take risks. The two keys for expressives that salespeople must keep in mind are the "must-have" of never being hurt emotionally and their underlying "want" is attention.

Expressives are animated and highly communicative.

- *Drivers*—Sometimes referred to as the director or dictator style, **drivers** are hard and detached from their relationships with others. Described as being cool, tough, and competitive in their relationships, drivers are independent and willing to run over others to get their preferred results. As they seek out and openly demonstrate power and control over people and situations, they are difficult to get close to and appear to treat people as things. Drivers are extremely formal, businesslike, and impatient, with a penchant for time and organization. They are highly opinionated, impatient, and quick to share those opinions with those around them. When attacked or confronted, drivers will dictate. Drivers exhibit a low tolerance for taking advice, tend to be risk takers, and favour making their own decisions. Although they are highly task oriented, drivers prefer to ignore facts and figures and instead rely on their own gut feelings in making decisions—after all, they do know it all. When working with drivers, salespeople should remember that this style's "must-have" is winning, and their fundamental "want" is results.
- *Analyticals*—The descriptive name for this style is derived from their penchant for gathering and analyzing facts and details before making a decision. **Analyticals** are meticulous and disciplined in everything they do. Logical and very controlled, they are systematic problem solvers and thus very deliberate and slower in pace. In stressful situations and confrontations, analyticals tend to withdraw. Many times, they appear to be nitpicky about everything around them. They do not readily let their feelings show nor are they spontaneous in their behaviours. As a result, they are often seen as being cool and aloof. Analyticals shy away from personal relationships and avoid taking risks. Time and personal schedules are close to being a religious ritual for the analytical. The two fundamentals that salespeople must keep in mind when working with this style are the "must-have" of being right and the underlying "want" is for analytical activities.

drivers Individuals who are low on responsiveness, high on assertiveness, and detached from relationships.

analyticals Individuals who are low on responsiveness and assertiveness, and are analytical, meticulous, and disciplined in everything they do.

MASTERING COMMUNICATION STYLE FLEXING

In addition to sensing and interpreting the customer's communication style, a salesperson must also be aware of his or her own personal style. Mismatched and possibly clashing styles can be dysfunctional and present significant barriers to communication and relationship building. To minimize possible negative effects stemming from mismatched styles, salespeople can flex their own style to facilitate effective communication. For example, an expressive salesperson calling on an analytical buyer would find considerable differences in both pace and relationship/task orientation that could hinder the selling process unless adjustments are made. Flexing his or her own style to better match that of the buyer enhances communication. In our example, the salesperson would need to adjust by slowing down his or her natural pace, reining in the level of spontaneity and animation, and increasing task orientation by offering more detailed information and analysis.

Adapting to buyers by flexing their own communication style has been found to have a positive impact on salespeople's performance and the quality of buyer–seller relationships. Nevertheless, flexing should not be interpreted as meaning an exact match between a salesperson's style and that of a customer. Not only is it not required, but exact matches could even be detrimental. For example, a buyer and seller with matching expressive styles could easily discover that the entire sales call regressed to little more than a personal discussion with nothing of substance being accomplished. However, a buyer and seller matched as drivers could find it difficult, if not impossible, to reach a decision that was mutually beneficial. Rather than matching the buyer's style, flexing implies that the salesperson should adjust to the needs and preferences of the buyer to maximize effectiveness. Growmark, an agricultural product and service organization with divisions in Canada and the United States, teaches its salespeople to flex throughout their interaction with a buyer by studying different behaviours a salesperson might demonstrate with each style of buyer (see the Appendix to this chapter).[6]

Study and compare the flexing behaviours that Growmark recommends that their salespeople demonstrate when working with each different buyer communication style. Note the differences in recommended salesperson behaviour and rationalize them in terms of the specific characteristics of each buyer's style. Overlaying and integrating these two sets of information will enhance the understanding of how to flex to different buyers and why that form of flexing is recommended.

It is not always possible to gain much information about a buyer's communication style, especially if the buyer is new. If this is the case, it may be more appropriate to assume that the buyer is an analytical driver and prepare for this style. If the buyer proves to be close to an amiable expressive, then the salesperson can easily adapt. It is much more difficult to prepare for the amiable expressive and then switch to an analytical-driver style.

3-8 Buying Teams

A single individual typically makes routine purchase decisions, such as straight rebuys and simpler modified rebuys. However, the more complex modified rebuy and new task purchase decisions often involve the joint decisions of multiple participants within a buying centre or team. **Buying teams** (also referred to as buying centres) use the expertise and multiple buying influences of people from different departments throughout the organization. At Xerox, for example, there are on average four customer employees involved in every Xerox sale.[7] As the object of the purchase decision changes, the makeup of the buying team may also change to maximize the relevant expertise of team members. The organization's size, as well as the nature and volume of the products being purchased, will influence the actual number and makeup of buying teams. The different members of a buying team will often have varied goals reflecting their individual needs and those of their different departments.

Buying team members are described in terms of their roles and responsibilities within the team.[8]

- *Initiators*—**Initiators** are individuals within the organization who identify a need or perhaps realize that the acquisition of a product might solve a need or problem.
- *Influencers*—
Individuals who guide the decision process by making recommendations and expressing preferences are referred to as **influencers**. These are often technical or engineering personnel.
- *Users*—**Users** are the individuals within the organization who will actually use the product being purchased. They evaluate a product on the basis of how it will affect their own job performance. Users often serve as initiators and influencers.
- *Deciders*—The ultimate responsibility for determining which product or service will be purchased rests with the **deciders**. Although buyers may also be deciders, it is not unusual for different people to fill these roles.
- *Purchasers*—**Purchasers** have the responsibility for negotiating final terms of purchase with suppliers and executing the actual purchase or acquisition.
- *Gatekeepers*—Members who are in a position to control the flow of information to and between vendors and other buying centre members are referred to as **gatekeepers**.

buying teams Teams of individuals in organizations that use the expertise and multiple buying influences of people from different departments throughout the organization.

initiators Individuals within an organization who identify a need.

influencers Individuals within an organization who guide the decision process by making recommendations and expressing preferences.

users Individuals within an organization who will actually use the product being purchased.

deciders Individuals within an organization who have the ultimate responsibility of determining which product or service will be purchased.

purchasers Organizational members who negotiate final terms of the purchase and execute the actual purchase.

gatekeepers embers of an organization who are in a position to control the flow of information to and between vendors and other buying centre members.

Although each of these influencer types will not necessarily be present on all buying teams, the use of buying teams incorporating some or all of these multiple influences has increased in recent years. One example of multiple buying influences is offered in the recent experience of an Executive Jet International salesperson selling a Gulfstream V corporate jet to a Chicago-based pharmaceutical company. For more than six months, the salesperson worked with a variety of individuals serving different roles within the buying organization:

- *Initiator:* The initiator of the purchase process was the chief operating officer of the corporation, who found that the recent corporate expansions had outgrown the effective service range of the organization's existing aircraft. Beyond pointing out the need and thus initiating the search, this individual would also be highly involved in the final choice based on her personal experiences and the perceived needs of the company.
- *Influencers:* Two different employee groups acted as the primary influencers. First were the corporate pilots who contributed a readily available and extensive background of knowledge and experience with a variety of aircraft types. Also playing a key influencer role were members from the capital budgeting group in the finance department. Although concerned with documented performance capabilities, they also provided inputs and assessments of the different alternatives by using their capital investment models.
- *Users:* The users provided some of the most dynamic inputs, as they were anxious to make the transition to a higher performance aircraft to enhance their own efficiency and performance in working at marketing/sales offices and plants that now stretched over North and South America. Primary players in this group included the vice presidents for marketing and for production/operations, in addition to the corporate pilots who would be flying the plane.
- *Deciders:* Based on the contribution and inputs of each member of the buying team, the chief executive officer would make the ultimate decision. Primarily travelling by commercial carriers, her role as decider was based more on her position within the firm rather than her use of the chosen alternative. As the organization's highest operating officer, she was in a position to move freely among all members of the buying team and make the decision on overall merits rather than personal feelings or desires.
- *Purchaser:* Responsibility for making the actual purchase, negotiating the final terms, and completing all the required paperwork followed the typical lines of authority and was the responsibility of the corporate purchasing department, with the director of purchasing actually assuming the immediate contact role. The purchasing office typically handles purchasing contracts and is staffed to draw up, complete, and file the related registrations and legal documents.
- *Gatekeepers:* This purchase decision involved two different gatekeepers within the customer organization: the executive assistant to the chief operating officer and an assistant purchasing officer. The positioning of these gatekeepers facilitated the salesperson's exchange of information and ability to keep in contact with the various members of the buying team. The COO's executive assistant moved easily among the various executives influencing the decision and was able to make appointments with the right people at the right times. However, the assistant purchasing officer was directly involved with the coordination of each member and bringing their various inputs into one summary document for the CEO. The salesperson's positive dealings and good relationships with each gatekeeper played a significant role in Executive Jet getting the sale.

A classic and all-too-common mistake among salespeople is to make repetitive calls on a purchasing manager over several months only to discover that a buying team exists and that someone other than the purchasing manager will make the ultimate decision. Salespeople must gather information to discover who is in the buying team, what their individual roles are, and which members are the most influential. This information might be collected

Gatekeepers, such as this administrative assistant, are in a position to control the flow of information to and between vendors and other buying centre members.

© CAP53/iStockphoto

from account history files, people inside the salesperson's organization who are familiar with the account sources within the client organization, and even other salespeople. A salesperson should work with all members of the buying team and be careful to address their varied needs and objectives properly. Nevertheless, circumstances sometimes prevent a salesperson from working with all members of the team, and it is important that the salesperson reaches those who are most influential.

3-9 Current Developments in Purchasing

Today's business organizations are undergoing profound change in response to ever-increasing competition and rapid changes in the business environment. The worldwide spread of technology has resulted in intense and increasingly global competition that is highly dynamic in nature. Accelerating rates of change have fragmented what were once mass markets into more micro and niche markets composed of more knowledgeable and demanding customers with escalating expectations. In response, traditional purchasing practices are also rapidly changing.

INCREASING USE OF INFORMATION TECHNOLOGY

Buyers and sellers alike are increasingly using technology to enhance the effectiveness and efficiency of the purchasing process. Business-to-business e-commerce is rapidly growing. Although EDI over private networks has been in use for some time, nearly all the current growth has been in Internet-based transactions.

Information technology electronically links buyers and sellers for direct and immediate communication and transmission of information and data. Transactional exchanges, such as straight rebuy decisions, can now be automated with Internet- and World Wide Web-enabled programs tracking sales at the point of purchase and capturing the data for real-time inventory control and order placing. By cutting order and shipping times, overall cycle times are reduced, mistakes are minimized, and working capital invested in inventories is made available for more productive applications. Further, the automation of these routine transactions allows buyers and salespeople to devote more time to new tasks, complex sales, and postsale service and relationship-building activities.

Customer relationship management (CRM) systems integrated with the Web allow reps to have a more informed conversation with prospects and customers by helping them to better understand customers. Sales organizations know keywords searched to find the seller's company, pages clicked on the company's website, and particular products and services buyers examined before asking for more information. Additionally, data collected on customer demographics, sales and customer service histories, and marketing preferences and customer feedback can be easily accumulated through a CRM system and used to better understand customers and provide customized offerings to best serve their needs. Celanese Corporation, a leading chemicals manufacturer, credits its CRM system with allowing sales conversations to advance based on the premise that the customer has a specific need it can fulfill.[9] Social networking technologies are likely to play an important role in CRM systems, making it more convenient for customers to provide information that goes into product planning and development, as well as provide deeper insights into customer buying motives.

In addition to facilitating exchange transactions, applications integrating the Internet are also being used to distribute product and company information along with training courses and materials. Several companies have begun publishing their product catalogues online as a replacement for the reams of product brochures salespeople have traditionally had to carry with them. The online catalogues can be easily updated without the expense of obsolete brochures and can be selectively downloaded by salespeople to create customized presentations and proposals.

BUYERS' ACCESS TO AND DEMAND FOR RELEVANT INFORMATION

With ever-expanding information technology, buyers have easier access to information on vendors and are utilizing technology to become more informed buyers. This has shifted some of the power to buyers, who can accompany more bidders, making the landscape even more competitive. As buyers increasingly undertake a larger share of the purchase process on their own, they are demanding that sellers make available to them relevant content to help them justify their buying decisions.

supply chain management The strategic coordination and integration of purchasing with other functions within the buying organization as well as external organizations.

In a survey of how customers choose, approximately two-thirds of respondents indicated that they do their own research rather than waiting for salespeople to contact them.[10] As such, buyers are demanding that information be made available to them via their laptops, desktops, iPads, and smartphones as they seek out more and more information prior to connecting with a salesperson. These buyers are looking for personalized dialogue that can help guide them through the decision process. For instance, content aimed at an economic buyer might include a return-on-investment (ROI) calculator. To help the analytical buyer understand the company's novel approach to solving a problem, a case study might prove valuable.[11]

Blogs, white papers, webinars, videos, recorded interviews, product demos, and presentations—providing anything from expert analysis and advice to product announcements—should be offered to targeted customers through media such as a company Web site, Twitter stream, or LinkedIn discussion group.[12] Logicalis, an integrated information and communication technologies provider, tries to gain attention as a thought leader by helping buyers understand cutting-edge IT topics by posting informative content on its own Web site and having a presence on Facebook and LinkedIn. Citrix Systems, a provider of virtualization and cloud-computing technologies, is using blogs to provide information to those searching for trends in cloud computing and virtualization, while LinkWare, a developer of electronic forms, posts relevant information on community sites that prospective customers visit.[13] The more streamlined and personalized the information the better, as buyers increasingly face information overload. Overwhelmingly, buyers are looking for information that proves how the seller's product will result in savings, enhance productivity, and positively affect profitability.

RELATIONSHIP EMPHASIS ON COOPERATION AND COLLABORATION

More than ever before, the business decisions one company makes directly affect decisions in other companies. Business in today's fast-paced and dynamic marketplace demands continuous and increased levels of interactivity between salespeople and buyers representing the customer organizations. This trend is further underscored by more and more buying organizations emphasizing long-term relationships with fewer suppliers so that they can forge stronger bonds and develop more efficient purchasing processes. As illustrated in "An Ethical Dilemma," this increasing level of buyer–seller interaction and interdependence can create challenging ethical decisions for the salesperson.

Rather than competing to win benefits at the expense of one another, leading organizations are discovering that it is possible for all parties to reduce their risk and increase the level of benefits each receives by sharing information and coordinating activities, resources, and capabilities.[14] For instance, Walmart and Sam's Club stores share information with suppliers on the products they supply. Procter & Gamble synchronizes its product data with Walmart, saving it an estimated $1 million annually.[15] These longer-term buyer–seller relationships are based on the mutual benefits received by and the interdependence between all parties in this value network. In addition to being keenly aware of changing customer needs, collaborative relationships require salespeople to work closely with buyers to foster honest and open two-way communication and develop the mutual understanding required to create the desired solutions. This suggests that salespeople understand the buyer's customers to determine how to help the buyer succeed by better serving their customers. Such understanding provides insights to challenges facing the buyer, enhances the salesperson's credibility, and helps to establish a strong business partnership.[16] Further, salespeople must consistently demonstrate that they are dependable and acting in the buyer's best interests.

SUPPLY CHAIN MANAGEMENT

Having realized that their success or failure is inextricably linked to other firms in the value network, many organizations are implementing **supply chain management** across an extended network of suppliers and customers. Beyond a buyer–seller relationship, supply chain management emphasizes the strategic coordination and integration of purchasing with other functions within the buying organization as well as external organizations, including customers, customers' customers, suppliers, and suppliers' suppliers. Such arrangements typically involve information sharing, joint planning, joint demand management and combined inventory of the other's performance capabilities and commitment to the relationship. These expanded agreements often involve **outsourcing** to a supplier certain activities that the buying organization previously performed. These activities are necessary for the day-to-day functioning of the buying organization but are not within the organization's core or distinct competencies. Outsourcing these activities allows the organization to focus on what it does best. However, these activities are typically among those in which the supplying organization specializes or even excels. As a result of the outsourcing agreement, the relationship gains strength and is further extended in such a way that all parties benefit over the long term. Outsourcing agreements place increased emphasis on the role of the salesperson to provide continuing follow-up activities to ensure customer satisfaction and nurture the buyer–seller relationship. Changes in customer needs must be continually monitored and factored into the supplier's market offerings and outsourcing activities.

An Ethical Dilemma

© Gallo Images-Heinrich van den Berg/Jupiter Images

Jamie Payne, a key account manager with Stern Suppliers Inc., has developed strong relationships with members of the buying teams at each of the 15 companies that comprise his account list. Fennel Steel Industries, a worldwide producer of large metal castings and forgings, has become Payne's largest account, providing 30 percent of his total annual sales volume. Last week, Payne took Fennel Steel's director of purchasing—an avid golfer—out for a day of golf at one of Prince Edward Island's best private golf clubs. On the tenth tee, Payne hit his best drive of the day, and the Fennel Steel buyer began admiring Payne's driver. It was a brand-new club that he had paid $499 for only a few days earlier. At the next tee box, Payne handed the club to the buyer and insisted that he try it out. He did and drilled his longest shot of the day straight down the fairway. The buyer handed the driver back to Payne with many positive exclamations including the comment that he could not wait to get one for himself. At that point, Payne tossed the driver back to the buyer saying, "It's in your bag. Just remember to think of me every time you use it."

If, like Jamie Payne, you were attempting to build a business relationship, how would you have handled this situation?

a) The same way that Jamie Payne did, to reward the buyer for all the business he sends my way.
b) Told the buyer where he could find the golf club and offered to take him golfing again to try it out when he got it.
c) Offered to purchase the club for the buyer in exchange for increasing his business with Stern Suppliers Inc.

management, and involve connecting discrete groups within and across organizations.[17] Salespeople must focus on coordinating their efforts with all parties in the network—end users and suppliers alike—and effectively work to add value for all members of the network.

INCREASED OUTSOURCING

Broader business involvement and expanded integration between organizations is a natural evolution as buyers and suppliers become increasingly confident

TARGET PRICING

Using information gathered from researching the marketplace, buyers establish a **target price** for their final products. For example, buyers determine the selling price for a new printing press should

outsourcing The process of giving to a supplier certain activities that the buying organization previously performed.

target price The price buyers determine for their final products through information gathered from researching the marketplace.

be $320,000. Next, they divide the press into its subsystems and parts to estimate what each part is worth in relation to the overall price. Using such a system, buyers might conclude that the maximum price they could pay for a lead roller platen would be $125 and then use this information when working with potential suppliers. In working with targeted pricing requirements, salespeople find they have two fundamental options. They can meet the required cost level, which often entails cutting their prices, or they can work with the buyer to better understand and possibly influence minimum performance specifications. Certain restrictive specifications might be relaxed as a trade-off for lower pricing. For example, a salesperson might negotiate longer lead times, fewer or less complex design features, or less technical support in exchange for lower prices. The latter option requires salespeople to have a high level of knowledge regarding their product's organizational capabilities, and customer applications and needs. Just as important is the ability to create feasible options and effectively communicate them to the buyer.

INCREASED IMPORTANCE OF KNOWLEDGE AND CREATIVITY

The increased interdependence between buyer and seller organizations hinges on the salesperson's capabilities to serve as a problem solver in a dynamic and fast-changing business environment. Buyers depend on the salesperson to provide unique and value-added solutions to their changing problems and needs. To shape such innovative solutions, salespeople must have broad-based and comprehensive knowledge readily available and the ability to use that knowledge

PROFESSIONAL SELLING IN THE 21ST CENTURY

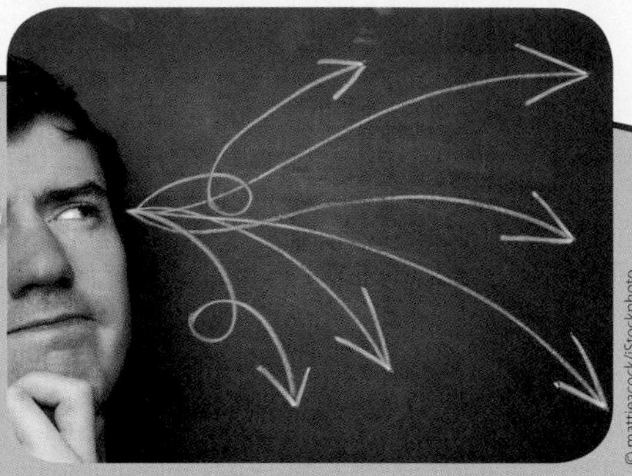
© mattjeacock/iStockphoto

Adding Value to Enhance Customer Relationships

Roy Chitwood, sales and sales management author, trainer, and consultant, and President of Max Sacks International, Seattle, provides some useful advice for offering customers added value.

Building long-term relationships with your clients involves more than simply understanding and meeting their needs in a one-time sale. Implicit in the definition of relationship building is the idea of adding value to the transaction, going beyond simply being an order taker to being an asset in the business or personal lives of your clients. By seeking to play an active role in your clients' success, you show that your firm is truly interested in helping them achieve their long term goals, not simply making a sale. Be willing to share your business knowledge for the common good with clients and firms with whom you can build alliances. Provide your distributors with all the marketing materials, points of value and support they need, not to just effectively sell your product, but to be successful in their business endeavours as a whole. Finally, build a strategic relationship with your clients based on creating solutions. Once you have established your own integrity and professionalism in the eyes of your customers by offering them capable, helpful, and effective staff, use of your experts, referrals and the wealth of your experience, you are ready to take the concept of adding value to the next level by building strong strategic relationships with them. When you and your client invest in your relationship to this depth, you can intuitively tailor your products to fit their needs and create new solutions at every stage as you observe their needs evolve and change. Within this relationship, you become a trusted adviser, helping them formulate key points of strategy and assisting them with creative solutions when problems arise.

in creative ways. This includes knowledge of one's own products and capabilities, as well as the products and capabilities of competitors. More important, the salesperson must possess a thorough understanding of product applications and the needs of the customer to work with the buyer in generating innovative solutions. For more on how to build relationships by adding value for customers see "Professional Selling in the 21st Century: Adding Value to Enhance Customer Relationships."[18]

APPENDIX CHAPTER 3

Recommended Flexing Behaviour for Different Communication Styles

Selling Task or Objective

SETTING AN APPOINTMENT

Selling to the Analytical

- Send a business letter with details about yourself and the company.
- Follow the letter with a phone call to confirm expectations and set an appointment.

Selling to the Driver

- Drivers may not take time to read your letter.
- Contact them by phone first and follow up with a letter.
- Keep the call businesslike and to the point by identifying yourself, explaining the business problem addressed by your product, and asking for an appointment.
- The letter should simply confirm the time and date of appointment and include materials the driver might review before the meeting.

Selling to the Amiable

- Send a letter with a personal touch stating who you are and why you are contacting him or her.
- The letter should include your experience working with clients the prospect knows by reputation or experience, your reliability and follow-through, and the quality of your product or service.
- Follow the letter with a personal phone call.
- Take time to be friendly, open, and sincere, and to establish trust in the relationship.

Selling to the Expressive

- Generally, a phone call is most appropriate.
- Make your call open and friendly, stressing quick benefits, personal service, your experience, and your company's experience with its products and services.
- If you send a letter, make it short and personal, stressing who you are, how you know of him or her, and what you are interested in talking about.

OPENING THE CALL

Selling to the Analytical

- Provide background information about you and the company.
- Approach in an advisory capacity, acknowledging buyer's expertise.
- Show evidence that you have done your homework on the buyer's situation.
- Offer evidence of having provided solutions in the past.
- Be conscious of how you are using the buyer's time.

Selling to the Driver

- Listen and focus on the driver's ideas and objectives.
- Provide knowledge and insight relevant to the driver's specific business problems.
- Be personable but reserved and relatively formal.
- Present factual evidence that establishes the business problem and resulting outcome.
- Maintain a quick pace. Drivers value punctuality and the efficient use of time.

Selling to the Amiable

- Engage in informal conversation before getting down to business.
- Demonstrate that you are personally interested in the amiable's work and personal goals.
- You will have to earn the right to learn more personally about the amiable.
- Demonstrate your product or service knowledge by referencing a common acquaintance with whom you've done business.

Selling to the Expressive

- Quickly describe the purpose of your call and establish credibility—you must earn the right to develop a business relationship with the expressive.
- Share stories about people you both know.
- Share information the expressive would perceive as exclusive.
- Share your feelings and enthusiasm for the expressive's ideas and goals.
- Once the expressive has confidence in your competence, take time to develop an open and trusting personal relationship.

GATHERING INFORMATION

Selling to the Analytical

- Ask specific, fact-finding questions in a systematic manner.
- Establish a comprehensive exchange of information.
- Encourage the buyer to discuss ideas while focusing on factual information.
- Be thorough and unhurried—listen.
- Explain that you are in alignment with his or her thinking and can support his or her objectives.

Selling to the Driver

- Ask, don't tell. Ask fact-finding questions leading to what the driver values and rewards.
- Make your line of questioning consistent with your call objective.
- Follow up on requests for information immediately.
- Support the buyer's beliefs; indicate how you can positively affect goals.
- Clarify the driver's expectations.

Selling to the Amiable

- Create a cooperative atmosphere with an open exchange of information and feelings.
- Amiables tend to understate their objectives, so you may need to probe for details and specifics about his or her goals.
- Listen responsively. Give ample amounts of verbal and nonverbal feedback.
- Verify whether there are unresolved budget or cost justification issues.
- Find out who else will contribute to the buying decision.
- Summarize what you believe to be the amiable's key ideas and feelings.

Selling to the Expressive

- Begin by finding out the expressive's perception of the situation and vision of the ideal outcome.
- Identify other people who should contribute to analysis and planning.
- Listen and then respond with plenty of verbal and nonverbal feedback that supports the expressive's beliefs.
- Question carefully the critical data you'll need.
- Keep the discussion focused and moving toward a result.
- If the expressive shows limited interest in specifics, summarize what has been discussed and begin to suggest ways to move the vision toward reality.

ACTIVATING THE NEED TO CHANGE

Selling to the Analytical

- Use the buyer's records to supply information.
- Use a logical approach.
- Illustrate with dollars and cents.

Selling to the Driver

- Be fast paced and businesslike.
- Be sure of your figures.
- Show the driver the bottom line.
- Appeal to rational thinking and avoid appealing to emotions.

Selling to the Amiable

- Address emotional needs in line with safety and comfort needs.
- Use the amiable's figures rather than your own.
- Do not push!

Selling to the Expressive

- Support the expressive's ideas and goals.
- Work toward his or her esteem needs.
- Supply data from people seen as leaders by the expressive.

ENGAGING IN THE SALES CONVERSATION

Selling to the Analytical

- Provide a detailed written proposal as part of your presentation.
- Include the strongest cost-benefit justifications
- Support with third-party data.
- Be reserved and decisive but not aggressive.
- Limit emotional or testimonial appeals.
- Recommend a specific course of action.
- Give the buyer chance to review all documents related to purchase and delivery.

Selling to the Driver

- Present your recommendation so that the driver can compare alternative solutions and probable outcomes.
- Provide documented options.
- Offer the best quality given the cost limitations.
- Be specific and factual without overwhelming the driver with details.
- Appeal to esteem and independence needs.
- Reinforce the driver's preference for acting in a forthright manner.
- Summarize content quickly, and then let the driver choose a course of action.

Selling to the Amiable

- Define clearly in writing and make sure the amiable understands the following:
  - What you can do to support the amiable's personal goals
  - What you will contribute and what the amiable needs to contribute
  - The support resources you intend to commit to the project
- Provide a clear solution to the amiable's problem with maximum assurances that this is the best solution and that there is no need to consider others.
- Ask the amiable to involve other decision makers.
- Satisfy needs by showing how your solution is best now and will be best in the future, and support it with references and third-party evidence.
- Use testimonials from perceived experts and others close to the amiable.

Selling to the Expressive

- Provide specific solutions to the expressive's ideas—in writing.
- Build confidence that you have the necessary facts, but do not overwhelm the expressive with details.
- Do not rush the discussion. Spend time developing ways to implement ideas.
- Appeal to personal esteem needs.
- Try to get commitments to action in writing.

EARNING COMMITMENT

Selling to the Analytical

- Ask for commitment in a low-key but direct manner.
- Expect to negotiate changes.
- Pay special attention to pricing issues.
- Work for commitment now to avoid the analytical's tendency to delay decisions.
- Cite data supporting your company's service records.
- Respond to objections by emphasizing the analytical's buying principles and objectivity.

Selling to the Driver

- Ask for the order directly.
- Put your offer in clear, factual terms.
- Offer options and alternatives.
- Be prepared to negotiate changes and concessions.
- Drivers sometimes attach conditions to a sale.
- Offer the driver time to consider the options.

- Anticipate objections in advance and come prepared with facts.
- Respond to objections based on the driver's values and priorities.

Selling to the Amiable

- Ask for the order indirectly—do not push.
- Emphasize the guarantees that offer protection to the amiable.
- Do not corner the amiable; he or she will want out if things go wrong.
- Guard against "buyer's remorse"—get a commitment even if you have to base it on a contingency.
- Stress your personal involvement after the sale.
- Encourage the amiable to involve others in the final purchase decision.
- Welcome objections and be patient and thorough in responding to them.
- When responding to objections,
  - Describe financial justification
  - Refer to experts or others the amiable respects
  - Keep in mind how the amiable feels about and will be affected by the purchase decision

Selling to the Expressive

- When you have enough information to understand the need and have tested the appropriateness of the recommendation, assume the sale and ask for the order in a casual and informal way.
- When the opportunity presents itself, offer incentives to encourage the purchase.
- Do not confuse the issue by presenting too many options or choices.
- Get a definite commitment. Be sure the expressive understands the decision to purchase.
- Save the details until after you have a firm buying decision. The expressive believes it is the salesperson's job to handle details.
- In handling objections,
  - Describe what others have done to get over that hurdle
  - Respond to the expressive's enthusiasm for his or her goals
  - Deal with how the recommendation meets with this buyer's options
  - Restate benefits that focus on the satisfaction a buying decision will bring

PROVIDING FOLLOW-UP

Selling to the Analytical

- Provide a detailed implementation plan.
- Maintain regular contact.
- Check to confirm satisfactory and on-schedule delivery.

Selling to the Driver

- Set up a communication process with the driver that encourages quick exchange of information about checkpoints and milestones.
- Make sure you have a contingency plan to responsively implement corrections and incorporate changes.
- Make sure there are no surprises.

Selling to the Amiable

- Immediately after the purchase decision is made, make a follow-up appointment.
- Initiate and maintain frequent contacts providing services, such as the following:
  - Periodic progress reports on installation
  - Arrangements for service and training
  - Introduction of new products and services
  - Listening carefully to concerns, even those that seem trivial

Selling to the Expressive

- As soon as the order is signed, reaffirm the schedule for delivery and your personal relationship with the buyer, and introduce the implementation person or team.
- A social situation, such as a lunch, can be a very effective opportunity for following up on business with this buyer.
- Work toward becoming an ongoing member of the buyer's team.
- In case of any complaints, handle them yourself. Never refer them to another in your organization without the buyer's consent.

CHAPTER 3 CASE

SELLING FOR RELATIONSHIPSFIRST INC.: UNDERSTANDING COMMUNICATION STYLE, BUYING TEAMS, AND BUYING NEEDS

Background

RelationshipsFirst Inc. is a relatively new entrant in the cloud computing business management software industry, having been in existence for a little over four years. It specializes in providing Web-based customizable customer relationship management software solutions that support an entire company, from accounting to Web capabilities. Its software is constructed around an individual customer record so that accounting, sales, support, shipping, and billing all access identical information for each interaction. The company currently serves a variety of businesses across a number of industries. Customer satisfaction is the company's top priority and it acts with integrity to fulfill this mission. Its technology is easy to learn and easy to use, and its information technology staff is extremely knowledgeable and customer friendly. The company currently employs more than 75 salespeople who call directly on businesses and organizations throughout Canada. Salespeople are trained to be customer-oriented problem solvers who seek to establish long-term relationships with customers. This approach has allowed RelationshipsFirst to experience steady sales gains since its beginning and it hopes to continue its upward growth trajectory.

Current Situation

Dawn, a recent college graduate who just completed the sales rep training program at RelationshipsFirst, is excited about her upcoming meeting with Red Meadows Nursery and Landscape, LLC of Winnipeg, Manitoba. Privately owned, Red Meadows serves the nursery and landscaping needs of its customers through its two large metro retail locations. Each location has a store manager, and several full- and part-time employees to assist with sales and operations. The company's owner serves as president and they also employ a director of marketing and sales, who among other things oversees a staff of five outside salespeople, a director of operations, a director of information technology (whose primary responsibility is to run the Web side of their business), and a director of accounting and finance. The outside sales force solicits both residential and commercial accounts and in large part is responsible for growing the non-retail business for Red Meadows.

A good friend of Dawn's, Kristen Lewis, happens to be neighbours with Adam Kean, Red Meadows' director of marketing and sales. In a recent conversation with Adam, Kristen mentioned Dawn and how she might be able to help him at Red Meadows. Adam suggested that Kristen have Dawn give him a call and subsequently Dawn was able to secure a meeting with Adam Kean the following Tuesday morning.

Dawn was delighted that Kristen provided her with this prospect and was confident that this would help her get off to a fast start at RelationshipsFirst. Dawn has been friends with Kristen since grade school. This is not unusual for Dawn, who has many friends and close relationships, likely because she shows such a sincere interest in others, particularly in their hobbies, interests, family, and mutual friends. She enjoys listening to the opinions of others and seems to get along with most everyone, generally avoiding conflict rather than submitting to others. Dawn credits her ability to communicate well orally (she loves to talk and socialize), get along well with others, and build a consensus, in part, for her landing a position in sales at RelationshipsFirst.

Prior to her meeting with Adam Kean, Dawn asked Kristen if she could meet her for lunch to find out a little more about Adam and Red Meadows. When Dawn finally arrived for lunch, late as usual, she wasn't able to learn as much about Red Meadows as she would have liked, but she did learn the following about Adam. Kristen indicated that Adam was a good neighbour, but he certainly wasn't a friendly, outgoing relationship builder such as Dawn. In fact, he tended to be rather cool, tough, and competitive when it came to relationships. He liked to be in charge of people and situations and was not willing to let others stand in the way of achieving his goals. Adam manages his time well, is impatient with others, and tends to be very business-like. He likes extreme sports and appears to have a penchant for taking risks. According to Kristen, at annual home owners' association meetings Adam tends to be the most outspoken individual in attendance. While opinionated, Adam rarely takes advice from others and prefers to make his own decisions.

Although Dawn believed she still had additional work to do before meeting with Adam, she was at least glad to know a little bit about the person she would be meeting. The more she knew about her buyer, she surmised, the better she could tailor her offering to meet his needs.

Questions

1. Based on your understanding of both Dawn and Adam, how would you characterize the communication style of each?
2. What, if any, preparations and style flexing should Dawn make to better relate to and communicate with Adam Kean?
3. Who all might be involved in the buying decision for Red Meadows with regard to Dawn's offering? For each, explain why and how.
4. Explain at least two needs that might be met by Red Meadows by purchasing the software offered by RelationshipsFirst.

Role Play

Situation: Read the case.

Characters: Dawn, sales rep for RelationshipsFirst Inc.; Adam Kean, director of marketing and sales, Red Meadows Nursery and Landscape, LLC.

Scene:

Location—Adam Kean's office at Red Meadows.

Action—Dawn meets with Adam to find out more about Red Meadows' operations and needs to see if she can help them. She is also trying to determine who else might be involved in the buying decision and what influence each might have. She has no plans to make a sale on this call.

CHAPTER 3

Role Play: Shoes Unlimited

Background

You are a sales representative for Shoes Unlimited, a manufacturer and marketer of an array of styles of men's and women's casual shoes, located in Red Deer, Alberta. You are responsible for calling on a variety of accounts throughout western Canada, many of which are independently owned shoe retailers, often in small cities and towns.

Current Situation

You recently scheduled a meeting with Joe Jackson, owner of Fantastic Footwear, an independent retail shoe store located in a small rural community in British Columbia. Joe contacted you after finding your company on the Internet. He is in the process of evaluating several suppliers for his soon-to-be-opened shoe store.

Before meeting with Joe, you have decided to prepare a series of questions to ask Joe to identify his situational, functional, social, psychological, and knowledge needs. When meeting with Joe you want to ask him several questions so that you can fully understand his needs and then demonstrate to him how you and your company can best satisfy those needs.

Role Play

Location: Joe Jackson's office at Fantastic Footwear

Characters: You, Shoes Unlimited sales representative; Joe Jackson, owner of Fantastic Footwear

Action: Using the questions you developed, have a conversation with Joe to assess his five general types of needs (ask at least one to two questions to assess each need).

Interactive, collaborative

conversations with customers are essential for gaining critical information and insight about customers' situations and enable salespeople to offer unique, added-value solutions for customers' needs.

what do you think?

Of all the skills and activities involved in selling, the most important for salesperson success is active listening.

1 2 3 4 5 6 7

strongly disagree strongly agree

4 Communication Skills

After completing this chapter, you should be able to

4-1 Explain the importance of collaborative, two-way communication in trust-based selling.

4-2 Explain the primary types of questions and how they are applied in selling.

4-3 Illustrate the diverse roles and uses of strategic questioning in trust-based selling.

4-4 Identify and describe the SPIN and ADAPT systems for effective questioning in a sales dialogue.

4-5 Discuss the four sequential steps for effective active listening.

4-6 Describe and interpret the different forms of verbal and nonverbal communication.

Introduction

As an accomplished sales trainer in the business-to-business marketplace, Al Simon identifies effective communication as the essential selling competency for successful selling performance. Simon places particular emphasis on the concept of collaborative, active listening. "Prospects want salespeople to listen to them, to understand their business. This point was driven home for me one day when I was on a sales call with a client to observe her performance. She did what I thought was a good job, asking several excellent questions and the prospect responded with a lot of valuable information. As we were leaving, the salesperson excused herself to visit the restroom. Standing there at the elevator with the prospect, he said to me, 'That salesperson seems very sharp.' I had to chuckle to myself, as the salesperson had not said much else besides asking questions!"

Based on Simon's experience, there is a significant difference between the communication skills of highly successful salespeople and those who are not so successful, and he asserts that the biggest difference is the ability to utilize active listing. Collaborative, active listening is much more involved than simply listening to the other party's message. It involves two-way engagement: listening with your eyes, your mind, and your whole being—not just your ears. It requires a higher level of concentration on the total message being exchanged, maintaining effective eye contact without staring, considering and evaluating the message being received, and actively responding and participating by paraphrasing back what you heard the prospect say and asking related questions to clarify and gain additional information and detail.

An additional communication skill Simon stresses as being critical for salespeople to master is the ability to stay with the prospect's thought process and not think too far ahead or behind. If a salesperson allows his or her mind to get ahead or behind what the prospect is saying, concentration is broken, the full message will not be properly received and considered, and the salesperson will be unable to follow up on what the prospect has just said. "If you are unable to remember conversation from even a few minutes back, it will be painfully obvious to the prospect that you aren't listening and don't care about their issues. How much business do you suppose you will win that way? To be effective in today's business climate, really listen to the prospect and then help them solve the problem."

Source: Al Simon, Sandler Training, Simon Inc. "Hearing versus Listening," *Sales and Marketing Management's SMM*, May 23, 2011. Reprinted with permission.

trust-based sales communication
Talking *with* rather than *at* the customer. A collaborative and two-way form of communication that allows buyers and sellers to develop a better understanding of the need situation and work together to co-create the best response for resolving the customer's needs.

Al Simon's experience with the potency of collaborative, active communication illustrated in this chapter's introduction is not uncommon. In reality, it is quickly becoming the norm for effective selling. On the one hand, selling is basically interpersonal communication. The skill and effectiveness of a salesperson's interpersonal communication are fundamental determinants of selling performance. On the other hand, effective communication continues to be one of the least understood and understudied skills for successful selling.

This chapter addresses the need to better understand and master the art of collaborative, two-way communication. First, we will examine the basic nature of **trust-based sales communication**. Building on this preliminary understanding, the text breaks down trust-based sales communication into its component and subcomponent parts to facilitate study, application, and mastery. The verbal dimension of communication is examined first with an emphasis on three communication subcomponents: (1) developing effective questioning methods for use in uncovering and diagnosing buyers' needs and expectations, (2) using active listening skills to facilitate the interchange of ideas and information, and (3) maximizing the responsive sharing of information with buyers in a way that fully explains and brings to life the benefits of proposed solutions. Finally, the nonverbal dimension of interpersonal communication is examined with an emphasis on its application and meaningful interpretation.

4-1 Sales Communication as a Collaborative Process

either people nor organizations buy products. Rather, they seek out the satisfaction and benefits that certain product features provide. Although traditional selling has been described as "talking *at* the customer," trust-based selling has been referred to as "talking *with* the customer." Trust-based sales communication is a two-way and naturally collaborative interaction that allows buyers and sellers alike to develop a better understanding of the need situation and work together to generate the best response for solving the customer's needs. Although trust-based selling has become the preeminent model for contemporary personal selling, the situation described in "An Ethical Dilemma" should serve as a reminder that some salespeople and sales organizations continue to practise more traditional and manipulative forms of selling.

Trust-based sales communication is the sharing of meaning between buying and selling parties that results from the interactive process of exchanging information and ideas. It is important to note that the purpose of sales communication is not agreement but rather the maximization of common understanding among participants. With this emphasis on establishing understanding, communication is fundamental throughout each stage of the selling process. Effective communication skills are needed to identify buying needs and to demonstrate to buyers how a salesperson's proposed solution can satisfy those needs better than competitors. The critical capabilities for effective selling include questioning, listening, giving information, nonverbal communication, and written communication skills. Although each of these skills is pervasive in everyday life, they are the heart and soul of the interpersonal exchange that characterizes trust-based selling.

Verbal Communication: Questioning

There are two ways to dominate or control a selling conversation. A salesperson can talk all the time, or can maintain a more subtle level of control by asking well-thought-out questions that guide the discussion and engage the customer. As highlighted in "Professional Selling in the 21st Century: Diagnostic Conversations Create Unique Value for the Buyer," salespeople should think like doctors, asking relevant questions to methodically diagnose the situation and problems before presenting solutions. To present a cure to a patient before understanding the problem would be malpractice. In a similar fashion, salespeople must be masters at thinking through what they need to know, planning the questions

© amana images inc./Alamy

An Ethical Dilemma

Kaitlin is excited about her internship as an account representative for Channel 15, a popular independent television station offering regional and syndicated popular programming, news, and weather. Kaitlin has just finished sales training and is sensing big differences compared to the trust-based selling process learned in her university selling class. Sales training at Channel 15 has focused on getting the programming schedule, audience statistics, pricing sheets, and this week's special promotions. She was also introduced to the Channel 15 selling model, a sample script she is expected to follow, and conducted several role plays. The script calls for Kaitlin to introduce herself and explain that she represents Channel 15, explain the different programming packages, and detail the special pricing available for each package. After explaining each program package and special pricing, the script requires her to close by asking the prospect if they would be interested in purchasing the package. If the answer is "yes," she is to write the contract and get the buyer's signature. If the answer is "no," she is to explain the next program package and pricing and ask for the order again. What should Kaitlin do?

a) Play it safe and follow the Channel 15 sales model.
b) Use the trust-based selling process to customize Channel 15's sales script.
c) Turn down the internship and look for something different.

PROFESSIONAL SELLING IN THE 21ST CENTURY

Diagnostic Conversations Create Unique Value for the Buyer

Jeff Thull, CEO and president of Prime Resource Group, emphasizes that the biggest problem for salespeople is their tendency to present their solutions too early and too often during a sales call. All too often, salespeople present their solution before they have fully explored and understand the customer's situation. As a result, the salesperson lacks relevance, fails to connect to the customer's reality, and thus fails to make the sale.

Selling professionals must change their thinking. Instead of being so quick to push a solution, salespeople should think more like doctors who ask questions to diagnose problems thoroughly prior to offering cures. Diagnostic conversations explore and evaluate the nature and full extent of a customer's problem. The focus is on physical symptoms from the buyer's reality with the goal of raising the customer's as well as the salesperson's awareness and understanding of the problem and its impact. The result of this enhanced and shared understanding is a solution that offers clear and unique value to the buyer and positively influences the sales outcome.

open-end questions
Questions designed to let the customer respond freely; the customer is not limited to one- or two-word answers but is encouraged to disclose personal or business information.

closed-end questions
Questions designed to limit the customer's responses to one or two words.

they need to ask, and then asking those diagnostic questions in a sequential manner that builds understanding of the situation for themselves as well as for the customer. They should know exactly what information they need and which type of question is best suited for eliciting that information from a prospective buyer.

Purposeful, carefully crafted questions can encourage thoughtful responses from a buyer and provide richly detailed information about the buyer's current situation, needs, and expectations. This additional detail and understanding is often as meaningful for the buyer as it is for the salesperson. That is, proper questioning can facilitate both the buyer's and the seller's understanding of a problem and its possible solutions.[1] For example, questions can encourage meaningful feedback regarding the buyer's attitude and the logical progression through the purchase decision process. Questioning also shows interest in the buyer and his or her needs and actively involves the buyer in the selling process. Questions can also be used tactically to redirect, regain, or hold the buyer's attention should it begin to wander during the conversation. In a similar fashion, questions can provide a convenient and subtle transition to a different topic of discussion and provide a logical guide promoting sequential thought and decision making.

Successful salespeople are experts at considering what information they need to know and purposefully planning and asking the questions they need to ask.

Questions are categorized by the results they are designed to accomplish. Does the salesperson want to receive a free flow of thoughts and ideas or a simple yes/no confirmation? Is the salesperson seeking a general description of the overall situation or specific details regarding emergent needs or problematic experiences with current suppliers? To be effective, a salesperson must understand which type of question will best accomplish his or her desired outcome. In this manner, questions can be put into two basic categories: (1) the amount of information and level of specificity desired and (2) the strategic purpose or intent.

4-2 Types of Questions Classified by Amount and Specificity of Information Desired

OPEN-END QUESTIONS

Open-end questions, also called nondirective questions, are designed to let the customer respond freely. That is, the customer is not limited to one- or two-word answers but is encouraged to disclose personal business information. Open-end questions encourage buyers' thought processes and deliver richer and more expansive information than closed-end questions. Consequently, these questions are typically used to probe for descriptive information that allows the salesperson to better understand the specific needs and expectations of the customer. The secret to successfully using open-end questions lies in the first word used to form the question. Words often used to begin open-end questions include *what*, *how*, *where*, *when*, *tell*, *describe*, and *why*?[2] "What happens when . . .", "How do you feel . . .", and "Describe the . . ." are examples of open-end questions.

CLOSED-END QUESTIONS

Closed-end questions are designed to limit the customer's response to one or two words. This type of question is typically used to confirm or clarify information gleaned from previous responses to open-end questions. Although the most common form is the yes/no question, closed-end questions come in many forms—provided the response is limited to one or two words. For instance, "Do you . . .", "Are you . . . ", "How many . . .", and "How often . . ." are common closed-end questions.

© khz/Shutterstock

dichotomous questions A directive form of questioning; these questions ask the customer to choose from two or more options.

probing questions Questions designed to penetrate below generalized or superficial information to elicit more articulate and precise details for use in needs discovery and solution identification.

evaluative questions Questions that use the open- and closed-end question formats to gain confirmation and to uncover attitudes, opinions, and preferences the prospect holds.

tactical questions Questions used to shift or redirect the topic of discussion when the discussion gets off course or when a line of questioning proves to be of little interest or value.

DICHOTOMOUS/ MULTIPLE-CHOICE QUESTIONS

Dichotomous questions and multiple-choice questions are directive forms of questioning. This type of question asks a customer to choose from two or more options and is used in selling to discover customer preferences and move the purchase decision process forward. An example of this form of question would be, "Which do you prefer, the _____ or the _____?"

Salespeople use purposeful questions to encourage thoughtful and detailed responses from prospects.

Types of Questions Classified by Strategic Purpose

PROBING QUESTIONS

Probing questions are designed to penetrate below generalized or superficial information to elicit more articulate and precise details for use in needs discovery and solution identification. Rather than interrogating a buyer, probing questions are best used in a conversational style: (1) requesting clarification ("Can you share with me an example of that?" "How long has this been a problem?"), (2) encouraging elaboration ("How are you dealing with that situation now?" "What is your experience with ______?"), and (3) verifying information and responses ("That is interesting, could you tell me more?" "So, if I understand correctly, _____. Is that right?").

EVALUATIVE QUESTIONS

Evaluative questions use open- and closed-end question formats to gain confirmation and to uncover attitudes, opinions, and preferences the prospect holds. These questions are designed to go beyond generalized fact finding and uncover prospects' perceptions and feelings regarding existing and desired circumstances as well as potential solutions. Exemplary evaluative questions include "How do you feel about _____?" "Do you see the merits of _____?" and "What do you think _____?"

TACTICAL QUESTIONS

Tactical questions are used to shift or redirect the topic of discussion when the discussion gets off course or when a line of questioning proves to be of little interest or value. For example, the salesperson might be exploring the chances of plant expansion only to find that the prospect cannot provide that type of proprietary information at this early stage of the buyer–seller relationship. To avoid either embarrassing

reactive questions
Questions that refer to or directly result from information the other party previously provided.

the prospect or himself or herself by proceeding on a forbidden or nonproductive line of questioning, the seller uses a tactical question designed to change topics. An example of such a tactical question might be expressed as "Earlier you mentioned that ______. Could you tell me more about how that might affect _____?"

REACTIVE QUESTIONS

Reactive questions are questions that refer to or directly result from information the other party previously provided. Reactive questions are used to elicit additional information, explore for further detail, and keep the flow of information going. Illustrative reactive questions are "You mentioned that ____. Can you give me an example of what you mean?" and "That is interesting. Can you tell me how it happened?"

These different groupings of question types are not mutually exclusive. As depicted in the guidelines for combining question types in Exhibit 4.1, effective questions integrate elements from different question types. For example, "How do you feel about the current trend of sales in the industry?" is an open-end (classified by format) question and evaluative (classified by purpose) in nature.

Regardless of the types of questions one might combine in a sales dialogue, the natural tendency is to overuse closed-end questions. Monitor the types of

EXHIBIT 4.1

Guidelines for Combining Types of Questions

Amount and Specificity of Information Desired	Strategic Objective or Purpose of Questioning: Explore and Dig for Details	Gain Confirmation and Discover Attitudes/Opinions	Change Topics or Re-direct Buyer's Attention	Follow Up Previously Elicited Statements
Discussion and Interpretation	*Open-end* questions designed to be *probing* in nature	*Open-end* questions designed to be *evaluative* in nature	*Open-end* questions designed to be *tactical* in nature	*Open-end* questions designed to be *reactive* in nature
Confirmation and Agreement	*Closed-end* questions designed to be *probing* in nature	*Closed-end* questions designed to be *evaluative* in nature	*Closed-end* questions designed to be *tactical* in nature	*Closed-end* questions designed to be *reactive* in nature
Choosing from Alternatives	*Dichotomous or multiple-choice* questions designed to be *probing* in nature	*Dichotomous or multiple-choice* questions designed to be *evaluative* in nature	*Dichotomous or multiple-choice* questions designed to be *tactical* in nature	*Dichotomous or multiple-choice* questions designed to be *reactive* in nature

questions you ask over the next several hours and see if you share the tendency to use more closed-end than open-end questions. It is not uncommon to find salespeople using an average of ten closed-end questions for every open-end question used in a sales conversation. This overuse of closed-end questions is dangerous in selling. The discovery and exploration of customer needs are fundamental to trust-based selling, and discovery and exploration are best done with open-end questions.

As previously discussed, closed-end questions certainly have their place in selling, but they are best used for clarification and confirmation, not discovery and exploration. An additional issue in overusing closed-end questions is that when they are used in a sequence, the resulting communication takes on the demeanour of interrogation rather than conversation.

4-3 Strategic Application of Questioning in Trust-Based Selling

Effective questioning skills are indispensable in selling and are used to address critical issues throughout all stages of the selling process. In practice, salespeople combine the different types of questions discussed earlier to accomplish multiple and closely related sales objectives:

- *Generate buyer involvement.* Rather than the salesperson dominating the conversation and interaction, purposeful and planned questions are used to encourage prospective buyers to participate actively in a two-way collaborative discussion.
- *Provoke thinking.* Innovative and effective solutions require cognitive efforts and contributions from each participant. Strategic questions stimulate buyers and salespeople to think thoroughly and pragmatically about and consider all aspects of a given situation.
- *Gather information.* Good questions result from advance planning and should be directed toward gathering the information required to fill in the gap between "What do we need to know?" and "What do we already know?"
- *Clarify and emphasize.* Rather than assuming that the salesperson understands what a buyer has said, questions can be used to clarify meaning further and to emphasize the important points within a buyer–seller exchange further.
- *Show interest.* In response to statements from buyers, salespeople ask related questions and paraphrase what the buyer has said to demonstrate their interest in and understanding of what the buyer is saying.
- *Gain confirmation.* The use of simple and direct questions allows salespeople to check back with the prospective buyer to confirm the buyer's understanding or agreement and gain his or her commitment to move forward.
- *Advance the sale.* Effective questions are applied in a fashion that guides and moves the selling process forward in a logical progression from initiation through needs development and through needs resolution and follow-up.

With the aim of simultaneously targeting and achieving each of these objectives, several systems have been developed to guide salespeople in properly developing and using effective questions. Two of the more prominent questioning systems are SPIN and ADAPT. Both of these systems use a logical sequencing—a sort of funnelling effect—that begins with broad-based, nonthreatening, general questions. Questioning progressively proceeds through more narrowly focused questions designed to clarify the buyer's needs and to propel the selling process logically toward the presentation and demonstration of solution features, advantages, and benefits.

© peepo/iStockphoto

Besides gaining information, effective questions can also be used to provoke thinking, show interest, and generate buyer involvement.

4-4 SPIN QUESTIONING SYSTEM

The **SPIN** system sequences four types of questions designed to uncover a buyer's current situation and inherent problems, enhance the buyer's understanding of the consequences and implications of those problems, and lead to the proposed solution.[3] SPIN is actually an acronym for the four types of questions making up the multiple question sequence: situation questions, problem questions, implication questions, and need-payoff questions.

SPIN A questioning system that sequences four types of questions designed to uncover a buyer's current situation and inherent problems, enhance the buyer's understanding of the consequences and implications of those problems, and lead to the proposed solution.

situation questions One of the four types of questions in the SPIN questioning system used early in the sales call that provides salespeople with leads to develop the buyer's needs and expectations fully.

problem questions One of the four types of questions in the SPIN questioning system that follows the more general situation questions to further probe for specific difficulties, developing problems, and areas of dissatisfaction that might be positively addressed by the salesperson's proposed sales offering.

implication questions One of the four types of questions in the SPIN questioning system that follows and is related to the information flowing from problem questions; they are used to assist the buyer in thinking about the potential consequences of the problem and understanding the urgency of resolving the problem in a way that motivates him or her to seek a solution.

need-payoff questions One of the four types of questions in the SPIN questioning system that is based on the implications of a problem; they are used to propose a solution and develop commitment from the buyer.

- *Situation questions.* This type of question solicits data and facts in the form of general background information and descriptions of the buyer's existing situation. **Situation questions** are used early in the sales call and provide salespeople with leads to develop the buyer's needs and expectations fully. Situation questions might include "Who are your current suppliers?" "Do you typically purchase or lease?" and "Who is involved in purchasing decisions?" Situation questions are essential, but they should be used in moderation as too many general fact-finding questions can bore the buyer. Further, their interrogating nature can result in irritated buyers.
- *Problem questions.* **Problem questions** follow the more general situation questions to probe further for specific difficulties, developing problems, and areas of dissatisfaction that might be positively addressed by the salesperson's proposed sales offering. Some examples of problem questions include "How critical is this component for your production?" "What kinds of problems have you encountered with your current suppliers?" and "What types of reliability problems do you experience with your current system?" Problem questions actively involve the buyer and can assist the person in better understanding his or her own problems and needs. Nevertheless, inexperienced and unsuccessful salespeople generally do not ask enough problem questions.
- *Implication questions.* **Implication questions** follow and relate to the information flowing from problem questions. Their purpose is to assist the buyer in thinking about the potential consequences of the problem and understand the urgency of resolving the problem in a way that motivates him or her to seek a solution. Typical implication questions might include "How does this affect profitability?" "What impact does the slow response of your current supplier have on the productivity of your operation?" "How would a faster piece of equipment improve productivity and profits?" and "What happens when the supplier is late with a shipment?" Although implication questions are closely linked to success in selling, even experienced salespeople rarely use them effectively.
- *Need-payoff questions.* Based on the implications of a problem, salespeople use **need-payoff questions** to propose a solution and develop commitment from the buyer. These questions refocus the buyer's attention on solutions rather than problems and get the buyer to think about the positive benefits derived from solving the problems. Examples of need-payoff questions are "Would more frequent deliveries allow you to increase productivity?" "If we could provide you with increased reliability, would you be interested?" "If we could improve the quality of your purchased components, how would that help you?" and "Would you be interested in increasing productivity by 15 percent?" Top salespeople effectively incorporate a higher number of need-payoff questions into sales calls than do less successful salespeople.

ADAPT QUESTIONING SYSTEM

As Figure 4.1 illustrates, the **ADAPT** questioning system uses a logic-based funnelling sequence of questions, beginning with broad and generalized inquiries designed to identify and assess the buyer's situation. Based on information gained in this first phase, further questions

FIGURE 4.1

Funnelling Sequence of ADAPT Technique for Needs Discovery

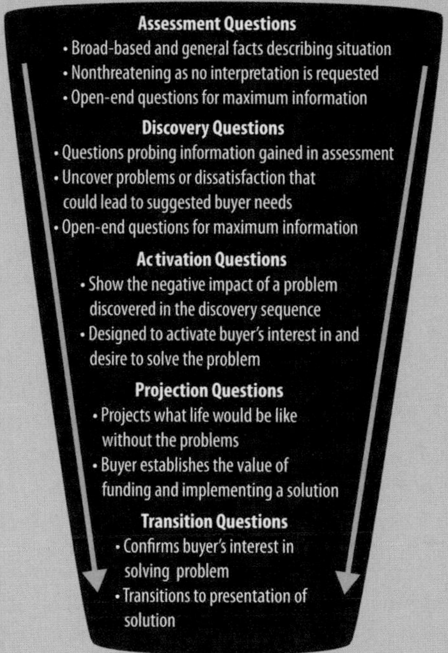

Assessment Questions
- Broad-based and general facts describing situation
- Nonthreatening as no interpretation is requested
- Open-end questions for maximum information

Discovery Questions
- Questions probing information gained in assessment
- Uncover problems or dissatisfaction that could lead to suggested buyer needs
- Open-end questions for maximum information

Activation Questions
- Show the negative impact of a problem discovered in the discovery sequence
- Designed to activate buyer's interest in and desire to solve the problem

Projection Questions
- Projects what life would be like without the problems
- Buyer establishes the value of funding and implementing a solution

Transition Questions
- Confirms buyer's interest in solving problem
- Transitions to presentation of solution

The ADAPT questioning technique logically sequences questions from broad and general inquiries through increasingly detailed questions for effective needs discovery.

are generated to probe and discover more details regarding the needs and expectations of the buyer. In turn, the resulting information is incorporated in further collaborative discussion in a way that activates the buyer's motivation to implement a solution and further establishes the buyer's perceived value of a possible solution. The last phase of ADAPT questioning transitions to the buyer's commitment to learning about the proposed solution and grants the salesperson permission to move forward into the presentation and demonstration of the sales offering. ADAPT is an acronym for the five stages of strategic questioning and represents what the salesperson should be doing at each stage: assessment questions, discovery questions, activation questions, projection questions, and transition questions.[4]

- *Assessment questions*. This initial phase of questioning is designed to be nonthreatening and to spark conversation that elicits factual information about the customer's current situation that can provide a basis for further exploration and probing. As illustrated in Exhibit 4.2, **assessment questions** do not seek conclusions—rather, at a macro or treetop level of focus, these questions should address the buyer's company and operation, goals and objectives, market trends and customers, current suppliers, and even the buyer as

ADAPT A questioning system that uses a logic-based funnelling sequence of questions, beginning with broad and generalized inquiries designed to identify and assess the buyer's situation

assessment questions One of the five stages of questions in the ADAPT questioning system that do not seek conclusions but rather should address the buyer's company and operations, goals and objectives, market trends and customers, current suppliers, and even the buyer as an individual.

EXHIBIT 4.2

Assessment Questions

These questions are designed to elicit factual information about the customer's current situation. These questions do not seek conclusions; rather, they seek information that describes the customer and his or her business environment. The information sought should augment or confirm precall research.

Examples:

1. Question—"What types of operating arrangements do you have with your suppliers?"
   Answer—We use a just-in-time (JIT) system with our main suppliers.
2. Question—"Who is involved in the purchase decision-making process?"
   Answer—I make the decisions regarding supplies....

Assessment questions are generally open end; however, closed-end questions are used when seeking confirmation or basic descriptive information. For example, "So, you currently work with 10 different suppliers?" or "How many years have you been in business?" Assessment questions are necessary for drawing out information early in the sales cycle.

discovery questions
One of the five stages of questions in the ADAPT questioning system that follows up on the assessment questions; they should drill down and probe for further details needed to develop, clarify, and understand the nature of the buyer's problems fully.

activation questions
One of the five stages of questions in the ADAPT questioning system used to activate the customer's interest in solving discovered problems by helping him or her gain insight into the true ramifications of the problem and to realize that what may initially seem to be of little consequence is, in fact, of significant consequence.

EXHIBIT 4.3
Discovery Questions

Discovery questions are used to uncover problems or dissatisfactions the customer is experiencing that the salesperson's product or company may be able to solve. Basically, these questions are used to distill or boil down the information gained from the preceding assessment questions and from precall research into suggested needs.

Examples:

1. Question—"I understand you prefer a JIT relationship with your suppliers—how have they been performing?"

   Answer—Pretty well . . . an occasional late delivery . . . but pretty well.

2. Question—"How do you feel about your current supplier occasionally being late with deliveries?"

   Answer—It is a real problem . . . for instance . . . .

The *suggested* needs gained from discovery questions are used as a foundation for the rest of the sales call. Yet a *suggested* need is usually not sufficient to close the sale. Often, a customer will believe that a particular problem does not cause any significant negative consequences. If this is the case, finding a solution to the problem will be a very low priority. The professional salesperson must then help the customer to reevaluate the impact of the *suggested* need by asking activation questions.

an individual. The information sought should augment or confirm precall research. Examples would include "What is the current level of your production?" "How long has the current equipment been in place?" "How many suppliers are currently being used?" "What are the growth objectives of the company?" and "What individuals have input into purchase decisions?"

- *Discovery questions.* As portrayed in Exhibit 4.3, these questions follow up on the responses gained from the preceding assessment questions. At a more micro and ground-level focus, **discovery questions** should drill down and probe for further details needed to fully develop, clarify, and understand the nature of the buyer's problems. Facts as well as the buyer's interpretations, perceptions, feelings, and opinions are sought about the buyer's needs, wants, dissatisfactions, and expectations relevant to product, delivery requirements, budget and financing issues, and desired service levels. The goal is to discover needs and dissatisfactions that the salesperson's sales offering can resolve. Examples of discovery questions might include "How often do these equipment failures occur?" "How well are your current suppliers performing?" "What disadvantages do you see in the current process?" "How satisfied are you with the quality of components you are currently purchasing?" and "How difficult are these for your operators to use?"
- *Activation questions.* The implied or suggested needs gained from discovery questions are not usually sufficient to gain the sale. Often, a buyer will believe that a particular problem does not cause any significant negative consequences; hence, the motivation to solve the problem will carry a low priority. Successful salespeople help the customer realistically evaluate the full impact of the implied need through the use of **activation questions**. As detailed in Exhibit 4.4, the objective is to activate the customer's interest in solving discovered problems by helping him or her gain insight into the true ramifications of the problem and to realize that what may initially seem to be of little consequence is, in fact, of significant consequence. Examples include "What effects do these equipment breakdowns have on your business operations?" "To what extent are these increases in overtime expenses affecting profitability?" "How will the supplier's inability to deliver on time affect your planned expansion?" and "When components fail in the field, how does that failure influence customer satisfaction and repurchase?"

EXHIBIT 4.4

Activation Questions

Activation questions are used to show the impact of a problem, uncovered through discovery questions, on the customer's entire operation. The objective is to activate the customer's interest in solving the problem by helping him or her to gain insight into the true ramifications of the problem and realize that what may seem to be of little consequence is, in fact, of significant consequence.

Examples:

1. Question—"What effect does your supplier's late delivery have on your operation?"

   Answer—It slows production .... Operating costs go up.

2. Question—"If production drops off, how are your operating costs affected, and how does that affect your customers?"

   Answer—Customer orders are delayed .... Potential to lose customers.

Activation questions show the negative impact of a problem so that finding a solution to that problem is desirable. Now the salesperson can help the customer to discover the positive impact of solving the problems by using projection questions.

projection questions One of the five stages of questions in the ADAPT questioning system used to encourage and help the buyer project what it would be like without the problems that have been previously discovered and activated.

- *Projection questions*. As a natural extension of the activation questions, **projection questions** encourage and facilitate the buyer in "projecting" what it would be like without the problems that have been previously discovered and activated. The use of good projection questions accomplishes several positive outcomes. First, the focus is switched from problems and their associated consequences to the upside—the benefits to be derived from solving the problems. What were initially perceived as costs and expenses are now logically structured as benefits to the buyer and his or her organization—the payoff for taking action and investing in a solution. Second—and equally important—the benefit payoff allows the buyer to establish the realistic value of implementing a solution. In this manner, the benefit payoff is perceived as a positive value received and serves as the foundation for demonstrating what the solution is worth—what the buyer would be willing to pay. As illustrated in Exhibit 4.5, projection questions encourage the buyer to think about how and why he or she should go about resolving a problem. In essence, projection questions assist the buyer by establishing the worth of the proposed solution. The customer, rather than the salesperson, establishes the benefits of

EXHIBIT 4.5

Projection Questions

Projection questions help the customer to project what life would be like without the problems or dissatisfactions uncovered through activation questions. This helps the customer to see value in finding solutions to the problems developed earlier in the sales call.

Examples:

1. Question—"If a supplier was never late with a delivery, what effects would that have on your JIT operating structure?"

   Answer—It would run more smoothly and at a lower cost.

2. Question—"If a supplier helped you meet the expectations of your customers, what impact would that have on your business?"

   Answer—Increased customer satisfaction would mean more business.

These questions are used to let the customer tell the salesperson the benefits of solving the problem. By doing so, the customer is reinforcing in his or her mind the importance of solving the problem and reducing the number of objections that might be raised.

solving the problem. This reinforces the importance of solving the problem and reduces the number of objections that might be raised. Examples of projection questions include "If a supplier was never late with a delivery, what effects would that have on your overall operation?" "What would be the impact on profitability if you did not have problems with limited plant capacity and the resulting overtime expenses?" "How would a system that your operators found easier to use affect your business operations?" and "If component failures were minimized, what impact would the resulting improvement in customer satisfaction have on financial performance?"

- *Transition questions.* **Transition questions** are used to smooth the transition from needs discovery into the presentation and demonstration of the proposed solution's features, advantages, and benefits. As shown in Exhibit 4.6, transition questions are typically closed-end and evaluative in format. These questions confirm the buyer's desire to seek a solution and give consent for the salesperson to move forward with the selling process. Examples include "So, having suppliers that are consistently on time is important to you—if I could show you how our company ensures on-time delivery, would you be interested?" "It seems that increasing capacity is a key to reducing overtime and increasing profitability—would you be interested in a way to increase capacity by 20 percent through a simple addition to your production process?" and "Would you be interested in a system that is easier for your operators to use?"

transition questions
One of the five stages of questions in the ADAPT questioning system used to smooth the transition from needs discovery into the presentation and demonstration of the proposed solution's features, advantages, and benefits.

4-5 Verbal Communication: Listening

Listening is the other half of effective questioning. As illustrated in "Professional Selling in the 21st Century: 'Feelings Questions' Are the Key for Collaborative Communication," asking the customer for information is of little value if the salesperson does not listen. Effective listening is rated among the most critical skills for successful selling. Yet most of us share the common problem of being a lot better at sending messages than receiving them. Considerable research identifies effective listening as the number-one weakness of salespeople.[5]

Poor listening skills have been identified as one of the primary causes of salesperson failure.[6] To get the information needed to best serve, identify, and respond to needs, and nurture a collaborative buyer–seller relationship, salespeople must be able to listen to

EXHIBIT 4.6
Transition Questions

Transition questions are simple closed-end questions that confirm the customer's desire to solve the problem(s) uncovered through the previous questions.

Examples:

1. Question—"So, having a supplier who is never late with deliveries is important to you?"

   Answer—Yes, it is.

2. Question—"If I can show you how our company ensures on-time delivery, would you be interested in exploring how it could work for your organization?"

   Answer—Yes, if I am convinced your company can guarantee on-time delivery.

The primary function of these questions is to make the transition from need confirmation into the sales presentation. In addition, these questions can lead to a customer commitment, provided the salesperson adequately presents how his or her company can solve the customer's problems.

Professional Selling in the 21st Century

"Feelings Questions" Are the Key for Collaborative Communication

John Kilch, financial representative with the Northwestern Mutual Financial Network, emphasizes that the questions he asks and the information he receives in the initial meeting will determine his ability to develop a lasting, mutually beneficial relationship with the person.

During John's first meeting with a prospect, called a "factfinder," he seeks to understand everything about the client: his or her fears, accomplishments, and information he or she has never told anyone. In doing so he asks a lot of "feeling" questions designed to enable prospects to open up and express their feelings and beliefs. "To be able to truly be an advisor to someone, you need to have an intricate understanding of their goals, thoughts, and feelings. You cannot expect someone to open up until you start asking questions about why a belief or goal is important and to be genuinely interested in their answers. Feeling questions help the prospect express themselves and provide more in-depth information and understanding by engaging the prospect in a two-way discussion instead of the more typical question-and-answer session directed at the prospect." But those in-depth responses have no value unless the salesperson is carefully listening to the full range of information being provided. Collaborative communication requires more than just good questions. The salesperson must be fully tuned in to what the buyer is saying, how they are saying it, and also participating in the conversation by asking related questions in order to elicit the detail required for complete understanding.

and understand what was said *and* what was meant. Nevertheless, situations similar to the one depicted in "An Ethical Dilemma" are all too common. As Figure 4.2 illustrates, effective listening can be broken down into six primary facets:

1. *Pay attention*—Listen to understand, not to reply. Resist the urge to interrupt, and receive the full message the buyer is communicating.
2. *Monitor nonverbals*—Make effective eye contact and check to see if the buyer's body language and speech patterns match what is being said.
3. *Paraphrase and repeat*—Confirm your correct understanding of what the buyer is saying by paraphrasing and repeating what you have heard.
4. *Make no assumptions*—Ask questions to clarify the meaning of what the buyer is communicating.
5. *Encourage the buyer to talk*—Encourage the flow of information by giving positive feedback and help the buyer stay on track by asking purposeful, related questions.
6. *Visualize*—Maximize your attention and comprehension by thinking about and visualizing what the buyer is saying.

The practised listening skills of high performance salespeople enable them to pick up, sort out, and interpret a greater number of buyers' verbal and nonverbal messages than lower performing salespeople can. In addition to gaining information and understanding critical to the relational selling process, a salesperson's good listening behaviours provide the added benefits of positively influencing the formation and continuation of buyer–seller relationships. A salesperson's effective use and demonstration of

social listening An informal mode of listening that can be associated with day-to-day conversation and entertainment.

serious listening A form of listening that is associated with events or topics in which it is important to sort through, interpret, understand, and respond to received messages

FIGURE 4.2

Six Facets of Effective Listening

Pay Attention
Listen to understand, not to reply; resist the urge to interrupt.

Monitor Nonverbals
Make effective eye contact and check to see if body language matches what is said.

Paraphrase and Repeat
Repeating buyers' concerns back to them confirms your understanding.

Make No Assumptions
Let buyers completely finish their thoughts; ask questions to clarify when needed.

Encourage Buyers to Talk
Give subtle and positive feedback to encourage flow of information; utilize questions to keep buyer on track and probe for details.

Visualize
Think about and visualize what the buyer is saying to maximize your attention and understanding.

Effective Listening

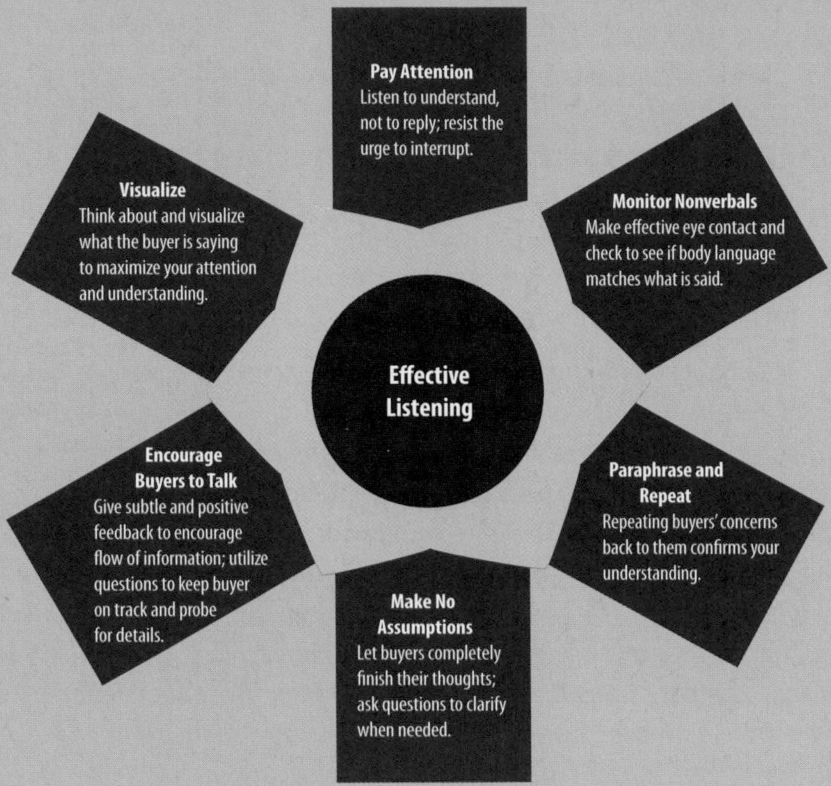

The six facets of effective listening enable salespeople to better pick up, sort out, and interpret buyers' verbal and nonverbal messages

good listening skills is positively associated with the customer's trust in the salesperson and the anticipation of having future interactions with the salesperson.[7] Clearly, effective listening is a critical component in trust-based, relational selling, and success requires continuous practice and improvement of our listening skills.

USING DIFFERENT TYPES OF LISTENING

Communications research identifies two primary categories of listening: *social* and *serious*.[8] **Social listening** is an informal mode of listening that can be associated with day-to-day conversation and entertainment. Social listening is characterized by low levels of cognitive activity and concentration and is typically used in conversation with a friend or a store clerk or listening to music, a concert, a television program, or even a play.

Effective listening requires more than just hearing what is being said.

The received messages are taken at face value and do not require a high degree of concentration or thinking to sort through, interpret, and understand. However, **serious listening** is associated with events or topics in which it is important to sort through, interpret, understand, and respond to received messages. The serious form of listening is often referred to as *active listening*, as it requires high levels of concentration and cognition about the messages being received. *Concentration* is required to break through the distractions and other interference to facilitate receiving and remembering specific messages. *Cognition* is used to sort through and select the meaningful relevant messages and interpret them for meaning, information, and response.

An Ethical Dilemma

Erin Sutton is an account manager for a large, Vancouver-based manufacturer of printing equipment and supplies. Erin feels that her 12 years of experience in the printing industry provide her with a level of expertise and knowledge much greater than most prospective buyers. This, combined with her unbridled impatience, often results in Erin interrupting buyers' statements, finishing their thoughts for them, and assuming she understands the buyers' needs better than the buyer does. Rather than allowing the buyer to fully describe what is going on and the nature of the buying organization's problems and needs, Erin often seems to be telling the buyer what his or her organization should be purchasing and using. Erin continues to sell products; however, her customer retention level is below average and her sales revenues have peaked out. Erin recognizes something is wrong and is seeking to adopt a new and more effective selling process. She has recently completed a trust-based selling program and is contemplating changing the way she sells in order to enhance her selling performance. What should Erin do?

a) Continue selling based on her experience and superior knowledge of what prospects need.
b) Use the selling process she is comfortable with and simply call on more prospects to increase her sales performance.
c) Learn to use effective questions to engage prospects; actively listen to gain understanding of a prospect's actual needs; develop unique solutions based on a prospect's specific needs.

ACTIVE LISTENING

Active listening in a selling context is defined as "the cognitive process of actively sensing, interpreting, evaluating, and responding to the verbal and nonverbal messages of present or potential customers."[9] This definition is very useful to those wanting to master active listening skills. First, it underscores the importance of receiving and interpreting both verbal and nonverbal cues and messages to better determine the full and correct meaning of the message. Second, it incorporates a well-accepted model of listening. As illustrated in Figure 4.3,[10] the **SIER** model depicts active listening as a hierarchical, four-step sequence of sensing, interpreting, evaluating, and responding.[11] Effective active listening requires each of these four hierarchical process activities to be carried out successfully and in proper succession.

- *Sensing*. Listening is much more than simply hearing. Nevertheless, the first activities in active listening are sensing (i.e., hearing and seeing) and receiving (i.e., paying attention to) the verbal and nonverbal components of the message being sent. Sensing does not occur without practice and should not be taken for granted. In fact, research indicates that most of us listen at only 25 percent of our capacity. Think about yourself. How often have you had to ask someone to repeat what he or she said or perhaps assumed you knew what the sender was going to say before he or she could say it? Increased concentration and attention can improve sensing effectiveness. Taking notes, making eye contact with the sender, and not interrupting can improve sensing skills. Let the sender finish and provide the full content of the message. This not only improves the concentration of the receiver but also encourages the sender to provide more information and detail.
- *Interpreting*. After the message is received, it must be correctly interpreted. Interpreting addresses the question of "What meaning does the sender intend?" Both content and context are important. That is, in addition

active listening The cognitive process of actively sensing, interpreting, evaluating, and responding to the verbal and nonverbal messages of present or potential customers.

SIER A model that depicts active listening as a hierarchical, four-step sequence of sensing, interpreting, evaluating, and responding.

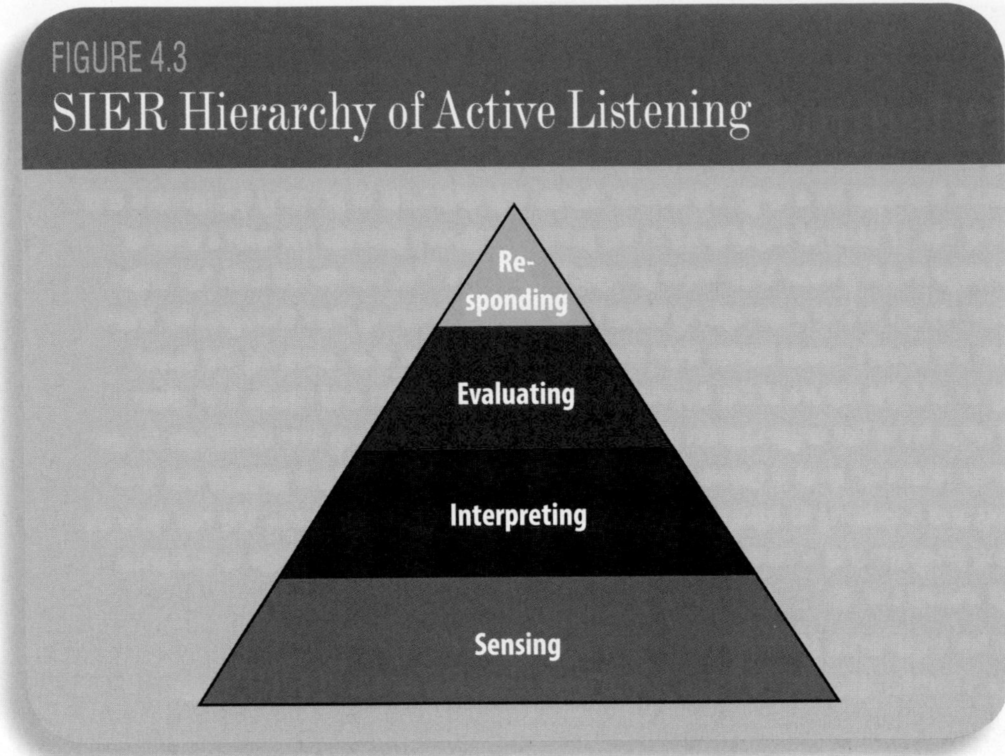

Active listening is a cognitive process of actively sensing, interpreting, evaluating, and responding to verbal and nonverbal messages from buyers and prospects.

to the semantic meaning of the words and symbols, we must consider the experiences, knowledge, and attitudes of the sender to understand fully what was meant. Hold back the temptation to evaluate the message until the sender is through speaking. Note the nonverbal and verbal cues along with possible consistencies and inconsistencies between them. Incorporate knowledge of the sender's background and previous relevant statements and positions into the message interpretation.

- *Evaluating*. Active listening requires the receiver to decide whether he or she agrees with the sender's message. The results from the interpretation stage are evaluated to sort fact from opinion and emotion. Too often, receivers complete this activity before receiving the full message, and on hearing something with which they disagree, the sender is effectively tuned out. As a result, communication is stifled. Evaluating can be improved through concentration and thoughtful consideration of the full message. Summarizing the key points as if they were going to be reported to others can further enhance evaluation skills. Searching for areas of interest rather than prejudging the message can also facilitate the evaluation process.
- *Responding*. Responding is both an expectation and a requirement for active listening to be effective. Collaborative, two-way communication requires that the listener respond to the sender. Responses provide feedback to the other party, emphasize understanding, encourage further elaboration, and can serve as a beginning point for the receiver to transition into the role of sender for the next message sent. Responses can take many forms. Nonverbal cues, such as nodding and smiling, can indicate that the sender's message was received. Responses in the form of restating and paraphrasing the sender's message can provide strong signals of interest and understanding. Asking questions can elicit additional details and clarification.

The SIER model provides a useful framework for evaluating communication accuracy and pinpointing the sources of problems. Similarly, it can be effectively used for

© MichaelDeLeon/iStockphoto

Salespeople maximize interpersonal communication by using active listening to show interest, evaluate, and respond to what the prospect is saying.

planning activities and behaviours designed to improve communication effectiveness. As the SIER model depicts, active listening is a hierarchical and sequential process. A person must sense the message before it can be interpreted. In turn, the message must be interpreted before it can be evaluated. Finally, it must be effectively evaluated before a proper response can be generated. When diagnosing a listening breakdown, look for the lowest level in the hierarchy where the breakdown could have originated and take proper action to remedy the problem. Exhibit 4.7[12] describes ten specific keys to effective listening that can be used in conjunction with the SIER model to pinpoint and improve listening problems.

4-6 Interpreting the Different Forms of Verbal and Nonverbal Communication

VERBAL COMMUNICATION: GIVING INFORMATION

Verbal information refers to statements of fact, opinions, and attitudes that are encoded in the form of words, pictures, and numbers in such a way that they

EXHIBIT 4.7

Ten Keys to Effective Listening

The Key Practice	The Weak Listener	The Strong Listener
1. Find areas of interest	Tunes out dry subjects	Actively looks for opportunities of common interest
2. Judge content, not delivery	Tunes out if the delivery is poor	Skips over delivery errors and focuses on content
3. Hold your fire until full consideration	Evaluates and enters argument before completion of message	Does not judge or evaluate until message is complete
4. Listen for ideas	Listens for facts	Listens for central themes
5. Be flexible	Takes intensive and detailed notes	Takes fewer notes and limits the theme to the central theme and key ideas presented
6. Work at listening	Shows no energy output; attention is faked	Works hard at attending the message and exhibits active body state
7. Resist distractions	Is distracted easily	Resists distractions and knows how to concentrate
8. Exercise your mind	Resists difficult expository material in favour of light recreational materials	Uses complex and heavy material as exercise for the mind
9. Keep an open mind	Reacts to emotional words	Interprets colour words but does not get hung up on them
10. Capitalize on the fact that thought is faster than speech	Tends to daydream with slow speakers	Challenges, anticipates, mentally summarizes, weighs evidence, and listens between the lines

© Getty Images/Jupiter Images

convey meaning to a receiver. However, many words and symbols mean different things to different people. Different industries, different cultures, and different types of training or work experience can result in the same word or phrase having multiple interpretations. For instance, to a design or production engineer, the word *quality* might mean "manufactured within design tolerance." However, to a customer it might be translated as "meeting or exceeding expectations." To maximize clarity and minimize misunderstandings, understand and use the vocabulary and terminology that corresponds with the perspective of the customer.

UNDERSTANDING THE SUPERIORITY OF PICTURES OVER WORDS

Studies in cognitive psychology have found that pictures tend to be more memorable than their verbal counterparts.[13] The fact that pictures enhance understanding and are more easily recalled than abstract words and symbols has several implications for effective selling.

- The verbal message should be constructed in a manner that generates a mental picture in the receiver's mind. For example, the phrase "Tropicana juices are bursting with flavour" is more visual than the more abstract version "Tropicana juices have more flavour." This can also be accomplished by providing a short and illustrative analogy or illustrative story to emphasize a key point and bring it alive in the buyer's mind.
- Rather than abstract words that convey only a broad general understanding, use words and phrases that convey concrete and detailed meaning. Concrete expressions provide the receiver with greater information and are less likely to be misunderstood than their abstract counterparts. For example, "This Web transfer system will increase weekly production by 2,100 units" provides more detail than "This Web transfer system will increase production by 10 percent." Similarly, "This conveyor is faster than your existing system" does not deliver the same impact as "This conveyor system will move your product from production to shipping at 15 metres per second as compared with your current system's 6 metres per second."
- Integrate relevant visual sales aids into verbal communication. Sales support materials that explain and reinforce the verbal message will aid the receiver's understanding and enhance recall of the message. As an additional benefit, such sales aids as samples, brochures, graphs, and comparative charts can be left with the buyer to continue selling until the salesperson's next call on the buyer.

Sales aids, such as samples, brochures, and charts, reinforce the verbal message and enhance the receivers' understanding and recall.

IMPACT OF GRAMMAR AND LOGICAL SEQUENCING

Grammar and logical sequencing are also important in the process of giving information to others. The use of proper grammar is essential in business and social communication. In its absence, the receiver of the message tends to exhibit three closely related behaviours. First, the meaning and credibility of the message are significantly downgraded. Second, the receiver begins to focus on the sender rather than the message, which materially reduces the probability of effective communication. Last, the receiver dismisses the sender and the sender's organization as being unqualified to perform the role of an effective supplier and partner. The importance of proper grammar should not be overlooked.

Similarly, whether one is engaged in simply explaining details or making a formal proposal, logical sequencing of the material is critical. The facts and details must be organized and connected in a logical order. This is essential to clarity and assists the receiver in following the facts. A discussion or presentation that jumps around runs the risk of being inefficient and ineffective. At best, the receiver will have to ask many clarification questions. At worst, the receiver will dismiss the salesperson as incompetent and close off the sales negotiation. Advance planning and preparation can improve organization. Outline what needs to be covered and organize it into a logical flow. The outline becomes the agenda to be covered and can serve as an aid for staying on track.

NONVERBAL COMMUNICATION

Nonverbal behaviours have been recognized as an important dimension of communication since medieval times. As early as 1605, Francis Bacon focused on the messages conveyed by *manual language*. Verbal communication deals with the semantic meaning of the message itself, whereas the nonverbal dimension consists of the more abstract message conveyed by how the message is delivered. **Nonverbal communication** consists of the conscious and unconscious reactions, movements, and utterances that people use in addition to the words and symbols associated with language. This dimension of communication includes eye movements and facial expressions; placement and movements of hands, arms, head, and legs as well as body orientation; the amount of space maintained between individuals; and variations in vocal characteristics. Collectively, the various forms of nonverbal communication carry subtle and explicit meanings and feelings along with the linguistic message and are frequently more informative than the verbal content of a message.[14]

Research indicates that highly successful salespeople are capable of picking out and comprehending a higher number of behavioural cues from buyers than less successful salespeople are able to sense and interpret. In addition, evidence shows that 50 percent or more of the meaning conveyed within the communication process stems from nonverbal behaviour.[15] As the nonverbal components of a message carry as much or more meaning than the language portions, it is critical for salespeople to sense effectively, interpret accurately, and evaluate fully the nonverbal elements of a message as well as the verbal components. In addition to sensing verbal messages, learn to sense between the words for the thoughts and feelings not being conveyed verbally.

FACIAL EXPRESSIONS

Possibly reflecting its central point of focus in interpersonal communication, the various elements of the face play a key role in giving off nonverbal messages. Frowning, pursed lips, and squinted eyes are common in moments of uncertainty, disagreement, and even outright skepticism. Suspicion and anger are typically

© Alex Mares-Manton/Getty

Fifty percent or more of the meaning conveyed in interpersonal communication comes through nonverbal behaviours. What nonverbal messages are being conveyed here?

accompanied by tightness along the jaw line. Smiles are indicative of agreement and interest, whereas biting of the lip can signal uncertainty. Raised eyebrows can signify surprise and are often found in moments of consideration and evaluation.

EYE MOVEMENTS

In North America and Western Europe, avoiding eye contact results in a negative message and is often associated with deceit and dishonesty. However, a sender's increased eye contact infers honesty and self-confidence. Increased eye contact by the receiver of the message signals increasing levels of interest and concentration. However, when eye contact becomes a stare and continues unbroken, either by glances away or blinking, it is typically interpreted as a threat or inference of power. A blank stare or eye contact directed away from the conversation can show disinterest and boredom. Repeated glancing at a watch or possibly an exit door often indicate that the conversation is about to end.

nonverbal communication The conscious and unconscious reactions, movements, and utterances that people use in addition to the words and symbols associated with language.

PLACEMENT AND MOVEMENTS OF HANDS, ARMS, HEAD, AND LEGS

Smooth and gradual movements denote calm and confidence, whereas jerky and hurried movements are associated with nervousness and stress. Uncrossed arms and legs signal openness, confidence, and cooperation. However, crossed arms and legs psychologically close out the other party and express disagreement and defensiveness. Increased movement of the head and limbs hints at increasing tension, as does the tight clasping of hands or fists. The placement of a hand on the chin or a tilted head suggests increased levels of evaluation, whereas nodding of the head expresses agreement. Growing impatience is associated with drumming of the fingers or tapping of a foot. Fingering the hair and rubbing the back of the neck signify increasing nervousness and apprehension.

BODY POSTURE AND ORIENTATION

Fidgeting and shifting from side to side is generally considered to be a negative message associated with nervousness and apprehension. Leaning forward or sitting forward on the edge of a chair is a general sign of increasing interest and a positive disposition in regard to what is being discussed. Similarly, leaning away can indicate disinterest, boredom, or even distrust. Leaning back with both hands placed behind the head signifies a perceived sense of smugness and superiority. A rigid erect posture can convey inflexibility or even defensiveness, whereas sloppy posture suggests disinterest in the topic. Similar to sitting backward in a chair, sitting on the edge of the table or the arm of a chair is an expression of power and superiority.

PROXEMICS

proxemics The personal distance that individuals prefer to keep between themselves and other individuals; an important element of nonverbal communication.

Proxemics refers to the personal distance that individuals prefer to keep between themselves and other individuals and is an important element of nonverbal communication. The distance that a person places between himself or herself and others implies a meaningful message and affects the outcome of the selling process. If a salesperson pushes too close to a prospect who requires more distance, the prospect may perceive the salesperson to be manipulative, intimidating, and possibly threatening. However, salespeople who put too much distance between themselves and the customer risk being perceived as rigidly formal, aloof, or even apprehensive.

Proxemics differs across cultures and regions of the world. For example, in North Africa and Latin America business is conducted at a much closer distance than in North America. As depicted in Figure 4.4, North Americans generally recognize four distinct proxemic zones. The *intimate zone* is reserved for intimate relationships with immediate family and loved ones. The *personal zone* is for personal relationships with close friends and associates. The *social zone* is for business client relationships and is the zone in which most business is conducted. The *public zone* is for the general public and group settings such as classrooms and presentations.

It is critical that salespeople understand proxemics and monitor the progression of their buyer–seller relationships so as to position themselves with different customers properly. Typically, salespeople begin working with a prospect at the far end of the *social zone*. As the salesperson–buyer relationship develops, the salesperson is in a position to move closer without violating the customer's space and causing him or her to become defensive.

As trust develops, salespeople are able to use interpersonal space to communicate and positively affect the sales outcome.

© Sisoje/iStockphoto

FIGURE 4.4

Personal Space and Interpersonal Communication

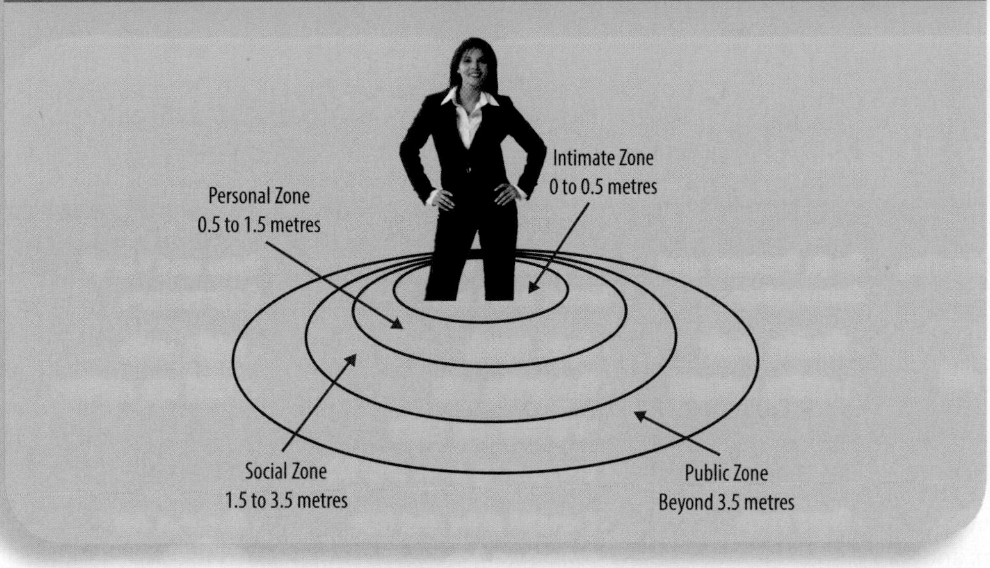

Personal Zone
0.5 to 1.5 metres
Intimate Zone
0 to 0.5 metres
Social Zone
1.5 to 3.5 metres
Public Zone
Beyond 3.5 metres

© rubberball/Jupiter Images

Individuals use four preferred spatial zones for interaction in different social and business situations.

VARIATIONS IN VOCAL CHARACTERISTICS

Nonverbal vocal characteristics, such as speaking rates, pause duration, pitch or frequency, and intensity, have been linked to communication effectiveness and selling performance. These voice characteristics convey direct as well as subtle and implied meanings and feelings that can complement or accent the corresponding verbal message.[16]

Speaking Rates and Pause Duration Within normal speaking rates, faster speakers are generally evaluated more favourably than slower speakers. Contrary to the often-cited fast-talking salesperson being perceived as high pressure, faster rates of speech and shorter pause duration are actually associated with higher levels of intelligence, credibility, and knowledge. Slower speakers are perceived as being less competent as well as less benevolent. However, speech rates that are jerky and beyond normal rates of speech can present problems in sensing and interpreting the complete message. Varying the rate of speech has also been found to be conducive to maintaining interest.

Pitch or Frequency Vocal pitch carries a great deal of information to the receiver. Varying pitch and frequency during the course of a message encourages attentiveness of the listener and accents certain forms of statements. A rising pitch during the message is associated with questions and can often be perceived as reflecting uncertainty. Just the opposite, a falling pitch is associated with declarative statements and completion of the message. Overall, high-pitched voices are judged as less truthful, less emphatic, less potent, and more nervous. Lower-pitched voices are considered more persuasive and truthful and have a positive impact on selling performance.

Intensity and Loudness Dominance, superiority, intensity, and aggression are commonly associated with loud voices, whereas soft voices characterize submission and uncertainty. However, it is the variability of intensity that has been found to be most effective in communication. Varying levels of loudness allow the sender to adapt to different situations and environments. Variation also increases the receiver's attention and can provide additional information inputs by accenting key points of a message.

USING NONVERBAL CLUSTERS

Nonverbal clusters are groups of related expressions, gestures, and movements. Similar to a one-word expression, a single isolated gesture or movement should not be taken as a reliable indication of the true intent or meaning of a message. Sensing and interpreting groups or clusters of nonverbal cues provides a more reliable indicator of the message and intent. When the individual behaviours and gestures begin to fit together, they form a common and unified message that the salesperson should consider. Common nonverbal clusters applicable to selling communication are described in Exhibit 4.8.[17]

nonverbal clusters
Groups of related nonverbal expressions, gestures, and movements that can be interpreted to better understand the true message being communicated.

Just as salespeople can interpret nonverbal messages to better understand communication with prospects and buyers, those same prospects and buyers can also sense and interpret the nonverbal messages the salesperson is sending. Consequently, it is important that salespeople monitor the nonverbal cues they are sending to ensure consistency with and reinforcement of the intended message.

EXHIBIT 4.8

Common Nonverbal Clusters

Cluster Name	Cluster Meaning	Body Posture and Orientation	Movement of Hands, Arms, and Legs	Eyes and Facial Expressions
Openness	Openness, flexibility, and sincerity	• Moving closer • Leaning forward	• Open hands • Removing coat • Unbuttoning collar • Uncrossing arms and legs	• Slight smile • Good eye contact
Defensiveness	Defensiveness, skepticism, and apprehension	• Rigid body	• Crossed arms and legs • Clenched fists	• Minimal eye contact • Sideways glances • Pursed lips
Evaluation	Evaluation and consideration of message	• Leaning forward	• Hand on cheek • Stroking of chin • Chin in palm of hand	• Tilted head • Glasses dropping to tip of nose
Deception	Dishonesty and secretiveness	• Patterns of rocking	• Fidgeting with objects • Increasing leg movements	• Increased eye movement • Frequent gazes elsewhere • Forced smile
Readiness	Dedication or commitment	• Sitting forward	• Hands on hips • Legs uncrossed • Feet flat on floor	• Increased eye contact
Boredom	Lack of interest and impatience	• Leaning head in palm of hands • Slouching	• Drumming fingers • Swinging a foot • Brushing and picking at items • Tapping feet	• Poor eye contact • Glances at watch • Blank stares

ISLAND VIEW TECH SOLUTIONS AND QUARTER & ASSOCIATES

Background

This case involves a salesperson representing the institutional sales division of Island View Tech Solutions, a leading reseller of technology hardware and software, and Dalton Genge, Director of Technology for Quarter & Associates, a prominent St. John's-based law firm specializing in corporate litigation. Quarter & Associates is preparing to move to larger facilities and wants to update its computer technology in the new facilities. Corner Brook-based Island View Tech Solutions has established itself as a major competitor in the technology marketplace specializing in value-added systems solutions for business institutions and government entities nationwide. This past year, Island View Tech Solutions has added sales and distribution centres in Burlington, Ontario, Halifax, Nova Scotia, and St. John's, Newfoundland and Labrador.

Current Situation

As an integral part of their move to new and larger facilities, Quarter & Associates want to replace their computers and information technology systems including laptop/desktop combinations for each of their 21 attorneys, desktop systems for their 10 staff members, along with archive and e-mail servers. Island View Tech Solutions specializes in this type of systems selling and uses their network of hardware and software providers in combination with their own in-house engineering, programming, and systems group to consistently provide higher value solutions than the competition.

In preparation for an initial meeting with Dalton Genge, the Island View Tech Solutions sales representative is outlining his/her information needs and developing a draft set of needs discovery questions. These needs discovery questions will be the focus of the meeting with Dalton Genge and enable Island View Tech Solutions to better identify and confirm the actual needs, desires, and expectations of Quarter & Associates in relation to new and expanded computer and information technology capabilities.

Questions

1. What information does the Island View Tech Solutions salesperson need in order to fully understand the technology needs of Quarter & Associates?
2. Following the ADAPT methodology for needs discovery questioning, develop a series of salesperson questions and anticipated buyer responses that might apply to this selling situation.

Role Play

Situation: Review the above Island View Tech Solutions–Quarter & Associates case and the ADAPT questions you developed in response to the questions associated with this case.

Characters: You, salesperson for Island View Tech Solutions; Dalton Genge, Director of Technology for Quarter & Associates

Scene:

Location—Dalton Genge's office at Quarter & Associates

Action—As a salesperson for Island View Tech Solutions, you are making an initial sales call to Dalton Genge for the purpose of identifying and detailing the specific needs and expectations Quarter & Associates has for new and expanded computers and information technology. Role play this needs discovery sales call and demonstrate how you might utilize SPIN or ADAPT questioning sequences to identify the technology needs.

CHAPTER 4

Role Play: Communication Skills: Port Wireless Inc.

Background

Port Wireless Inc. specializes in providing wireless information technology for businesses having 10 to 500 employees and needs for wireless communication, information processing, and digital data transmittal. The company offers a full range of services ranging from the one-time design of applications for smartphones and digital devices to the design and building out of full enterprise systems. As a business development specialist for Port Wireless, you are making an initial sales call to Wally Stevens, technology manager for Island Claims & Adjusters, LLC. As a preferred provider for inspection and adjusting insurance claims across Atlantic Canada, Island Claims serves as an outsource provider of claims and adjusting services to many of the top 25 property and casualty insurance companies and has experienced rapid growth over the last five years. The company currently employs 65 people: 50 adjusters out in the field, 10 assistants located at company headquarters in Summerside, PEI, and 5 administrative and executive staff members.

The purpose of this initial call is to assess Island Claim's current use and needs for wireless communication and data services. According to the initial information you gained from a short phone conversation with Stevens, Island Claims is currently using a variety of different smartphones on Sprint's cellular and data service. However, they are exploring a combination of custom-designed apps for the iPad 4 for use by their adjusters in the field. This combination would enable adjusters to complete and submit data forms complete with pictures and eliminate the added processing required in their current use of paper-based forms and records. During the phone conversation, Stevens mentioned that some of the benefits are obvious; nevertheless, they have concerns about the custom apps and transitioning to a fully digital system.

Role Play

Location: Wally Stevens' office at Island Claims & Adjusters.

Action: Role play this needs discovery sales call and demonstrate how you might utilize SPIN or ADAPT questioning sequences to identify the needs and concerns of the prospect.

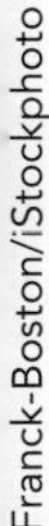
Franck-Boston/iStockphoto

SELL

what do you think?

The best salespeople do not have to spend time prospecting.

1 2 3 4 5 6 7
strongly disagree — strongly agree

Spending time with

the best prospects and customers is one of the keys to salesperson success.

5 Strategic Prospecting and Preparing for Sales Dialogue

After completing this chapter, you should be able to

5-1 Discuss why prospecting is an important and challenging task for salespeople.

5-2 Explain strategic prospecting and each stage in the strategic prospecting process.

5-3 Describe the major prospecting methods and give examples of each method.

5-4 Explain the important components of a strategic prospecting plan.

5-5 Discuss the types of information salespeople need to prepare for sales dialogue.

Introduction

Most salespeople have to spend time prospecting to generate business from new customers and to increase sales from existing customers. One study found that about 50 percent of sales leads are identified by salespeople themselves and about 50 percent are produced by marketing and other partners.[1] Another study indicated that the time salespeople spend prospecting has increased from 19 percent in 2006 to 24 percent in 2011.[2] Successful salespeople employ an effective strategic prospecting process that employs the most appropriate technology at each stage.

CAN Financial sells financial and marketing products to independent financial advisers. The company CEO was identifying potential customers at different events and assigning them to salespeople. Most of these leads were not good sales opportunities and the company did not have a process for tracking the leads once assigned to a salesperson. This approach was not very effective and salespeople were not happy with the leads they were receiving.

The company decided to develop a strategic prospecting process that integrated the marketing function with the latest technology. E-mail marketing campaigns were created to generate and nurture leads from a database of 50,000 independent financial advisers. The financial advisers that responded to an e-mail message were sent to a Web site to answer five questions to determine if they were qualified prospects. The questions addressed the length of time in business, income level, regulatory requirements, licences held, and range of financial services offered. Those scoring above 190 were assigned to a salesperson. The salesperson contacted the qualified sales lead and invited the financial adviser for an office visit. This approach increased the number of office visits by 43 percent and almost half of those visiting the office became new clients.

The entire strategic prospecting process is tracked using GreyMS lead management software and on the firm's CRM system. CAN Financial is very pleased with its new process. Salespeople are able to focus on the best sales opportunities with more qualified prospects being converted into new customers. The company plans to continue improving its strategic prospecting process in the future.

Adapted from: Henry Canaday, "The Same Team," *Selling Power* (January/February 2011): 51-52.

The CAN Financial example illustrates the importance and complexity of identifying the best sales opportunities. Most salespeople, as with those at CAN Financial, have to cultivate new business if they are to sustain the sales growth objectives their company establishes. However, salespeople typically achieve sales growth objectives by finding the right balance between getting new customers and generating additional business from existing customers. Various prospecting approaches are available, with each having advantages and disadvantages. New technological advances are increasing the number of tools salespeople can use to determine the best sales opportunities. The purpose of this chapter is to examine the importance and challenges of prospecting, introduce the strategic prospecting process, present different prospecting methods, and discuss preparation for sales dialogue.

5-1 The Importance and Challenges of Prospecting

Prospecting is extremely important to most salespeople. Salespeople who do not regularly prospect are operating under the assumption that the current business with existing customers will be sufficient to generate the desired level of future revenue. This is a shaky assumption in good times, but it is especially questionable in the tough economic environment of recent years. As market conditions change, existing customers may buy less. Or customers may go out of business. Some customers might be acquired by another firm, with the buying decisions now being made outside the salesperson's territory. The salesperson could also simply lose customers because of competitive activity or dissatisfaction with the product, the salesperson, or the selling firm. Because there is typically a considerable time lag between the commencement of prospecting and the conversion of prospects to customer status, salespeople should spend time prospecting on a regular basis. Otherwise, lost sales volume cannot be regained quickly enough to satisfy the large majority of sales organizations—those that are growth-oriented.

strategic prospecting A process designed to identify, qualify, and prioritize sales opportunities, whether they represent potential new customers or opportunities to generate additional business from existing customers.

sales funnel or **pipeline** A representation of the trust-based sales process and strategic sales prospecting process in the form of a funnel.

Despite its importance, salespeople often find it difficult to allocate enough time to prospecting. Many salespeople do not like to prospect because of their fear of rejection. Today's buyers are busy, and many are reluctant to see salespeople. Buyers may not want to take the time to see a salesperson for several reasons:

1. They may have never heard of the salesperson's firm.
2. They may have just bought the salesperson's product category and currently have no need.
3. Buyers may have their own deadlines or other issues, and not be in a receptive mood to see any salespeople.
4. Buyers are constantly getting calls from salespeople and do not have time to see them all.
5. Gatekeepers in any organization screen their bosses' calls and sometimes are curt and even rude.

Salespeople can overcome the challenges of prospecting and become more effective in determining the best sales opportunities by following a strategic sales prospecting process, using a variety of prospecting methods, developing a strategic prospecting plan, and preparing for sales dialogue with prospects. Sometimes the stress of prospecting can produce difficult situations, as presented in "An Ethical Dilemma."

5-2 The Strategic Prospecting Process

The first step in the trust-based sales process presented in Chapter 1 is strategic prospecting. **Strategic prospecting** is a process designed to identify, qualify, and prioritize sales opportunities, whether they represent potential new customers or opportunities to generate additional business from existing customers. The basic purpose of strategic prospecting is to help salespeople determine the best sales opportunities in the most efficient way. Effective strategic prospecting helps salespeople spend their valuable selling time in the most productive manner.

The strategic prospecting process (illustrated in Figure 5.1) is often viewed as a **sales funnel** or **sales pipeline** because it presents the entire trust-based sales process and the strategic prospecting process in

© iStock/Thinkstock

An Ethical Dilemma

Sam Johnson has sold uniforms for The Uniform Company for the past 10 years. He has had the same sales territory during this period and has developed strong relationships with his customers. During good economic times, his customers expanded their businesses and purchased more uniforms from him. The poor economic climate of the past few years has changed his situation dramatically, because current customers are buying less. His sales manager, Mary Hamilton, suggested that he focus on generating new customers and asked him to report his prospecting efforts to her each month. Sam is reluctant to call on new prospects, but has made some half-hearted calls to prospects over the past few months with little success. However, he exaggerates and fabricates information in the reports he submits to Mary Hamilton. Mary Hamilton has scheduled a ride-along with Sam and wants to accompany him on some sales calls to prospects included in his reports. What should Sam do?

a) Tell Mary that he could not get any appointments with these prospects during the period of her visit.
b) Actually call on the prospects he has put in his reports and try to set up appointments during Mary's visit.
c) Tell Mary that he is reluctant to call on new prospects and has fabricated some of the information in his reports.

the form of a funnel. The funnel is very wide at the top, as salespeople typically have a large number of potential sales opportunities. As salespeople move through the strategic prospecting process and the other stages in the trust-based sales process, the funnel narrows because only the best sales opportunities are pursued and not all sale opportunities result in a sale or new customer relationship. For the most productive salespeople, the sales funnel is normally much wider at the bottom than it is for less productive salespeople. The most productive salespeople pursue the best sales opportunities and translate a larger percentage of these opportunities into actual sales than less productive salespeople do. We will now discuss each step in the strategic prospecting process.

GENERATING SALES LEADS

The first step in the strategic prospecting process is to identify sales leads. **Sales leads** or **suspects** are organizations or individuals who might possibly purchase the product or service a salesperson offers. This represents the realm of sales opportunities for a salesperson. For example, if a salesperson sells copiers in business markets, any organization that might need a copier would be a sales lead. Although more sales leads are usually better than fewer leads, the identified organizations

> The most productive salespeople pursue the best sales opportunities and translate a larger percentage of these opportunities into sales than less productive salespeople do.

represent different types of sales opportunities. For example, large organizations might represent better sales opportunities because they probably need more copiers than smaller organizations. Other organizations may have just purchased copiers or are very satisfied with their current copiers, which would mean they do not represent good sales opportunities. If salespeople

sales leads or **suspects** Organizations or individuals who might possibly purchase the product or service a salesperson offers.

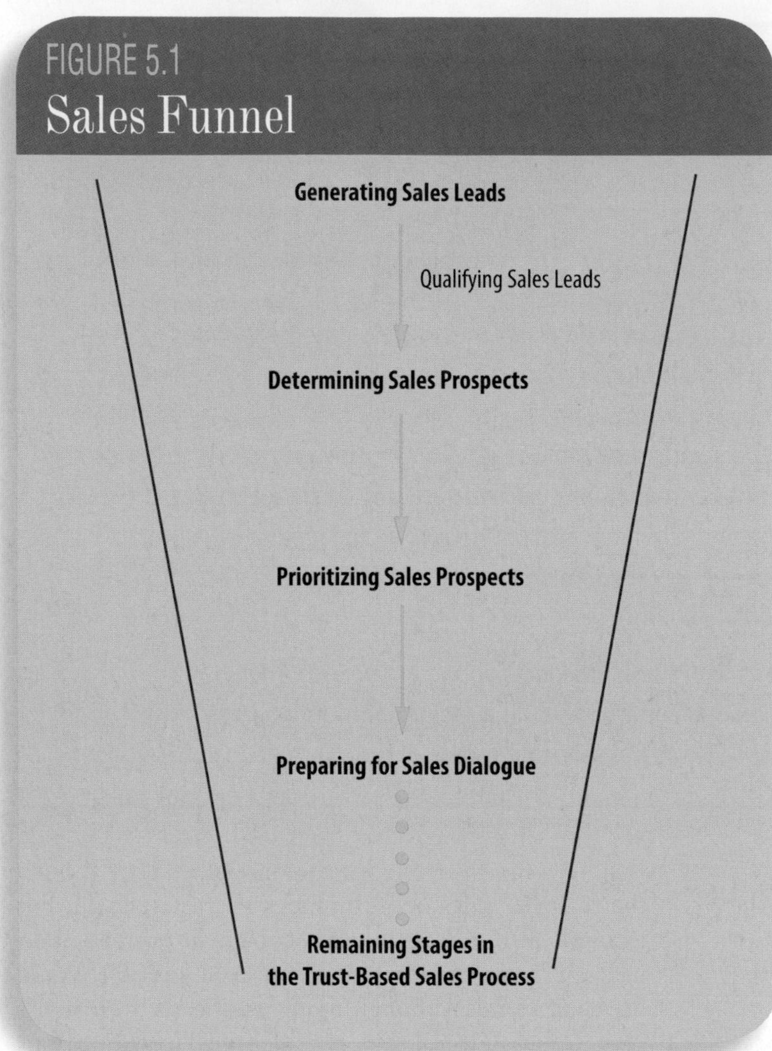

The sales funnel presents the trust-based sales process and highlights the major steps of the strategic prospecting process.

qualifying sales leads The salesperson's act of searching out, collecting, and analyzing information to determine the likelihood of the lead being a good candidate for making a sale.

sales prospect An individual or organization that has a need for the product or service, has the budget or financial resources to purchase the product or service, and has the authority to make the purchase decision.

ideal customer profile The characteristics of a firm's best customers or the perfect customer.

merely generate leads and pursue most of them, they are likely to be spending a great deal of their time with organizations that are unlikely to purchase from them.

DETERMINING SALES PROSPECTS

The most productive salespeople evaluate sales leads to determine which ones are true prospects for their product or service. This evaluation process is usually called **qualifying sales leads**. Salespeople search for, collect, analyze, and use various types of screening procedures to determine if the sales lead is really a good sales prospect. Although specific companies define sales prospects in different ways, a **sales prospect** is typically an individual or organization that

- has a need for the product or service
- has the budget or financial resources to purchase the product or service
- has the authority to make the purchase decision

Those that meet these criteria move down the sales funnel (see Figure 5.1) into the sales prospect category, while those that do not are set aside. In the CAN Financial process, those scoring above 190 on five key questions were considered to be qualified prospects. About 14 percent of the financial advisers who responded to a marketing e-mail were found to be qualified prospects. Salespeople who spend the time and effort qualifying their leads limit the time wasted on making calls with a low probability of success and focus their efforts on the more fruitful opportunities.

PRIORITIZING SALES PROSPECTS

Even though the qualifying process has culled out the least promising sales leads, the remaining prospects do not all represent the same sales opportunity. The most productive salespeople prioritize their sales prospects to ensure that they spend most of their time on the best opportunities. One approach is to create an **ideal customer profile** and then analyze sales prospects by comparing them with this ideal customer profile. Those that most closely fit the profile are deemed to be the best sales prospects. Another approach is to identify one or more criteria, evaluate sales prospects against these criteria, and either rank all of the sales prospects based on this evaluation or place the sales prospects into A, B, and C categories, with A sales prospects representing the best sales opportunities. The CAN Financial salespeople prioritized their sales prospects according to their score on the five qualifying questions. Financial advisers with the highest scores were the best sales prospects.

PREPARING FOR SALES DIALOGUE

The final step in the strategic prospecting process is to prepare for the initial contact with a sales prospect by planning the sales dialogue. The information accumulated to this point in the process is helpful, but additional information is usually required to increase the chances of success in the initial sales dialogue. The types of additional information required are discussed later in this chapter.

5-3 Prospecting Methods

Many different sources and methods for effective strategic prospecting have been developed for use in different selling situations. A good selling organization and successful salespeople will have a number of ongoing prospecting methods in place at any given time. The salesperson must continually evaluate prospecting methods to determine which methods are bringing in the best results. New methods must also be evaluated and tested for their effectiveness. Many popular prospecting methods are presented in Exhibit 5.1.

COLD CANVASSING

Cold canvassing occurs when salespeople contact a sales lead unannounced with little if any information about the lead. **Cold calling** is the most extreme form of cold canvassing because salespeople merely knock on doors or make telephone calls to organizations or individuals. This is a very inefficient prospecting method. Typically, a very small percentage of cold calls produce, or lead to future sales dialogue with, qualified prospects. Because there is so much rejection, many salespeople do not like to cold call sales leads.

Using referrals or introductions can improve the success of cold calling. A **referral** is a sales lead a customer or some other influential person provides. Salespeople are often trained to ask customers and others for the names and contact information of potential prospects. Sometimes salespeople can also obtain sufficient information to qualify the lead as a good sales prospect. Additionally, salespeople can get permission to use the person's name when contacting the prospect. In some cases, the person might agree to provide an **introduction** by writing a letter or making a phone call to introduce the salesperson to the prospect. An example of an effective referral approach is presented in "Professional Selling in the 21st Century: Referred Lead Prospecting."

cold calling Contacting a sales lead unannounced and with little or no information about the lead.

referral A name of a company or person given to the salesperson as a lead by a customer or even a prospect who did not buy at this time.

introduction A variation of a referral in which, in addition to requesting the names of prospects, the salesperson asks the prospect or customer to prepare a note or letter of introduction that can be sent to the potential customer.

NETWORKING

Salespeople can use various types of networking as effective methods for prospecting. Many salespeople join civic and professional organizations, country clubs, or fraternal organizations, and these

EXHIBIT 5.1
Prospecting Methods

Cold Canvassing	Networking	Company Sources	Published Sources
• Cold calling	• Centres of influence	• Company records	• Directories
• Referrals	• Noncompeting salespeople	• Advertising inquiries	• Commercial lead lists
• Introductions	• Electronic networking	• Telephone inquiries	
		• Trade shows	
		• Seminars	

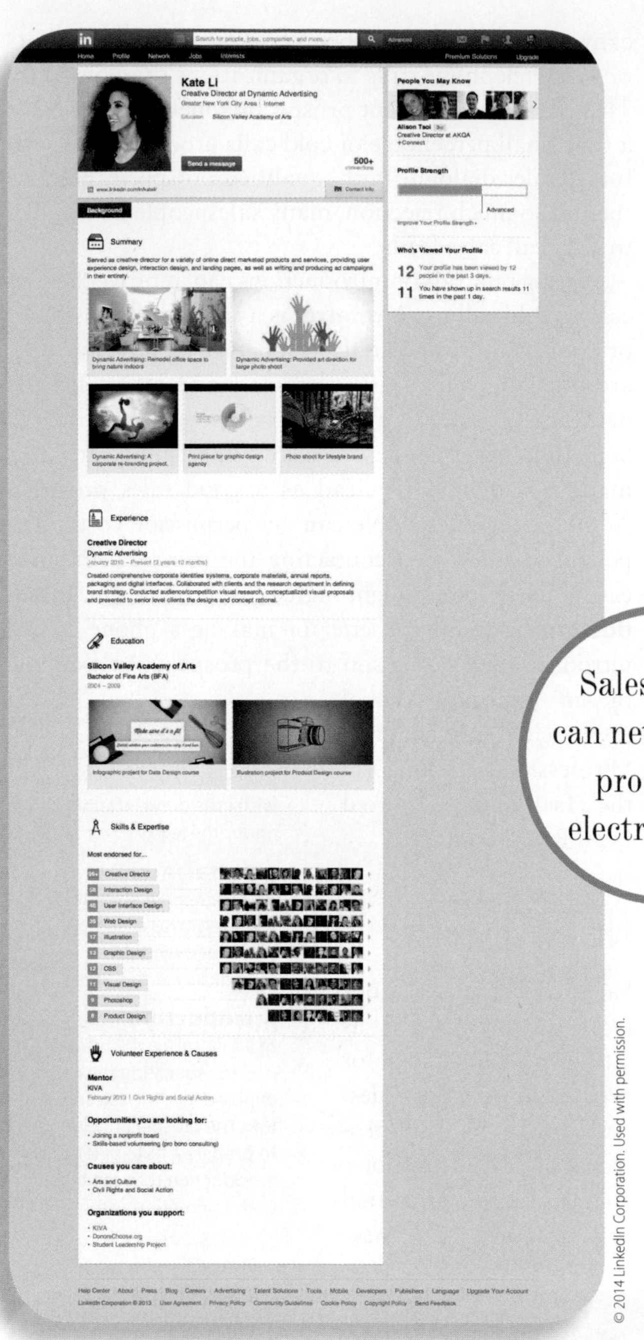

centres of influence Well-known and influential people who can help a salesperson prospect and gain leads.

noncompeting salespeople Salespeople selling noncompeting products.

electronic networking Using Web sites designed to help salespeople identify and gather information about prospects.

memberships provide the opportunity for them to build relationships with other members. Sometimes these relationships yield prospects. Some members might be influential people in the community or other organizations, making them **centres of influence** for the salesperson and potentially providing help in locating prospects. Accountants, bankers, attorneys, teachers, business owners, politicians, and government workers are often good centres of influence.

Networking with salespeople from noncompeting firms can also be a good source of prospects. Business Networking International (BNI), which has several active chapters throughout Canada, is a formal organization with each local group consisting of **noncompeting salespeople**. The basic purpose of this organization is for the members to generate prospects for one another. There are other sales and marketing organizations that salespeople can join to create the opportunity to identify prospects by networking with members.

It is important for salespeople to strike up conversations with other sales representatives while waiting to see buyers. Noncompeting salespeople can be found everywhere and can help in getting valuable information about prospects. An example of how noncompeting salespeople can help each other was demonstrated when a Hershey Chocolate salesperson went out of his way to tell a noncompeting sales representative from Hormel Foods about a new grocery store going into his territory. Hormel Foods is a manufacturer of food and meat products for consumers throughout the world. The Hormel representative was the first of his competitors to meet with the new grocery store management team and was given valuable shelf space that his competitors could not get. A few months later, the Hormel sales representative returned the favour when he found out that an independent convenience store was changing hands. The Hershey salesperson was able to get into the new owner's store early and added valuable shelf space for his products. The operating principle of "you scratch my back and I scratch yours" works when information flows in both directions.

> Salespeople can network for prospects electronically.

Electronic Networking

New developments in technology have produced a variety of Web sites that allow salespeople to engage in **electronic networking**. Some of the sites are free, but others charge fees for some or all services provided. The specifics of each site differ, but all make it possible for salespeople to network online for prospects and obtain various types of information about the prospects. The most popular sites include LinkedIn (www.linkedin.com), Jigsaw (www.jigsaw.com), Spoke Software (www.spoke.com), and Plaxo (www.plaxo.com). The use of electronic networking is likely to increase in the future as technology continues to advance.

© CJG - Technology/Alamy

Professional Selling in the 21st Century

Referred Lead Prospecting

Tom Raisor is managing director at Northwestern Mutual Financial Network (NMFN). He has been with NMFN for 32 years and is currently involved in sales as well as in training all salespeople in his region. Tom discusses the referred lead prospecting approach that he uses and teaches:

The basic objective of our referred lead prospecting approach is to get favourable introductions to the best prospects for our financial products and services. It is extremely important that a salesperson understand the market and be able to identify an ideal prospect. In general, an ideal prospect is a person who is responsible, interested in taking care of family and/or employees, and doing well financially.

Prior to a client meeting, the salesperson prepares a list of five to six people that the client knows who are likely to be good prospects. We call this a feeder list and use Web sites, Facebook, LinkedIn Groups, and other sources to identify these leads. At the end of the meeting, the salesperson presents the feeder list to the client and asks which of these people meet the criteria for an ideal prospect. We also ask the client to give reasons for those selected as the best prospects.

Then, for each person selected from the feeder list, the salesperson asks if the client would be willing to let the person know by e-mail, phone, or in person that the NMFN salesperson will be contacting them in the near future. This approach has been very successful for our salespeople. The feeder list helps the client identify the best prospects and the favourable client introduction increases the likelihood of getting to talk to the prospect.

Personal Selling and Social Media Various forms of social media, such as Facebook, MySpace, Twitter, and blogs, have become mainstream forms of communication for individuals and businesses alike. Since social media is top of mind for most businesses, and with sales organizations' emphasis on external communications, the pressure to stay current is high. However, sales experts agree that sale reps and managers must apply some type of filter so that social media remains a sales tool and not a distraction to the sales rep.[3]

"Social networking is a strategy for marketing promotions and relationship management. It is not a prospecting tool. A lot of the maintenance functions involved with social media tools are going to slide down to the lowest paid person who is competent to do them."[4] In other words, sales reps should not be focusing on daily tweets and Facebook updates. Some experts believe that these new communication tools are doing a disservice to salespeople; they are tools of communication and not meant to replace the sales process.

Participating in trade shows is an effective prospecting method.

© Stockbyte/Jupiter Images

COMPANY SOURCES

Many companies haveresources or are engaged in activities that can help their own salespeople with strategic prospecting. **Company records** can be a useful source of prospects. Salespeople can also review company records to identify previous customers who have not placed an order recently. Contacting previous customers to determine why they have stopped ordering could provide opportunities to win back business. Examining the purchasing behaviour of existing customers can also help in identifying opportunities to sell additional products to specific customers.

company records Information about customers in a company database.

advertising inquiries Sales leads generated from company advertising efforts.

inbound telemarketing A way to locate prospects in which the prospect calls the company to get information.

outbound telemarketing A way to locate prospects in which the salesperson contacts the prospect by telephone.

trade shows Events at which companies purchase space and set up booths that clearly identify each company and its offerings and that are staffed with salespeople who demonstrate the products and answer questions.

Advertising inquiries are potentially a good source of prospects. For example, one manufacturer's rep in the natural gas industry speaks highly of his company's advertising plan. The company advertises only in trade magazines that it believes buyers read. The salesperson's territory includes Alberta, Manitoba, and Saskatchewan. The advertising message is simply "If we can help you with any of your natural gas needs (e.g., flow meters, odorizers), please give us a call." These leads are then turned over to the salesperson who calls on that territory. One salesperson cannot cover territories of this size. The advertising program qualifies the prospect (with the help of the telephone) before the salesperson is sent out on the call.

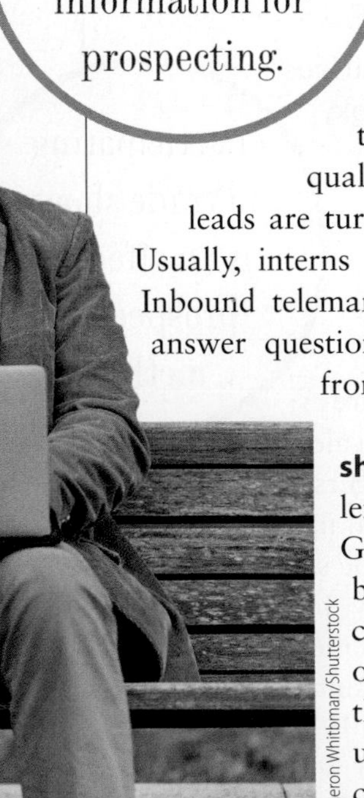
© Cameron Whitman/Shutterstock

Online directories provide salespeople with useful information for prospecting.

The CAN Financial strategic prospecting process used e-mail marketing campaigns to identify sales leads and potential prospects. More companies are using online advertising as a way to generate sales leads. Expenditures for online advertising to obtain sales leads increased from $12.5 billion in 2005 to over $22.7 billion in 2009, with additional growth since 2009.[5] AP Under Inc. is one company that has used Web-based marketing effectively. The company redesigned its Web site to include interactive features that created a dialogue with visitors. It worked on the site's search engine optimization to get into the top five listings for healthcare audit-related terms and started a company blog. These efforts increased traffic to its Web site from 10 to 15 visits per week to 1,500–2,000, generated qualified sales prospects, and increased new business by $2 million. This Web-based marketing approach has replaced cold calling as the major source of new customers.[6]

Many organizations today use both inbound (prospect calls the company) and outbound (salesperson contacts the prospect) telemarketing. **Inbound telemarketing** involves a telephone number (usually a toll-free number) that prospects or customers can call for information. Companies distribute toll-free numbers by direct mail pieces (brochures), advertising campaigns, and their **outbound telemarketing** program. Some companies use both inbound and outbound telemarketing to serve their market. They use outbound telemarketing to generate and then qualify leads for their salesforce. Qualified leads are turned over to experienced salespeople. Usually, interns do all the outbound telemarketing. Inbound telemarketing is used to resolve problems, answer questions from prospects, and take orders from existing customers.

Attending conventions and **trade shows** presents salespeople with excellent opportunities to collect leads. Generally, the company purchases booth space and sets up a stand that clearly identifies the company and its offerings. Salespeople are available at the booth to demonstrate their products or answer questions. Potential customers walk by and are asked to fill out information cards indicating an interest in the company or one of its products. The completed information card provides leads for the salesperson. Trade shows can stimulate interest in products and provide leads. For example, bank loan officers attend home improvement trade shows and can offer the homeowner immediate credit to begin a project. Those who sign immediately may be offered a lower interest rate.

Firms can use **seminars** to generate leads and provide information to prospective customers. For example, a financial planner will set up a seminar at a local hotel to give a presentation on retirement planning, inviting prospects by direct mail, word of mouth, or advertising on local television and radio. The financial consultant discusses a technique or investment opportunities that will prepare the audience for retirement. Those present will be asked to fill out a card expressing their interest for follow-up discussions. The financial consultant hopes this free seminar will reward him or her with a few qualified prospects.

PUBLISHED SOURCES

Published lists and **directories** offer an inexpensive, convenient means of identifying leads. Telephone books today contain a business section that lists all the community's businesses. This list is usually broken down further by business type. Manufacturers, medical facilities, pharmacies, and grocery stores, to name a few, can be easily identified by using the business pages of the phone book. Many other directories exist, such as Board of Trade directories, chamber of commerce directories, trade association lists, *Moody's Industrial Directory*, and *Standard & Poor's Register of Corporations, Directors, and Executives*. Directories are a wealth of information if used correctly. A salesperson must remember that when these lists are published they become obsolete. Companies change their names, merge with others, and even change addresses. Salespeople must verify information from published sources before using it. Exhibit 5.2 lists some of the directories that salespeople have at their disposal.

A large variety of list providers offer **commercial lead lists** designed to focus on virtually any type of business or individual. Available on paper or in convenient computer formats, commercial lead lists range from simple listings of names, addresses, and phone numbers to more detailed listings with a full profile of the different entities included in the list. Leading providers include infoCANADA (www.infocanada.ca), Scott's Directories (www.scottsdirectories.com), *Canada Business Directory* (http://canadabusinessdirectory.ca), and Industry Canada (www.ic.gc.ca).

5-4 Developing a Strategic Prospecting Plan

The most productive salespeople use a variety of prospecting methods and follow the strategic prospecting process by generating leads, qualifying them to identify true prospects, and then prioritizing these prospects so that they pursue the best sales opportunities. The use of a strategic prospecting plan can help salespeople continually improve their prospecting effectiveness.

A **strategic prospecting plan** should fit the individual needs of the salesperson. As illustrated in Figure 5.2, the focal point of a prospecting plan should be the goal stating the number of qualified prospects to be generated. Formalized goals serve as guides to what is to be accomplished and help to keep a salesperson on track. The plan should also allocate an adequate and specific daily or weekly time period for prospecting. Having specific times set aside exclusively for prospecting helps to prevent other activities from creeping in and displacing prospecting activities. A good **tracking system** should also be a part of the prospecting plan. A tracking system can be as low-tech as a set of index cards or employ one of the many computerized and online contact management or customer relationship management software

seminars A presentation salespeople give to generate leads and provide information to prospective customers who are invited to the seminar by direct mail, word of mouth, or advertising on local television or radio.

directories Electronic or print sources that provide contact and other information about many different companies or individuals.

commercial lead lists Lists that focus on virtually any type of business or individual; they range from simple listings of names, addresses, and phone numbers to more detailed listings with a full profile of the different entries included in the list.

strategic prospecting plan A salesperson's plan for gathering qualified prospects.

tracking system Part of the strategic prospecting plan that records comprehensive information about the prospect, traces the prospecting methods used, and chronologically archives outcomes from any contacts with the prospect.

EXHIBIT 5.2
List of Secondary Lead Sources

1. *Canadian Business Resource*, published by Canadian Newspaper Services International, maintains a database of 2,500 of Canada's largest firms and all firms listed on the TSX and TSX Venture exchanges. It also maintains more than 40,000 contact names that are downloadable to subscribers' contact management software from www.cbr.ca.
2. *Moody's Industrial Directory* is an annual publication with a wide range of statistical information about particular firms that might be prospects for a specific product or service. Names of executives, description of the company business, and a brief financial statement for more than 10,000 publicly held firms are available at www.moodys.com.
3. *Standard & Poor's Register of Corporations, Directors, and Executives* is an excellent source of personal information about individuals in companies. Such information can be used for qualifying prospects and for learning enough about them to plan an effective approach and presentation. This annual publication lists names, titles, and addresses for 50,000 firms. See www.standardandpoors.com.
4. *Canadian Trade Index*, published by Canadian Manufacturers and Exporters, is available in print, on CD-ROM, and online at www.ctidirectory.com. It lists more than 30,000 manufacturers, distributors, and industrial service companies and features nearly 100,000 product listings under 20,000 headings.
5. *Polk City Directory* supplies detailed information on individuals living in specific communities. Polk publishes more than 1,100 directories covering 6,500 communities throughout Canada and the United States. The local chamber of commerce should have access to this directory. See www.citydirectory.com.
6. *Hoover's Business Directory*, available from Dun & Bradstreet Canada in print form or on CD, lists and profiles more than 20,000 of Canada's largest companies and maintains more than 60,000 key contact names. See www.dnb.ca/salesmarketing/keybusinessdir.html.
7. *World Scope: Industrial Company Profiles* (Wright Investors' Service) provides extensive coverage of 5,000 companies from 25 countries, within 27 major industry groupings. See www.wisi.com.
8. Frasers.com provides a comprehensive online directory and search tool for Canadian manufacturers and industrial distributors and their products and services. It also lists international companies that sell in the Canadian marketplace. A separate website lists trade shows in Canada and the United States. See www.frasers.com/public/home.jsf.
9. Scott's Directories publishes separate directories for many sectors: corporate (140,000 manufacturers, distributors, banks, construction companies, etc.), medical (100,000 doctors, dentists, hospitals, etc.), government (federal, provincial/territorial, municipal), associations (10,000 listings), schools (various types), and residential (12 million listings, available by segment). Directories are available in print, on CD-ROM, or online. See www.scottsinfo.com.

applications. Exhibit 5.3 shows an example of a simple but effective paper-and-pencil tracking form. The tracking system should record comprehensive information about the prospect, trace the prospecting methods used, and chronologically archive outcomes from any contacts with the prospect. A fourth element of the prospecting plan is a system for analyzing and evaluating the results of prospecting activities. Continuous evaluation should be employed to ensure the salesperson is meeting prospecting goals and using the most effective prospecting methods. The fifth and final element of a prospecting plan should be a program to review and stay up-to-date on product knowledge and competitor information to emphasize and underscore that the salesperson's products and services offer the best solutions to customer needs and problems. Self-confidence is critical to success in selling, and a base of comprehensive knowledge and understanding is the key to believing in yourself.

As with all phases of the sales process, salespeople must exercise judgment and set priorities in prospecting. A limited amount of time is available for prospecting, and a better understanding of the concepts and practices illustrated in this chapter can help a salesperson be more productive. An added bonus is that the sales process is more enjoyable for salespeople calling on bona fide prospects who can benefit from the salesperson's offering.

FIGURE 5.2

Prospecting Plans Are the Foundation for Effective Prospecting

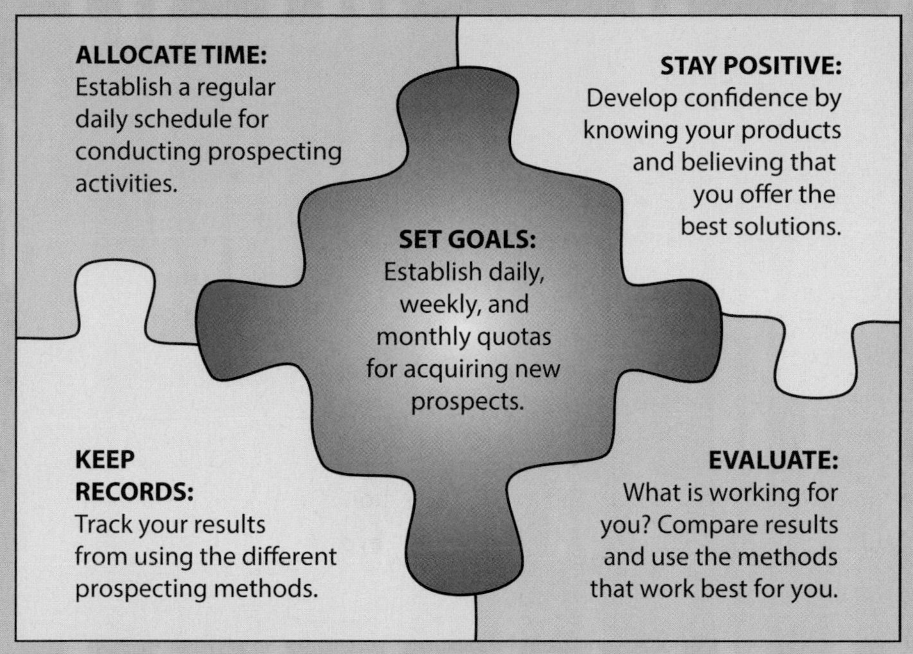

The strategic prospecting plan sets goals, allocates specific times to be used for prospecting, and continuously evaluates results to maximize the effectiveness of prospecting time and effort.

5-5 Gathering Prospect Information to Prepare for Sales Dialogue

Once potential customers are identified, the salesperson must begin the process of collecting information. During this stage, the salesperson gathers information about the prospect that will be used to formulate future sales interactions. Buyer's needs, buyer's motives, and details of the buyer's situation should be determined. Some organizations spend a great amount of time determining the salesperson's and buyer's communication styles. Effectively sensing and interpreting customers' communications styles allows salespeople to adapt their own interaction behaviours in a way that facilitates buyer–seller communication and enhances relationship formation. An example of collecting information about prospects and current customers before meeting with them is presented in "Professional Selling in the 21st Century: Preparing for Sales Dialogue."

The more a salesperson knows about a prospect, the better chance the salesperson has to make a sale. Over time, the salesperson should be able to accumulate knowledge about the prospect. The information that the salesperson needs varies with the kind of product that he or she is selling. As a rule, a salesperson needs to know a few basic things about his or her customers (e.g., the prospect's name, correct spelling, and correct pronunciation). A salesperson can learn a great deal about a customer over time by collecting bits and pieces of information, sorting them out, and developing a personalized presentation for the customer.

> The most effective salespeople set prospecting priorities.

OBTAINING INFORMATION ON THE BUYER

A salesperson must do some preliminary homework once a company has been identified as a potential client. The first stage of information gathering is to concentrate on

EXHIBIT 5.3

Personal Prospecting Log

PERSONAL PROSPECTING LOG

Name Tom Jenkins

Team Charlottetown Commercial Date 4/16

1st Contact	Organization	Contact Person	Source of Lead	Phone	Date of Appointment	Outcome of Call	Follow-Up Activity
3/02/12	Cummins Engine	Tyler Huston	Personal contact	902-444-1234	4/11 8:30 a.m.	Need info on printer	Send in mail
9/01/11	Costco Katya Epstein	Referral Tom Oats John Deere	902-888-4111	Will call with dates/times	Liked our numbers; decision next week	Send info on satisfied customers	
9/02/11	Ball-Foster	MaryLou Hinkle	Called in on 800#	902-365-4242	4/13 Lunch	Great lunch, need proposal	Will work up proposal, set date and present
4/19/12	Ontario Systems	Darrell Beaty	Referral	902-223-4117	4/19 4 p.m.		
4/17/12	Tom's Grocery	Sharon Bristow	Referral Stacey Jones Saskatoon Saskatchewan	905-452-4422	4/17 8 a.m.		
2/02/12	Shopper's Drug Mart	Isabelle Chen	Direct mail sent back 6/02	905-663-2214	4/16 Lunch	Didn't seem impressed, need more work	Need more contact with Alice PACER GAME?
2/03/12	Davis & Davis	Frank Chapman	800# call in	905-211-8811	Bob Evans 4/15 Breakfast	Will include their DP department at next call	Schedule DP
3/03/12	ABB	Jerome Parker	Personal contact	905-927-4321	4/14 2 p.m.	Liked our proposal	Call Monday for answer
3/03/12	Thomson Consumer Electronics	Doug Lyon	Phone	905-212-4111	4/15 3 p.m.	Had bad experience with us several years ago	This one will take time

Professional Selling in the 21st Century

Preparing for Sales Dialogue

Eric Bassett is an account executive for ValPak. He sells advertising for the ValPak Cooperative Direct Mail Program to owners of local small and medium-sized businesses in an assigned sales territory. Preparing for sales dialogue with prospects and existing customers is critical for sales success. Eric discusses how he gets the information he needs to be successful:

Once I have identified a good prospect, I gather as much information as possible before contacting the prospect to schedule an appointment. I use the Secretary of State Business Registry and the Better Business Bureau Web site to make sure I have the correct name and contact information for the business owner. Then, I typically perform an Internet search for recent articles about the business and review its Web site to understand the current situation and future plans of the prospect. I also check Facebook, because more personal information about the business owner is sometimes provided. Once I have gathered the information I need, I call the business owner to set up an appointment and to collect some additional information, such as the type of current advertising and its effectiveness, who are their customers and where do they come from, and if there are other people involved in the decision-making process who should be involved in our meeting. This type of preparation increases my chances for converting the prospect into a ValPak customer

Once this prospect becomes a customer, I work hard to build good relationships, but am always looking for opportunities to increase business with each customer. Before calling on an existing customer, I review the amount and type of advertising the customer has done with ValPak in the past. I try to assess the short-term and long-term ROI from the past advertising efforts. My focus is to determine what is working or not working as well as desired. This analysis makes it possible for me to be able to identify and suggest specific changes to improve the customer's ROI from advertising with ValPak. My customers are usually very impressed with how prepared I am for the meetings I have with them, and this helps me increase business with them.

the individual prospect. Several questions need to be answered that will identify how the buyer will behave toward the salesperson. Exhibit 5.4 details some of the questions that a salesperson needs to ask.

It is not unusual for gatekeepers to prohibit the salesperson access to the buyer over the phone if the salesperson mispronounces the buyer's name. Mail is thrown away without being opened if the name is misspelled or the title is incorrect.

Precall information should be used to develop a rapport with the prospect and eventually to tailor the presentation to fit the buyer's needs. A salesperson can establish a relationship with a prospect by discussing such mutual points of interest as an alumni association with the same university or support for the same athletic team. Information gathering must be done thoughtfully; it can take many sales calls and months to gather all the useful information a salesperson needs.

GATHERING INFORMATION ON THE PROSPECT'S ORGANIZATION

Gathering information about the prospect's company helps salespeople better understand the environment in which they will be working. Exhibit 5.5 details some of the questions that provide useful information about the prospect's organization. Is the prospect currently buying from a single supplier? How long has the prospect been buying from this supplier? If the answer

EXHIBIT 5.4

Information to Gather on a Prospect and Whom to Contact

Information Needed	How to Collect Information
The prospect's name.	Correct spelling and pronunciation can be gathered by asking the receptionist or secretary to verify information.
The prospect's correct title.	This can be determined by asking the gatekeepers to verify.
Is this prospect willing to take risks? Are they confident with decision making?	The salesperson may have to ask the prospect about willingness to take risks.
Is the prospect involved in the community? Does the prospect belong to any clubs or professional organizations?	The salesperson may be able to observe club or organizational honours displayed in the office.
Does the prospect have hobbies or interests he or she is proud of (e.g., coin collector, sports enthusiast)?	Observation of the office might give away this information.
What is the prospect's personality type? Easygoing? All business?	Observation and experience with the buyer will give the answer to the salesperson.
Where was the prospect educated? Where did this prospect grow up?	Look for a degree or diploma on the wall. The salesperson may have to ask for this information.

EXHIBIT 5.5

Gathering Information about the Organization

Information Needed	How to Collect Information
What type of business are we dealing with: manufacturer, wholesaler, retailer, government, educational, medical, financial institution?	This can be gathered from a directory.
To what market does the company sell? Who are the organization's primary competitors? What does the company make and sell?	Annual reports may be helpful in answering these questions.
From whom does the prospect presently buy? Do they buy from a single vendor? Multiple vendors? How long have they purchased from their suppliers? What problems does the company face? In what volume does the company buy? What is the organization's financial position?	The salesperson may have to ask for this information.

is 20 years and he or she is extremely satisfied with the current salesperson, products, and services, then the prospect should be thanked for his or her time, and the salesperson should move on to other accounts.

SOURCES OF INFORMATION

A good salesperson uses all available information sources to gather valuable information. Lists and directories will have names, addresses, phone numbers, and other key information. Secretaries and receptionists can be a friendly source of information and can certainly be used to verify name, title, pronunciation, and correct spelling. Also, noncompeting salespeople can help a salesperson fill in information on accounts.

The Web can be a valuable tool as companies provide more than enough vital information for a salesperson. Quite often, companies have employees responsible for seeking critical Web information daily about the company's clients and competitors. Salespeople have access to a large quantity of current information and should use it to gain an edge over their competitors. The use of social media as a valuable information source for salespeople has been increasing in recent years. Facebook, LinkedIn, and blogs are especially useful information sources. Many companies are also accumulating information about prospects and making it readily available to salespeople using the latest technology. Two examples are illustrative:

- Cintas has created a virtual office of various types of prospect information. Salespeople can access this information electronically and get useful information before contacting a prospect.[7]

© alejandro dans neergaard/Shutterstock

An Ethical Dilemma

Garett Williams is a Business Development Manager for a community bank. His job is to create new banking relationships with small firms in the local area. Many of these small firms have had relationships with the large national banks for many years. However, Garett knows that if he can find out about a firm's current banking relationship and get an appointment with the firm's owner, he has a good chance of getting some business for his bank. The problem is that many of the small firm owners are reluctant to provide any information about their banking relationships and often are not willing to agree to an appointment.

Garett recently read about the large losses incurred by some national banks in their risky derivatives trading. Although these losses were not expected to have any impact on their relationships with business clients, Garett thought he might be able to use this situation to help him get appointments and banking information from the small business owner. So, Garett would call a small business prospect and ask them if they were familiar with the losses at the large national banks. If the prospect's response indicated minimal knowledge of the situation, he would explain the problem and discuss how these losses could have a negative effect on business customers of the national bank. He would then ask the prospect if they had any relationships with the large national banks and the specifics of these relationships. Many of the prospects were now willing to share this information and many agreed to schedule an appointment to meet with Garett. Garett increased the number of his appointments and was able to translate these into significant increases in business for his bank. What should Garett Williams do?

a) Garett should continue this approach, because it has been very successful for him.
b) Garett should continue this approach, but he should acknowledge that the derivative trading losses at the large national banks are not expected to have any negative impact on banking relationships with their small business clients.
c) Garett should discontinue this approach and create a more ethical one, even if it is not as effective as this approach.

EXHIBIT 5.6
Customer Profile

1. Name of Business ______________________________
2. Address ______________________________
3. Phone ______________________________
4. Name of Buyer(s) ____________ Title ______________

   Personality, Hobbies, Interests ______________________________

   ____

   ____

   ____
5. Source of Prospect (i.e., referral, cold call) ______________________________
6. Other Key People ______________________________

   Receptionists ______________________________

   Personality, Hobbies, Interests ______________________________

   Secretaries ______________________________

   Personality, Hobbies, Interests ______________________________

   Department Heads ______________________________

   Personality, Hobbies, Interests ______________________________

   Other Influencers—Who? ______________________________

   Personality, Hobbies, Interests ______________________________
7. What products does the company produce? ______________________________
8. History and current standing in the industry ______________________________
9. How many employees? ______________________________
10. Extent of operations—local, regional, national, international ______________
11. Is buying done by individuals or committee? ______________________________
12. Does the company buy from single or multiple sources? ______________

- Several pharmaceutical firms are pilot testing the use of smartphone applications (apps). Salespeople can make a few clicks on a smartphone and get information about whether or not a physician has had any changes in patient population or prescribing habits, and even any physician engagements with digital media.[8]

The use of new and emerging technologies will certainly improve the availability of prospect information for salespeople in the future.

Even the most thorough preparation usually will not provide salespeople with all of the desired prospect information. The additional information is typically collected through questioning the prospect during sales dialogues. This can be an effective approach, but must be done in a considerate and professional manner or problems can occur, as illustrated in "An Ethical Dilemma." The information salespeople collect about prospects prior to the first meeting and throughout the trust-based sales process should be accumulated and updated on a regular basis. Although some salespeople do this manually, as illustrated in Exhibit 5.6, the use of contact management, salesforce automation (SFA), and customer relationship management (CRM) systems is increasing. These technologies are being improved continuously and are valuable tools for salespeople.

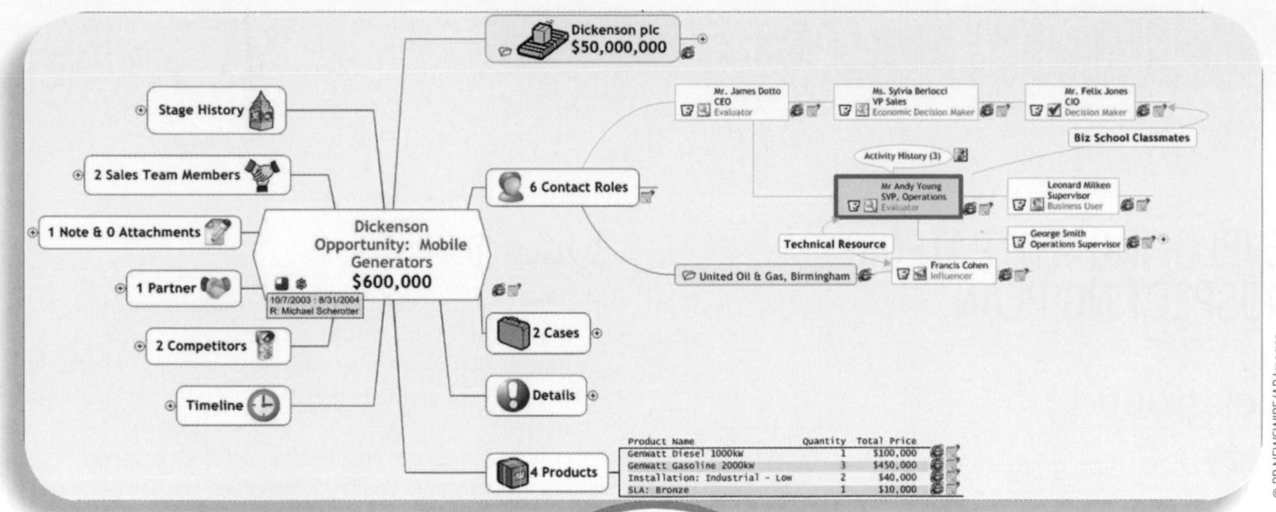

© PR NEWSWIRE/AP Images

DETERMINING OTHER BUYERS' INFLUENCES

As products become more complex, we often see an increase in the number of buying influencers and decision makers involved in the purchase. The salesperson should attempt to determine the various buying influencers. For example, if a salesperson concentrates on the purchasing agent in an organization and ignores other key players (e.g., department head, data processing) in the decision-making process, the salesperson risks selling to the wrong person.

Salespeople can use different software programs to assemble information about prospects.

The salesperson must use observation and questioning to determine the role of each member of the buying team and the amount of influence each exerts; each member's needs should be determined before or during the presentation. Department heads may be interested in how the product will benefit their department, whereas the CFO may care only about the price. During group presentations, all the members of the buying party must feel involved. The salesperson must be sure to direct questions and comments to all potential decision makers in the group.

If a salesperson has only one contact (e.g., purchasing agent) in an organization, he or she runs the risk that the key contact could die, get fired, change jobs, be transferred, or retire. By having contact with many influencers in an organization, the salesperson will always have a number of people who have had previous experiences to pass on to the new purchasing agent or team member. In the first instance, the salesperson must start the entire relationship process again; in the second, the salesperson will have help keeping the relationship in place.

Visit **www.nelson.com/student** to find the resources you need today!

Located at the back of the textbook are rip-out Chapter Review cards. Make sure you also go online to check out other tools that SELL offers to help you successfully pass your course.

- Flashcards
- Glossary
- PowerPoint Notes
- Role-Play Videos
- Games
- Interactive Quizzing

CHAPTER 5 CASE

DEVELOPING A STRATEGIC PROSPECTING PLAN

Background

Colleen King graduated from Memorial University and was hired as a sales representative for the Connector Company. The Connector Company is a transportation broker that links companies needing products shipped with trucking firms to carry the shipments. After an initial training program, Colleen was given a couple of existing company customers and a small list of leads to get her started. She began by serving the shipment needs of the existing customers. This gave her some confidence, but she realized that for her to be successful, she must begin prospecting and try to identify the best sales opportunities. The Connector Company provides an ongoing list of leads that can be accessed by all salespeople. Once a salesperson contacts one of these leads, no other salesperson can contact them. Colleen started her prospecting by contacting these leads.

Current Situation

Colleen has been calling a number of leads each day, but has not been very successful in generating much business. She feels like she is wasting much of her time on leads that are not good sales opportunities. The leads provided by her company are not qualified in any way and the training program she attended focused on cold calling as the basic prospecting method. Colleen took a professional selling class in university and remembered that the chapter on prospecting emphasized the need to follow the strategic prospecting process to identify the best sales opportunities. She found her professional selling textbook, went to the chapter on prospecting, and decided to create a strategic prospecting plan.

Questions

1. What methods should Colleen use to generate sales leads beyond those provided by her company?
2. How should Colleen qualify the leads provided by her company and those she generates herself? What is the profile of an ideal prospect?
3. How should Colleen prioritize her qualified prospects?
4. What information should Colleen collect to prepare for sales dialogue with a prospect?
5. Colleen used LinkedIn during university and wanted to employ it in her strategic prospecting process. How can she best use LinkedIn?

Role Play

Situation: Read case and prepare a strategic prospecting plan.

Characters: Colleen and her sales manager.

Scene: Colleen has implemented her strategic prospecting plan and been very successful. She has been the top seller in her office for the past two months. Her sales manager is impressed and he asks her what she is doing to be so successful. She indicates that her success is due to spending most of her time with the best sales opportunities. He wants to talk to her about her strategic prospecting plan and sets up a meeting.

Location—Sales manager's office.

Action—Role play the meeting between Colleen and her sales manager. The sales manager should ask many questions and Colleen will respond to these questions. The use of LinkedIn has been valuable to Colleen and no other salespeople at the Connector Company are using LinkedIn, so make sure the role of LinkedIn is included in the role play.

Role Play: Strategic Prospecting and Preparing for Sales Dialogue: Prospecting and Gaining Prospect Information

Background

Preston Adams has just completed the sales training program for the Office Equipment Division of Xerox. Adams has been assigned a territory in New Brunswick that includes the metro areas of Fredericton, Saint John, and Moncton. The company once commanded a significant market share in these markets. However, because of a problem with a previous salesperson in these markets three years ago, Xerox has not been directly working this particular region of central Illinois. Although a large number of Xerox machines are still in use across this territory, it has been a while since a salesperson has called on any accounts. As with any geographic area, a lot of changes have likely occurred, with existing companies moving or even going out of business and new companies opening up.

Current Situation

Adams's sales manager, Eric Waits, is coming in two weeks to spend three days in the field with Adams calling on prospective accounts. Adams is working to develop a list of leads that he can qualify and then contact to set up the sales calls he will be making with his manager.

Role Play

Situation: Read the role play.

Characters: Preston Adams, salesperson for Xerox Business Machines Division; Jerri Spencer, office manager with purchasing responsibilities for Moncton-based McKelvey and Walters, Attorneys-at-Law.

Scene:

Location—Preston Adams's office at Xerox Business Machines Division.

Action—In the course of Adams's prospecting activities, Spencer and the McKelvey and Walters law firm have come up as a strong prospect for Xerox's new line of professional copiers. McKelvey and Walters operate a large office in Moncton that occupies most of two floors in the Planter's Bank Building and a branch office in Saint John. They were previously a customer of Xerox, but the information that Adams has obtained indicates that they are using an unspecified variety of different brands of copiers.

Role play the phone conversation between Adams and Spencer as Adams introduces himself and his company to Spencer, gathers needed information to better qualify the prospect, and asks for an appointment for an initial sales call.

© HomeStudio/Shutterstock

In sales,

you have to show up to be successful. But before you show up, you have to do your homework.

what do you think?

Salespeople with great presentation skills can overcome a lack of planning for sales calls.

1 2 3 4 5 6 7

strongly disagree — strongly agree

6

Planning Sales Dialogues and Presentations

After completing this chapter, you should be able to

6-1 Explain why it is essential to focus on the customer when planning sales calls.

6-2 Understand alternative ways of communicating with prospects and customers through canned sales presentations, written sales proposals, and organized sales dialogues and presentations.

6-3 Discuss the nine components of the sales dialogue template that can be used for planning an organized sales dialogue or an organized sales presentation.

6-4 Explain how to write a customer value proposition statement.

6-5 Link buying motives to benefits of the seller's offering, support claims made for benefits, and reinforce verbal claims made.

6-6 Engage the customer by setting appointments.

Introduction

College students and professional salespeople have a lot in common: Performance is largely determined by preparation. The best salespeople know that their success depends on their ability to properly plan for customer encounters. According to Tom Reilly, a leading sales trainer, consultant, and writer, 95 percent of top salespeople routinely plan their sales calls. Mr. Reilly estimates that the large majority of less successful salespeople fail to plan their customer visits adequately, displaying an attitude of, "I'm talented. I go with the flow. I'm able to wing it."

Kevin Davis, a leading trainer of Fortune 500 salesforces, reinforces the concept of the salesperson as a student, noting that understanding customer needs, buying environment, and how the sales offering fits into the buyer's world is essential for the value-adding salesperson. In today's fast-changing, information-rich business world, top salespeople must be inquisitive and able to assess their own efforts when it comes to precall preparation. For example, salespeople should ask themselves if they are fully prepared in terms of what information they will need from the buyer, what they will want to convey to the buyer, what support information they will need, and what obstacles they will need to overcome. Their precall preparation must be guided by a firm objective that specifies the customer action sought as a result of the upcoming call.

Sales technology is assisting precall planning far beyond checking out the prospect's Web site. While customer Web-site searches can yield valuable information, other sources are rapidly growing in popularity. For example, LinkedIn has become a powerful tool for researching companies and individuals within those companies. Prospective buyers often seek advice on potential vendors on LinkedIn, and sales organizations are monitoring the site as part of precall preparation. InsideView.com offers an online tool that monitors LinkedIn and Twitter for relevant sales opportunities and prospect information. Google (Google.com/finance and Google alerts) and Hoover's (www.hoovers.com) also offer salespeople efficient ways for preparing for sales calls. With an abundance of information at their fingertips, salespeople have no excuse for arriving unprepared for a sales call. With most business decision makers starved for time, showing up unprepared is essentially an insult to the buyer. Top salespeople already know this, and they would not dare insult their prospects or existing customers.

Sources: Kevin Davis, *Slow Down, Sell Faster!* (New York: American Management Association, 2011); and Tom Reilly, *Value-Added Selling*, 3rd ed. (New York: McGraw-Hill, 2010).

6-1 Customer-Focused Sales Dialogue Planning

Buyers are generally well informed and have little time to waste. This means that salespeople must invest a significant amount of time in planning sales calls on prospective and existing customers so that they can communicate in a clear, credible, and interesting fashion. A **sales call** takes place when the salesperson and buyer or buyers meet in person to discuss business. This typically happens in the customer's place of business, but it may occur elsewhere, such as in the seller's place of business or at a trade show.

As defined in Chapter 1, **sales dialogue** comprises business conversations between buyers and sellers that take place over time as salespeople attempt to initiate, develop, and enhance customer relationships. The term *sales conversation* is used interchangeably with sales dialogue. Some sales calls involve **sales presentations** as part of the dialogue. Sales presentations are comprehensive communications that convey multiple points designed to persuade the prospect or customer to make a purchase.

Ideally, sales presentations focus on customer value and take place only after the salesperson has completed the ADAPT process (introduced in Chapter 4). As a reminder, the ADAPT process means the salesperson has assessed the customer's situation; discovered his or her needs, buying processes, and strategic priorities; activated the buyer's interest in solving a problem or realizing an opportunity; helped the buyer project how value can be derived from a purchase; and then made a transition to the full sales presentation. Salespeople who attempt to make a sales presentation before building a foundation through sales dialogue risk being viewed as noncustomer-oriented and overly aggressive.

sales call An in-person meeting between a salesperson or sales team and one or more buyers to discuss business.

sales dialogue Business conversations between buyers and sellers that occur as salespeople attempt to initiate, develop, and enhance customer relationships. Sales dialogue should be customer focused and have a clear purpose.

sales presentations Comprehensive communications that convey multiple points designed to persuade the customer to make a purchase.

Courtesy of Michael Schell (www.tlp1.com)

The importance of focusing on the customer when planning sales dialogues is reflected in the popular trade book* Buyer Approved Selling *by Michael Schell.

Consistent with the trust-based sales process introduced in Chapter 1 (see Figure 1.5), sales dialogue planning efforts should focus on customer value. Salespeople must have a basic understanding of the value they and their companies can deliver to customers. Further, they must recognize that what constitutes value will typically vary from one customer to the next. Finally, as the process continues and relationships are established with customers, salespeople must work continually to increase the value their customers receive. Throughout the process, selling strategy must focus on customer needs and how the customer defines value.

To better understand the process of planning sales dialogues and presentations, we will now discuss the three most common approaches: the canned sales presentation, the written sales proposal, and organized sales dialogues and presentations. Each of these alternatives varies greatly in terms of how much customization and customer interaction is involved. A planning template that serves as a guide for sales dialogues and comprehensive presentations will then be presented. The chapter concludes with a discussion of how to foster better sales dialogues when attempting to initiate relationships with customers.

6-2 Sales Communications Formats

In planning customer encounters, salespeople must decide on a basic format, such as a canned sales presentation, a written sales proposal, or an organized sales dialogue. Exhibit 6.1 summarizes the types of communications sales professionals use. A salesperson might use one or more of these formats with a particular customer. Each format has unique advantages and disadvantages. To be successful, these communications must be credible and clear. In addition, the salesperson must communicate in the right environment at an appropriate time to maximize the probability of a successful outcome.

For any of the three communications types, salespeople must plan to be as specific as possible in developing their sales message. For example, it is better to tell a prospect "This electric motor will produce 4800 RPM and requires only one hour of maintenance per week" than to say "This motor will really put out the work with only minimum maintenance."

EXHIBIT 6.1
Types of Sales Communications

Canned Presentations

- These include scripted sales calls, and memorized and automated presentations.
- They can be complete and logically structured.
- The downside is that to not vary from buyer to buyer; they should be tested for effectiveness.

Written Sales Proposals

- The proposal is a complete self-contained sales presentation.
- Written proposals are often accompanied by sales calls before and after the proposal is submitted.
- Thorough customer assessment should take place before a customized proposal is written.

Organized Sales Dialogues and Presentations

- They address individual customer and different selling situations.
- They allow flexibility to adapt to buyer feedback.
- They are the most frequently used format by sales professionals.

CANNED SALES PRESENTATIONS

Canned sales presentations include scripted sales calls, memorized presentations, and automated presentations. The telemarketing industry relies heavily on scripted sales calls, and memorized presentations are common in trade show product demonstrations. Automated presentations often incorporate computer graphics, video, or slides to present the information to the prospect.

When done right, canned presentations are complete and logically structured. Objections and questions can be anticipated in advance, and appropriate responses can be formulated as part of the presentation. The sales message varies little from customer to customer, except that some sales scripts have "branches" or different salesperson responses based on how the customer responds. Canned presentations can be used by relatively inexperienced salespeople, and using this format might boost the confidence of some salespeople. Canned sales presentations should be tested for effectiveness, ideally with real customers, before they are implemented with the entire salesforce.

Canned sales presentations make an implicit assumption that customer needs and buying motives are essentially homogeneous. Therefore, canned presentations fail to capitalize on a key advantage of personal selling—the ability to adapt to different types of customers and various selling situations. The salesperson can only assume the buyer's need and must hope that a lively presentation of product benefits will cause the prospect to buy. The canned presentation can be effective, but is not appropriate for many situations—simply because customer opportunity to interact is minimized. During a memorized presentation,

canned sales presentation Sales presentations that include scripted sales calls, memorized presentations, and automated presentations.

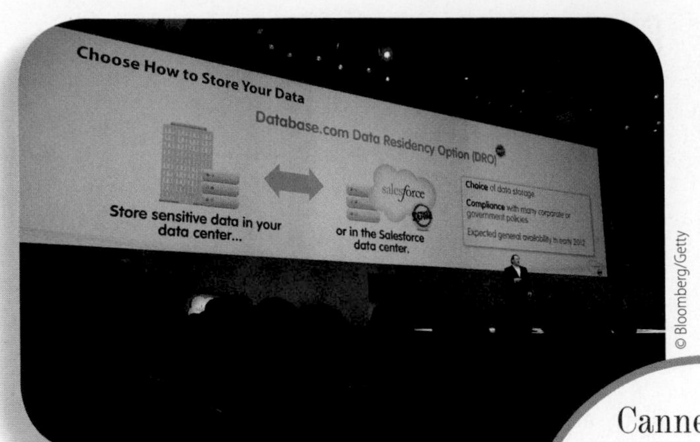

© Bloomberg/Getty

Canned sales presentations include scripted presentations to customers at industry trade shows.

the salesperson talks 80 to 90 percent of the time, only occasionally allowing the prospect to express his or her feelings, concerns, or opinions. Canned presentations do not handle interruptions well, may be awkward to use with a broad product line, and may alienate buyers who want to participate in the interaction.

Despite its limitations, the canned sales presentation can be effective in some situations. If the product line is narrow and the salesforce is relatively inexperienced, the canned presentation may be suitable. Also, many salespeople find it effective to use a sales dialogue to introduce their company, to demonstrate the product, or for some other limited purpose.

Buyers expect clear, informative sales messages, and they are less tolerant of sloppy communication.

WRITTEN SALES PROPOSALS

The second basic type of sales communication is the **written sales proposal**. The proposal is a complete self-contained sales presentation, but it is often accompanied by sales dialogues before or after the proposal is delivered. In some cases, the customer may receive a proposal and then request that the salesperson make a sales call to further explain the proposal and provide answers to questions. Alternatively, preliminary sales dialogues may lead to a sales proposal. In any event, the sales proposal should be prepared after the salesperson has made a thorough assessment of the buyer's situation as it relates to the seller's offering.

written sales proposal
A complete self-contained sales presentation on paper, often accompanied by other verbal sales presentations before or after the proposal is delivered.

The sales proposal has long been associated with important, high-dollar-volume sales transactions. It is frequently used in competitive bidding situations and in situations involving the selection of a new supplier by the prospect. One advantage of the proposal is that the written word is usually viewed as being more credible than the spoken word. Written proposals are subject to careful scrutiny with few time constraints, and specialists in the buying firm often analyze various sections of the proposal.

Sales proposal content is similar to other comprehensive sales presentations, focusing on customer needs and related benefits the seller offers. In addition, technical information, pricing data, and perhaps a timetable are included. Most proposals provide a triggering mechanism, such as a proposed contract to confirm the sale, and some specify follow-up action to be taken if the proposal is satisfactory.

With multimedia sales presentations becoming more routine, it is natural to think that written sales proposals would be declining in importance. Actually, the opposite is true. With the widespread use of multimedia, the standards for all sales communication continue to rise. Buyers expect clear, informative sales messages, and they are less tolerant of sloppy communication. Because everyone knows that word processing programs have functions to check spelling and grammar, for example, mistakes are less acceptable than ever.

Because written communication provides a permanent record of claims and intentions, salespeople should be careful not to overpromise but still maintain a positive and supportive tone. No buyer wants to read a proposal full of legal disclaimers and warnings, yet such information may be a necessary ingredient in certain written communication. As with all communication, salespeople should try to give buyers the information they need to make informed decisions.

Writing Effective Proposals

Whether the proposal is in response to a buyer's request for proposals (RFP) or generated to complement and strengthen a sales presentation, it is essential that the proposal be correctly written and convey the required information in an attractive manner. Tom Sant, an author and consultant who works with many Fortune 100 companies, gives these reasons why proposals may fail:[1]

1. Customer does not know the seller.
2. Proposal does not follow the customer-specified format.
3. Executive summary does not address customer needs.
4. Proposal uses the seller's (not the customer's) company jargon, which forces readers to interpret the message.
5. Writing is flat, technical, and without passion. A technical data dump is not effective.
6. Generic material does not match the targeted prospect, indicating a lack of customer-focused consultative selling.
7. Proposal is not convincing, and does not substantiate claims made.
8. Proposal has poor layout and glaring grammatical errors.
9. Proposal does not address key decision criteria. Don't assume what is important to the buyer—ask!
10. Proposal is vague, lacking specifics in key areas such as pricing and buyer/seller roles and responsibilities.

Clearly, developing a quality proposal takes time and effort. When beginning the proposal-writing process, it is important for the salesperson to adopt the right mindset with a key thought of "Okay, this will take some time to get the details down, but it will be worth it." To reinforce this mindset, consider the tips for creating effective sales proposals given in Exhibit 6.2.[2]

Breaking the proposal down into its primary and distinct parts can simplify the process of writing an effective proposal. Five parts common to most proposals are an executive summary, customer needs and proposed solution, seller profile, pricing and sales agreement, and an implementation section with a timetable.

EXHIBIT 6.2
Tips for Creating Effective Sales Proposals

- When writing a proposal, pretend you are one of the buyer's decision makers and decide what you need to know to make a decision.
- Think of the proposal as an in-depth conversation with the buyer's decision makers.
- Give the decision makers all the information they need to make an informed decision.
- Avoid boilerplate proposals that use the same wording for all customers.
- Avoid so-what proposals that do not give customers the financial justification for buying your product.
- Realize that you must educate the buyer and provide information accordingly.
- Ensure that your proposal has a logical flow that the customer can easily follow.

Executive Summary This summary precedes the full proposal and serves two critical functions. First, it should succinctly and clearly demonstrate the salesperson's understanding of the customer's needs and the relevance of the proposed solution. An effective summary will spell out the customer's problems, the nature of the proposed solution, and the resulting benefits to the customer. A second function of the summary is to build a desire to read the full proposal. This is important as many key members of the organization often read little more than the information provided in the summary. A question new salespeople commonly ask refers to the length of the executive summary. A good rule of thumb is that an executive summary should be limited to two typewritten pages—especially if the main body of the report is fewer than 50 pages.

Customer Needs and Proposed Solution This section is typically composed of two primary parts. First, the situation analysis should concisely explain the salesperson's understanding of the customer's situation, problems, and needs. Second, the recommended solution is presented and supported with illustrations and evidence on how the proposed solution uniquely addresses the buyer's problems and needs. The emphasis in this section should be on the benefits resulting from the solution and not on the product or service being sold. It is important that these benefits be described from the perspective of the customer. Proprietary information required in the proposal can be protected in a

organized sales dialogue Also known as the organized sales presentation. Unlike a canned sales presentation, an organized sales dialogue has a high level of customer involvement.

organized sales presentation A sales presentation that allows a salesperson to implement appropriate sales strategies and tactics based on customer research or information gathered during previous sales calls. Organized sales presentations feature a high-level two-way dialogue with the customer.

number of ways. The most common method is to place a notice on the cover (i.e., "Confidential" or "For Review Purposes Only"). Many technology companies ask the prospect to sign a nondisclosure agreement that is part of the overall document and, in some instances, the selling organization will even copyright the proposal.

Seller Profile This section contains information that the customer wants to know about the selling company. This section offers a succinct overview and background of the firm, but the emphasis should be on the company's capabilities. Case histories of customers for whom the company solved similar problems with similar solutions have proved to be an effective method to document and illustrate organizational capabilities and past successes.

Pricing and Sales Agreement The previous sections are designed to build the customer value of the proposed solution. Once this value has been established, the proposal should "ask for the order" by presenting pricing information and delivery options. This information is often presented in the form of a sales agreement for the buyer to sign off on and complete.

Implementation and Timetable The purpose of this section is to make it as easy as possible for the buyer to make a positive purchase decision. In effect, this section should say "if you like the proposal and want to act on it, this is what you do." There may be a contract to sign, an order form to fill out, or instructions regarding whom to call to place an order or request further information. A timetable that details a schedule of key implementation events should also be included.

Evaluating Proposals Before Submission In the customer's eyes, the standards for written sales proposals are high. Poor spelling and grammatical mistakes send a negative message that the seller has little regard for attention to detail. The quality of a salesperson's written documents is a surrogate for that salesperson's competence and ability as well as the capabilities and overall quality of the organization. If the proposal does not properly interpret the buyer's needs or fails to make a compelling case to justify the purchase, the odds of success are low. Although a well-written proposal is no guarantee of making the sale, a poorly written proposal will certainly reduce the probability of success.

Since the stakes are usually high when written sales proposals are used, it is a best practice to evaluate proposals carefully before they are submitted to the customer. In fact, it is a good idea to build the evaluative criteria into the proposal writing process early on, then use the criteria shown in Exhibit 6.3[3] as a final check before submitting a sales proposal.

ORGANIZED SALES DIALOGUES

In most situations, the process of converting a prospect into a customer will take several sales conversations over multiple encounters. These conversations constitute an **organized sales dialogue**. For example, salespeople often speak by telephone with a qualified prospect to get an appointment for a later meeting. The second conversation with the customer typically focuses on fact finding and parallels the ADAPT process. The next step would come after the salesperson has developed a tailored solution for the customer.

The salesperson may make a comprehensive sales presentation but, in this case, it is designed for dialogue with the customer throughout. To reiterate, this is not a one-way presentation or monologue—it is a sales dialogue with a high level of customer involvement. This type of comprehensive presentation is commonly called an **organized sales presentation**.

Before making comprehensive sales presentations, salespeople often have several conversations with prospects to better understand their situation and needs.

© Image Source/Jupiter Images

EXHIBIT 6.3

Evaluating Sales Proposals

It is a best practice to evaluate sales proposals before they are submitted to the customer. Five important dimensions for evaluating proposals are reliability, assurance, tangibles, empathy, and responsiveness.

Reliability reflects your (the seller's) ability to identify creative, dependable, and realistic solutions and strategies and match them to the buyer's needs and wants.

Does the proposal

1. Clearly articulate proposed solutions and strategies?
2. Provide creative and innovative solutions and strategies for the buyer?
3. Present solutions and strategies appropriate for the buyer's business operation and organization?
4. Provide financial justifications that support the proposed solutions and strategies?

Assurance builds the buyer's trust and confidence in your ability to deliver, implement, produce, and provide the benefits.

Does the proposal

1. Provide adequate specifications and benefits that substantiate ability and capability statements?
2. Present techniques, methodologies, or processes for ensuring quality performance?
3. Concisely and adequately define project or implementation roles and responsibilities?
4. Clearly identify and define all fees, prices, and expenses for completing the project?

Tangibles enhance and support the communication of your message and invite readership by its overall appearance, content, and organization.

Does the proposal

1. Provide a logical flow of information and ideas and sense of continuity for solving the buyer's business problems?
2. Convert the intangible elements of the solutions or strategies into tangibles?
3. Demonstrate high standards for excellence in format, structure, grammar, spelling, and appearance?
4. Provide positive indicators to differentiate the proposing organization from their competition?

Empathy confirms your thorough understanding of the buyer's business and his or her specific needs and wants.

Does the proposal

1. Clearly identify the buyer's specific needs and wants?
2. Demonstrate a thorough understanding of the buyer's business operation and organization?
3. Provide solutions and strategies that fit within the buyer's business goals?
4. Identify and discuss financial and nonfinancial benefits in terms of their impact on the buyer's unique operation and organization?

Responsiveness developed in a timely manner demonstrates a willingness to provide solutions for the buyer's needs and wants and to help measure results.

Does the proposal

1. Reflect a genuine willingness to understand the buyer's business operation and organization and provide viable and flexible solutions and strategies?
2. Reflect the proposing organization's willingness to work closely with the buyer by enthusiastically asking questions, gathering information, presenting options, and reviewing draft proposals?
3. Lead to the proposing organization thoroughly reviewing the final proposal with the buyer and responding to his or her questions or clarifying any outstanding issues and concerns?
4. Describe the proposed solutions or strategies within the buyer's budget and implementation time frames?

Organized sales dialogues may precede or follow other sales communications, such as a written sales proposal. Sales dialogues are much more than mere conversation—they are a chance for the salesperson to seek information or action from the prospect and to explore the business reasons the prospect has for continuing the dialogue with the salesperson (e.g., solving a problem or realizing an opportunity). Feedback from the prospect is encouraged, and therefore this format is less likely to offend a participation-prone buyer. "An Ethical Dilemma" demonstrates the problem for a salesperson who is not willing to ask questions and gain feedback.

An Ethical Dilemma

Tom Lawrence was not one who liked to do a lot of precall planning or ask questions of his prospects. Lawrence had a good idea about which of his products' features were hot buttons for most prospects. During each of his sales calls, he hammered home those features that he thought were important to most of his prospects. His sales manager made calls with him for a few days and made the observation that Lawrence should do more questioning and listening and sell only those features and benefits that were relevant to each prospect. Lawrence stated: "I feel that is a waste of time. Most of my buyers are busy. They don't have time to answer questions all day. I'm the expert; I should know what they need." What are the dangers in the way Lawrence thinks? What can his sales manager do to help Lawrence change?

When the situation calls for a full sales presentation, the organized sales presentation is usually favoured over both the canned presentation and the written proposal. Such an approach allows much-needed flexibility to adapt to buyer feedback and changing circumstances during the presentation. Organized presentations may also include some canned portions. For example, a salesperson for Caterpillar may show a videotape to illustrate the earth-moving capabilities of a bulldozer as one segment of an organized presentation. Because of its flexibility during the sales call and its ability to address various sales situations, the organized presentation is the most frequently used format for professional sales presentations.

One reality of this presentation format is that it requires a knowledgeable salesperson who can react to questions and objections from the prospect. Dr. Tony Alessandra, internationally known author, trainer, and sales consultant, confirms this in "Professional Selling in the 21st Century: Being Prepared for Sales Calls." Further, this format may extend the time horizon before a purchase decision is reached, and it is vulnerable to diversionary delay tactics by the prospect. Presumably, those who make these arguments think that a canned presentation forces a purchase decision in a more expedient fashion. Overall, however, most agree that the organized presentation is ideal for most sales situations. Its flexibility allows a full exploration of customer needs and appropriate adaptive behaviour by the salesperson. By fully participating in the dialogue, both buyer and seller have an opportunity to establish a mutually beneficial relationship.

The trust-based relational selling presentation often referred to as the need-satisfaction/consultative model is a popular form of an organized presentation. Figure 6.1 highlights the three stages of the trust-based selling process and the participation levels of the salesperson and buyer.

The first stage of the process, the need development stage, is devoted to a discussion of the buyer's needs. During this phase the buyer should be talking 60 to 70 percent of the time. The salesperson accomplishes this by using the first four questioning techniques of the ADAPT process.

The second stage of the process (need awareness) is to verify what the buyer thinks his or her needs are and to make the buyer aware of potential needs that may exist. For instance, fast-food restaurants were

PROFESSIONAL SELLING IN THE 21ST CENTURY

Courtesy of Dr. Alessandra. Used with permission.

Being Prepared for Sales Calls

Dr. Tony Alessandra, internationally known author, trainer, and sales consultant, knows that sales call preparation is essential for sales effectiveness:

Being fully prepared for the sales interview has a number of advantages for both you and the customer. By being prepared, you are better able to react to the demands of the sales transaction. You can talk about those service benefits that relate directly to the needs of the buyer. You can bring the proper materials to the interview so that it progresses smoothly and efficiently. It saves time for the buyer because he is not burdened by an inefficient interview or salesperson. You are able to set realistic call objectives and develop a sales strategy around them. You impress the buyer with your knowledge, preparation, strategy, and confidence. In other words, preparing for sales interviews leads to more, bigger, and better sales. It spells success! There's an old adage—"If you fail to plan then you are planning to fail." In sales, this couldn't be truer. Your research and preparation will educate you so that you will be of service to your client. If you don't prepare yourself, you might as well be calling everyone cold without even knowing their names. It's not a very attractive alternative. Preparation and planning are like studying a map: You'll know which road to take with your prospect to get where you both want to go.

Source: Dr. Tony Alessandra, "Preparing for the Sales Call," http://www.assessmentbusinesscenter.com/media/articles/article_prep_sales_call.pdf, accessed June 15, 2012.

generally slow to recognize the need to offer more low-fat and low-carbohydrate menu items until their sales volume suffered. Others, such as Subway, gained a competitive advantage by working with their suppliers to formulate a significant number of menu alternatives for the health-conscious consumer. The need-awareness stage is a good time to restate the prospect's needs and to clarify exactly what the prospect's needs are. During this stage, the participation level for the buyer and salesperson has reached a balance in which both individuals are interacting equally.

In the final stage, the need fulfillment, the salesperson must show how his or her product and its benefits will meet the needs of the buyer. During this stage, the salesperson will do more of the talking by indicating what specific product will meet the buyer's needs. For this stage to be successful, the salesperson has to identify the features of a product and explain the advantages of those features to demonstrate the benefits of the product. By letting the customer talk and practising active listening, the salesperson will better understand the needs of the customer. The salesperson, by being a good listener early in the process, will now have a better chance to gain the buyer's interest and trust by talking about specific benefits the buyer has confirmed as being important.

By fully participating in the dialogue, both buyer and seller have an opportunity to establish a mutually beneficial relationship.

FIGURE 6.1

The Trust-Based Selling Process: A Need-Satisfaction Consultative Mode

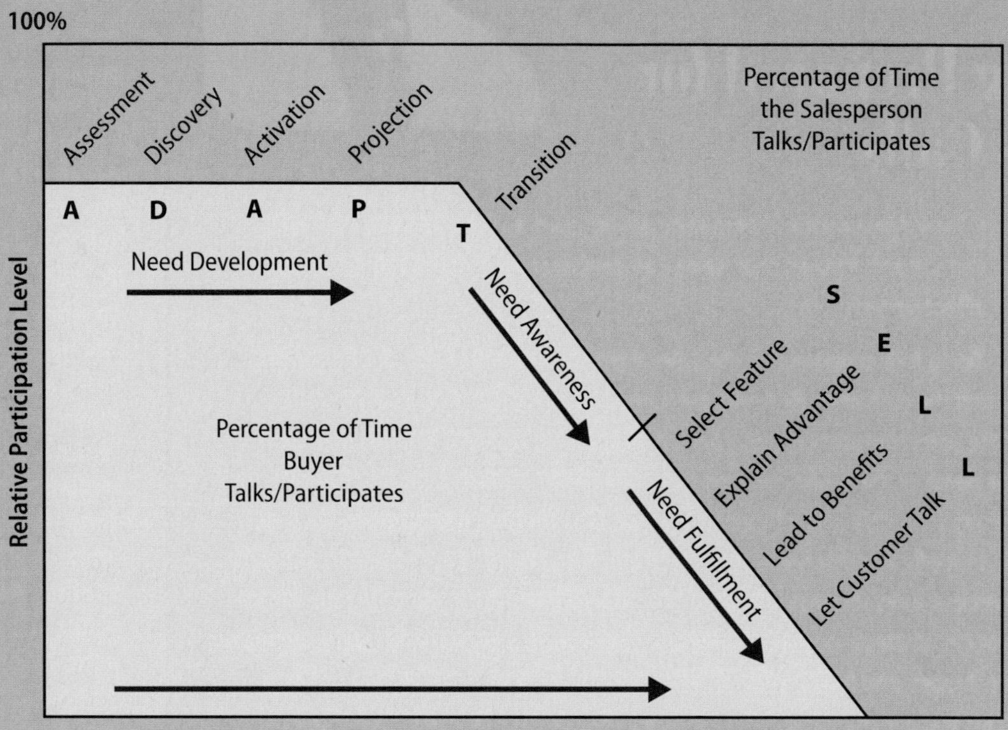

At some points in the two-way sales dialogue, the customer will do more talking; at other points, the salesperson will do more of the talking.

6-3 Sales Dialogue Template

ales dialogues are not scripted in advance as canned sales presentations are; however, salespeople should think ahead about what questions and statements to include in the conversation and be prepared to hold up their end of the conversation with an appropriate amount of detail. A **sales dialogue template** (see Exhibit 6.4) is a useful tool to ensure that all pertinent content areas are covered with each prospect. The template is flexible and can be used either to plan a comprehensive organized sales presentation or to guide sales dialogues of a more narrow scope. The template is not meant to be a script for a sales encounter, but rather an aid in planning and assembling the information required of the salesperson.

sales dialogue template A flexible planning tool that assists the salesperson in assembling pertinent information to be covered with the prospect.

By addressing the issues noted in the template, salespeople can facilitate trust-building by demonstrating their competence and expertise, customer orientation, candour, dependability, and compatibility. It is true that trust is built through behaviour not just by planning and having good intentions; however, salespeople who are aware of what it takes to earn the customer's trust in the planning stages have a better chance of earning that trust in subsequent encounters with the customer. The sales dialogue template is organized into nine sections, each of which is discussed individually.

SECTION 1: PROSPECT INFORMATION

This section is used to record specific information on the prospect, such as the company name, the key decision maker's name and job title, and the type of business. In most business-to-business situations, it is critical to know who else is involved in the buying decision and what role he or she plays, such as gatekeeper, user, or influencer. (Refer to Chapter 3 if you need to review the buying team concept.) It is also important that the salesperson makes sure all the key players are receiving the appropriate information and getting the proper attention they deserve. A mistake salespeople often make is not identifying all the buying influencers.

EXHIBIT 6.4
Sales Dialogue Template

1. Prospect Information:

A. Company Name: ______________________ Type of Business: ______________________

Key-Person Information

B. Prospect's Name (Key Decision Maker): ______________________ Job Title: ______________________

C. Other people involved in the purchase decision:

Names/Job Title	*Departments*	*Role in Purchase Decision*

2. Customer Value Proposition: A brief statement of how you will add value to the prospect's business by meeting a need or providing an opportunity. Include a brief description of the product or service:

A. Product/Service That Delivers Value:

____

____

B. Value Proposition Statement:

____

____

____

3. Sales Call Objective (must require customer action, such as making a purchase, supplying critical information, etc.):

____

____

Continued

EXHIBIT 6.4
Sales Dialogue Template—*Continued*

4. Linking Buying Motives, Benefits, Support Information, and Other Reinforcement Methods:
(Repeat for each person who will be involved in the upcoming sales call.)

A. *Buying motives:* What is most important to the prospect(s) in making a purchase decision? **Rational** motives include economic issues, such as quality, cost, service capabilities, and the strategic priorities of the prospect's company. **Emotional** motives include fear, status, and ego-related feelings. List all relevant buying motives in order of importance.	B. *Specific benefits matched to buying motives:* Benefits to be stressed are arranged in priority order (sequence to be followed unless prospect feedback during the presentation indicates an alternative sequence). Each benefit should correspond to one or more buying motives.	C. *Information needed to support claims for each benefit.*	D. *Where appropriate, methods for reinforcing verbal content* (Audio/visual, collateral material, illustrations, testimonials, etc.).
1. ____________ →	____________ →	________ →	
2. ____________ →	____________ →	________ →	
3. ____________ →	____________ →	________ →	
4. ____________ →	____________ →	________ →	

5. Current Suppliers (If Applicable) and Other Key Competitors:

Competitors	*Strengths*	*Weaknesses*

6. Beginning the Sales Dialogue:

Plans for the first few minutes of the sales presentation:

Introduction, thanks, agenda agreement, then begin ADAPT as appropriate or transition into other sales dialogue or presentation:

Assessment ____________________

Discovery ____________________

Activation ____________________

Project ____________________

Transition to Presentation ____________________

Note: The ADAPT process may take place over several sales conversations during multiple sales calls. In other cases, it may be concluded in a single sales call, then immediately followed by a sales presentation during the same sales call.

Continued

EXHIBIT 6.4
Sales Dialogue Template—*Continued*

7. Anticipating Prospect Questions and Objections, with Planned Responses:

Questions/Objections	*Responses*

8. Earning Prospect Commitment:

A preliminary plan for how the prospect will be asked for a commitment related to the sales call objective:

9. Building Value through Follow-Up Action:

Statement of follow-up action needed to ensure that the buyer–seller relationship moves in a positive direction:

6-4 SECTION 2: CUSTOMER VALUE PROPOSITION

In this section, the salesperson develops a preliminary **customer value proposition**, which is a statement of how the sales offering will add value to the prospect's business by meeting a need or providing an opportunity. Essentially, the customer value proposition summarizes the legitimate business reason for making the sales call by answering the prospect's question, "Why should I spend my time with you?" A good customer value proposition clearly states why the customer will be better off by doing business with the salesperson and his or her firm but at this point does not try to list all of the reasons.[4]

customer value proposition A statement of how the sales offering will add value to the prospect's business by meeting a need or providing an opportunity.

At the planning stage, the customer value proposition is preliminary. The salesperson has good reason to believe that customer value can be enhanced by delivering on the contents of the proposition, but the true value of the proposition will be accepted or rejected by the customer as the sales process moves along. It is during this sales dialogue process that the actual customer value to be delivered will be refined and modified. This section of the template provides a point of departure for planning purposes and assumes that the value proposition is likely to be modified before the purchase decision. In writing the preliminary customer value proposition, salespeople should attempt the following:

1. Keep the statement fairly simple so that the direction for upcoming sales dialogues is clear.
2. Choose the key benefit(s) likely to be most important to the specific customer who is the audience for this particular dialogue or presentation. (At this point, it is not necessary to list all the benefits of their offerings.)
3. Make the value proposition as specific as possible on tangible outcomes (e.g., improvements to revenues, cost containment or reduction, market share, process speed and efficiency) or the enhancement of the customer's strategic priority.
4. Reflect product or service dimensions that add value, whether or not the customer pays for them. For example, some companies offer delivery, installation, and training along with the purchase of their products. Added value may also accrue from what the seller's sales team provides (e.g., work in the field with a distributor's salespeople or certification training for the buyer's technicians).
5. Promise only what can be consistently delivered. Strictly speaking, a customer value proposition in the planning stage is not a guarantee; rather, it is a belief based on the salesperson's knowledge and best judgment. As the sales process moves along, appropriate guarantees can be made.

Using these points as a guide, the following is an example of a customer value proposition that could provide clear direction for planning an upcoming sales presentation or a series of sales dialogues:

> *"ABC Company can improve its market share by a minimum of four percentage points in a one-year period in its Vancouver and Calgary markets by implementing our customer satisfaction and retention training for its customer service personnel."*

In contrast, here is an example of a poorly constructed customer value proposition:

> *"By adopting our customer satisfaction and retention programs, ABC Company will see a dramatic increase in its market share."*

This second proposition opens the salesperson to a potential barrage of questions:

> *Dramatic increase in market share? What's dramatic?*
>
> *We operate in 22 markets. Are you saying that we will increase market shares in all 22 markets?*
>
> *What do you mean by programs? Are you referring to training programs?*

In the planning stages, salespeople may or may not be fully aware of the prospect's needs and priorities—and, until they are aware of these needs and priorities, the sales dialogue should focus on the first two stages of the ADAPT process: assessing the prospect's situation and discovering his or her needs. Unless these stages are completed, the customer value proposition will not contain enough detail to be useful. Done correctly, a customer value proposition will portray the seller's company in a favourable light and give the customer reasonable expectations of the selling company. As illustrated in "An Ethical Dilemma," this sometimes requires caution in communicating the customer value proposition.

SECTION 3: SALES CALL OBJECTIVE

Section 3 asks the salesperson to determine the objective for his or her sales call. Salespeople must have an objective for each sales call. Basically, sales call objectives state what salespeople want customers to do as a result of the sales call. The objectives should be specific enough to know whether or not they have been accomplished at the conclusion of the call, and they should require customer actions, such as placing an order, agreeing to participate in a test market, or supplying specific information useful to the salesperson. Many salespeople think that they have only one objective: to get an order. Other legitimate sales call objectives do exist. For instance, during an introductory call the objective may be simply to introduce the salesperson and his or her company and to gather information on the buyer's needs. Eventually, the major sales presentation objective will be to earn a commitment from the customer by making a sale, but this is not always the only objective.

After the sale is made, the objective may be to follow up and determine whether or not the customer is satisfied with the salesperson's efforts. The salesperson can also look for openings to cover additional objectives. Gwen Tranguillo of Hershey's always looks for ways to introduce other products in her presentation if the buyer expresses interest. Tranguillo made

An Ethical Dilemma

Ivan Khan, a sales representative for a manufacturing equipment company, had given a lot of thought to a recent training session on precall preparation planning. The trainer told the sales representatives, "Use the template we provide to be sure you have included all of the relevant information in planning your sales calls. Don't develop a script from the template. Make it your own and add your own ways of doing things to make it more effective." Ivan knew that customer value propositions should be as specific as possible and should not overpromise on what could be delivered to the customer. Ivan also knew that customer cost savings in the range of 5–15 percent were possible, but that actual savings would depend on the situation. Ivan was strongly considering stating the 15 percent savings figure early in his sales dialogues as an average savings, which would make a lot more prospects willing to listen to a full sales presentation. What should Ivan do?

a) Be conservative and continue to state the average savings as 5–15 percent. Be prepared to show the customer how to maximize savings.
b) Go with the 15 percent figure and back it up with testimonials from customers that had achieved 15 percent savings.
c) Early in the sales dialogue, learn more about the customer's situation and then estimate the potential cost savings for the customer.

a major sales presentation on a Halloween display of king-size candies and found that the buyer was very interested in adding more king sizes immediately. She shifted gears and gained a commitment on the new king-size display and later in the presentation went back to her Halloween proposal. At the very least, the heart of any presentation should be to advance the process toward an order.

6-5 SECTION 4: LINKING BUYING MOTIVES, BENEFITS, SUPPORT INFORMATION, AND OTHER REINFORCEMENT METHODS

In Section 4 of the planning template, the prospect's buying motives are linked to specific benefits offered. For each benefit identified, the salesperson will also assemble the information needed to support the claims to be made in the upcoming dialogue or presentation. In some cases, verbal claims must be reinforced with audio-visual portrayal, illustrations, printed collateral material, or testimonials from satisfied customers, as appropriate to the situation.

Buying motives refer to the most important factors from the customer's perspective in making a purchase decision. In other words, what will motivate the buyer to make a purchase? Buying motives may be rational or emotional, or a combination of both rational and emotional. **Rational buying motives** typically relate to the economics of the situation, including cost, profitability, quality, services offered, and the total value of the seller's offering that the customer perceives. **Emotional motives**, such as fear, the need for security, the need for status, or the need to be liked, are sometimes difficult for salespeople to uncover as prospects are generally less likely to share such motives with salespeople. In business-to-business selling, rational motives are typically the most important buying motives, but salespeople should not ignore emotional motives if they are known to exist.

In linking benefits to buying motives, benefits should be distinguished from features. **Features** are factual statements about the characteristics of a product or service, such as "This is the lightest electrical motor

buying motives A need-activated drive to search for and acquire a solution to resolve a need or problem; the most important factors from the customer's perspective in making a purchase decision.

rational buying motives Typically relate to the economics of the situation, including cost, profitability, quality, services offered, and the total value of the seller's offering as perceived by the customer.

emotional buying motives Include such motives as security, status, and the need to be liked; sometimes difficult for salespeople to uncover these motives.

features Qualities or characteristics of a product or service that are designed to provide value to a buyer.

benefits The added value or favourable outcome derived from features of the product or service the seller offers.

in its performance category." **Benefits** describe the added value for the customer—the favourable outcome derived from a feature. For example, "The lightweight motor supports your mobile repair service strategy in that it is very portable. The ease of use allows your technicians to complete more service calls per day, thus increasing your profitability." To make such a claim about increasing profitability, the salesperson would need to gather specific information to support it. For example, in this case the claim that technicians can complete more service calls per day because the motor is easy to use might call for competitive comparisons and actual usage data or a demonstration.

Some situations may lead the salesperson to decide that a product demonstration and testimonials from satisfied customers will reinforce the spoken word. In other cases, third-party research studies or articles in trade publications might be used to reinforce oral claims. Another powerful option is material developed by the salesperson, such as a break-even chart showing how quickly the customer can recoup the investment in the new product or service. A note of caution: It is always a good idea to use these types of sales support materials sparingly—some prospects do not react positively to information overload. Chapter 7 discusses in greater detail sales tools and how they can enhance the sales effort.

SECTION 5: COMPETITIVE SITUATION

Understanding the competitive situation is essential in planning sales dialogues and presentations. Because buyers make competitive comparisons in their decision processes, salespeople should be prepared for it. This section of the planning template asks the salesperson to identify key competitors and to specify their strengths and weaknesses. By knowing their own product's strengths and weaknesses as well as those of their competitors, salespeople are better equipped to articulate customer value relative to their competitors. This competitive positioning is important, as most major purchase decisions are made in a highly competitive business environment. If the prospect is already buying a similar product, knowledge about the current supplier can give the salesperson critical insight into which buying motives and product attributes are likely to be affecting the buyer's decisions.

SECTION 6: BEGINNING THE SALES DIALOGUE

Section 6 addresses the critical first few minutes of the sales call. During this period, salespeople will greet the prospect and introduce themselves, if necessary. There is typically some brief polite conversation between the salesperson and buyer as the salesperson is welcomed to the buyer's office, then both parties are usually eager to get down to business as quickly as possible. It is recommended that the salesperson propose an agenda, to which there may or may not have been previous agreement. Then, depending on the situation, the salesperson will proceed with questions designed to assess the prospect's situation, discover their needs, or make a transition into a sales dialogue or presentation. A typical first few minutes might sound like this:

Buyer: Come on in, Pat. I am John Jones. Nice to meet you. *(Introduction/greeting.)*

Seller: Mr. Jones, I am Pat Devlin with XYZ Company. Nice to meet you, too. I appreciate the time that you are spending with me today. *(Thanks, acknowledges importance of the buyer's time.)*

Buyer: Glad you could make it. We have had a lot of cancellations lately because of the bad weather. Did you have any problems driving over from Montreal? *(Polite conversation may last for several minutes depending on the buyer–seller relationship and on how much the buyer wants to engage in this sort of conversation.)*

Seller: Not really, it was pretty smooth today. I know you are busy, so I thought we could talk about a couple of key ways I think we can really help you build market share with your end-user market. How does that sound? *(A simple illustration of getting the buyer to agree to the agenda.)*

Buyer: Sure, let's get right to it. What do you have in mind?

Seller: Well, based on our phone call last week, I believe that our training programs for your customer service representatives can improve your customer satisfaction ratings and customer retention. I can share the details with you over the next 20 minutes or so. *(Transition to a sales dialogue or presentation based on customer needs and customer value.)*

In planning the first few minutes of the sales call, salespeople should remind themselves to be friendly and positive. They should also remain flexible in terms of their proposed agenda—customers like to have an agenda but sometimes want to modify it. The salesperson should be prepared to make an adjustment on the spot. For example, in the previous dialogue, the prospect might have said, "Yes, I want to hear about your training programs for our customer service reps, but I am also interested in your thoughts on how we can build a service-based culture across our entire marketing organization." The salesperson might respond accordingly, "I would be happy to do that. In fact, let me start with an overview that shows you the big picture from a strategy and company culture perspective, then later I will show you how the customer service training piece fits into the overall strategy. How does that sound?"

These first few minutes are critical in the trust-building process. By showing sensitivity to customer needs and opinions, and by asking questions to clarify the customer's perspective, salespeople demonstrate a customer orientation. Salespeople can demonstrate their expertise and competence by being sharp and well prepared. First impressions are crucial in all human interactions, so time spent on planning the first few minutes is a good investment on the salesperson's part. But remember that the planning template is not intended as a script. It is imperative that salespeople

© Fuse/Jupiter Images

Planning the first few minutes of a sales dialogue can help the salesperson make a positive impression and build trust by exhibiting a customer orientation and demonstrating his or her sales expertise.

think logically—and from the buyer's point of view—in planning what to say after greeting the customer. For more on how to initiate effective dialogue with customers, see "Professional Selling in the 21st Century: Tips for Developing Dialogue with Customers."

INITIATING CONTACT

When you are planning the first few minutes of the sales dialogue or presentation, there are few ironclad rules. Instead, the situation and the prospect's preferences dictate the appropriate sequence—but a few general rules do apply:

- Following an adequate introduction of the salesperson and the salesperson's company, the salesperson should use questions, careful listening, and confirmation statements to clarify and define explicit customer needs and motives as related to his or her offering.
- The salesperson should present benefits in order of importance according to the prospect's needs and motives, and these benefits may be repeated during the presentation and at the conclusion of the presentation.
- If the sales presentation is a continuation of one or more previous sales calls, the salesperson should make a quick summary of what has been agreed on in the past, moving quickly into the prospect's primary area of interest.
- As a general rule, the salesperson should not focus on pricing issues until the prospect's needs have been defined and the salesperson has shown how those needs can be addressed with the product or service being sold. After prospects fully understand how the product or service meets their needs, they can make informed judgments on price/value issues.

Obviously, the first few minutes of the sales call will be greatly influenced by previous interaction (if any) between the buyer and the salesperson. For example, if previous sales calls have established buyer needs and the buyer has agreed to a sales presentation, the first few minutes will be quite different than if this is the first sales call on this prospect. The ADAPT questioning process (refer to Chapter 4) can be used in part or whole to acquire needed information and make a transition to the sales dialogue or presentation. As a guide, the salesperson should respect the buyer's time and get to the presentation as soon as circumstances allow. The salesperson should not rush to get to the presentation and certainly should not launch into a presentation without establishing buyer needs and interest in it.

© Jeff Thrower/Shutterstock

Professional Selling in the 21st Century

Tips for Developing Dialogue with Customers

Geoffrey James, whose "Sales Source" is the world's most popular sales blog, offers straightforward advice on how to initiate effective dialogue with customers:

Be patient. If you lack patience, you'll be frustrated whenever things take longer than you'd like. Customers will sense your frustration and hesitate to buy. Engage with customers as equals. The client conversation should contain a feeling of mutuality rather than talking down or being subservient to your clients. Self-disclose when appropriate. Human beings buy from human beings. Rather than talking purely business, it's OK to occasionally bring up family, hobbies, or whatever will be of real interest to you and your clients. Enthusiasm is contagious. If you are enthusiastic about yourself, your firm and your product, your customers will pick up your enthusiasm and believe in your ability to improve their lives. It's fine to have your own perspective, do your own research and develop expertise in your own offerings—but approach every customer with the assumption that the customer knows more about their own business than you do. Use your time with the customer to hear about the real situation she is experiencing. And never, ever lecture.

Sources: Geoffrey James, "3 Ways to Annoy Your Customers (Plus 3 Better Ways)," Inc. online at http://www.inc.com/geoffrey-james/3-ways-to- irritate-customers-and-3-better-tactics.html, May 18, 2012; Geoffrey James "12 Customer Dos and Don'ts," Inc. online at http://www.inc.com /geoffrey-james/12-customer-dos-donts.html, March 12, 2012; Geoffrey James, "7 Most Powerful Sales Tools," Inc. online at http://www.inc .com/geoffrey-james/7-most-powerful-sales-tools.html, May 23, 2012.

SECTION 7: ANTICIPATING QUESTIONS AND OBJECTIONS

For reasons to be explained fully in Chapter 8, prospects will almost always have questions and objections that salespeople must be prepared to answer. In the planning stages, salespeople can prepare by asking themselves, "If I were the buyer, what would I want to be certain about before I make a purchase?" By anticipating these issues and preparing responses, salespeople can increase their chances of ultimate success.

SECTION 8: EARNING PROSPECT COMMITMENT

As sales dialogues and presentations progress, there eventually comes a critical time to ask for a customer's purchase decision. In many cases, this is an obvious point in the sales conversation, but at other times the salesperson may feel the need to probe to see if the timing is right. Earning a commitment from a customer, as discussed in Chapter 8, should be a natural step in the conversation, not a forced or high-pressure attempt by the salesperson. Although circumstances will dictate exactly when and how commitment will be sought, a preliminary action plan for seeking customer commitment should be part of the overall planning process. Most buyers expect the salesperson to seek a commitment— and, if the commitment is sought at the right time, buyers appreciate that effort from the salesperson.

SECTION 9: BUILDING VALUE THROUGH FOLLOW-UP ACTION

Finally, the salesperson must always be looking for ways to enhance the relationship and move it in a positive direction. The salesperson should always make a note of any promises that he or she has made during the sales calls and especially during the proposal presentation. The buyer may ask for information that the salesperson is not prepared to give during the presentation. By taking notes, the salesperson ensures that the appropriate follow-up activities will happen.

This planning template for sales dialogues and presentations is an extremely useful tool for all salespeople, especially inexperienced salespeople. It guarantees that all the appropriate steps are covered and that all the pertinent information needed is collected. Using this template will make the task of customizing sales dialogues and presentations easier.

6-6 Engaging the Customer

Most initial sales calls on new prospects require an appointment. Requesting an appointment accomplishes several desirable outcomes. First, the salesperson is letting the prospect know that he or she thinks the prospect's time is important. Second, there is a better chance that the salesperson will receive the undivided attention of the prospect during the sales call. Third, setting appointments is a good tool to assist the salesperson in effective time and territory management. The importance of setting appointments is clearly proclaimed in a survey of secretaries, administrative assistants, and other "gatekeepers" responsible for scheduling appointments. A majority of respondents thought that arriving unannounced to make a sales call is a violation of business etiquette.[5] Given this rather strong feeling of those who represent buyers, it is a good idea to request an appointment if there is any doubt about whether one is required. See "An Ethical Dilemma" for a demonstration of the importance of trust and why misleading a gatekeeper can damage future customer relationships.

A salesperson can request an appointment by phone, mail (including e-mail), or personal contact. By far, setting appointments by telephone is the most popular method. Combining mail and telephone communications to seek appointments is also commonplace. Regardless of the communication vehicle used, salespeople can improve their chances of getting an appointment by following three simple directives: give the prospect a reason why an appointment should be granted; request a specific amount of time; and suggest a specific time for the appointment. These tactics recognize that prospects are busy individuals who do not spend time idly.

In giving a reason that the appointment should be granted, a well-informed salesperson can appeal to the prospect's primary buying motive as related to one of the benefits of the salesperson's offering. Be specific. For example, it is better to say that "you can realize gross margins averaging 35 percent on our product line" than "our margins are really quite attractive."

An Ethical Dilemma

© Jose Luis Pelaez Inc/Blend Images/Getty

After working a year in customer service with an office supply wholesaler, Paul Compean moved into an outside sales position. He is doing a great job with existing accounts, having shown steady sales volume increases in recent months. When it comes to gaining new customers, Paul is doing fine when he gets referrals from other customers or when he receives leads generated at trade shows. On the other hand, Paul is struggling with gaining new customers through cold calls. When cold-calling, Paul has been trained to tell gatekeepers that his company can provide fast delivery and possibly save prospects money on office supplies. He is contemplating changing the message to guarantee money savings, even though he knows that savings will not be possible in all cases. What should Paul do?

a) Try the guaranteed cost savings tactic. After all, he needs to gain new customers and the old tactics are not working.
b) Avoid untruthful tactics in all phases of the sales process, including when trying to set up appointments.
c) Be truthful with gatekeepers, but bend the truth if necessary to get the appointment.

© i love images/Jupiter Images

Most buyers and gatekeepers prefer that salespeople make an appointment for their initial sales call. Telephone calls are the most popular means of arranging appointments.

Specifying the amount of time needed to make the sales presentation alleviates some of the anxiety a busy prospect feels at the idea of spending some of his or her already scarce time. It also helps the prospect if the salesperson suggests a time and date for the sales call. It is very difficult for busy individuals to respond to a question such as, "What would be a good time for you next week?" In effect, the prospect is being asked to scan his or her entire calendar for an opening. If a suggested time and date is inconvenient, the interested prospect will typically suggest another. Once a salesperson has an appointment with the prospect and all the objectives have been established, the salesperson should send a fax or an e-mail that outlines the agenda for the meeting and reminds the buyer of the appointment.

CHAPTER 6 CASE

NIMBLEFOOT

Background

Nimblefoot is a manufacturer of women's running shoes, which are sold through major sporting goods chain stores and specialty stores. Nimblefoot has targeted Trailrunner, a regional specialty store chain, as a potential prospect for its latest product. Nimblefoot's sales representative, Corey Whyte, hopes to replace a competitor's product in the Trailrunner stores. Corey has begun planning his upcoming sales call on Maria Tupper, head buyer at Trailrunner. At a recent trade show, Corey had a brief conversation with Maria and learned that Trailrunner's management is interested in improving the profitability of the chain. Further, Maria made it clear that Trailrunner would only be interested in high-quality products.

Current Situation

Corey and his sales manager, Gabrielle Bellows, have been discussing the plans for the upcoming call on Trailrunner. Gabrielle asked Corey to give her a summary of Trailrunner's key buying motives and the related benefits that Nimblefoot could offer. In addition, Gabrielle wanted to review the information that would be required to support any claims made for the benefits, as well as additional ideas for how to reinforce the verbal content of Nimblefoot's sales message. Corey supplied Gabrielle with the requested information, as shown in Exhibit A. Gabrielle is now

EXHIBIT A

Trailrunner's Buying Motives and Nimblefoot's Benefits

Trailrunner's Buying Motives	Related Nimblefoot Benefits	Support Information	Reinforcement of Verbal Content
Improve profitability	1. Profit margin is 6% higher than product to be replaced.	1. Cost and retail prices	1. Example income statement with and without new Nimblefoot product
	2. Nimblefoot product has significantly higher turnover rate than replacement product, thus improving total annual profitability.	2. Use historical data for existing product, projected turnover data for Nimblefoot.	2. Spreadsheet to illustrate multiplier effect of new Nimblefoot product with lower turnover rate. High-quality product
High-quality product	1. Durable synthetic material features a waterproof, breathable upper	1. Nimblefoot Website	1. Customer interviews on Nimblefoot Website
	2. Support around arch and extra width through the forefoot creates better shock absorption	2. Nimblefoot Website	2. Customer interviews on Nimblefoot Website
	3. Proprietary outsole gives best durability in high-wear areas.	3. Nimblefoot Website	3. Article from *Running World* magazine

reading over Exhibit A and plans to give Corey some feedback tomorrow morning.

Questions

1. In the role of Gabrielle Bellows, what specific comments and suggestions do you have for Corey Whyte?
2. Should a customer value proposition be developed before completing the information in Exhibit A?

Role Play

Characters: Gabrielle Bellows, sales manager, and Corey Whyte, sales representative

Scene:

Location—Gabrielle Bellows's office

Action—One student plays the role of Gabrielle Bellows, and one student plays the role of Corey Whyte. Gabrielle has told Corey that she thinks it would be a good exercise to act out the presentation of the key benefits shown in section four of the template. She said to Corey "I will act like the Trailrunner buyer, and you try to convince me that your benefits are significant. Be as specific as you can."

Questions

After completing the role play, address these questions:

1. What were the strengths of Corey Whyte's performance?
2. How could Corey's performance be improved?
3. How important is sales call planning in determining sales call performance?

CHAPTER 6

Role Play: Planning Sales Dialogues and Presentations: Kindle Versus Nook

Background

For this role play, students will assume one of three roles: (1) sales representative for Amazon's Kindle; (2) sales representative for Barnes and Noble's Nook; or (3) a buyer for a major university that is considering the purchase of e-readers for students. Prior to the role play, all students should conduct a comparison of the features and benefits of the Kindle and the Nook. To do the comparison, begin by using a search engine such as Google. Enter "Kindle vs. Nook" to find features and benefits of both products.

Role Play

Characters: One Kindle representative, one Nook representative, and a buyer for the university

Scene 1:

Location—The buyer's office

Action—Both sellers present their products to the buyer with a focus on explaining their product's benefits to the buyer.

After completing the role play, address the following questions:

1. Did the sellers demonstrate that they knew the difference between features and benefits?
2. Did the sellers have sufficient information to be convincing?
3. Can you suggest additional ways that the sellers could improve their sales communications?

what do you think?

Salespeople should explain all of their product's features and benefits to buyers.

1 2 3 4 5 6 7
strongly disagree — strongly agree

Salespeople are

likely to be more successful if they engage the buyer and focus on creating value during sales dialogue.

7 Sales Dialogue

Creating and Communicating Value

After completing this chapter, you should be able to

7-1 Describe the key characteristics of effective sales dialogue.

7-2 Describe the differences among features, potential benefits, and confirmed benefits, and describe the role they play in benefits selling.

7-3 Describe how verbal support can be used to communicate value in an interesting and understandable manner.

7-4 Discuss how sales aids can engage and involve buyers.

7-5 Explain how salespeople can support product claims.

7-6 Discuss the special considerations involved in sales dialogue with groups.

Introduction

The past 10 years have witnessed a remarkable transformation in the professional selling landscape. Competition is tougher, buyers are more demanding, and pressures on margins have increased, while product differences have been steadily whittled nearly out of existence.

Faced with these daunting challenges, many savvy sales organizations have turned to outside sales-training consultants to deliver the skills and knowledge necessary to gain an edge over ever-shifting customer demands. By working with hundreds of companies in a broad range of industries, top sales trainers enjoy a rare perspective on what does—and doesn't work—in the 21st-century sales marketplace.

Sam Reese, president and CEO of Miller Heiman, one of the world's top sales training organizations, says that his clients frequently comment on losing business when, with no apparent warning, a familiar buying process will erode, leaving them out in the cold.

"That's the number one thing we hear," Reese explains. "They'll say, 'Hey, I've been doing business with this client for 10 years, and then somehow we find we're not in the position we need to be in. New people are involved in the buying process. We now have all these new restrictions placed on us, and our guy in purchasing isn't calling the shots anymore.' That's a big one."

Naturally, two straight years of economic stagnation have only hastened this trend, driving upper-level executives to pay much closer attention to every dollar going out the door. As upper-level decision makers take greater interest in every purchase, product evaluators and purchasing agents located lower on the corporate ladder lose much of the power they once wielded to make value-based buying decisions.

Effective value selling today requires leapfrogging the low-level customer agents to sell to those upper-level folks who are genuinely empowered to buy based on more than simply product specs and price. But as Reese notes, selling to senior-level executives is a game with a different set of rules; success frequently means abandoning some of the tried and no-longer-true tactics that have been drilled into salespeople for generations.

"All the tactics and techniques around manipulation are out," he says. "That doesn't work anymore. You have to have the right product and the right solution, and it's a gradual process of making sure you meet all the customer's requirements. If you're selling the right way, you're not dealing with people who can be manipulated that way."

In contrast with the traditional hard-close route, Reese emphasizes the greater need today for respect and openness in the buyer-seller interaction.

"If you really believe in what you do, you want companies to make their decisions with all the information available. You want that because you passionately believe your company is the best at providing them with a solution. If you don't want that, then you need to take a hard look at what you're doing and what your company's doing. To me that's the definition of manipulation—hoping things don't surface for you to address that might put you at a disadvantage and make you weak because you can't deliver what the customer needs.

"Sales-training organizations have often spent most of their time teaching people how to know their products, their company and their competitors very well," he explains. "That needs to change. We need to teach people how to understand their customers' businesses. That's what makes the difference in whether you're perceived by the customer as yet another vendor peddling product—which is where you don't want to be—or as a true strategic resource who understands the customer's issues, challenges and opportunities."

Effective sales training today may be more forward-thinking, customer-focused and sophisticated than ever before, but it's also more complex, more demanding and frankly, more challenging to implement across a sales organization than the manipulative, hard-closing approaches that used to predominate. That's why sales trainers themselves have to work harder today, Reese says, not only to get the salespeople on board, but to create company-wide change that supports the new approach.

Ultimately, says Reese, what strategy a company employs to train its sales force reflects that company's attitude about the sales function and the job the salespeople themselves perform.

"For a long time, a lot of companies have really considered their salespeople as little more than glorified order-takers," he says. "But now that's changing and we're saying, 'No, they're not just order-takers, they're a real strategic asset.' Smart companies recognize that the sales force can be their most powerful strategic weapon. The way you sell can provide a huge strategic advantage—or disadvantage, for that matter. In the past, very few companies even understood this. But today that's changing, and the organizations that understand the concept and are putting powerful tools in the hands of the salespeople are the ones that are succeeding. And that's no coincidence."

Source: Malcolm Fleschner "The Value-Added Ladder," Selling Power, *http://www.sellingpower.com/content/article.php?a=6242.*

The purpose of this chapter is to examine the keys to effective sales dialogue. The chapter provides an opportunity to apply what has been learned about building trust (Chapter 2), understanding buyers (Chapter 3), and communication skills (Chapter 4). It also builds on the information gathered during the prospecting stage of the sales process (Chapter 5) and the sales dialogue template and section on "Beginning the Sales Dialogue" presented in Chapter 6. Chapter 8 expands on this chapter by addressing how to resolve buyer concerns and earn a commitment from a sales dialogue.

7-1 Effective Sales Dialogue

Preparing and completing this phase of the sales process successfully has been compared to doing surgery in that it is complex and requires preparation, knowledge, and skill.[1] Before conducting surgery, the doctor has acquired a great deal of relevant information from a variety of sources and developed a comprehensive understanding of the patient's problems and needs. Based on this understanding of the patient's needs, the surgeon uses his or her training and skills in combination with an assortment of tools to conduct a surgical procedure unique to the individual patient's needs. Continuing the analogy, up to the point of the presentation in the selling process the salesperson has been developing his or her knowledge and understanding of the buyer's situation and needs. Now, in the form of an effective presentation, the salesperson presents a solution that is specific and customized to the needs of the buyer, illustrates and demonstrates the benefits of the solution, and confirms the buyer's belief in and desire to obtain the benefits.

Good salespeople are very much like good surgeons in that they are serious in what they do and leave nothing to chance. They work with the prospective buyer to identify, diagnose, and clarify unsatisfied needs or problems and then show the buyer how much better the situation would be by purchasing the proposed product or service. As discussed previously, it will normally take several sales calls to complete a sales dialogue. Many firms plan for multiple sales calls in their sales process. For example, salespeople at Northwestern Mutual Financial Network conduct an initial "fact finding" sales call to identify the financial situation and objectives of potential clients. Then, one or more subsequent sales calls are used to present strategies for achieving these financial objectives.

© Yuri Arcurs/Shutterstock

Salespeople must diagnose customer problems before prescribing solutions.

Professional selling classes often require students to role play a sales dialogue. This has been found to be an effective way for students to learn about and develop skills for a sales dialogue. We will cover a complete sales dialogue in one sales call in this chapter and Chapter 8.

The keys to effective sales dialogue are presented in Exhibit 7.1. The importance of planning and practising were emphasized in Chapter 6. This planning and practice should focus on an organized sales dialogue and not a canned sales presentation. Salespeople who practise asking questions, getting different responses, and adapting to these responses appropriately are better prepared to be successful in a real sales dialogue. Proper planning and practice provide an important foundation for effective sales dialogue. We discuss the remaining keys in the rest of this chapter.

EXHIBIT 7.1

Keys to Effective Sales Dialogue

The most effective sales dialogues

1. Are planned and practised by salespeople.
2. Encourage buyer feedback.
3. Focus on creating value for the buyer.
4. Present value in an interesting and understandable way.
5. Engage and involve the buyer.
6. Support customer value through objective claims.

7-2 Needs-Gap Analysis

The simple fact that a qualified prospect has a need that can be met by the salesperson's product or service does not necessarily translate into a purchase. Need alone is not sufficient. A prospect will buy after concluding that by purchasing the salesperson's product, he or she will be substantially better off. Given the high level of competition in most industries, salespeople must have a clear understanding of their customers' needs to be considered seriously. Using a questioning sequence, such as SPIN or ADAPT (for a full discussion of these see Chapter 4, "Communication Skills"), the salesperson explores the buyer's situation to identify missed opportunities, dissatisfactions, needs, and problems. The salesperson must ask questions, probe for details, and listen carefully to what the prospective buyer says. This may take more than one sales call, depending on the amount of probing and clarifying that must take place to understand the prospect's needs. The salesperson's primary goal is to uncover the prospect's specific needs or problems and then focus on what products or services will solve the problem or meet the specific needs.

Based on the prospective buyer's identified and confirmed needs, the salesperson reviews possible product and service options to select or create a solution that best satisfies the buyer's requirements. The salesperson describes and builds desire for the recommended solution by detailing features of the solution as they relate to the prospective buyer's specific needs and demonstrating the benefits provided by each relevant feature. Features and benefits are linked to the buyer's specific needs in a way that generates the buyer's desire to purchase and acquire the recommended solution.

LINKING SOLUTIONS TO NEEDS

It is unlikely that the customer will be interested in every detail of the salesperson's product or service offering, and certainly some aspects will be more important to a particular prospect than will others. Essentially, salespeople should strive to communicate three crucial factors: (1) how buyer needs will be met or how an opportunity can be realized as a result of a purchase, (2) how the product features translate, in a functional sense, into benefits for the buyer, and (3) why the buyer should purchase from you as opposed to a competitor salesperson. To assist salespeople in effectively communicating these three factors, most sales training programs emphasize a form of benefit selling, sometimes referred to as **FAB** (for features, advantages, and benefits).

Benefit Selling

Any given product or service comprises multiple features that have the capability to produce different potential benefits and confirmed benefits. **Features** are traditionally defined as a quality or characteristic of a product or service that is designed to provide value to a buyer. Features answer the question, "What is it?" A benefit is the value provided by a feature to the buyer, and addresses the always present question, "What's in it for me?" However, not all benefits will be valued at the same level by all buyers, thus the categorization of *potential benefits* versus *confirmed benefits*. A **potential benefit** describes a general form of value that is assumed to be of importance by the salesperson but is not yet acknowledged as such by the buyer. Once the prospective buyer acknowledges the importance of a benefit to his or her buying situation, it is a **confirmed benefit**. Because confirmed benefits represent customer value that is provided by the proposed solution, some sales programs refer to one or more confirmed benefits as the value proposition.

Research tells us that buyers do not purchase products and features. Rather, buyers purchase the value and satisfaction provided to them in the form of relevant benefits. Consequently, features have very little persuasive power. Salespeople can be more effective by selling benefits rather than features. However, to be most effective and gain the buyer's confirmation, stated benefits must be relevant to the prospective buyer's needs and phrased in a format that clearly translates the benefit from a generic one-size-fits-all description to a unique and customized benefit that has immediate meaning for the prospective buyer. While the one-size-fits-all benefit statements do not require much thinking on the part of the salesperson, they typically do not pass from potential benefits to confirmed benefits. As illustrated in Exhibit 7.2, benefit statements that build on the salesperson's understanding and appreciation of the buyer's situation and are tailored to the individual buyer's needs and expectations are more likely to be confirmed by the buyer as being important.

FAB A form of selling that focuses on the features, advantages, and benefits of a product.

features Qualities or characteristics of a product or service that are designed to provide value to a buyer.

potential benefits A general form of value that is assumed by the salesperson to be of importance but is not yet acknowledged as such by the buyer.

confirmed benefits The benefits the buyer indicates are important and represent value.

By themselves, features and potential benefits risk the buyer thinking or asking, "So what?" Confirmed benefits are persuasive and advance the sale forward on the basis of creating added value for the buyer. This is the foundation of benefit selling. In benefit selling, the salesperson describes the benefits as they relate to specific needs of the prospective buyer and limits the role of features to simply supporting and evidencing the presence of confirmed benefits. This combination of a specific feature and its meaningful benefit statement is referred to as a selling point. As the following illustrate, selling points should be phrased in a conversational tone and clearly describe the benefit in a manner that emphasizes its applicability and importance to the individual buyer:

- "This copier automatically selects the paper size that best matches your original document. Based on the experience of other customers using this model, it will speed up reproduction of longer reports and reduce waste. This not only will save you money by reducing waste, but also will increase the efficiency of your office staff, which you expressed as one of your major concerns."
- "The design of this golf club will give you an expanded sweet spot for maximum ball contact. This not only will increase the distance of your shots but also will provide the improved accuracy that you are looking for."
- "Our unique use of overnight express for merchandise delivery reduces your need for backup inventory while eliminating the possibility for being out of stock and disappointing customers, which you mentioned was costing you business."

Most sales trainers and successful salespeople agree that showing the buyer potential benefits of relevant features will sometimes lead to successful sales calls. A sale may be made but, if not, at least the dialogue has been advanced in a positive manner, which sets the stage for subsequent sales calls. However, without question, the chances of a successful sales call are greatly improved by getting the buyer to agree that one or more benefits are indeed important to him or her.

The use of confirmed benefits is further explained in "Professional Selling in the 21st Century: Using Confirmed Benefits." In selecting specific features and

EXHIBIT 7.2

Features, Potential Benefits, and Confirmed Benefits

Salesperson in Golf Shop Selling Titleist Golf Balls to a Weekend Golfer.	Confirmed Benefit?	Explanation
Feature: Solid 1.58″ diameter core **Potential Benefit:** Higher initial velocity and launch angle.	No	The typical weekend golf customer would not immediately see how the benefit of higher velocity and launch angle will benefit him or her.
Feature: Solid 1.58″ diameter core **Potential Benefit:** Provides more distance on shots for the typical golfer and lowers your score.	Yes	Longer shots and lower scores are a primary interest of the typical weekend golfer. Customers can immediately understand the benefit to themselves.
Selling a New Frito-Lay Snack to a Regional Supermarket Chain.	**Confirmed Benefit?**	**Explanation**
Feature: Daily delivery **Potential Benefit:** Retailer can reduce inventory costs.	No	This prospective buyer considers inventory costs a regular cost of doing business. The potential benefit is not perceived as being important.
Feature: Daily delivery **Potential Benefit:** Assures product freshness, which will lead to high customer satisfaction.	Yes	Prospective customer places tremendous emphasis on customer satisfaction. Consequently, this potential benefit is confirmed as being valuable.

benefits to be stressed, salespeople should focus on any unique benefits not offered by the competition, as long as the benefits are of interest to the prospective buyer. These might include product benefits and nonproduct benefits, such as delivery, financing, extraordinary customer service, or additional sales support available to the buyer.*

Encouraging Buyer Feedback

In a productive sales dialogue, the salesperson continually assesses and evaluates the reactions and responses of prospective buyers. The SPIN or ADAPT questioning processes are designed to get the buyer to provide feedback to specific questions the salesperson asks. During the presentation portion of a sales dialogue, the most successful salespeople encourage buyer feedback. In contrast, less successful salespeople often rush through the entire presentation from beginning to end and never stop to invite feedback from the buyer. Feedback from the prospective buyer provides the salesperson with important information measuring the climate between the salesperson and the buyer, the buyer's level of interest in the product's features and benefits, whether the salesperson has successfully responded to the buyer's concerns, and how well the presentation is progressing toward the buyer making a purchase decision.

As detailed and discussed in Chapter 4, the observant salesperson can receive a great deal of continual feedback in the form of the buyer's nonverbal cues. In addition to observing nonverbal cues, high-performing salespeople

*Page 165–167: From Ingram/Laforge/Avila/Schwepker. *Professional Selling*, 4E. © 2008 South-Western, a part of Cengage Learning, Inc. Reproduced by permission. www.cengage.com/permissions.

PROFESSIONAL SELLING IN THE 21ST CENTURY

© mediaphotos/Vetta/Getty

Using Confirmed Benefits

Todd Harrett is Senior Account Executive for Northern Continental Logistics. He helps manufacturing customers with annual sales of $50 million to $1 billion improve processes throughout their supply chain. Todd discusses the importance of identifying the confirmed benefits of all members of the buying centre at each prospect:

The supply chain services I provide impact many different business functions, such as warehousing, logistics, accounting, finance, and information technology. It is important for me to interact with the appropriate people in the relevant functions for each prospect. Because each business function has a different perspective, I must identify the confirmed benefits for each functional area. If I do this successfully, I am usually able to create a lot of value for the prospect and am much more likely to get the sale. If I do not, it is much less likely I will get the sale. Let me provide two examples.

I received a referral to a company that makes large utility vehicles and was able to get a meeting with the logistics manager to learn about the company's supply chain. During our meeting, I identified the confirmed benefits of the logistics manager, but these were limited to only his responsibilities. Many of the services I can provide would have created value for the company, but the distribution manager was not interested in them. I tried to get meetings with managers from other functional areas in the firm, but was unable to do so. Even though I could meet the needs of the logistics manager, I could not offer the prospect enough total value to get the sale.

In another situation, the president of a local manufacturing company referred me to the person responsible for the shipping and receiving department. I indicated to the president that my services impact financial and operational aspects of the business beyond shipping and receiving, so I requested and got meetings with managers from accounting and information technology. Each of the managers I met with had different confirmed benefits which I identified and was able to provide. Meeting the needs of the individual business functions allowed me to increase my value proposition to the firm. The sales process was longer, but the increased value for the firm led to me getting the sale and selling more services.

check-backs or **response checks** Questions salespeople use throughout a sales dialogue to generate feedback from the buyer.

incorporate verbal probes at key points to evaluate the buyer's interest and assess the progress of the sales dialogue. These verbal probes are typically confirmatory forms of questions in search of simple "yes" or "no" responses from the buyer.

The phrases **check-backs** or **response checks** have become common names for this form of questioning—seeking feedback from the buyer. Although feedback can be sought at any point in the conversation, check-backs are commonly employed at two key points: (1) after a specific feature–benefit sequence to confirm the benefit and better assess the prospective buyer's level of interest, and (2) following the response to an objection in order to evaluate the level to which the salesperson has handled the problem. Exhibit 7.3 provides an illustrative selection of check-back examples that salespeople indicate are typical of those they commonly use.

The effective use of check-backs offers a number of advantages. Probably the most evident is increased buyer interaction. Asking for buyer feedback helps to ensure that the dialogue remains a two-way, collaborative exchange. The effective use of response-checks also

EXHIBIT 7.3

Illustrative Examples of Check-Backs

- "How does this sound to you?"
- "Does this make sense to you so far?"
- "Would this feature be useful to you in your current operations?"
- "What do you think?"
- "So is this something that would be valuable to you?"
- "Isn't that great?"
- "Do you like this colour?"
- "From your comment, it sounds as if you would want the upgraded memory. Is that correct?"
- "Does that answer your concern?"
- "Would this be an improvement over what you are doing right now?"
- "Is this what you had in mind?"

helps the salesperson evaluate the level of the buyer's understanding and keeps the salesperson on the right track. If feedback indicates a lack of understanding—or even worse, a lack of interest—on the part of a prospective buyer, the salesperson must make changes to improve alignment with the needs and expectations of the buyer. In contrast, positive feedback indicating a high level of understanding and interest on the part of the buyer would signal the salesperson to stay the course and advance the presentation toward gaining the buyer's purchase commitment. A series of positive response-checks indicates that the buyer is nearing a purchase decision. The more positive affirmations a salesperson receives in relation to his or her response-checks, the easier the final purchase decision becomes and the more confident the prospective buyer is in having made the appropriate decision. Specific examples of check-backs within a sales dialogue will be presented at appropriate places in the remainder of this chapter.

Creating Customer Value

After the introductory part of a sales call, the salesperson must try to determine what the buyer considers to be of value. A salesperson can use the SPIN or ADAPT questioning strategies (discussed in Chapter 4 and included in the sales dialogue template in Chapter 6) to understand the buyer's situation and to identify needs, problems, or opportunities important to the buyer. The salesperson must ask questions, probe for details, and listen carefully to what the prospective buyer is saying. This may take more than one sales call depending on the amount of probing and clarifying that must take place to understand the prospect's needs. The salesperson's primary goal is to uncover the prospect's specific needs or problems and then focus on what products or services will solve the problem or meet the specific needs. As discussed in Chapter 6, features are the characteristics of a product and benefits are the favourable outcome from a feature or the value received by the buyer. Most products have many features and benefits, but the buyer generally is not interested in all of a product's features and benefits. Confirmed benefits are those benefits the buyer has indicated are of interest. A major purpose of the use of the SPIN or ADAPT questioning process is to help the salesperson identify the confirmed benefits for the buyer. Then, the salesperson presents a recommended solution by emphasizing product features that will produce the confirmed benefits the buyer desires.

Product features and confirmed benefits are linked to the buyer's specific needs in a way that generates the buyer's desire to purchase and acquire the recommended solution. The importance of focusing on confirmed benefits to create value for buyers is illustrated previously in this chapter in "Professional Selling in the 21st Century: Using Confirmed Benefits." The "Beginning the Sales Dialogue" section in Chapter 6 provides an effective introduction to a sales call. The sales dialogue would then transition into a stage where the salesperson identifies the confirmed benefits the buyer desires. An example of this interaction using the ADAPT questioning process is presented here.

Seller: What are you currently doing to improve your customer satisfaction ratings and customer retention?
(Assessment question)

Buyer: We are trying to do a number of things, such as improving our products, providing faster deliveries, and offering better customer service.

Seller: How are these efforts working?
(Discovery question)

Buyer: Our product and delivery improvements have been effective, but we have received a number of complaints about our customer service.

Seller: What types of customer service complaints have you received?
(Discovery question)

Buyer: Most of the complaints are that our representatives do not act professionally and cannot resolve customer issues in a timely manner. But, when I talk to our representatives, they suggest that the customers are very demanding and difficult to deal with.

Seller: What has been the impact of these customer service problems on your business?
(Activation question)

Buyer: The impact has been twofold. First, although we have not yet lost any customers, our customer satisfaction ratings have gone down, so we could lose customers in the future. Second, we have lost some of our best customer service reps because they got tired of dealing with irate customers. Losing these reps just added to the customer service problems we have been having.

Seller: So, if we could find a way to help your reps deal with difficult customers, it would improve your customer service and reduce the turnover of your reps?
(Projection question)

Buyer: That would be a big help to us.
(The seller has identified a confirmed benefit.)

Seller: Mr. Jones, have you ever provided any training to your customer service reps?
(Assessment question)

Buyer: Yes, we sent our reps to a public customer service training program a few months ago. But the reps said the program was very general and did not address the issues they face.

Seller: Do you think your reps would find a training program customized to their situation useful?
(Activation question)

Buyer: A customized program would be received well by our reps and would be valuable to them.
(The seller has identified another confirmed benefit.)

Seller: Have you ever considered online training?
(Assessment question)

Buyer: We thought about it, but many of our reps were not receptive to the idea of online training.
(The buyer has indicated that online training is NOT a confirmed benefit.)

Seller: It seems like a customized customer service training program that focused on dealing with difficult customers would improve your service to existing customers and help reduce turnover of your customer service reps. Do you think this type of training program would be valuable to your business?
(Transition question)

Buyer: I would certainly be interested in this type of program.

This sales dialogue example illustrates the value of the ADAPT questioning process to help salespeople identify confirmed benefits and transition into the presentation of a solution to solve the problems the buyer expresses. This presentation should focus on a customized training program that emphasizes dealing with difficult customers (confirmed benefits), but it should not be an online training program (benefit not confirmed). This example sales dialogue will be continued later in this chapter.

Sometimes salespeople do not focus on the confirmed benefits of the buyer. This might produce a sale in the short run, but could lose a customer in the long term. Creating and communicating value is also important in maintaining relationships with existing customers, because changes can occur in a customer's situation. For example, Match Eyewear had been doing business with a large

Salespeople need to vary the pitch and speed of their speech during sales dialogue.

© Julie Weiss/iStockphoto

account. This customer had made some changes in its business objectives and was ready to stop doing business with Match Eyewear. The Match Eyewear sales team found out about this and met many times with the customer. These meetings identified the new value needed by the customer. Match Eyewear addressed the new value requirements by improving its service and support offerings and communicating these changes effectively. The customer was retained and Match Eyewear used this situation to develop a stronger relationship with this customer.[2]

7-3 Interesting and Understandable Sales Dialogue

Once confirmed benefits have been identified, the salesperson needs to present key selling points in a manner that is interesting and understandable to the buyer. The presentation should focus on the buyer and is intended to gain and hold the buyer's attention, and to increase the buyer's understanding and retention of the information provided by the salesperson. **Verbal support** elements include voice characteristics, examples and anecdotes, and comparisons and analogies. Using these elements appropriately can produce interesting and understandable sales dialogue.

VOICE CHARACTERISTICS

The key aspects of **voice characteristics** are the pitch and speed of speech. Varying and changing pitch on key words adds emphasis and increases impact. It is analogous to putting different colours and hues into your voice. The increased intensity and vividness grab attention, hold interest, and help the buyer remember what is said. Fluctuating the speed of speech can add emphasis and guide the buyer's attention to selected points of the presentation. Important details—especially quantitative information—should be provided at a slower, more careful pace. Less critical information can be presented at a faster pace to grab the buyer's attention and redirect his or her interest. Changes in volume can be used to add emphasis to an important phrase or topic, and a softer volume—almost a whisper—can build intrigue and pull the prospect into the conversation. Altering volume from loud to soft can better grab and hold the buyer's interest while simultaneously adding clarity and emphasis to increase understanding.

verbal support The use of voice characteristics, examples and anecdotes, and comparisons and analogies to make sales dialogue interesting and understandable.

voice characteristics The pitch and speed of speech, which salespeople should vary to emphasize key points.

example A brief description of a specific instance used to illustrate features and benefits of a product or service.

anecdote A type of example that is provided in the form of a story describing a specific incident or occurrence.

As emphasized in "Professional Selling in the 21st Century: Energizing Sales Dialogues," a salesperson can know his or her product inside and out, but if there is no energy and passion in his or her voice, the potential for making the sale will be seriously impaired. As voice coach Jeffrey Jacobi emphasizes, "Your voice and how you use it determines how people respond to you. The sound of your voice relays to people whether you are confident, likable, boring, unpleasant, honest, or even dishonest."[3] Voice quality can be used to bring excitement and drama to the presentation by doing three things: varying the pitch, fluctuating the speed, and altering the volume.

EXAMPLES AND ANECDOTES

An **example** is a brief description of a specific instance used to illustrate features and benefits. Examples may be either real or hypothetical and are used to further explain and emphasize a topic of interest. A production equipment salesperson might further explain the purpose of an infrared guidance control by using the following example:

> *If the feedstock coming off the main paper roll gets out of line by as little as 1.5 millimetres, the infrared guidance control will sense it and automatically make the correct adjustments. This prevents a paper jam from shutting down your package printing line and costing lost time and wasted product.*

An **anecdote** is a type of example presented in the form of a story describing a specific incident or occurrence. Stories can be very effective in keeping a buyer interested and helping the buyer understand the solution a salesperson presents. The production

Professional Selling in the 21st Century

© Joshua Hodge Photography/E+/Getty

Energizing Sales Dialogues

Eric Brown is a manager for Malone Training Solutions. He has extensive sales experience in service industries and now provides sales training and coaching for client firms. Eric discusses the importance of using voice characteristics, nonverbal communication, and stories to energize sales dialogues:

Salespeople represent the voice of the company—its products, services, and promises. But, communicating our knowledge of products and services in ways that resonate with buyers is challenging. Buyers rely on us to help identify and solve problems for them. Translating the complexities of our products into stories of effective problem-solving helps buyers visualize the results from using our products. We convey confidence and passion for our suggested solution through variation in the speed, pitch, and tonality of our voice, and the nonverbal cues we communicate.

The first time I experienced the positive impact of voice characteristics, nonverbal cues, and stories was during a sales meeting with a retail business owner. I was very interested in the owner and success of her business. The speed, pitch, and tone of my voice changed as we discussed potential problems and I told stories of possible solutions. My body language aligned with my voice characteristics to reinforce my curiosity and concern. After lowering my voice as we talked about an especially painful problem, the owner became emotional and said: "I've never talked with someone who cared so much about my business and helping me solve these difficult problems." This experience confirmed to me that demonstrating our desire to help buyers can be done best by varying our voice characteristics, aligning our message with our body language, and using stories to support our recommended solutions.

equipment salesperson might use an anecdote such as the following:

> *One of my customers was having a problem with paper jams that were shutting down the firm's package printing line. Similar to your situation, there was a lot of lost production time and wasted product. We installed the infrared guidance control, which automatically adjusts the paper roll when it gets off by as little as 1.5 millimetres. This reduced paper jams, resulting in less wasted product and more production time for the customer.*

A salesperson's use of examples and anecdotes keeps the buyer interested, brings clarity into the presentation, and improves the buyer's understanding and retention of what the salesperson is presenting. The use of an example and anecdote in a sales dialogue example for customer service training follows.

> **Seller:** Customized training programs can be very effective. For example, one of our clients increased customer satisfaction ratings by 25 percent after we implemented a customized program for their reps. (*Example*). Is this the type of improvement you are looking for? (*Check-back*)

> **Seller:** Customers of the XYZ Company were very dissatisfied with the service the firm's reps provided. We reviewed the customers' complaints, met with the customer service reps, identified the main problems, and created a specific training program to deal with the key problems. After completion of the sales training program, customer complaints decreased by 75 per cent (*anecdote*). What do you think about these results? (*Check-back*)

© JMS WENN Photos/Newscom

Salespeople can use comparisons to communicate effectively with buyers.

COMPARISONS AND ANALOGIES

A **comparison** is a statement that points out and illustrates the similarities between two points. Comparisons increase the buyer's level of interest and understanding of information. A salesperson wanting to add emphasis and meaning to his or her verbal description of the Honda S2000's performance capabilities might use a direct comparison to the performance capabilities of a competitive model that the prospective buyer might also be considering:

> *You have the performance specifications on both cars, and as you can see . . . the 6-second 0 to 60 performance of the S2000 outperforms the Audi TT by a good 10 percent. This is a large difference in performance.*

A salesperson for Newell-Rubbermaid might illustrate the benefits of setting up an end-of-aisle display of special occasion containers by using the following comparison to the store manager's sales goals for the product category:

> *Sales data from stores similar to yours indicate that adding an end-of-aisle display for these seasonal containers will increase their sales by 35 to 40 percent during the fourth-quarter holiday season. This would certainly help you achieve—and possibly exceed—the store's goal of a 20-percent increase for this general product category.*

Medical products salespeople use comparisons in their role as consultants to doctors. The salespeople will provide a direct comparison of existing products to new products that will be introduced in the near future. Doctors find these comparisons valuable and, in some cases, find the new product valuable enough to postpone non-emergency surgery until the new product is available.[4]

comparison A statement that points out and illustrates the similarities between two points.

analogy A special and useful form of comparison that explains one thing in terms of another.

An **analogy** is a special and useful form of comparison that explains one thing in terms of another. Analogies are useful for explaining something complex by allowing the buyer to better visualize it in terms of something familiar that is easier to understand. A BMW salesperson presenting to an Air Force pilot the option of an in-car global positioning system map and tracking system might use the following analogy:

> *Having the onboard map and tracking system is like having a friendly flight controller with you on every trip. You will always know exactly where you are and what route you should travel to reach your destination. You will never get lost or be delayed because you took the wrong turn.*

An example of a comparison and an analogy in a sales dialogue example is presented here.

> **Seller:** We will incorporate your reps throughout the design and execution of our training program. This gives the reps some ownership in the program. Our competitors, in contrast, develop their programs based on what management tells them is important. (*Comparison*). Do you think your reps would respond well to being included in all aspects of the training program? (*Check-back*)
>
> **Seller:** Developing a customized sales training program is like planning for a family vacation. Everyone in the family is likely to be more excited about the vacation if they are involved in all aspects of the planning process. (*Analogy*). What do you think about involving your reps in all aspects of the training program? (*Check-back*)

7-4 Engaging and Involving the Buyer

Simply informing the prospect about the benefits and their value to the buyer is seldom sufficient to generate the level of interest and desire required to result in a purchase decision. To maximize the

sales aids The use of printed materials, electronic materials, and product demonstrations to engage and involve buyers.

visual materials Printed materials, photographs and illustrations, and charts and graphs used as sales aids.

effectiveness of the sales dialogue, salespeople use various **sales aids** to engage and involve the buyer throughout the sales interaction. These sales aids also help to capture and hold the buyer's attention, boost the buyer's understanding, increase the believability of the claims, and build the buyer's retention of information (see Exhibit 7.4). Not all sales aids are suitable for all products, selling situations, or buyers. Nor should a salesperson feel the need to use each and every tool in any given sales call. A salesperson should use the sales aids that will engage and involve each buyer most effectively in a particular sales dialogue. Many times, the selling organization provides these sales tools. However, experienced salespeople are quick to comment that some of their most effective sales aids are those that they developed themselves for specific prospects and selling situations.

TYPES OF SALES AIDS

Sales aids allow the salesperson to involve one or more of the buyer's senses in the presentation, help to illustrate features and confirmed benefits, and add clarity and dramatization to increase the effectiveness of a sales dialogue. The types of sales aids available to a salesperson include visual materials, electronic materials, and product demonstrations.

Visual Materials

Visual materials represent a variety of sales aids intended to engage and involve buyers visually. The major types of visual materials are printed materials, photographs and illustrations, and charts and graphs. Exhibit 7.5 provides salespeople with a number of tips for preparing printed materials and visuals.

Printed materials include such items as brochures, pamphlets, catalogues, articles, reprints, reports, testimonial letters, and guarantees. Well-designed printed materials can help the salesperson communicate, explain, and emphasize key points during a sales dialogue. They are designed to summarize important features and benefits and can be effectively used not only during the presentation but also left behind as reminder pieces for the buyer

EXHIBIT 7.4

Reasons for Using Sales Aids

- Capture prospective buyer's attention.
- Generate interest in the recommended solution.
- Make presentations more persuasive.
- Increase the buyer's participation and involvement.
- Provide the opportunity for collaboration and two-way communication.
- Add clarity and enhance the prospect's understanding.
- Provide supportive evidence and proof to enhance believability.
- Augment the prospect's retention of information.
- Enhance the professional image of the salesperson and selling organization.

EXHIBIT 7.5

Tips for Preparing Visual Materials

- Visual materials should be kept simple.
- When possible, use phrases and let the buyer's mind complete the sentences.
- Use the same layout and format throughout to tie the presentation together.
- Check for typographical and spelling errors.
- Use colours sparingly and for functional rather than decorative purposes.
- Leave plenty of white space; do not crowd the page.
- Each visual should present only one idea.
- Try to use a maximum of seven words per line and seven lines per visual.
- Where possible, use graphics (charts and graphs) rather than tables.
- Use bullet points to emphasize key points.
- Never read the presentation directly from the visual.
- Clearly label each visual with titles and headings to guide the prospective buyer.

© John W Banagan/Photographer's Choice/Getty

Printed materials are effective sales aids.

after the salesperson has left. When printed materials are left with a buyer, the salesperson's name and contact information should be clearly printed on the material or an attached business card.

Photographs and illustrations are easy to produce and relatively inexpensive. Using images allows the salesperson to present a realistic portrayal of the product or service. Many products cannot be taken into a prospective buyer's office because of their size. A detailed image can give the prospect an idea of the product's appearance and size. Line drawings and diagrams can show the most important details of a product. Images are most effective when they illustrate and simplify a more complex product or feature and make it easy to communicate information about size, shape, construction, and use.

Charts and graphs are useful in showing trends and illustrating relationships. As such, they can show the prospect what the problem is costing them or how a solution might work. Charts and graphs often illustrate relationships by using bars, lines, circles, or squares. For example, a salesperson for an office equipment vendor might get the cost figures associated with the buyer's use of an outside copy centre for the previous two years. The salesperson could then use this information in a comparative bar graph to better illustrate the savings possible if the buyer owned a copier. Salespeople for a leading medical technology company use a chart format to compare the features and benefits of their product versus the competitors' equipment the buyer is considering. The chart format succinctly and effectively supports statements of superiority made during the presentation.

Electronic Materials

Electronic materials include all sales aids in electronic format. These span individual slides and videos to complete multimedia presentations. As technology continues to develop, more options to use electronic materials become available to salespeople. Two examples are customized electronic presentations and online sales aid libraries.

Salespeople today can customize graphic presentations for each buyer. Customizing and enriching presentations by using electronic multimedia can be done inexpensively and in a fairly short time. Microsoft PowerPoint, for example, allows the salesperson to quickly build a complete, high-impact graphic presentation customized for an individual prospect. These powerful multimedia presentations might include pictures of products, as well as product demonstrations and competitive comparisons. The use of video has the advantage of both sound and action. The buyer can be taken on a virtual tour of the selling organization and see the product being produced or simultaneously see and hear a personal message from the president of the selling organization as well as testimonials from satisfied customers.

A rapidly growing trend is the development and use of online libraries of sales aids. Selling organizations typically develop these libraries for their salespeople's exclusive use. For example, GlaxoSmithKline provides salespeople with before-and-after slides to depict the effectiveness of a topical cream product. The slides show how the skin of most patients clears up after using the cream for three days. Hewlett-Packard maintains an extensive online database

electronic materials Sales aids in electronic format, such as slides, videos, or multimedia presentations.

and library of sales aids that include product brochures and specification sheets, graphics, proposal templates, competitive comparisons, and an archive of PowerPoint presentations. Content can be downloaded and printed as is or customized to better fit a specific need.

Leading pharmaceutical companies are using electronic materials in two interesting ways. First, iPad applications (apps) have been developed by some firms to facilitate interaction between sales reps and doctors. The salesperson can use the app to visually illustrate how a drug works in the body and to respond to questions a doctor might have. Second, doctors are very busy and may not have time to interact with a salesperson during an office visit. In these cases, the sales rep can give the physician a card with a URL on it and invite the doctor to view a presentation electronically, engage in an online discussion, or participate in a live electronic presentation at a more convenient time. These and other forms of "e-detailing" are being explored by many pharmaceutical firms.[5]

Product Demonstrations

The product itself is often the most effective sales tool because it provides the prospective buyer with an opportunity for hands-on experience. When the actual product does not lend itself to being demonstrated, models can be used to represent and illustrate key features and benefits of the larger product. The value of an actual product demonstration is applicable to all types of products and services. For example, Boeing salespeople use scale models to give the buyer a detailed and realistic feel for the aircraft, which cannot be tucked into the salesperson's briefcase. As the sale progresses, the prospective buyer's team will be given actual hands-on experience with the real product. Simmons and Sealy, leading manufacturers of quality sleep products, require that their registered dealers have demonstration models of mattress sets on display and available for customers to try out. Major vendors of office furniture will set up a model office so that the prospective client can experience its actual use. Pharmaceutical companies provide doctors with samples of the product for trial use with selected patients.

Multimedia sales aids are being used more in sales dialogue.

© Blend Images - Andersen Ross/Getty

As detailed in Exhibit 7.6, the salesperson should make sure the product being demonstrated is typical of what is being recommended. Furthermore, it should be checked to ensure that it is in good working order before the demonstration and that setup and removal do not detract from the presentation. The last thing the salesperson wants is to have to apologize for poor appearance or inadequate performance.

Whenever possible, it is important to have the buyer use the product instead of the salesperson demonstrating its use. For example, buyers often realize that many new software products have features that could be valuable to their firm. However, they may be reluctant to make a purchase because they think it will be too hard for their employees to learn to use the software. A salesperson could demonstrate the software to show how easy it is to use, but it would be more effective to have the buyer use the software to experience firsthand its ease of use.

USING SALES AIDS IN THE PRESENTATION

Practise! Practise! Practise! Rehearsal of the presentation is the final key to conducting effective sales dialogue. Understand what features are relevant and what benefits are meaningful to the prospective buyer in terms of value to be realized. Be confident in developing and using multiple sales aids to add impact to the presentation itself. Using the SPES Sequence can facilitate the effectiveness of presentation tools and sales aids: S = *State selling point and introduce the sales aid*; P = *Present the sales aid*; E = *Explain the sales aid*; S = *Summarize*.[6]

State the Selling Point and Introduce the Sales Aid

State the full selling point, including the feature and potential benefit, and then introduce the sales aid. For instance, "To demonstrate this benefit, I would like you to take a look at this video" or "This graph summarizes the increased performance you will experience with the

EXHIBIT 7.6
Guidelines for Product Demonstrations

- Ensure the appearance of the product is neat and clean.
- Check for problem-free operation.
- Be confident and able to demonstrate the product skillfully.
- Practise using the product before the demonstration.
- Anticipate problems and have backup or replacement parts on hand.
- Make sure that setup and knockdown are easy and quick.

Honda S2000." This prepares the buyer for the visual aid and informs him or her that attention is required.

Present the Sales Aid

Present the sales aid to the customer and allow a few moments for examination and familiarization before saying anything. For example, when using printed materials, place the material directly in front of the customer and allow it to be reviewed momentarily in silence. Allow the customer to review the sales aid and satisfy his or her natural curiosity before using it.

Explain the Sales Aid

No matter how carefully a sales aid is prepared, it will not be completely obvious. The customer will not necessarily understand the significance unless the salesperson provides a brief explanation. Do not rely on a chart or graph to illustrate fully the points being supported. Similarly, a prospect might enjoy a product demonstration yet totally miss the information or experience supporting the presentation. The salesperson should point out the material information and explain how it supports his or her points.

Summarize

When you have finished explaining the significance of the sales aid, summarize its contribution and support and remove the sales aid. If not removed, its presence can distract the prospective buyer's attention from subsequent feature and benefit points.

The use of the SPES Sequence to use a sales aid in a customer service training program sales dialogue is presented here.

Seller: You mentioned earlier that your reps are not well prepared to deal with irate customers. I would like to show you a short video from a training program we developed for another firm. The video illustrates how we use role plays to help reps develop the skills to interact with irate customers effectively. (*State the selling point and introduce the sales aid*)
(*The salesperson shows the video to the buyer*)

Seller: Did you notice how everyone involved in the training program watched the role play carefully and was able to contribute comments to improve the interaction with the irate customer? (*Explain the sales aid*)

Buyer: The role-play exercise did get everyone involved and produced some good ideas for improvement.

proof providers The use of statistics, testimonials, or case histories to support product claims.

Seller: Although this is just one type of exercise we employ in our training programs, the role play produced some guidelines that all reps could use to deal with irate customers more effectively. (*Summarize*). Do you think this type of exercise would be valuable to your reps? (*Check-back*)

Salespeople can increase the success of a sales dialogue by using appropriate sales aids effectively.

7-5 Supporting Product Claims

s discussed earlier in this chapter, confirmed benefits answer the buyer's question, "What is in it for me?" In a similar fashion, **proof providers**, such as statistics, testimonials, and case histories,

statistics Facts that lend believability to product claims and are used as proof providers.

testimonials Proof providers that are in the form of statements from satisfied users of the selling organization's products and services.

can be used to preempt the buyer from asking, "Can you prove it?" or "Who says so?" Claims of benefits and value produced and provided to the buyer need to be backed up with evidence to highlight their believability.

STATISTICS

Statistics are facts that lend believability to claims of value and benefit. When available, statistics from authoritative, third-party sources carry the highest credibility. Among others, third-party sources include independent testing organizations and labs (e.g., *Consumer Reports*, Underwriters Laboratories of Canada), professional organizations (e.g., The Risk Management Society), research companies (e.g., PricewaterhouseCoopers), institutions (e.g., University of Toronto), and various governmental entities (e.g., Statistics Canada, Industry Canada). Statistics prepared by the selling organization as well as the salesperson can also be useful in providing evidence for claims. Facts and statistics are most powerful when they fairly represent all sides to the story and are presented in printed form rather than simply stated orally. The printed word not only carries more credibility but also is convenient and can be left as a reminder to aid the prospect's retention of information.

© PR NEWSWIRE/AP Images

TESTIMONIALS

Testimonials are similar to statistics, but in the form of statements from satisfied users of the selling organization's products and services. Supportive statements from current users are excellent methods to build trust and confidence. They predispose the prospective buyer to accept what the salesperson says about the benefits and value a recommended solution offers, and they reduce the prospect's perceived risk in making a purchase decision.

Salespeople can use testimonials to support their product claims.

Written testimonials are especially effective when they are on the recommending user's letterhead and signed. However, testimonials that list customers, trade publications, trade associations, and independent rating organizations along with one-sentence comments in a presentation can also be effective. For instance:

- "The Canadian Dental Association has endorsed the new Laserlite drilling system as being safe and painless for the patient."
- "In January, *Fortune* magazine recognized CDW as the top-rated technology vendor on the basis of services provided to the buying customer."
- "The *RIMS Quality Scorecard* rated Arthur J. Gallagher & Co. as the highest-rated insurance broker in North America in terms of value and service provided to its clients."

As shown in "An Ethical Dilemma," the power of testimonials sometimes tempts salespeople to misuse them.

Testimonials are used extensively across industry and product/service types. To maximize their effectiveness, testimonials should be matched according to relevance and recognition to the prospective buyer. It is critical that the organization or person providing the supporting testimony be known or recognized by the prospect, above reproach, and in a position of respect.

An Ethical Dilemma

© Leonardo Patrizi/iStockphoto

Karen Dillane is a new sales representative for the local newspaper. She sells advertising for the print and digital versions of the newspaper to local small business owners. This is a difficult task, because small businesses have limited advertising budgets and many are not knowledgeable about or comfortable with advertising on the digital version of the newspaper. Karen has had a few successes and wants to get some written testimonials to use in her sales dialogues. She helped Dan Lustig, owner of a local restaurant, increase sales significantly by advertising in the print and digital newspaper. Dan agreed to write a testimonial over a month ago, but has not yet prepared it. When she asks him about it, he says he will do it soon. Karen knows that he is a very satisfied customer and would give her a positive recommendation, so she prepares a written testimonial letter from him and signs his name on it. She has found this testimonial letter to be very effective, because it has helped her get several new clients. Karen continues to try to get the testimonial letter from Dan, but he never gets around to it. What should Karen do?

a) Continue to use the testimonial letter she has prepared, because it has been very effective for her.
b) Take the testimonial letter she has prepared to Dan and see if he will sign it.
c) Stop using the testimonial letter she has prepared and wait until Dan prepares the testimonial he has promised.

case histories A testimonial in story or anecdotal form used as a proof provider.

CASE HISTORIES

Case histories are basically a testimonial in story or anecdotal form. Their added length allows more detail to be presented to further clarify an issue or better itemize the proof for a given statement. Case histories can also break the monotony of a long presentation. Like their counterpart testimonials, case histories should be used only when they clearly illustrate a particular point and are appropriate for the prospective buyer. Unrelated or tangential stories not only distract the customer but also can be a source of irritation that works against credibility building. Case histories should be short and to the point, lasting no more than a minute. They should support the presentation rather than becoming the centre of attention.

Salespeople are increasingly involved in group sales dialogue.

7-6 Group Sales Dialogue

Sales dialogue with groups is fairly commonplace in business-to-business selling. For example, retail chains often employ buying committees when considering the addition of new products for their stores. Hospitals use cross-functional teams comprising medical and administrative personnel to choose vendors such as food service providers. A group of marketing and upper-management people usually make the decision about which advertising agency will be chosen. Corporations

© Fuse/Jupiter Images

presselling Salespeople present their product or service to individual buyers before a major sales dialogue with a group of buyers.

often depend on representatives from several departments to make purchase decisions that affect all employees, such as the choice of insurance providers.

Interacting with groups presents special challenges and opportunities. In addition to the basic fundamentals of planning and delivering sales dialogue to individual buyers, there are additional strategies and tactics that can enhance sales dialogue with groups.

When selling to groups, salespeople can expect tough questions and should prepare accordingly. Although buyer questions are part of most sales dialogues, whether with individuals or groups, they are particularly crucial when multiple buyers are involved. Most buying groups are assembled to tap the individual expertise and interests of the group members. For example, a buying committee for a company's computer information system could include technical specialists; finance and accounting personnel; and representatives from production operations, logistics, management, and marketing. All of these individuals are experts and demand in-depth information to make a decision. In some situations, this calls for a sales team to address all questions adequately, while in other cases, an individual salesperson has the cross-functional expertise required to make the sale.

When selling to a group, salespeople should take every opportunity of **preselling** to individual group members before the group presentation. Preselling to individual buyers or subgroups of buyers takes place before a major sales presentation to the entire group. Buying procedures in a given company may or may not allow preselling. If it is an option, the salesperson should work with the individuals composing the buying group before presenting to the group as a whole. By doing so, the salesperson can better determine individual and group interests and motives and possibly build a positive foundation for the group presentation. Preselling can also reveal the roles of the individuals in the buying centre, as discussed in Chapter 3. Knowing who the decision maker is, along with the other roles, such as users and influencers, is crucial for success in group sales interactions. In the following discussion, we will focus on two key areas: tactical suggestions for group presentations and handling questions in group settings.

SALES TACTICS FOR SELLING TO GROUPS

Assuming that the salesperson or sales team has planned a comprehensive sales dialogue and done as much preselling as possible, some specific sales tactics can enhance presentations to groups. Sales tactics for group presentations fall into three general categories: arrival tactics, eye contact, and communication tips for presentation delivery.

Arrival Tactics

Try to arrive at the location for the meeting before the buying group arrives. This provides an opportunity to set up and check audio-visual equipment, prepare collateral material for distribution to the group, and become familiar and comfortable with the surroundings. It also sets the stage for the salesperson to greet individuals from the buying team personally as they enter the room. In a symbolic way, it also signals territorial command, or that the salesperson is in charge of the meeting. Although the control of the meeting is typically shared with the buying group, arriving first sends a message that the salesperson is prepared to start promptly at the appointed time, thus showing respect for the buyer's time.

From the very beginning, the salesperson is hoping to connect with each individual in the group, rather than connecting only at the group level. By arriving first, the salesperson may have the opportunity to talk briefly with each individual. If nothing more, a friendly greeting, handshake, and introduction can help establish a rapport with individuals in the group. When not allowed to arrive first, salespeople should attempt individual introductions when joining the group. If that is not practical, salespeople must try to engage each individual through eye contact and, if appropriate, introductory remarks early in the presentation that recognize the individual interests of those present. For example, a salesperson for a food service company might begin a presentation to a hospital with the following:

> *Thank you for the opportunity to discuss our food service programs with you today. In planning for our meeting, I recognize that the dietary group is most concerned about the impact of any proposed change on the quality of patient care. Linda [the head dietician], I believe we have a program that will enhance the quality of care that your patients receive. John [the head of finance], we will also propose an efficient, cost-effective alternative ....*

Opening remarks such as these, when kept brief, can be most effective in building involvement with all individuals in a small group.

Eye Contact

For both small and large groups, establishing periodic eye contact with individuals is important. With small groups, this is easily accomplished. With larger groups, especially formal presentations in which the salesperson is standing and the group is sitting, there may be a tendency to use the so-called overhead approach. This method calls for looking just over the heads of the group, with the idea that those seated farthest from the presenter will feel included as part of the group. This method should be avoided. It might be fine for a formal speech to a large audience in a convention hall, but it is far too impersonal for groups of 10 to 25 individuals. Also avoid a rapid scanning from side-to-side. This gives the appearance of nervousness and is ineffective in connecting with individual group members. The most effective eye contact is to try to connect with each individual or small subgroups for a few seconds, moving through the entire group over the course of the presentation. Professional entertainers often use this method to connect with audience members, and salespeople can do the same.

Communications Tips

When selling to groups, it is essential to make all members of the group feel that their opinions are valuable. It is also important to avoid being caught in the middle of disagreements between members of the buying group. For example, if one member likes the salesperson's proposal and another thinks it is too expensive, any resolution of this disagreement must be handled carefully. Although the salesperson may present information that resolves the issue, in some cases, disagreements among group buying members may be resolved outside the meetings. It is to the salesperson's advantage if disagreements can be handled during the presentation, as it keeps the sales process moving; unresolved issues can stall the sales process. As an example of how salespeople can play a peacemaker role, consider this exchange:

Buyer A: "I really like this system and think we should install it as soon as possible."

Buyer B: "I like it too, but it is way too expensive. Is there a less expensive alternative?"

Buyer A: "Sure, but it will not do the job."

Salesperson: (*Directed to Buyer B*) "Could I add something here? I believe we have a cost-effective system and that our lease-to-purchase plan reduces the capital expenditure and allows a favourable payback period. Could we take another look at the numbers?"

Salespeople must be diplomatic as participants in discussions that might develop between members of the buying group. This sometimes means remaining silent while the discussion comes to a resolution, and sometimes it means playing an active role. There are no hard and fast rules in this area, and salespeople must simply use their best judgment to guide their actions.

In delivering group presentations, it is important to maintain contact with group members. Thus, reading or overreliance on densely worded slides should be avoided. Think of slides and other audio-visual aids as support tools, not as a "roll-and-scroll" presentation to be read to the group. Natural movement can also enhance contact with the group. Too much pacing about can be detrimental to holding the group's attention, just as remaining tethered to a laptop can detract from group communication. When possible, salespeople should stand to the left of visual aids, as people read right-to-left. When standing to the left, it is easier to direct attention to the visual aids while momentarily deflecting attention away from the speaker. In this way, the salesperson becomes an unobtrusive narrator and the visual aid has maximum impact.

Body language can add to or detract from sales effectiveness in the group setting. In general, your posture should reflect an energetic, relaxed person. Conventional wisdom dictates that presenters should avoid contact with their own bodies while presenting. Salespeople who stuff their hands in their pockets, scratch their heads, or cross their arms are creating distractions to their own messages.

HANDLING QUESTIONS IN GROUP DIALOGUE

Just as is the case with sales dialogue to individuals, questions from buyers in a group are an important part of the buyer–seller interaction that leads to a purchase decision. Salespeople should recognize that questions fill information gaps, thus allowing buyers to make better decisions. In a group setting, questions can also add a dramatic element, making the presentation more interesting for those in attendance. To the extent that it is possible, salespeople should anticipate group questions and then decide whether to address the question before it arises or wait and address the question should it arise during the presentation.

To effectively handle questions that arise during the meeting, salespeople should listen carefully. Questions should be answered as succinctly and convincingly as possible. By listening carefully to the question, salespeople show respect for the person asking the question. At the same time, they are helping direct the attention of the group to the question. As the question is posed, it is important for the salesperson to maintain eye contact with the person asking the question. Again, this demonstrates respect for the person and for his or her right to ask questions. This may require some practice, as salespeople may be tempted to glance at sales materials or perhaps their watch when the attention is shifted to the person asking the question. To do so could insult the questioner, who may feel slighted by the lack of attention.

In answering questions during a group dialogue, salespeople should listen carefully, answer directly, and address the individual asking the question as well as the others in the group.

In many cases, it is a good idea to repeat or even restate the question. This will ensure that everyone understands the question. It also signals a shift from the individual back to the group. Additionally, it allows the salesperson to state the key issue in the question succinctly. This is often important because not all questions are well formulated and they are sometimes accompanied by superfluous information. Consider this dialogue:

Buyer: "You know, I have been thinking about the feasibility of matching our Brand X computers with Brand Y printers. Not too long ago, matching multiple brands would have been a disaster. Are you telling me now that Brand X computers are totally compatible with Brand Y printers?"

Seller: "You are asking whether your computers are compatible with our printers. Is that right? Yes, they are—with no special installation requirements."

When restating questions, salespeople must be careful to capture the essence of the buyer's concern accurately. Otherwise, they could be perceived as avoiding the question or trying to manipulate the buyer by putting words in his or her mouth. Therefore, when in doubt, it is a good practice when restating a question to seek buyer confirmation that the restated question is an accurate representation of the original question. For example, salespeople might say, "Ms. Jackson, as I understand the question, you are concerned about the effectiveness of our seasonal sales promotion programs. Is that correct?"

When answering questions, there are three guidelines. First, a salesperson should not attempt to answer a question until he or she and the group members clearly understand the question. Second, salespeople should not attempt to answer questions that they are not prepared to answer. It is far better to make a note and tell the group you will get back to them with the answer than to speculate or give a weak answer. Third, salespeople should try to answer questions as directly as possible. Politicians are often accused of not answering the questions posed during press conferences, but rather steering the answer toward what they want to talk about. Salespeople will quickly lose credibility if they take a long time to get to the point in their answer. To answer convincingly, start with a "yes" or "no," then explain the exceptions to the general case. For example, saying, "Yes, that is generally the case. There are some exceptions, including . . ." is preferred to answering "Well that depends . . ." and then explaining all of the special circumstances only to conclude with "but, generally, yes, that is the case."

When answering questions, it is important to address the entire group rather than just the individual who asked the question. Otherwise, salespeople may lose the attention of other group members. When salespeople conclude their answers, they have the option of going back to the person who asked the question, continuing their presentation, or taking a question from another group member. Salespeople can rely on their common sense and experience to decide what is appropriate in a given situation.

In larger groups, it is particularly important to avoid getting locked into a question-and-answer dialogue with one person if other people are showing an interest in asking questions. Indeed, it is important to take all questions, but it is also important to spread the opportunity to ask questions around the room, coming back to those who have multiple questions until all questions are answered. If one person is a dominant force within the buying group, other group members will typically defer their questions until that person has asked all of their questions at different points in the presentation.

When selling to a group, salespeople should have a clear objective for their presentation. To get the group to take the desired action, salespeople must make a convincing case, motivate the group to take action, and make it easy for the group to take the desired action. Some of the methods for handling buyer objections and earning a commitment that will be discussed in Chapter 8 will prove useful for accomplishing these tasks.

In some cases, the group will want to deliberate and let the salesperson know of their decision at a later time. This is not uncommon, because the group may need a frank discussion without outsiders to reach a final decision. Should this occur, salespeople should be certain that the group has all the information they need or offer to provide the needed information promptly and offer to follow-up within a specified time period.

The process for planning and delivering a group sales dialogue is much the same as it is for sales dialogue with individuals. By paying attention to the special considerations in this section, salespeople can build on their experience with sales interaction with individuals and engage in effective sales dialogue with groups.

Visit **www.nelson.com/student** to find the resources you need today!

Located at the back of the textbook are rip-out Chapter Review cards. Make sure you also go online to check out other tools that SELL offers to help you successfully pass your course.

- Flashcards
- Glossary
- PowerPoint Notes
- Role-Play Videos
- Games
- Interactive Quizzing

CHAPTER 7 CASE

OFFICE FURNITURE COMPANY

Background

The Ennismore Furniture Company specializes in providing customers with office furniture solutions that are customized and designed to address productivity and aesthetic needs. It sells office furniture from the leading manufacturers, but creates value by analyzing the specific needs of each customer and then developing a customized design to meet these needs. There are several competitors in the office furniture industry, but most of them focus on low prices. Customers usually pay more for an Ennismore Furniture Company solution, but receive more value in terms of increased productivity and business effectiveness.

Current Situation

Arnold & Associates is a small, but growing, accounting firm. The company plans to add more office staff and to increase the number of its accountants. This planned growth means that the firm will have to find new office space, because it will have outgrown its current location. Because it plans continued growth in the future, it is looking for a new office that will accommodate current and future growth objectives. Arnold & Associates also wants to purchase new and better furniture for its new office. You are a sales representative for the Ennismore Furniture Company and have been meeting with partner Sarah Arnold, as well as accountants and staff, at Arnold & Associates. Based on these meetings, you have identified the following office furniture needs:

1. Arnold & Associates has typically met with clients at their offices. It would like to have most client meetings in the future at its new office. This means they desire furniture that facilitates these meetings and communicates a professional and customer-friendly image.

2. Their current office furniture did not provide much storage for accountants or staff. Thus, important documents were stored at the end of a long hallway. Employees wasted a lot of time trying to retrieve important documents. Thus, they desire furniture that provides more storage for each employee.

3. Technology is changing at a rapid pace, so furniture that can be easily adapted to new technologies is very important.

4. As Arnold & Associates continues to grow, it will probably have to reorganize itself and is likely to need to adapt the physical office to different organizational arrangements. Office furniture that is adaptable to different configurations is important. You have created an office equipment design for Arnold &Associates that addresses each of the issues presented above and are preparing for a meeting with the partner, Sarah Arnold, the office manager, and a representative for the firm's accountants. You know that a competitor has already made a presentation to the same group and their offer will cost less than what you will be able to charge.

Questions

1. How will you try overcoming the lower price offer by a competitor?
2. What specific value can you offer Arnold & Associates?
3. How can you most effectively communicate the value of your proposed office equipment design?
4. What sales aids could you use to make your presentation more engaging and effective?

Role Play

Situation: Read the Ennismore Equipment Company case.

Characters: Sarah Arnold, partner; Tricia MacDonald, office manager; Jessica Attaway, accountant representative

Scene:

Location—Current Arnold & Associates office.

Action—Role play this meeting. Be sure to address the specific needs identified earlier, to communicate effectively with each person in the meeting, and to incorporate sales aids appropriately.

After completing the role plays, address the following questions:

1. How would you evaluate the role play in terms of interesting, understandable, and engaging sales dialogue? What improvements would you recommend?
2. How well did you involve each person in the meeting? What improvements would you recommend?
3. Evaluate the effectiveness of each sales aid used. What improvements in the use of sales aids would you recommend?

Role Play: Sales Dialogue: Creating and Communicating Value: Chemong Insurance and National Networks

Background

The Chemong Insurance Company has 3,200 sales agents spread across five regions that cover all of Canada. The company is moving toward the development of a national network that would tie each of the agent offices together with the regional offices and corporate headquarters. The improved communication capability will allow all company personnel to have full access to customer records and form the core of a comprehensive customer relationship management system that is to be rolled out in 18 months.

Current Situation

Jim Roberts is a network account specialist for National Networks, a specialist in large corporate network solutions, and has been working with the technology-buying group at Chemong Insurance for several months now. Roberts has worked through several meetings with the buying group members and has a meeting scheduled for next Wednesday to present his recommendations and demonstrate why they should select National Networks as the supplier for this sizable project. Joyce Fields (director of information systems), John Harris (comptroller and CFO), Javid Quadri (director of agent services), and Dianne Sheffield (director for customer services) will make the final decision. Roberts also knows that one other competitor will be making a presentation in hopes of landing the project. The equipment both vendors are proposing is virtually identical because of the detailed specifications that Chemong Insurance had included in the RFP. Prices are also likely to be pretty similar. The decision will most likely come down to the services each competitor includes in the proposals. Based on the information that Roberts has collected from different sources, he has come up with a comparison of customer services National Networks and the competitor offer (see the following table).

Role Play

Situation: Read the role play Background and Current Situation.

Characters: Jim Roberts—salesperson for National Networks; Joyce Fields—director of information systems for Chemong Insurance; John Harris—comptroller and CFO for Chemong Insurance; Javid Quadri—director of agent services for Chemong Insurance; Dianne Sheffield—director for customer services for Chemong Insurance

Scene:

Location—A conference room at Chemong Insurance

Action—As described, Jim Roberts is presenting the National Networks proposal for a corporate computer network linking Chemong Insurance's corporate offices with each of its five regional offices and 3,200 sales agents out in the field.

Role play Roberts's presentation of each of the feature–benefit sets incorporating sales aids suitable for use in the group presentation.

Features	Capability of National Networks	Capability of Competitor	Benefits
Service and repair centres	175 affiliated service and repair centres across Canada	21 affiliated service and repair centres across Canada	Ensures fast and reliable repairs for hardware and software
Installation and testing	Installation and testing done by National Networks employees	Installation and testing outsourced to several different companies	Knowledge that all installations will be done the right way
Customer call centre	24 hours, 7 days per week, and staffed by National Networks employees	24 hours, 7 days per week, and staffed by an outsource commercial provider	Knowledgeable staff always available to assist Chemong Insurance employees with problems

After completing the role plays, address the following questions:

1. What other sales tools and aids might prove useful to Roberts in presenting his proposed solution to the Chemong Insurance buying team?
2. How might Roberts employ other tactics for selling to a group to increase the effectiveness of his presentation and advance the sale toward getting an order?

what do you think?

Earning commitment is the most important stage of the selling process.

1 2 3 4 5 6 7

strongly disagree — strongly agree

Sales resistance

is a normal part of any sales conversation and should be viewed as an opportunity to sell.

8

Addressing Concerns and Earning Commitment

After completing this chapter, you should be able to

8-1 Explain why it is important to anticipate and overcome buyer concerns and resistance.

8-2 Understand why prospects raise objections.

8-3 Describe the five major types of sales resistance.

8-4 Explain how the LAARC method can be used to overcome buyer resistance.

8-5 Describe the recommended approaches for responding to buyer objections.

8-6 List and explain the techniques for earning commitment that secure commitment and closing.

Introduction

FUSION Performance Marketing is a full-service performance improvement company that specializes in highly creative and results-oriented incentive systems. Its incentive planning process is focused on exceeding clients' sales and marketing goals and providing those clients with a solid return on investment. Simply stated, FUSION delivers results. FUSION provides its clients with the power to move their:

- business forward
- audience to a higher level of performance
- bottom line

FUSION's sales cycle is extremely long, ranging from three months to four or five years. Each prospective client has different challenges and objectives, requiring FUSION to develop custom solutions specific to each client's unique needs. Since the client is spending millions of dollars on these programs, the buying decision is lengthy and challenging. Given this scenario, the opportunities for resistance are rampant and the struggle to earn commitment is lengthy and arduous. For Jim Micklos, vice president of business development with FUSION, overcoming concerns and earning the commitment comes down to three key factors:

- Breadth and depth of client relationships
- Unique solutions to client challenges
- Delivering maximum value

Overcoming resistance starts with the initial presentation. First, we open with a factual comment that we are not sure if we can help, but we'll find out together. This approach immediately reduces the client's anxiety about meeting with a "sales rep" trying to sell them something. Early in the presentation, we detail our steps to success. We clearly define our sales process, thereby providing the prospect with a clear orientation about what to expect when (satisfying) (answering) concerns about surprises and taking away clients' fears about sharing real information. As part of the sales process, we emphasize that any costs that are incurred are paid by FUSION. Clients invest only if they decide to implement a solution. Resistance often comes in the form of the status quo, not necessarily the competition. We use key industry facts to transition the prospect into a place where they will listen to the solutions FUSION can deliver. Finally we contrast the future by using FUSION versus the present, providing financial models that pinpoint the value FUSION delivers. Earning commitment on multi-million dollar programs is difficult but much easier if we have a thorough

sales resistance A buyer's objections to a product or service during a sales presentation.

understanding of the client's situation. Following the process outlined above dramatically improves FUSION's rate of success.

Addressing Concerns

An objection or **sales resistance** is anything the buyer says or does that slows down or stops the buying process. The salesperson's job is to uncover these objections and answer them to the prospect's or client's satisfaction. It is very difficult for a salesperson to earn commitment if doubt or concern remain on the buyer's part. Thus, the salesperson must uncover and overcome any and all objections. In doing so, the salesperson strengthens the long-term relationship and moves the sales process closer to commitment.

Good salespeople will anticipate their buyers' concerns.

At the very least, it creates open dialogue between the salesperson and the prospect.

A brief discussion follows on why it is important for salespeople to anticipate and negotiate buyer concern. Following a discussion of why prospects raise objections, this chapter covers the five major types of objections. Next, different approaches to handling sales resistance are explained. Finally, techniques to earn commitment are reviewed.

8-1 Anticipating and Negotiating Concerns and Resistance

Over the years, many sales forces were taught that sales resistance was bad and would likely slow down or stop the selling process. Salespeople were also told that if they received resistance, then they had not done a good job explaining their product or service.

These notions have changed over the years, and objections are now viewed as opportunities to sell. Salespeople should be grateful for objections and always treat them as questions. The buyer is just asking for more information. It is the salesperson's job to produce the correct information to help buyers alleviate their concern. Inexperienced salespeople need to learn that sales resistance is a normal, natural part of any sales conversation. The prospect that does not question price, service, warranty, and delivery concerns is probably not interested.

Although many salespeople fear sales resistance from their prospects or customers, it should be viewed as a normal part of the sales process. At a minimum, the salesperson has the prospect involved. The salesperson can now start to determine customer interest and measure the buyer's understanding of the problem. In some situations, a salesperson cannot overcome resistance (e.g., delivery dates do not match; technology does not fit). Under these circumstances, the successful salesperson gracefully ends the sales call while leaving open the option for further business.[1] Finally, if the sales resistance is handled correctly, the outcome can lead to customer acceptance.

8-2 REASONS WHY PROSPECTS RAISE OBJECTIONS

There are many reasons why prospects will raise objections.

1. The prospect wants to avoid the sales interview. Some prospects do not want to create any more work for themselves than they already have. Granted, a sales interview takes time and buyers already have a busy schedule handling normal day-to-day tasks. Buyers may want to avoid the salesperson because they view his or her call as an interruption in their day. Most buyers do not have the time to see every salesperson who knocks on their door.
2. The salesperson has failed to prospect and qualify properly. Sometimes, poor prospects slip through the screening process. The prospect may have misunderstood the salesperson's intentions when asked for the interview. The salesperson should attempt to qualify the prospect during the sales call. For example, a computer software company used telemarketing to qualify prospects. Leads were turned over to the salesforce for in-person visits. The major

product line was an inventory control package that cost $20,000. The salesperson asked the owner of the company if she had a budget for this project. The owner answered $5,000. The salesperson gave the owner the names of a couple of inexpensive software companies, thanked the owner for her time, and moved on. The owner was not about to spend $20,000 and said so early in the sales conversation. That resistance actually helped the salesperson. What if this condition had stayed hidden for four to six weeks while the salesperson continued to call on the owner? Both the salesperson's and owner's time would have been wasted.

3. Objecting is a matter of custom. Many purchasing agents have a motto never to buy on the first call with a salesperson. Trust has not yet been developed and a thorough understanding of the salesperson, his or her company, and the products has not been created. The buyer will need most of this information to make a decision. Many buyers may say no during the first few calls to test the salesperson's persistence.
4. The prospect resists change. Many buyers like the way that they are currently doing business. Thus, buyers will tell the salesperson that they are satisfied with what they have now. Many prospects simply resist change because they dislike making decisions. Prospects may fear the consequences of deciding and dread disturbing the status quo. A purchase usually involves dismissing the present supplier and handling all of the arrangements (price, terms, delivery, and product specifications) to move the new supplier in smoothly. Once a buyer is comfortable with his or her suppliers, he or she will generally avoid new salespeople until a major need arises.
5. The prospect fails to recognize a need. The prospect may be unaware of a need, uninformed about the product or service, or content with the present situation. In any case, the lack of need creates no motivation to change suppliers. Many purchasing agents were content with their overnight mail service and were slow to recognize the fax machine as a viable solution to getting information to their customers quickly. The poor quality of the reproduced document also turned away many buyers. Only when the need for the information outweighed the aesthetics of the document did the buyers readily embrace the fax machine.
6. The prospect lacks information. Ultimately, all sales resistance comes back to the fact that the prospect simply lacks the information he or she needs to make a decision comfortably. The salesperson must view this as an opportunity to put the right information in front of the buyer. As Jim Micklos suggests in the opening vignette, the relationship must include a "thorough understanding of the client's situation." If the salesperson diagnoses correctly and presents the right information, then the resistance problem can be more easily overcome. Exhibit 8.1 summarizes why prospects raise objections and lists strategies for dealing with them.

8-3 TYPES OF SALES RESISTANCE

Although there appears to be an infinite number of objections, most fall into five or six categories. Buyers use delay techniques to avoid taking immediate action.

EXHIBIT 8.1
Why Prospects Raise Objections and Strategies for Dealing with Them

- Buyer wants to avoid the sales interview.
  Strategy: Set appointments to become part of the buyer's daily routine.
- Salesperson has failed to prospect and qualify properly.
  Strategy: Ask questions to verify prospect's interest.
- Buyer will not buy on the first sales call.
  Strategy: A regular call on the prospect lets the prospect know the salesperson is serious about the relationship.
- Prospect does not want to change the present way of doing business.
  Strategy: Salesperson must help the prospect understand there is a better solution than the one the prospect is presently using.
- Prospect has failed to recognize a need.
  Strategy: Salesperson must show evidence that sparks the prospect's interest.
- Prospect lacks information on a new product or on the salesperson's company.
  Strategy: Salesperson must continually work to add value by providing useful information.

© Oliver Childs/iStockphoto

Secretaries, assistants, receptionists, and even voicemail can block the access to your prospect; they can be the gatekeepers.

Comments such as "Give me a couple of weeks to think it over" can save the buyer the discomfort of saying no at the end of a presentation. "Your price is too high" or "I have no money" are easy ways for purchasing agents not to buy a salesperson's offering. Price is probably the most often cited objection and usually is not the most important issue. It is obvious that buyers do not buy merely based on price; if this were true, then the lowest price supplier would get all of the business and eventually be the only supplier left selling the product. "No need at this time" is another typical objection. The buyer may not be in the market to purchase at this time.

It is not unusual for salespeople to encounter product objections. Most buyers have fears associated with buying a product. The buyer may be afraid that the product will not be as reliable as the salesperson said it would. Not only do the salespeople have to demonstrate that their product will perform at the level they say it will, but they must also show how it stacks up to the competition. A competitor introducing a new technology (e.g., e-commerce) may change the way a salesperson competes on a particular product line (e.g., office products).

Many buyers are constantly assessing their supplier on service (e.g., delivery, follow-up, warranties, guarantees, repairs, installation, and training). If the service is good and department heads are not complaining, the buyer is likely to stay with the status quo. Service is one variable that companies and salespeople can use to differentiate their product. Enterprise Rent-a-Car will deliver cars to the home of the renter and has made this difference a factor in its advertising. A salesperson for a wholesale distributor may make the point to a prospect that their fresh fruit, fish, and meat can be delivered daily when their competitors deliver only three times per week.

need objection Resistance to a product or service in which a buyer says that he or she does not need the product or service.

Many buyers will feel intense loyalty to their present suppliers and use this as a reason not to change. Buyers may be equally committed to the salesperson from whom they are currently buying. As a nonsupplier to the company, the salesperson must continue to call on the buyer and look for opportunities to build trust with the prospect. The salesperson may want to investigate whether the buyer has had any previous bad experience with his or her company that is causing the buyer not to do business with the company. Some salespeople and their buyers will not hit it off. The salesperson has to recognize these feelings and move on if several calls do not result in a sale.

At first glance, an inexperienced salesperson may be overwhelmed with the thought of how he or she will handle all the different types of objections buyers will raise. Salespeople need to develop skills in evaluating objections.[2] It does not take long, however, for a salesperson to learn that most objections fall into just a few categories. When preparing to buy a product or service, a prospect generally obtains information in five areas: need, product or service features, company or source, price, and timing of the buy. Objections could come from any of these areas, as shown in Exhibit 8.2.

Need Objections

Without a need, prospects have little or no reason to talk to a salesperson. If the prospect has been qualified properly, the salesperson believes the prospect has a need for the product. Many buyers have been conditioned to say automatically, "I do not need your product" (i.e., **need objection**). This may be the result of the buyer being out of budget or not having the time to look at your product or proposal. Other buyers may respond, "We are getting along just fine without your product. No one in my company is asking for your product. Call back in a few months and maybe something will change."

The salesperson has a tough challenge ahead if the buyer sincerely believes they have no need. It is the salesperson's job to establish a need in the buyer's mind; if the salesperson cannot do this then, logically, an objection can be expected.

EXHIBIT 8.2
Types of Objections

No need	Buyer has recently purchased or does not see a need for the product category. "I am not interested at this time."
Product or service objection	Buyer may be afraid of product reliability. "I am not sure the quality of your product meets our needs." Buyer may be afraid of late deliveries, slow repairs, etc. "I am happy with my present supplier's service."
Company objection	Buyer is intensely loyal to the present supplier. "I am happy with my present supplier."
Price is too high	Buyer has a limited budget. "We have been buying from another supplier that meets our budget constraints."
Time or delay	Buyer needs time to think it over. "Get back with me in a couple of weeks."

Many prospects do not know they have a specific need for a product until a situation occurs that makes them aware of it (i.e., engineering calls and needs a special software package). Therefore, objections to the need require the salesperson to stimulate the need awareness of the prospect with relevant information—features and benefits that pique the prospect's interest. Exhibit 8.3 summarizes a number of the no-need objections.

EXHIBIT 8.3
Possible Need Objections

"I have all I can use (all stocked up)."
"I do not need any."
"The equipment I have is still good."
"I am satisfied with the company we use now."
"We have no room for your line."

Product or Service Objections

Often the product or service lacks something that the buyer wants and the salesperson cannot deliver. A competitive advantage for a large software firm (Ontario) is that it has 24-hour 800 service available to all its customers. The firm's number-one competitor offers only 8:00 a.m. to 8:00 p.m. call-in phone service. For those clients that run three shifts and need 24-hour service, the choice is easy: they buy from Ontario.

Other prospect objections could be simply emotional—the prospect does not like the way the product looks or feels (i.e., **product or service objection**). Still others have a problem with the product's performance characteristics (i.e., "I need a copier that has colour and staples in the bin"). The salesperson also must do an adequate job of fact-finding and qualifying. Many of these issues can be resolved by knowing what the prospect is looking for.

Objections toward the product centre on understanding the fit between the product and the customer's needs. The salesperson's job is to learn what product features are important to the buyer and sell those features. Products are bundles of benefits that customers seek to fit their needs. Tying the benefits to the customer's needs helps the prospect bridge the gap from no-need to need. Exhibit 8.4 summarizes a number of product or service objections.

Company or Source Objections

Marty Reist is a manufacturer's representative for a small company in the sporting goods industry. He has to sell against many large competitors. Sales representatives

product or service objection Resistance to a product or service in which a buyer does not like the way the product or service looks or feels.

EXHIBIT 8.4
Possible Product or Service Objections

"I do not like the design, colour, or style."

"A maintenance agreement should be included."

"Performance of the product is unsatisfactory (e.g., the copier is too slow)."

"Packaging is too bulky".

"The product is incompatible with the present system (e.g., we prefer Apple over IBM)."

"The specifications do not match what we have now."

"How do I know if you will meet our delivery requirements?"

"The product is poor quality."

from Nike, Titleist, and Reebok probably do not have to work as hard to get past the gatekeepers. Reist, in contrast, must justify his existence every day. "I have never heard of your company" (i.e., **company or source objection**) is something Reist must continually overcome.

Other buyers may be happy with their present supplier. It is not unusual for buyer–seller relationships to last 10 to 15 years and even longer. Robert Carroll, a former sales representative from Monsanto Agricultural Division, heard the following quote from many of his farmers and farm co-ops, "I'm perfectly happy with Monsanto; my crops look good. I've been buying from them for years, and they have always treated me right." This is one of the hardest objections to overcome, especially if the prospect feels genuine loyalty to his or her present supplier.

company or source objection Resistance to a product or service that results when a buyer has never heard of or is not familiar with the product's company.

price objection Resistance to a product or service based on the price of the product being too high for the buyer.

Professional salespeople never criticize their competitors. The salesperson can point out any superior features their product or service might have. They can also ask for a single order and ask for an evaluation against the present supplier.

Another form of source objection is a negative attitude a buyer might have about the salesperson's company or the poor presentation of a previous salesperson. A buyer might remember a late or damaged order the company did not properly handle. A former salesperson may have made promises to the buyer and did not follow through on them. The salesperson must investigate any and all source objections. The salesperson may uncover source problems that can be overcome with time. Exhibit 8.5 outlines typical company or source objections.

Price Objections

Most sales experts agree that price is the most common form of buyer resistance.[3] This objection has the prospect saying that they cannot afford the product, the price is too high, or the product is not in their budget at this time (i.e., **price objection**). This objection may be a request for the salesperson to justify to the prospect how they can afford the product or how they can work it into their budget. Most salespeople feel the price objection is an attempt by the buyer to get the salesperson to lower his or her price. The salesperson must address the price objection by citing how the benefits (value) outweigh the cost. To do this, the product's value must be established before the salesperson spends time discussing price.[4] Many companies never sell as the low-cost option. Stryker Medical sells hospital beds and stretchers to hospitals and emergency rooms. Stryker never offers the lowest cost. Stryker's salespeople almost always hear the price objection. First, they have to educate their prospects and customers that their

EXHIBIT 8.5
Company or Source Objections

"Your company is too small to meet my needs."

"I have never heard of your company."

"Your company is too big. I will get lost in the shuffle."

"Your company is pretty new. How do I know you will be around to take care of me in the future?"

"Your company was recently in the newspaper. Are you having problems?"

products last 25 to 50 percent longer than their competitor's products. They can demonstrate with evidence their product will still be around 5 to 10 years after their competitor's has been discarded. If one of their stretchers is $1,500 more than their competitor's, they must break down the price over the entire life of the stretcher. They can actually show a savings over time. By providing the right information, Stryker can show value over the competitor's offering.

Price objections probably occur more frequently than any other type. Price objections may be used to cover the real reason for a reluctance to buy. Probing and asking questions are the salesperson's tools to get to the real reasons for a buyer's objection. Exhibit 8.6 summarizes a number of price objections.

Time Objections

Buyers use the **time objection**, or as some salespeople call it the *stalling objection*, to put off the decision to buy until a later date. Many inexperienced salespeople hear this technique and believe the prospect is going to buy in the future but not today. Some buyers use this technique to get rid of salespeople so that the buyer does not have to reject the salesperson and his or her sales proposal formally. Sometimes proposals are very complex and the buyer does need time to think them over. The salesperson must be sensitive to this and not push too hard to get an answer until the buyer has had adequate time to make a decision. It is acceptable for the salesperson to review the reasons to act now or soon. Waiting can have consequences (e.g., prices rise, a new tax begins the first of the year) and the buyer should be made aware of these. Exhibit 8.7 illustrates possible time objections.

EXHIBIT 8.6
Price Objections

"We cannot afford it."

"I cannot afford to spend that much right now."

"That is 30 percent higher than your competitor's comparable model."

"We have a better offer from your competitor."

"I need something a lot cheaper."

"Your price is not different enough to change suppliers."

EXHIBIT 8.7
Time Objections

"I need time to think it over."

"Ask me again next month when you stop by."

"I am not ready to buy yet."

"I have not made up my mind."

"I do not want to commit myself until I have had a chance to talk to engineering (or any other department)."

8-4 USING LAARC: A PROCESS FOR NEGOTIATING BUYER RESISTANCE

The term **LAARC** is an acronym for listen, acknowledge, assess, respond, and confirm and describes an effective process for salespeople to follow to overcome sales resistance. The LAARC method is a customer-oriented way to keep the sales dialogue positive. In the early days of sales, buyers and sellers were not always truthful with each other, and manipulation was the norm. Although being persuasive is necessary to be an effective sales representative, having such a singular focus can have a detrimental effect on customer rapport and relationships.[5] Salespeople who said whatever it took to get an order—who overpromised and underdelivered and misrepresented their offering—were sometimes looked on favourably by their selling organization. Professional sellers today want to keep the dialogue open and build goodwill by adding value to their proposition. By listening to buyers' concerns and negotiating through open dialogue, the seller increases the likelihood of purchase decisions being made on a favourable basis, and this leads to long-term relationships. Thus, it is the salesperson's job to communicate and demonstrate value when sales resistance arises.

time objection Resistance to a product or service in which a buyer puts off the decision to buy until a later date.

LAARC An acronym for listen, acknowledge, assess, respond, and confirm that describes an effective process for salespeople to follow to overcome sales resistance.

Here is a description of LAARC:

- *Listen:* Salespeople should listen to what their buyers are saying. The ever-present temptation to anticipate what buyers are going to say and cut them off with a premature response should be avoided. Learning to listen is important—it is more than just being polite or professional. Buyers are trying to tell the salesperson something that they consider important.
- *Acknowledge:* As buyers complete their statements, salespeople should acknowledge that they received the message and that they appreciate and can understand the concern. Salespeople should not jump in with an instantaneous defensive response. Before responding, salespeople need a better understanding about what their buyers are saying. By politely pausing and then simply acknowledging their statement, a salesperson establishes that he or she is a reasonable person—a professional who appreciates other people's opinions. It also buys a salesperson precious moments for composing his or her thoughts and thinking of questions for the next step.
- *Assess:* This step is similar to assessment in the ADAPT process of questioning. This step in dealing with buyer resistance calls for salespeople to ask assessment questions to gain a better understanding of exactly what their buyers are saying and why they are saying it. Equipped with this information and understanding, salespeople are better able to make a meaningful response to the buyer's resistance.
- *Respond:* Based on his or her understanding of what and why the buyer is resisting, the salesperson can respond to the buyer's resistance. Structuring a response typically follows the method that is most appropriate for the situation. The more traditional methods of response (see Exhibit 8.8) include forestalling, direct denial, indirect denial, translation (or boomerang), compensation, question, third-party reinforcement (or feel-felt-found), and "coming to that." In "An Ethical Dilemma," MaryAnne Noffke considers using one technique to handle sales resistance that should never be used by a professional salesperson.

These techniques have been used both positively and negatively. Professional salespeople use these techniques to add value to their proposal. For instance, the translation or boomerang technique can be used quite effectively if the salesperson has gathered the appropriate information to support his or her response. The buyer might state, "Your company is too big, and we might slip through the cracks as a small customer." The salesperson might respond, "That is exactly why you want to do business with us. We are larger, and we are going to be able to offer you all of the levels of expertise you said you needed. Smaller companies will not be able to do this, and you will eventually have to search for another supplier. We are one-stop shopping, and we will make sure you will not fall through the cracks." Here, the salesperson took a reason not to buy and translated it into a reason to buy. Much dialogue had to go on before this for the salesperson to be able to provide the proper information to overcome the concern. Exhibit 8.8 includes examples of

An Ethical Dilemma

MaryAnne Noffke has been in sales for several years and had run into a number of difficult sales objections. She saw several orders go to her competitors because of her inability to answer these objections effectively. MaryAnne brought this issue up with her sales manager and he advised her to tell the prospect she was going to cover the concern later in the presentation. Her manager said even though she did not have an answer hopefully her prospect would forget and not bring up the objection again. How should MaryAnne handle this situation?

a) MaryAnne should obey orders and do what her sales manager suggested.
b) MaryAnne should tell her sales manager she is uncomfortable with his suggested tactic.
c) MaryAnne should tell her boss she will try his advice to keep him happy, but not try it once in the field.

EXHIBIT 8.8

Techniques to Answer Concerns

Technique	How It Works	Example
Forestalling	Take care of the objection before the prospect brings it up.	Many of my customers have had a concern going into my presentation that we do not have a warranty program. Let me put this to rest: we have one-, three-, and five-year warranty programs that match our competitors. I hope this answers your concern.
Direct denial	A rather harsh response that the prospect is wrong.	You have heard incorrectly. We are not raising prices.
Indirect denial	Softening the blow when correcting a prospect's information.	We have heard that rumour, too—even some of our best customers asked us about it. Our senior management team has guaranteed us our prices will hold firm through the rest of the year.
Translation or boomerang	Turn a reason not to buy into a reason *to* buy.	Buyer: Your company is too small to meet our needs. Salesperson: That is just the reason you want to do business with us. Because we are smaller, you will get the individual attention you said you wanted.
Compensation	Counterbalance the objection with an offsetting benefit.	Yes, our price is higher, but you are going to get the quality you said that you needed to keep your customers happy.
Questioning or assessing	Ask the buyer assessment questions to gain a better understanding of what they are objecting to.	Your concern is price. Can you please tell me who you are comparing us with, and does that quote include any service agreement?
Third-party reinforcement	Use the opinion or data from a third-party source to help overcome the objection.	Bill Middleton from Dial Electronics had the same concern going in. Let me tell you why he is comfortable with our proposal. . . .
Feel-felt-found	Salesperson relates that others actually found their initial opinions to be unfounded.	Buyer: I do not think my customers will want to buy a product with all those features. We generally sell scaled-down models. Salesperson: I can certainly see how you feel. Lisa Richardson down the road in Brandon felt the same way when I first proposed that she go with these models. However, after she agreed to display them in the front of her store, she found that her customers started buying the models with more features—and that, in turn, provided her with larger margins. In fact, she called me less than a week later to order more!
Coming-to-that	The salesperson tells the buyer that he or she will be covering the objection later in his or her presentation.	Buyer: I have some concerns about your delivery dates. Salesperson: I am glad you brought that up. Before fully discussing our delivery, I want to go over the features that you said were important to you that will help you better understand our product. Is that okay?

how a salesperson might respond to buyer concerns in a professional manner.

- *Confirm:* After responding, the salesperson should ask confirmatory questions—response-checks to make sure that the buyer's concerns have been adequately met. Once this is confirmed, the presentation can proceed. In fact, experience indicates that this form of buyer confirmation is often a sufficient buying signal to warrant the salesperson's attempt to gain a commitment.

8-5 RECOMMENDED APPROACHES FOR RESPONDING TO OBJECTIONS

A brief description of traditional methods for responding to objections follows. Exhibit 8.8 summarizes how each technique works.

Forestalling

When salespeople hear an objection arising repeatedly, they may decide to include an answer to the objection within their sales presentation before it is voiced by the prospect (i.e., **forestalling**). Marty Reist of MPRS Sales Inc. often tells his prospects he realizes he is not Nike, Titleist, or Reebok, but his size has not kept him from providing outstanding service to his customers. Reist can add a third-party testimonial to back up his statements and put his prospect's mind at ease. This technique should be used only when there is a high probability that the prospect will indeed raise the objection.[6]

forestalling A response to buyer objections in which the salesperson answers the objection during the presentation before the buyer has a chance to ask it.

direct denial A response to buyer objections in which the salesperson tells the customer that he or she is wrong.

indirect denial A response to buyer objections in which the salesperson takes a softer, more tactful approach when correcting a prospect or customer's information.

translation or **boomerang** A response to buyer objections in which the salesperson converts the objection into a reason the prospect should buy.

Direct Denial

When using the **direct denial** technique to handle sales resistance, the salesperson is directly telling the customer that he or she is mistaken. Prospects may have incorrect facts or may not understand the information they have. The prospect might say the following:

Prospect: I hear you do not offer service agreements on any of your products.

The salesperson, knowing this is not true, cannot soft-pedal his or her answer. In this situation, the prospect is clearly incorrect and the direct denial is the best solution.

Salesperson: I am sorry, that is not correct. We offer three- and five-year service contracts, and our warranty is also five years.

The important part of using the direct denial is not to humiliate or anger the prospect. The direct denial should be used sparingly, but it may be easier to use when the salesperson has a good feel for the relationship that he or she has with the buyer.

Indirect Denial

Sometimes it is best not to take an objection head on. The indirect approach takes on the objection, but with a softer, more tactful approach. With the **indirect denial**, the salesperson never tells the prospect directly that he or she is wrong. The best way to use this method is to think of it as offering sympathy with the prospect's view and still managing to correct the invalid objection of the buyer. An example follows:

Prospect: I heard that your emergency room beds are $4,000 more than your competitor's.

Salesperson: Many of our customers had a similar notion that our beds are much more expensive. The actual cost is only $1,200 higher. I have testimonials from other hospitals stating that our beds last up to five years longer. You'll actually save money.

The salesperson here tries to soften the blow with the opening sentence. Then the salesperson must correct the misconception. Techniques can be combined as the salesperson adds information from a third party to lend credibility to his or her statement.

Translation or Boomerang

The **translation** or **boomerang** method converts the objection into a reason that the prospect should buy. What the salesperson is trying to do is to take a reason not to buy and turn it into a reason to buy. Marty Reist of MPRS Sales Inc. offers the following advice:

Whenever I hear the objection "I don't think your company is large enough to meet our service needs," I immediately come back with "that is exactly the reason you should do business with us. We are big enough to meet your service needs. In fact, you will be calling an 800 number with a larger company and you won't know who you'll get to help you. With our company, anytime you have a problem, question, or concern, you'll call me and talk to a familiar voice."

Another example using the price objection might go like this:

Buyer: "Your price appears to be high."
Salesperson: "Our high price is an advantage for you; the premium sector of the market not only gives you the highest margin but it is also the most stable sector of the market."

The goal of the translation or boomerang method is to turn an apparent deficiency into an asset or reason to buy.

Compensation

There may be a time when a salesperson has to admit that his or her product does have the disadvantage that the prospect has noticed. The **compensation** technique is an attempt to show the prospect that a benefit or an advantage compensates for an objection. For example, a higher product price is justified by benefits, such as better service, faster delivery, or higher performance.

A buyer may use the objection that your company's lead time is 14 days compared with 10 days for your main competitor. The salesperson's response could be: "Yes, our required lead time is 14 days, but we ship our orders completely assembled. This practically eliminates extra handling in your warehouse. My competitor's product will require assembly by your warehouse workers."

With the compensation method, the objection is not denied at all—it is acknowledged and then balanced by compensating features, advantages, and benefits.

compensation A response to buyer objections in which the salesperson counterbalances the objection with an offsetting benefit.

questioning or **assessing** A response to buyer objections in which the salesperson asks the buyer assessment questions to gain a better understanding of what the buyer is objecting to.

Questioning or Assessing

Another potentially effective way to handle buyer resistance is to convert the objection into a question. This technique calls for the salesperson to ask **questions** or **assess** to gain a better understanding of the precise nature of the buyer's objections. Sometimes it is difficult for the salesperson to know the exact problem. This technique is good for clarifying the real objection. This technique can also be effective in resolving the objection if the prospect is shooting from the hip and does not have a strong reason for the objection. In "Professional Selling in the 21st Century: Poppin' the Question," Dave Voelker describes how "too often salespeople want to rush the sales process without doing all of the proper ground work. Effective questioning and listening will lead to less sales resistance and more closes." Exhibit 8.9 illustrates the questioning method as a tool to overcome sales resistance.

EXHIBIT 8.9
Questioning (Assessing) to Overcome Sales Resistance

Example 1

Buyer:	I am not sure I am ready to act at this time.
Salesperson:	Can you tell me what is causing your hesitation?

Example 2

Buyer:	Your price seems to be a little high.
Salesperson:	Can you tell me what price you had in mind? Have other suppliers quoted you a lower price?

Example 3

Buyer:	Your delivery schedule does not work for us.
Salesperson:	To whom are you comparing me? Can you please tell me what delivery schedule will work for your company?

© davidf/iStockphoto

Professional Selling in the 21st Century

Poppin'the Question

David Voelker, an independent sales consultant, makes a case for taking the time to do all the appropriate groundwork.

Think back to the minute you decided she was the one for you—the one you wanted to spend the rest of your life with. So, did you ask her then? Probably not. Instead, you took time to make her aware of your feelings and to learn more about her. Endless dinners, movies, telephone hours and, simply put, time to get to know her came next. You needed to be sure you two would be a match. How about her family and her friends? What was most important to her and what could potentially be a deal breaker? By the time you "popped the question," you knew the answer. All the ground work had been properly laid in preparation for this one magic moment. And she said, "Yes!"

Too often in sales we want to rush the process. We trade an initial "good feeling" for a genuine buying signal. We hurry the process and attempt to rush the decision. Let's face it—all the signals can be wasted if we skip important facts we must know about our prospect. Listen, and then listen some more. By the time you ask for the close, you should be hearing wedding bells in the distance.

third-party reinforcement A response to buyer objections in which the salesperson uses the opinion or data from a third-party source to help overcome the objection and reinforce the salesperson's points.

Third-Party Reinforcement: Feel-Felt-Found

The **third-party reinforcement** technique uses the opinion or research of a third person or company to help overcome and reinforce the salesperson's sales points. Salespeople today can use a wide range of proof statements. Consumer reports, government reports, and independent testing agencies can all be used to back up a salesperson's statement. Secondary data such as this, or experience data from a reliable third party, could be all that is needed to turn around a skeptical prospect. A salesperson must remember that this technique will work only if the buyer believes in the third-party source that the salesperson is using.

A version of using third-party reinforcement is the feel-felt-found method. Here, the salesperson goes on to relate that others found their initial beliefs to be unfounded after they tried the product. Salespeople need to practise this method—when used in the correct sequence, it can be very effective. Again, the strength of the person and company being used as an example is critical to how much influence the reference will have on the prospect.

Coming-to-That or Postpone

Salespeople need to understand that objections may and will be made to almost everything concerning them, their products, and their company. Good salespeople anticipate these objections and develop effective answers, but sometimes it may make sense to cover an objection later in the presentation, after additional questioning and information is provided. The salesperson should evaluate how important the concern is to the prospect—and, if the objection seems to be critical to the sale, the salesperson should address it immediately.

Once the salesperson has answered all the buyer's questions and has resolved resistance issues that have come up during the presentation, the salesperson should summarize all the pertinent buying signals (i.e., fair price, acceptable delivery dates, and good service agreement).

Summarizing Solutions to Confirm Benefits

The mark of a good salesperson is the ability to listen and determine the customer's exact needs. It is not unusual for salespeople to incorporate the outstanding benefits of their product into the sales presentation. A salesperson can identify many potential benefits for each product and feature. However, it does not make sense for a salesperson to talk about potential benefits that the buyer may not need. The salesperson must determine the confirmed benefits and make these the focal point of the sales summary before asking for the business. A salesperson must be alert to the one, two, or three benefits that generate the most excitement to the buyer. The confirmed benefits of greatest interest to the buyer deserve the greatest emphasis. These benefits should be summarized in such a way that the buyer sees a direct connection in what he or she has been telling the salesperson over the course of the selling cycle and the proposal being offered to meet his or her needs. Once this is done, it is time to ask for the business.

8-6 Securing Commitment and Closing

Ultimately, a large part of most salespeople's performance evaluation is based on their ability to gain customer commitment, often called closing sales. Because of this close relationship between compensation and getting orders, traditional selling has tended to overemphasize the importance of gaining a commitment.[7] In fact, there are those who think that just about any salesperson can find a new prospect, open a sale, or take an order. These same people imply it takes a trained, motivated, and skilled professional to close a sale. They go on to say that the close is the keystone to a salesperson's success, and a good salesperson will have mastered many new ways to close the sale. This outmoded emphasis on closing skills is typical of transaction selling techniques that stress making the sales call at all costs.

Another popular but outdated suggestion to salespeople is to "close early and often." This is particularly bad advice if the prospect is not prepared to make a decision, responds negatively to a premature attempt to consummate the sale, and then (following the principles of cognitive consistency) proceeds to reinforce the prior negative position as the salesperson plugs away, firing one closing salvo after another at the beleaguered prospect. Research tells us that it will take several sales calls to make an initial sale, so it is somewhat bewildering to still encounter such tired old battle cries as "the ABCs of selling, which stand for Always Be Closing." Research based on more than 35,000 sales calls over a 12-year period suggests that an overreliance on closing techniques actually reduces the chance of making a sale.[8]

Manipulative closing gimmicks are less likely to be effective as professional buyers grow weary of the cat-and-mouse approach to selling that a surprising number of salespeople still practise. It is also surprising to find many salespeople who view their customers as combatants over whom victory is sought. Once salespeople who have adversarial, me-against-you attitudes make the sale, the customer is likely to be neglected as the salesperson rides off into the sunset in search of yet another battle with yet another lowly customer.

One time-honoured thought that does retain contemporary relevance is that "nobody likes to be sold, but everybody likes to buy." In other words, salespeople should facilitate decision making by pointing out a suggested course of action but should allow the prospect plenty of mental space within which a rational decision can be reached.[9] Taken to its logical conclusion, this means that it may be acceptable to make a sales call without asking for the order. Salespeople must be cognizant, however, of their responsibility to advance the relationship toward a profitable sale, lest they become the most dreaded of all types of salespeople—the paid conversationalist.

It has already been mentioned that the salesperson has taken on the expanded roles of business consultant and relationship manager, which is not consistent with pressuring customers until they give in and say yes. Fortunately, things have changed to the point that today's professional salesperson attempts to gain commitment when the buyer is ready to buy. The salesperson should evaluate each presentation and attempt to determine the causes of its success or failure with the customer. The difference between closing and earning commitment is that commitment is more than just securing an order. Commitment signals the beginning of a long-term relationship.

GUIDELINES FOR EARNING COMMITMENT

Earning commitment is the culmination of the selling process. However, it should not be viewed as a formal stage that comes only at the end of the presentation. Many salespeople fail to recognize early buyer commitment by focusing on their presentation rather than on the comments the buyer is making. **Commitment signals** are favourable statements that may be made by the buyer, such as

- "I like that size."
- "That will get the job done."
- "The price is lower than I thought it would be."
- "I did not realize you delivered every day."

These statements should be considered green lights that allow the salesperson to move the process forward. Positive statements by the buyer should start the process of determining the best time to close. Ultimately the salesperson should ask for the order when the buyer has enough information to make an informed decision. Making sure the buyer has the right information to make an intelligent decision is the main goal of a salesperson's sales presentation. Normally the earning commitment question is asked when the sales presentation is completed and all the questions and sales resistances have been successfully addressed. Commitment may also be determined through the use of trial commitments.

Throughout the presentation, it is appropriate to determine a prospect's reaction to a particular feature or product. At this time, a trial commitment is a question designed to determine a prospect's reaction without forcing the prospect to make a final "yes or no" buying decision. The trial commitment is an effort to elicit how far along the prospect is in his or her decision making. Confirmation on the prospect's part on key features helps the salesperson determine how ready the prospect is to buy. A trial commitment can be used many times throughout a salesperson's presentation to test the buyer's level of commitment and for the salesperson to gain confirmed benefits. Exhibit 8.10 summarizes both verbal and nonverbal buying signals.

commitment signals Favourable statements a buyer makes during a sales presentation that signal buyer commitment.

Open-end questions are a good way to test a prospect's readiness to buy. A salesperson might ask during his or her presentation, "What do you think of our computer's larger memory capacity?" The answer to this will help direct the salesperson to his or her next sales points. However, many statements buyers make should be considered red lights, or formal objections. The salesperson must consider each of these objections and work to overcome them. Red light statements might include the following:

- "I am not sure that will work."
- "The price is higher than I thought it would be."
- "Your delivery schedule does not work for us."
- "I do not see the advantage of going with your proposal."

Red-light statements are commitment caution signals and must be resolved to the buyer's satisfaction before asking for a commitment. Closing early and often and having a closing quota for each sales call are traditional methods that buyers do not like. Nathan Schmidt in "Professional Selling in the 21st Century: Listening Leads to Earning Commitment" states that it is better to replace numerous closing efforts with better listening skills. The salesperson should put himself or herself in the buyer's shoes and think about how he or she would like to be hammered with many closes throughout a sales presentation, particularly if a few red lights are introduced. Many times, the best method for earning commitment is simply to ask for the business. If the prospect has been qualified properly and a number of confirmed benefits have been uncovered, then naturally the next step is to ask for the business.

EXHIBIT 8.10
Favourable Buying Signals

When the prospect:

- Makes a positive statement about the product
- Asks who else has bought the product
- Asks about price, delivery, installation, dates, or service
- Asks about methods of payment
- Begins to study and handle the product
- Appears more relaxed
- Begins to interact more intently with the salesperson

TECHNIQUES TO EARN COMMITMENT

Some sales trainers will try to teach their salesforces literally hundreds of commitment techniques. One trainer recommended to his salesforce that the salespeople learn two new commitment techniques per week. Then at the end of the year, they would have more than 100 commitment techniques ready to use. Relationship managers today do not need many commitment techniques. A few good ones will suffice. Five techniques that are conducive to relationship building follow:

© nicolas/iStockphoto

PROFESSIONAL SELLING IN THE 21ST CENTURY

Listening Leads to Earning Commitment

Nathan Schmidt, Senior Sales Representative for PCE Insurance Group, has learned over the years that listening skills are critical for success in earning commitment. Nathan states,

It takes time to develop trust with a client. I try to ask several early questions of the buyer which gets them to talk about their present situation and any problems they may have at this time when dealing with their insurance issues. When it is time to present, I can use the information I gathered to make sure during my presentation that I am providing the right information that will reduce the risk in their decision-making process. I close when the buyer has enough information to make an intelligent decision. That comes from good listening and by providing my prospect (client) the right information. Once the information has been thoroughly reviewed by my buyer, then I attempt to earn their commitment.

1. **Ask for the Order/Direct Commitment.** It is not unusual for inexperienced salespeople to lose an order simply by not asking the customer to buy. Professional buyers report that an amazing number of salespeople fear rejection. When the buyer is ready to buy, the salesperson must be prepared to ask for the buyer's commitment. The **direct commitment** technique is a straightforward request for an order. A salesperson should be confident if he or she has covered all the necessary features and benefits of the product and matched these with the buyer's needs. At this time, the salesperson cannot be afraid to ask "Tom, can we set up an office visit for next week?" or "Mary, I would like to have your business; if we can get the order signed today, delivery can take place early next week." Many buyers appreciate the direct approach. There is no confusion as to what the salesperson wants the buyer to do.
2. **Legitimate Choice/Alternative Choice.** The **alternative or legitimate choice** technique asks the prospect to select from two or more choices. For example, "Will the HP 400 or the HP 600 work best for you?" An investment broker might ask his or her prospect, "Do you feel your budget would allow you to invest $1,000 a month or would $500 a month be better?" The theory behind this technique suggests buyers do not like to be told what to do but do like making a decision among limited choices.
3. **Summary Commitment.** A very effective way to gain agreement is to summarize all the major benefits the buyer has confirmed during the sales calls. Salespeople should keep track of all the important points covered in previous calls so they can emphasize them again in summary form.

In using the summary commitment technique, a computer salesperson

direct commitment A selling technique in which the salesperson asks the customer directly to buy.

alternative or legitimate choice A selling technique in which the salesperson asks the prospect to select from two or more choices during a sales presentation.

summary commitment A selling technique in which the salesperson summarizes all the major benefits the buyer has confirmed during the sales calls.

T-account or **balance sheet commitment** A selling technique in which a salesperson asks the prospect to brainstorm reasons on paper of why to buy and why not to buy.

success story commitment A selling technique in which a salesperson relates how one of his or her customers had a problem similar to the prospect's and solved it by using the salesperson's product.

might say, "Of course, Tom, this is an important decision, so to make the best possible choice, let us go over the major concepts we have discussed. We have agreed that Thompson Computers will provide some definite advantages. First, our system will lower your computing costs; second, our system will last longer and has a better warranty, thus saving you money; and finally, your data processing people will be happier because our faster system will reduce their workload. They will get to go home earlier each evening."

Good salespeople are never in a hurry to earn commitment!

The **summary commitment** is a valuable technique because it reminds prospects of all the major benefits that have been mentioned in previous sales calls.

4. **The T-Account or the Balance Sheet Commitment.** The **T-account commitment** or **balance sheet commitment** is essentially a summary commitment on paper. With the T-account commitment, the sales representative takes out a sheet of paper and draws a large "T" across it. On the left-hand side, the salesperson and buyer brainstorm the reasons to buy. Here, the salesperson will list with the buyer all the positive selling points (benefits) they discussed throughout the selling process. Once this is completed, the salesperson asks the buyer for any reasons that he or she would not want to purchase. Visually, the left-hand side should help the buyer make his or her decision, as shown in Exhibit 8.11. This will not work if the weight of the reasons not to buy outweighs the reasons to buy. In the example in Exhibit 8.11, the buyer wants to act but does not have the money at this time.

5. **Success Story Commitment.** Every company has many satisfied customers. These customers started out having problems, and the sales representative helped solve these problems by recommending the product or products that matched the customer's needs. Buyers are thankful and grateful when the salesperson helps solve problems. When the salesperson relates a story about how one of his or her customers had a similar problem and solved it by using the salesperson's product, a reluctant buyer can be reassured that the salesperson has done this before successfully. If the salesperson decides to use the customer's name and company, then the salesperson must be sure to get permission to do so. A **success story commitment** may go something like this: Tom, thanks for sharing your copier problems with me. I had another customer you might know, Betty Brown, who had the same problem over at Thompson Electronics. We installed the CP 2000 and eliminated the problem completely. Please feel free to give Betty a call. She is very happy with our solution.

Some companies will use the success story commitment by actually taking the prospect to a satisfied customer. The salesperson may leave the prospect alone

EXHIBIT 8.11
T-Account Close

Reasons to Buy	Reasons Not to Buy
• Daily delivery schedule meets our needs	• Because of extra services
• Warranty agreement is longer than the one I have now (five years versus three years)	• Your price *is too high; I can't afford it*
• You provide a training program	
• Your service department is located in our city	

EXHIBIT 8.12
Techniques to Earn Commitment

1. Direct commitment—Simply ask for the order.
2. Legitimate choice/alternative choice—Give the prospect a limited number of choices.
3. Summary commitment—Summarize all the confirmed benefits to which there has been agreement.
4. T-account/balance sheet commitment—Summary close on paper.
5. Success story commitment—Salesperson tells a story of a business that successfully solved a problem by buying his or her products.

with the satisfied customer so the two can talk confidentially. A satisfied customer can help a salesperson earn commitment by answering questions a reluctant prospect needs answered before he or she can purchase. Exhibit 8.12 shows a summary of relationship-building earning commitment techniques.

PROBE TO EARN COMMITMENT

Not every attempt to earn commitment will be successful. Successful salespeople cannot be afraid to ask a prospect why he or she is hesitating to make a decision. It is the salesperson's job to uncover the reason why the prospect is hesitating by asking a series of questions that reveal the key issues. For instance, a buyer may state that he or she is not ready to sign an order. The salesperson must ask, "Mary, there must be a reason why you are reluctant to do business with me and my company. Do you mind if I ask what it is?" The salesperson must then listen and respond accordingly. A salesperson cannot be afraid to ask why a prospect is reluctant to purchase.

TRADITIONAL METHODS

Sales trainers across the nation teach hundreds of techniques to earn commitment. Exhibit 8.13 is a summary of the traditional commitment techniques. The vast majority of these are not conducive to building a strong buyer–seller relationship. As prospects become more sophisticated, most will be turned off by these techniques and they will be ineffective.

standing-room-only close A sales closing technique in which the salesperson puts a time limit on the client in an attempt to hurry the decision to close.

assumptive close A sales closing technique in which the salesperson assumes that an agreement has been reached, places the order form in front of the buyer, and hands him or her a pen.

fear or emotional close A sales closing technique in which the salesperson tells a story of something bad happening if the purchase is not made.

continuous yes close A sales closing technique that uses the principle that saying yes gets to be a habit; the salesperson asks a number of questions formulated so that the prospect answers yes.

minor-points close A sales closing technique in which the salesperson seeks agreement on relatively minor issues associated with the full order.

EXHIBIT 8.13
Traditional Commitment Method

Method	How to Use It
standing-room-only close	This close puts a time limit on the client in an attempt to hurry the decision to close. "These prices are good only until tomorrow."
assumptive close	The salesperson assumes that an agreement has been reached. The salesperson places the order form in front of the buyer and hands him or her a pen.
fear or emotional close	The salesperson tells a story of something bad happening if the purchase is not made. "If you do not purchase this insurance and you die, your wife will have to sell the house and live on the street."
continuous yes close	This close uses the principle that saying yes gets to be a habit. The salesperson asks a number of questions, each formulated so that the prospect answers yes.
minor-points close	Seeks agreement on relatively minor (trivial) issues associated with the full order. "Do you prefer cash or charge?"

"An Ethical Dilemma" illustrates that sometimes buyers will put a condition on the close.

Research has clearly shown that buyers are open to consultative techniques of handling objections (e.g., questioning and assessing, direct denial with facts, and so on) and earning commitment (e.g., asking for the order in a straightforward manner, summarizing key benefits). However, buyers have stated that standard persuasive (traditional) tactics that have been used for years are unacceptable. They now view traditional techniques of handling objections (e.g., forestalling, postponing) and earning commitment (e.g., standing-room only, fear) as overly aggressive and unprofessional.[10]

© iStock/Thinkstock

An Ethical Dilemma

Emily Ellison has just returned from a sales call at a local school system. Her company sells office equipment and the school system's buyer made her an interesting proposition. He told her she could close the sale if her firm donated $2,000 needed for new band uniforms. Emily took this information back to her boss, who said "Go ahead and do it, but keep this quiet so other school systems don't ask for the same treatment." This will be a $75,000 sale for Emily, her biggest of the year. Emily was worried the word would get out and other prospects would start asking for donations. What should Emily do next, now that she has been told by her boss to accept the order? How would you handle this situation?

a) Obey orders and process the order.
b) Tell your boss that you are uncomfortable making that type of sale and that you no longer want to be involved.
c) Tell your boss that you don't think the situation is fair but go ahead and do it anyway—ultimately it's her call to make.

CHAPTER 8 CASE

MARTICHENKO ENGINEERING

Background

Rob Dwhytie sells for Martichenko Engineering. He has been calling on Hudson Distributors for close to two years. Over the course of 15 calls, he has sold nothing to date. During an early call, Dwhytie had Hudson's engineers in to look over and test the quality of his products. The tests and the engineers' responses were positive. He thinks that he is extremely close to getting an order. Dwhytie knows that Hudson is happy with its present supplier, but he is aware that they have received some late deliveries. Tom Harris, Hudson's senior buyer, has given every indication that he likes Dwhytie's products and Dwhytie.

Current Situation

During Dwhytie's most recent call, Harris told him that he'd need a couple of weeks to go over Dwhytie's proposal. Harris really didn't have any major objections during the presentation. Dwhytie knows his price, quality, and service are equal to or exceed Hudson's present supplier.

Questions

1. Harris told Dwhytie that he needed a couple of weeks to think about his proposal. How should Dwhytie handle this?
2. What should Dwhytie have done during the sales presentation when Harris told him that he needed to think it over?
3. What techniques should Dwhytie have used to overcome the forestalling tactic?

Role Play

Situation: Read Case 8; Martichenko Engineering

Characters: Rob Dwhytie, sales representative; Tom Harris, senior buyer

Scene 1:

Location—Harris's office

Action—Harris has just stated that he needs a couple of weeks to go over Dwhytie's proposal.

Role play how Dwhytie should respond to Harris needing two weeks to think it over.

Scene 2:

Location—Harris's office

Action—Dwhytie is summarizing his product's advantages (i.e., price, quality, service).

Role play Dwhytie's summary and his asking for the order.

Upon completion of the role play, address the following questions:

1. Why do buyers hesitate and ask for more time to think over proposals?
2. How hard should Dwhytie press to get Harris to act now?

CHAPTER 8

Role Play: Addressing Concerns and Earning Commitment: ACampbell Engineering

Dan Harris has been selling for ACampbell Engineering for six months. Most of the first four months were spent in training learning ACampbell's products. He spent another two weeks learning their selling process and shadowed one of their senior reps for a couple of weeks. He has barely been in the field a month and is feeling frustrated. Dan was given a hot lead the first day in the field (Parker Distributors), and the past four weeks he has made seven calls on Parker. Dan feels he is close to getting an order from Parker. Dan knows Parker is fairly happy with their present supplier, but he is aware that they have received several late deliveries. Karen Williams, Parker's senior buyer, has given every indication that she likes ACampbell's products and Dan.

During Dan's most recent call, Williams told him she'd have to have a couple of weeks to go over his proposal. Williams really didn't have any major objections during his presentation. Dan knows his price, quality, and service are equal to or exceed Williams's present supplier. Williams did say she wasn't looking forward to calling their present supplier to tell them about doing business with ACampbell Engineering if she decided to change.

Role Play

Location: Karen Williams's office

Action: Role play Karen Williams telling Dan Harris she needs a couple of weeks to think over his proposal. Discuss the sales resistance of forestalling Williams is using and how Dan is going to overcome the objection (use LAARC). Also, role play Williams's concern telling her present supplier they are switching suppliers.

© iStock/Thinkstock

Repeat business

is the lifeline of an organization.

9

Expanding Customer Relationships

After completing this chapter, you should be able to

9-1 Explain how to follow up to assess and take action to ensure customer satisfaction by using the latest technology.

9-2 Discuss how to expand collaborative involvement.

9-3 Explain how to add value and enhance mutual opportunities.

Introduction

As the following vignette illustrates, customer relationships can be enhanced by adding value after the initial sale.

Wausau Paper, located in Mosinee, Wisconsin, is a principal producer of premium printing, writing, and technical specialty papers, as well as towel and tissue products, which does more than $1 billion a year in sales. Its success, in part, has come from its ability to create a competitive advantage in an environment in which its customer base has become increasingly price sensitive, thanks to Michael Nelson, Wausau's vice president of sales and marketing.

Nelson has instituted what he refers to as the "Value Delivery Framework," in which salespeople are asked to develop strategic relationships with key customers by closely incorporating Wausau Paper into those customers' businesses. According to Nelson, the objective is to "get beyond the traditional product orientation by collaborating with customers on the key dimensions of innovation, supply chain, and working-capital efficiencies and turnkey marketing programs, all in an effort to create value." The result has been an increase in customers who commit to multi-year partnerships.

This strategy has allowed for negotiating price on the front end of long-term agreements so that salespeople can concentrate on improving customers' business. For instance, salespeople at Wausau were able to help one consumer packaged-goods customer move into the ecosensitive product market. This helped the customer to gain first-mover advantage. In another example, Wausau was able to help a customer improve its forecasting, which enabled Wausau to improve this customer's service at reduced inventory levels. Wausau currently works closely with 15 to 20 percent of its customers and hopes to grow that to about 35 percent of its customers. The remaining customers are not interested in working closely with Wausau, as their main concern is price.

The change in strategy at Wausau has resulted in several changes in the way its salespeople operate. Salespeople now focus on managing their customers' business. They must understand factors that impact the customer's profits and losses and how Wausau can affect their customer's bottom line. Since reps are now compensated on customer profitability and other business-related metrics, they take actions to add value to their customers by helping them find the best ways to utilize Wausau's offerings. As such, strong, ongoing relationships are developed with customers.

Source: Adapted from Heather Baldwin, "Deeper Value Delivery," Selling Power, 30 (September–October, 2010): 16–17.

In traditional selling, salespeople too often thought that their job was over when they closed the sale. Once the order was obtained, they moved on to the next prospect. Any follow-up or customer service was minimal. The lifeline of an organization today is repeat business. It is important to acquire new customers, but it is critical to keep your existing customer base happy. In research involving 80,000 business customers, the number-one characteristic found to define a world-class salesperson is someone who personally manages the customer's satisfaction by being accountable for the customer's desired results.[1] Not following up with a new customer is a shortsighted attitude toward selling, for it fails to consider the importance of developing and maintaining a customer for your company.

building goodwill The process of converting new customers into lifetime customers by continually adding value to the product.

adding value The process of improving a product or service for the customer.

Research indicates that successfully retaining customers is critical for all companies' success. Salespeople's post-sale service behaviours are positively related to relationship quality and share of customer business.[2] Relationship marketing efforts can lead to longer term, broader, and deeper customer relationships, which results in increases in sales, profits, and positive word of mouth.[3] Companies that invest 10 percent or more of their revenue in customer experience have greater referral rates, superior customer satisfaction scores, and better retention rates than those companies that invest less in customer experience.[4] Another study finds that it takes only a slight decline in attention from a salesperson to lead to an opportunity to consider alternative suppliers.[5]

A salesperson can convert new customers into highly committed lifetime customers in several ways. Examples include (1) **building goodwill** by continually **adding value** to the product or service through appropriate follow-up, (2) handling complaints in a timely and thoughtful manner, and (3) processing requests for rush deliveries willingly and assuring the customer that the salesperson will do everything possible to make that request happen. However, it is just as easy for a salesperson to alienate a new customer by putting the focus on the short-term order and not the long-term activities that create a partnership. This can be done by overpromising and underdelivering, using exaggeration to get an order, and blaming everyone else for problems. Exhibit 9.1 reviews relationship enhancers and detractors that can strengthen or destroy a relationship.

Relationship-oriented salespeople, such as those at Wausau Paper illustrated in the opening vignette, are creating bonds with their customers that will partially isolate them from competitive pressures or at least minimize the importance of easily altered and matched competitive variables, such as price. This chapter explains the importance of follow-up to assess customer satisfaction. Next, harnessing technology to enhance follow-up and buyer–seller relationships is covered. This is followed by a discussion of why it is the salesperson's job to take action (i.e., be proactive) before problems arise and not wait for complaints (i.e., be reactive) to ensure customer satisfaction. We then discuss the importance of collaborative involvement and working to add value for the buyer. Finally, we review the value of customer service.

EXHIBIT 9.1
Relationship Enhancers and Detractors

Enhancers	Detractors
Focus on long term	Focus on short term
Deliver more than promised	Overpromise and/or underdeliver
Call regularly	Call sporadically
Add value	Show up only for another order
Keep communication lines open	Be unavailable to the customer
Take responsibility for problems	Lie, exaggerate, blame someone else

9-1 Assess Customer Satisfaction

Keeping customers satisfied is important as it leads to customer trust and, ultimately, share of customer. Research shows that customer satisfaction is in part affected by salespeople's reliability and responsiveness as demonstrated by returning phone calls promptly, fulfilling commitments, satisfying customer requests, and being readily available. Furthermore, salespeople who regularly, clearly, and concisely communicate product information to customers can enhance their satisfaction.[6] Such research points to the need to be diligent in following up and properly communicating with customers to build, maintain, and enhance customer relationships.

Unfortunately, many companies do a poor job understanding and satisfying their customers. Results from an annual study of business executives conducted by the Strativity Group Inc. include the following:[7]

- More than 65 percent do not have a dedicated customer experience management role.
- Nearly 73 percent of respondents do not have a clear definition of the customer experience that is well communicated in their companies.
- Fewer than one-third (28.8 percent) of respondents provide employees with the tools and authority to solve customer problems.
- Nearly 76 percent do not have employees who are well-versed in how to delight customers.
- Slightly more than 56 percent believe that their companies do not deserve their customers' loyalty.

Salespeople today use several technologies to stay in touch with customers.

John Haack, senior vice president of marketing and sales for Saint-Gobain Containers (a glass container manufacturer), knows the importance of enhancing customer relationships as opposed to focusing solely on current sales. With such customers as Anheuser-Busch, Quaker Oats, and Kraft, Haack says, "Making the sale is only the beginning. After that, you have to keep track of the process every step of the way. You have to make sure the product gets delivered on time and that everyone involved with the customer knows their customer's expectations." Haack continues, "Anybody can move product. I can go out and sell a ton of something, but if it is not right for that particular customer, it is just going to end up back on my doorstep as a major problem."[8]

Clearly, professional salespeople, such as John Haack, view their customer base as far too valuable an asset to risk losing it through neglect. In maintaining and enhancing customer relationships, salespeople are involved in performing routine postsale follow-up activities and in enhancing the relationship as it evolves by anticipating and adapting to changes in the customer's situation, competitive forces, and other changes in the market environment. For instance, many salespeople do field research, conduct brainstorming sessions, and provide sales leads obtained through a network of business contacts. Activities like these demonstrate a service commitment. The objective in this step is to create a strong bond with customers that will diminish the probability of customers terminating the relationship. In effect, the salesperson earns the business through a number of successive trials and strengthens his or her position as time passes through follow-up calls and by adding value.

Furthering this notion, Darrell Beaty of Ontario Systems (a collections software company) states, "We spend too much time and effort learning about our prospects to not follow through and assess satisfaction." Figure 9.1[9] demonstrates the time and commitment Beaty puts in to earn an order from a prospect. Beaty states, "We cannot be afraid to ask a customer, 'How are we doing?'" This practice should go on monthly, quarterly, and yearly. Sometimes, the salesperson will not like the answers that he or she gets from the customers. New customers generally feel special because they have received a lot of attention. Long-term customers may feel neglected because the salesperson has many new customers and cannot be as attentive as he or she was previously. Routine follow-up questions, such as "How are we doing?" can

© Neustockimages/iStockphoto

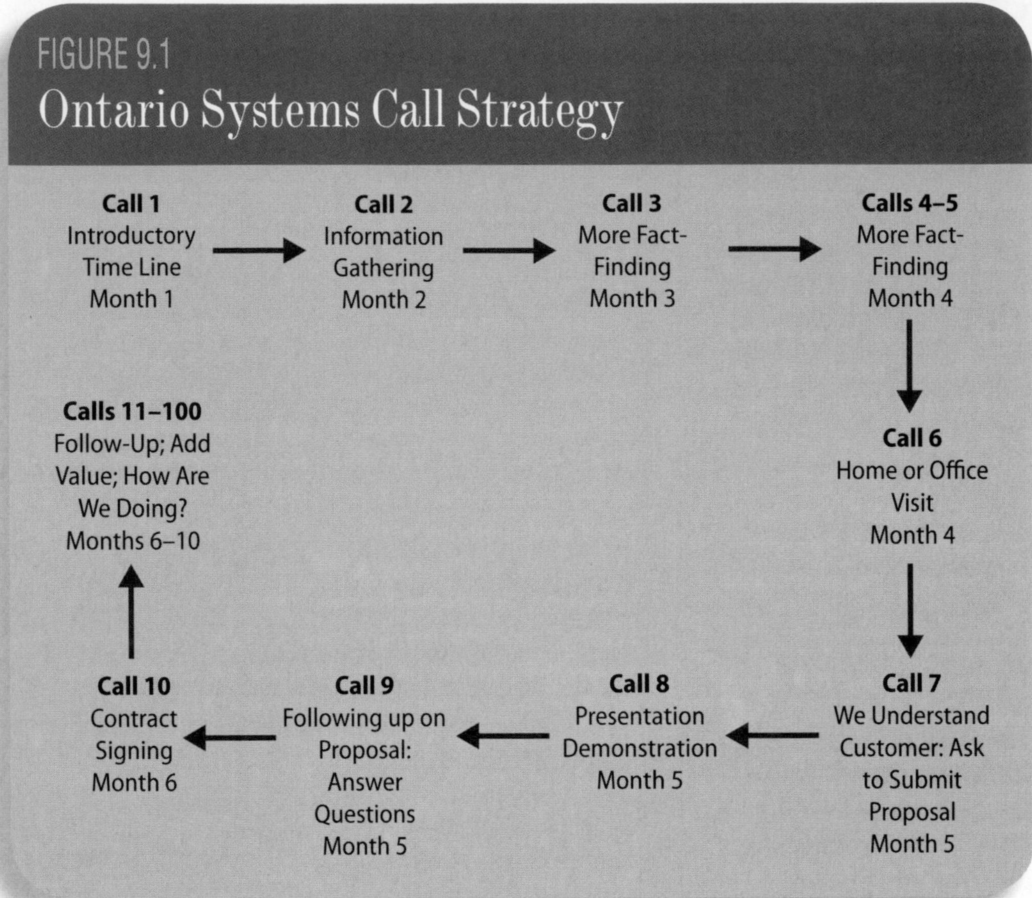

FIGURE 9.1
Ontario Systems Call Strategy

It takes many calls to earn commitment from a prospect. It can take months and even years to establish the trust needed to earn an order.

interact The salesperson acts to maximize the number of critical encounters with buyers to encourage effective dialogue and involvement between the salesperson and buyer.

connect The salesperson maintains contact with the multiple individuals in the buying organization who influence purchase decisions and manages the various touch points the customer has in the selling organization to ensure consistency in communication.

know The salesperson coordinates and interprets the information gathered through buyer–seller contact and collaboration to develop insight regarding the buyer's changing situation, needs, and expectations.

go a long way in letting a customer know that the salesperson cares and is willing to make sure that the customer is satisfied.

HARNESS TECHNOLOGY TO ENHANCE FOLLOW-UP AND BUYER–SELLER RELATIONSHIPS

Building buyer–seller relationships is easier said than done. Developing and nurturing customer relationships demands that salespeople do more than simply discover the buyer's needs and respond to them with a sales offering that resolves those needs. Relationships are formed over time through multiple buyer–seller interactions in which the seller wins the trust of the buyer. One survey found that one of the most important things buyers look for in sellers is accountability. They want someone whom they can rely on during the entire sales process and who will not abandon them after the sale is finalized.[10] Another study uncovered nearly 80 reasons why customers dislike salespeople, with the fourth most important ranked reason being a lack of salesperson follow-up.[11] The results of these studies emphasize the importance of effective follow-up by the salesperson. As discussed in this chapter and illustrated in Figure 9.2, effective salesperson follow-up should include specific components designed to interact with, connect with, know, and relate with customers.

- **Interact**—The salesperson acts to maximize the number of critical encounters with buyers to encourage effective dialogue and involvement between the salesperson and buyer.
- **Connect**—The salesperson maintains contact with the multiple individuals in the buying organization influencing purchase decisions and manages the various touch points the customer has in the selling organization to ensure consistency in communication.
- **Know**—The salesperson coordinates and interprets the information gathered through buyer–seller contact and collaboration to develop insight regarding the buyer's changing situation, needs, and expectations.

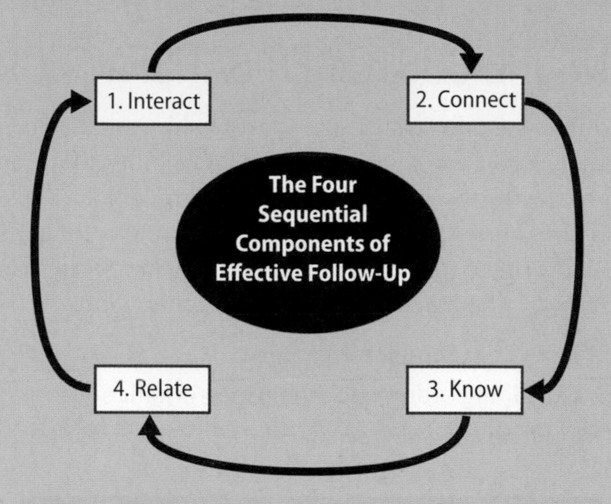

Effective salesperson follow-up should include specific components designed to interact with, connect with, know, and relate with his or her customers.

- **Relate**—The salesperson applies relevant understanding and insight to create value-added interactions and generate relationships between the salesperson and buyer.

Salespeople employ a variety of technology-based salesforce automation tools to better track the increasingly complex combination of buyer–seller interactions and to manage the exchange, interpretation, and storage of diverse types of information. Among the more popular salesforce automation tools are the many competing versions of PC- and Internet-based software applications designed to record and manage customer contact information. PC-based software applications such as Maximizer, Goldmine, and ACT!, and Internet-based applications such as Netsuite and Salesforce.com enable salespeople to collect, file, and access comprehensive databases detailing information about individual buyers and buying organizations. In addition to providing explicit details about customers and the multiple individuals influencing purchasing decisions within any given account, these databases also provide an archive of the interactions and

Relationships are formed over time through multiple buyer–seller interactions in which the seller wins the trust of the buyer.

purchasing decisions taking place over time. Salespeople using these systems have found them to be invaluable in helping them track and better service their accounts to ensure and enhance customer satisfaction. By better understanding every transaction and buyer–seller interaction, salespeople can be more effective in communicating with each individual customer throughout the lifetime of the account.

The advent of the Internet has allowed these customer contact management tools to be used in multiorganization intranets and extranets. An **intranet** is an organization's dedicated and proprietary computer network offering password-controlled access to people within and outside the organization (e.g., customers and suppliers). **Extranets** are proprietary computer networks created by an organization for use by the organization's customers or suppliers and linked to the organization's internal systems, informational databases, and intranet.

relate The salesperson applies relevant understanding and insight to create value-added interactions and generate relationships between the salesperson and buyer.

intranet An organization's dedicated and proprietary computer network that offers password-controlled access to people within and outside the organization (e.g., customers and suppliers).

extranet Proprietary computer networks created by an organization for use by the organization's customers or suppliers and linked to the organization's internal systems, informational databases, and intranet.

Internet-activated and integrated with an organization's intranet and extranets, customer contact

customer relationship management (CRM) system A system that dynamically links buyers and sellers into a rich communication network to establish and reinforce long-term, profitable relationships.

systems are transposed to full **customer relationship management (CRM) systems**. These systems dynamically link buyers and sellers into a rich communication network. Salespeople and buyers have immediate, 24/7 access to one another and one another's organizations. Problems can be resolved online, routine ordering procedures can be automated, and information such as product brochures and spec sheets, inventory availability, price lists, and order status can be exchanged. Salespeople can use the Web to view everything that is relevant to any account. This can include information in the organization's databases (e.g., purchasing history, credit rating) as well as pertinent information such as news stories, stock prices, and research reports from sources outside the organization (e.g., Hoover's, Standard & Poor's, etc.).

CRM systems enable salespeople to build and integrate multiple forms of customer information and create highly influential customer interactions that establish and reinforce long-term, profitable relationships. The benefits to salespeople learning to use these advanced, integrated systems effectively are self-evident. Every time a salesperson and buyer interact in a positive manner, the corresponding relationship is enriched. This enrichment translates to improved service levels, increased customer satisfaction, and enhanced revenues from loyal customers. For example, after a series of mergers and acquisitions, Honeywell Aerospace found customers telling them that it was difficult to do business with them. Two different Honeywell sales reps, for instance, might call on the same customer in the same day. After implementing a CRM system, customer satisfaction with Honeywell improved 38 percent, its on-time service request closure rate improved from 45 to 83 percent, and its sales opportunity rate improved. Moreover, Honeywell credits the CRM system with a 100 percent annual revenue improvement, from $45 million to $100 million in the sales of its after-market spare parts.[12]

ENSURE CUSTOMER SATISFACTION

Exhibit 9.2 illustrates the partnership-enhancement activities and the salesperson's responsibility that goes along with them. Specific relationship-enhancement activities vary substantially from company to company but are critical to the success of building long-term relationships. These activities include the following:

- Providing useful information
- Expediting orders and monitoring installation
- Training customer personnel

EXHIBIT 9.2
Relationship-Enhancement Activities

Partnership-Enhancement Activities	Salesperson Responsibility
Provide useful information	• Relevant • Timely • High quality
Expedite orders/monitor installation	• Track orders • Inform on delays • Help with installation
Train customer personnel	• Train even when contract does not call for it
Correct billing errors	• Go over all orders • Correct problem before customer recognizes it
Remember the customer after the sale	• Set up a regular call schedule • Let customer know you will be back
Resolve complaints	• Preferably prevent the need to complain • Ask customer how he or she wants complaint resolved

- Correcting billing errors
- Remembering the customer after the sale
- Resolving complaints

Traditional selling focuses on getting the order. In a sense, the sales process was over once the order was signed. The salesperson's job was to focus on getting the next order, and it was left to others in the organization to deliver and install the product. However, the relational sales process shown in Figure 9.3 indicates that many activities must take place after the sale, and it is the salesperson's responsibility to oversee and participate in all of the follow-up activities. By being actively involved during this stage, the salesperson increases the odds that a long-term relationship will develop. Joseph Sparacino, senior vice president and national sales manager for Omega Performance, discusses how salespeople can provide follow-up activities to increase customer satisfaction and build long-term customer relationships in "Professional Selling in the 21st Century: Building Relationships Through Follow-Up."

PROVIDE USEFUL INFORMATION

Many buyers feel neglected once they place an order with a company. They were given a lot of attention before they placed the order, but after the order was placed the salesperson disappeared. Once an economic relationship is established, the salesperson must continually provide timely, relevant, high-quality information to his or her customers. The job of educating the buyer never stops, and salespeople are responsible for updating customers and pointing out additional opportunities that will benefit them. Information that will help customers solve their problems also is a must.

By providing useful information, the salesperson is demonstrating a commitment to the buyer. The salesperson is showing that he or she is in the relationship for the long term and that he or she values the partnership. The salesperson should remember to provide information not only to the buyer but also to the secretaries, receptionists, administrative assistants, department heads, and other influential members of the buyer's organization.

Several postsale follow-up methods can be used to provide helpful information. First, however, salespeople should try to determine the customer's preferred method of receiving this information and provide it in that manner if possible. Perhaps one of the best ways to provide useful information is by a personal visit. After the sale is made, it is critical to follow up personally and make sure that the customer is completely satisfied with all the promises that have been made (e.g., delivery, installation done properly, courteous installers). This is the only strategy that provides face-to-face communication and thus affords the salesperson the opportunity to read the customer's body language. When a salesperson takes the time to make a well-planned

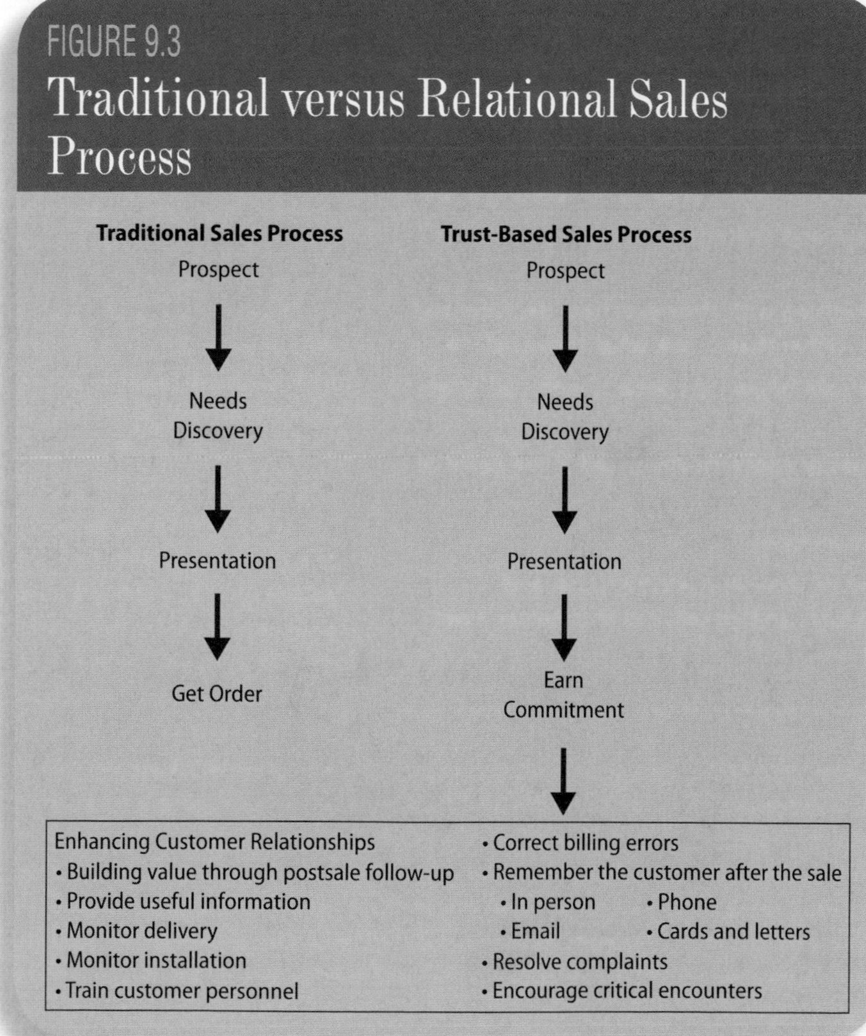

Traditional selling focuses on getting the order. The relational sales process indicates that many activities must take place after the sale.

Professional Selling in the 21st Century

Building Relationships Through Follow-Up

Joseph (Joe) Sparacino, senior vice president and national sales manager for Omega Performance, who is responsible for leading his teams in sales, consulting, and service activities for client relationships across the United States, discusses activities involved in providing exquisite customer service after the sale. According to Joe, long-term relationship building can be enhanced after the sale by:

- Foreseeing and planning post-sale customer needs prior to completing a sale.
- Developing a post-sale long-term vision and strategy for ensuring customer satisfaction.
- Making certain that customers are delighted with their purchase decision and think in terms of "Look what I bought" rather than "Look what they sold me."
- Planning and executing periodic post-sale follow-up contacts with customers to assess their level of satisfaction.
- Touching base with customers on issues or concerns discussed at the point of the initial sale.
- Recalling and recognizing customer milestones.
- Regularly evaluating the products and/or services customers use, and recommending new or upgraded products and/or services that better meet their needs.

personal follow-up visit, he or she indicates to the prospect that he or she really cares. A good salesperson will use the follow-up call to keep the customer informed of new developments in the industry, new products, or new applications. Providing this information may bring about future sales. When a salesperson makes a follow-up call, he or she should always have an objective for the sales call. The salesperson should be sure not to spend too much time on gossip sessions or chitchat. It is the salesperson's job to add value, not waste the customer's time. While the personal visit can be a very engaging method, perhaps its biggest weakness is that it can be time consuming.

An efficient option for providing useful information after a sale is to use the telephone. The telephone is a quick and efficient way to contact customers. The cell phone has provided salespeople with an opportunity to stay in touch with customers while on the road. A salesperson can easily make 7 to 10 phone calls per hour, and the cost is minimal. Although a personal note to a customer is always appropriate, the telephone has the advantage of a two-way exchange of information. The phone can be used to verify delivery, inform the customer of any changes (e.g., price, delivery schedule), and check for problems in general.

Electronic and social media provide an efficient and cost-effective way to continuously keep in touch with customers. When getting pertinent company and buyer information, the salesperson should also get e-mail addresses. Salespeople are able to include not only text, but also sound and video to e-mail messages they send to customers. Social networking sites such as LinkedIn and Facebook allow salespeople to keep in touch with customers by posting updates, information, and feature reviews. These tools, along with Twitter, allow salespeople to have brief interactions with customers between calls to provide information, address customer concerns, and simply get to know customers on a more personal basis. Moreover, information gleaned from using social media's search features can provide salespeople with insights on industry trends, or the preferences of prospects or customers.

Finally, a handwritten thank-you card to a customer is an inexpensive and convenient form of customer follow-up. It should always be used in conjunction with the other follow-up methods. The mail can also be used to send out new promotional material, information about new products, and trade publication articles that may be of interest to customers. Periodically, a salesperson could send his or her customers a short survey that asks "How are we doing?" Exhibit 9.3 summarizes the strengths and weaknesses of follow-up methods. Checking the customer's level of satisfaction might highlight an area of concern that the salesperson can take care of before it becomes a major problem.

EXPEDITE ORDERS AND MONITOR INSTALLATION

Generally, salespeople will set estimates on product delivery times. The salesperson must work to prevent a delay in delivery. The salesperson's job is to track the order status and inform the customers when delays occur. It is unpleasant to inform a buyer of a delay, but the information allows buyers to work around the inconvenience and plan accordingly. Waiting until the delivery date to announce a delay is inconsiderate and hurts the trust built between the salesperson and buyer.

Many problems with shipping and the delivery of an order are out of the salesperson's control. However, today's sophisticated tracking systems allow salespeople to track orders and find out what is causing the delay. The salesperson must keep the customer up-to-date on the delivery status and any possible delays.

Monitoring order processing and after-sale activities is critical to enhancing the relationship with a customer. Customers often have done a poor job of forecasting, run short of product, and may expect their salesperson to bring their emergency to a happy conclusion. Although it is not always possible to speed up orders, the salesperson should investigate and attempt to do everything possible to help the customers. If the buyer sees concern on the salesperson's part and knows that the salesperson is attempting to help the buyer, then the relationship will be strengthened, even if the order cannot be pushed through as quickly as the buyer had hoped.

Depending on the industry, salespeople generally do not help with installation. Nevertheless, some salespeople believe that it is in their best interest to supervise the installation process and to be available when customers have questions. Typically, installers do not have the same relationship with the customer and may not have the type of personality to deal with difficult situations. The salesperson can act as the buffer between the installation team and the customers.

EXHIBIT 9.3

Methods to Provide Useful Information

Method	Strength	Weakness
1. Personal call	Best for interactive face-to-face communication; view body language	Most time consuming Most expensive Customers will not always see salesperson
2. Telephone	Can make 7–10 calls per hour Cell phones allow call to be made from anywhere Inexpensive Immediate feedback	May interrupt your customers Cannot evaluate facial expressions
3. Mail	One more touch that lets the customers know you are thinking about them	Customers get a lot of mail Customer may not see it if secretary opens and tosses mail One-way communication
4. Electronic and social media	Efficient Inexpensive Immediate feedback	Customer may not use social media tools One way communication Impersonal

TRAINING CUSTOMER PERSONNEL

Companies are always looking for ways to gain a competitive advantage. Once the order is placed, traditional salespeople are happy to get their commission or bonus and move on to their

© Ciaran Griffin/Jupiter Images

Corken, a worldwide manufacturer and marketer of compressors and pumps, provides yearly in-house product training programs, as well as assistance for initial startups and on-site training for plant personnel.

next conquest. Relationship managers understand the real work begins once the order is signed. Training customer personnel may or may not be included in the price terms of the agreement. Salespeople may use this to gain the competitive edge they need. For example, instead of training only one person as stated in the sales terms, the salesperson gladly trains three people for the same price. Adding value should always be a priority with any salesperson.

When the product is technical, customer training may require the assistance of the company trainer or engineer. The salesperson still has a key role as he or she knows the customer best and should serve as the facilitator to ensure that all the parties have been properly introduced and start off in a positive manner. The salesperson should schedule the training sessions as conveniently as possible for the customer. Customer education is an integral part of the marketing strategy of Ontario Systems Corporation, a collections software company. What separates Ontario from its competitors is its ability to provide timely training and education for all its customers. Ontario knows that service after the sale is crucial, which is why it provides an 800 telephone number for 24-hour service. Each year, Ontario strengthens its relationships with customers by providing one week of training, seminars, and goodwill at its home office. Ontario understands the importance of the team approach to providing outstanding customer service.

> Complaints will never be completely eliminated by any company, but they must be addressed and resolved.

CORRECT BILLING ERRORS

Billing errors could turn into customer complaints if not found in a timely fashion and corrected. A salesperson should go over all orders and billing records to ensure proper billing has been sent to the customer. A customer will know the salesperson has his or her best interests in mind if the salesperson corrects problems without being prompted by the customer. As seen in "An Ethical Dilemma," it is possible that a billing error may result in an ethical dilemma.

REMEMBER THE CUSTOMER AFTER THE SALE

Customer follow-up methods should be used to express appreciation for the purchase and to develop the relationship after the sale further. Customers consistently cite poor service and lack of follow-up as the primary reasons that buyers stop buying. At one branch office of Wallace Computer Services, a saying hangs above the door: "Remember the Customer between Calls."

Personal visits should be the primary method to follow up after the sale. It is the most costly but also the most effective. This method allows face-to-face, two-way communication. The customer's body language can also be observed.

The telephone can also be used to follow up a sale. Most salespeople send a written follow up thanking the customer for his or her business. The telephone can then be used to reinforce the written message. The customer can give verbal feedback, and the salesperson can ask questions and use probing techniques that cannot be used with written correspondence. It is important not to forget the customer after the sale.

An Ethical Dilemma

© iStock/Thinkstock

Evan Celler is a sales representative for a manufacturer of windshield wipers that calls on automotive supply shops and various retail outlets. In reviewing an invoice scheduled to be submitted to one of his newest customers, he noticed a pricing error. The price should have included a quantity discount. Evan recalls mentioning the opportunity for earning quantity discounts to this customer when taking the customer's first order several months ago, but recalls not much was made of it since at that time this customer had no intent to place a large order. If Evan were to obtain this higher price, he would realize a significantly larger commission on this order. Given that this customer was relatively new, there was some question as to whether the customer would even realize he was not receiving a quantity discount. If you were Evan, what would you do?

a) Contact my billing department and have them correct the invoice prior to sending it.
b) Keep quiet, but if the customer questions the price, then inform the customer that billing made an error and that I will have them send out an invoice that includes the quantity discount.
c) Take my increased commission and treat myself to a nice dinner out since I deserve it; if the customer questions the price, tell the customer that quantity discounts take effect only after a customer has been buying from our company for at least nine months, so they will be eligible for a quantity discount very soon.

RESOLVE COMPLAINTS AND ENCOURAGE CRITICAL ENCOUNTERS

Complaints will never be completely eliminated by any company. Nevertheless, it is every company's hope that it can reduce the frequency of complaints. Complaints typically arise because the product did not live up to the buyer's expectations. Research shows that companies that systematically monitor, track, and address service failures, instances in which buyer expectations are not met, are rewarded with more satisfied customers and greater customer retention.[13] Buyers complain for any number of reasons: (1) late delivery, (2) wrong order sent (e.g., too many, too few), (3) product performs poorly, or (4) nobody at the salesperson's company takes the buyer's problems seriously. See Exhibit 9.4 for a more comprehensive list of complaints.

Many times, the complaint is not the fault of the salesperson (e.g., late delivery, wrong order, product performs poorly). However, this is not a concern to buyers as they expect the salesperson to resolve it. Traditional salespeople have been known to pass the blame when complaints arise. A salesperson would be better off to tackle the complaint by accepting responsibility and promptly fixing the problem. Salespeople get into trouble by overpromising what their product can do, being overly optimistic about delivery dates, and not being attentive to their customers when they do complain. Many complaints can be avoided by giving customers a reasonable expectation of what a company's product or service can do for them.

If periodic meetings are taking place between the buyer and seller after the sale, then in all probability, most of the important issues are being discussed. Salespeople must ask their buyers to be candid with them and encourage the buyer to discuss tough issues (e.g., late deliveries, damaged products), especially in areas where the salesperson's organization is providing less than satisfactory performance. Some buyers will not complain because they feel it will not do any good. Others will not complain because they feel that the salesperson should be in tune with their problems or concerns and recognize these problems on their own.

EXHIBIT 9.4

Typical Customer Complaints

1. Late delivery
2. Damaged merchandise
3. Invoice errors
4. Out of stock—back orders
5. Shipped incorrect product
6. Shipped incorrect order size
7. Service department unresponsive
8. Product does not live up to expectations
9. Customer not informed of new developments
10. Customer's problems not taken seriously
11. Improper installation
12. Need more training
13. Price increase—no notice
14. Cannot find the salesperson when needed
15. Unreturned phone calls

If a salesperson encourages critical encounters and acts accordingly to defuse a situation in which the buyer's expectations have not been met, then this will help with future meetings and sessions where **critical encounters** are discussed. If the salesperson does not act on these issues, then future meetings with the buyer will not uncover problem areas because the buyer is convinced nothing will be done to solve them.

Some salespeople tell the customer what he or she wants to hear to get the order but cannot deliver on promises made, as seen in "An Ethical Dilemma." Complaints can be avoided by being truthful when presenting a product's capabilities. Providing sales support can eliminate problems with late deliveries, wrong orders being sent, and the feeling that the salesperson does not care about the customer's complaints. The following section provides an outline on how to handle customer complaints.

A Procedure to Handle Complaints

Customer complaints must be handled quickly and with great sensitivity. Customers do not care about all the problems the company is experiencing and the reasons why the salesperson is providing less-than-stellar customer service. The reason that relationship selling is such a critical part of retaining customers is because

An Ethical Dilemma

© Justin Horrocks/iStockphoto

Steph Clark of Imaging Inc. had been working on making a sale to her newest customer for over six months. Finally, her customer was ready to purchase a copier but requested to take delivery in two days as one of the conditions of the sale. Typically it takes at least four full days for delivery. Steph knew that there was a 25 percent chance that the copier would be delivered on time. She feared that if she told the customer she may not be able to meet the requested delivery date she would lose the deal, and all her hard work would go to waste. Besides, she thought, the customer would likely take delivery even if the copier arrived late. If you were Steph, what would you do?

a) Not mention that the copier may not arrive on time, close the deal, and hope for the best. If the copier does not arrive in two days, blame it on shipping.

b) Find out why it is so important to have the copier in two days, explain that the chances of getting it that soon are slim, and see if I can help in any way should the copier not arrive within two days.

c) Contact my shipping department and see if it is possible to get a rush delivery. If so, no worries. If not, explain to the customer why the two-day delivery date cannot be met.

the salesperson must have an open communication line with the customer and encourage feedback, either positive or negative. Research has shown that 96 percent of customers will not complain and 63 percent of these dissatisfied customers will not repurchase.[14] Thus, salespeople must build relationships to the point where buyers will not hesitate to speak their mind if they are unhappy with the service. If the customer does not complain, then the salesperson does not know what it is that he or she needs to fix.

One study has indicated that, if a company fails to deal with customers and prospects who complain, those customers will tell on average up to 10 people about their bad experience; with e-mail and Internet, this negative feedback can spread to an even larger number of people. Satisfied customers, in contrast, tell only four or five others about their positive experience.[15] Another study showed that a company has a 40 percent chance of winning back upset customers—which indicates that the effort to make amends is worth it.[16] Recent research in consumer services suggests that satisfactory handling of customer complaints is key to customer recommendations of a firm to others.[17] A general procedure for handling customer complaints follows.

Salespeople don't want to make customers feel like the one in this picture! They need to make customers feel welcome to complain.

Build the Relationship to the Point That Your Customers Are Comfortable Complaining

Salespeople have been overheard saying to their customers, "Had I known that you were unhappy with our service, I could have fixed it." The buyer typically responds, "Well, I gave you plenty of signals; why were you not aware of the problems I was having when we were doing business?" The buyer and salesperson must work together to develop a trust so that whenever something comes up, either person feels comfortable speaking up. Open communication channels are a must for good customer service. Companies today cannot be afraid to ask their clients, "How are we doing?" Some companies are conducting 30-, 60-, and 90-day customer satisfaction follow-up visits after the sale. Beyond that, salespeople maintain quarterly follow-ups, even if only by phone. This at least tells customers that the salesperson is interested in them and wants to service their account well.

© Jon Carter

Listen Carefully and Get the Whole Story

The salesperson must listen carefully to what is being said and what is not being said. Good salespeople let the customer know that they are happy the complaint has been brought to their attention. Chances are that the customer will not complain again if he or she is made to feel uncomfortable with the initial complaint. The salesperson must be careful not to interrupt early in the discussion. The customer must be allowed to vent his or her frustration. Once the customer stops complaining, the salesperson may have to probe and ask follow-up questions to get the whole story. For instance, the buyer may not have told the salesperson whom he or she talked to at the salesperson's company about the problem, and this information may be helpful to the salesperson in solving the complaint. This is a good time to show empathy. The salesperson should apologize for any inconvenience and let the buyer know that he or she is happy that the problem was brought up.

critical encounters
Meetings in which the salesperson encourages the buyer to discuss tough issues, especially in areas in which the salesperson's organization is providing less than satisfactory performance.

The salesperson must make the buyer aware that he or she is anxious to resolve the problem and keep the buyer as a satisfied customer.

Ask Customers How They Would Like Their Complaint Resolved

Many salespeople attempt to solve the complaint without understanding what the customer wants them to do. For example, a salesperson may reason that the last customer wanted a 20 percent discount to make things better. "Thus, I will offer this unhappy buyer the same thing." The salesperson may be surprised to find out the buyer wanted something totally different to resolve the problem. The salesperson cannot be afraid to ask the customer what it will take to make him or her happy. A salesperson could say something like, "Theresa, we value you and your company's business. I am sorry for the inconvenience we caused you. Can you please tell me what we can do to solve this problem and keep you as a satisfied customer?" Then, the salesperson must listen carefully. The buyer may simply want an apology. He or she may want a discount; still other buyers might ask for another product to be substituted until the regular shipment arrives. Salespeople typically find that the customer is not demanding as much as they thought he or she might have been, considering the circumstances of the complaint. The solution should centre on what the customer wants and not what the salesperson thinks is appropriate. When salespeople provide customers with choice in the complaint resolution process, they are likely to increase customers' perceived control over the process and ultimately enhance customer satisfaction.[18]

© SteveLuker/iStockphoto

Salespeople must maintain open, two-way communication with customers after the initial sale to build a relationship.

Gain Agreement on a Solution

Once the salesperson hears what the customer wants, they must agree on a solution. Sometimes, the salesperson can do exactly what the customer asks. Other times, the buyer may be asking for an unrealistic solution. The salesperson's focus should always be on trying to do exactly what the customer wants. When that is not possible, the salesperson's message should concentrate on what he or she can do for the customer and then do it in a timely manner.[19] The conversation might sound like, "Jim, I'm sorry for the inconvenience we caused you. Thanks for your suggestions on what we need to do to resolve the problem. Here are a couple of things we can do—which of these will work better for you?" The salesperson is telling the buyer that he or she cannot do exactly what the buyer asked, but the salesperson can do the following. Good salespeople always focus on the positive.

Take Action—Educate the Customer

Once an agreement is reached, the salesperson must take action and solve the customer complaint in a timely fashion. The communication lines must be kept open to the customer (e.g., letting him or her know when the repair people will be arriving). Monitor complaint resolution and keep the customer up-to-date on progress. This is also a good time to convey that steps have been taken to ensure that the problem will not occur again.

If customers have unrealistic expectations of the services provided, then this would be a good time to educate the customers so that they have realistic expectations of the services the company will provide. Some salespeople promise the moon to secure an order and then let the customer down when the product or service does not meet expectations. This is not the way to develop a trusting relationship.

Follow Through on All Promises—Add Value

Whatever promises are made, good salespeople must make sure that they are kept, and this is a good time to

EXHIBIT 9.5
General Procedures for Handling Complaints

1. Build the relationship to the point that the customer is comfortable complaining.
2. Listen carefully and get the whole story.
3. Ask the customer what he or she would like you to do.
4. Gain agreement on a solution. Tell the customer what you can do; do not focus on what you cannot do.
5. Take action; educate the customer so he or she has realistic expectations.
6. Follow through on all promises. Add value.

go beyond what has been promised. Those salespeople who overdeliver what is promised will truly impress their customers and build stronger relationships faster than their competitors.[20] By exceeding expectations and adding value, the salesperson helps ensure repeat business. Exhibit 9.5 summarizes the procedures for handling complaints.

9-2 Expand Collaborative Involvement

Early in the selling process, the salesperson determines the specific needs of the buyer so that a good match can be made between the product's attributes and the needs of the buyer. This is done through effective questioning and listening to the buyer. Once the sale is made, the salesperson must continue to maintain open, two-way communication with the buyer. Periodic meetings with the buyer allow for this feedback. Furthermore, the methods discussed for obtaining information can be used to keep the line of communication between the buyer and seller open. Collaborative discussion becomes the most effective tool when dealing with customers and their problems. If the customer believes the salesperson is sincere, listens carefully, and responds accordingly to his or her concerns, then an already trusting relationship will become stronger.

Great salespeople work hard to provide quality customer service.

collaborative involvement A way to build on buyer–salesperson relationships in which the buyer's organization and the salesperson's organization join together to improve an offering.

A salesperson's goal is to work with customers who have entered into a strategic alliance with the salesperson's firm. This is done by building trust over a long time. The salesperson should always be looking for ways to take the relationship to a higher level and create a stronger bond. One way to accomplish this goal is to expand the **collaborative involvement** between the buyer's and salesperson's organizations. The salesperson may take a group of engineers along on a sales call and introduce them to the buyer's engineers. It may be possible for the engineers to work together to enhance the product offering. Customers often know the strengths and weaknesses of the product they use and can provide some insight into how improvements can be made.

Another example of a company's attempt to expand collaborative involvement is to host a week-long series of seminars, training sessions, and social engagements with its customers to expand the relationship. Brainstorming sessions with customers demonstrate a willingness to listen, show that the company cares, and often result in better ways to serve customers. Any time the salesperson can involve additional personnel from the buyer's company during relationship building, chances are that the relationship will become stronger.

9-3 Work to Add Value and Enhance Mutual Opportunities

To build mutually satisfying relationships between buyers and sellers, professional sales-people must work toward adding value and enhancing mutual opportunities for the customer. This can be done by reducing risk through repeated displays of the seller's ability to serve the customer. By demonstrating willingness to serve the customer, the seller reduces the buyer's risk—both real and perceived. A good relationship is one that has few, if any, unpleasant surprises.

Salespeople must also establish high standards and expectations. Many relationships fail because of unmet expectations. The higher the customer's expectations, the better, provided the seller can meet or exceed those expectations. Salespeople should ensure that the customer's expectations are reasonable by clearly and honestly conveying the firm's offering, and continually work to improve performance.

Finally, salespeople must monitor and take action to improve customer satisfaction. Salespeople must never let up on this. Doing so only invites competitor challenges. A good salesperson must always look for cracks in the relationship and patch them before insurmountable problems occur. All relationships require work, and taking a good customer for granted is foolish. It should be remembered that the salesperson must continually add value to the relationship or he or she will run the risk of losing the customer.

PROVIDE QUALITY CUSTOMER SERVICE

Every salesperson is looking for a competitive edge to help him or her differentiate his or her products in the eyes of customers. Many of the products that a salesperson sells have essentially the same features and benefits as the competitors'. Chris Crabtree of Lanier once said, "A copier is a copier, is a copier. There is just no difference between what I have to offer and my competitors. We all charge about the same price. In fact, I can match any price my competitor puts on the table. That leaves only one attribute for me to differentiate on—service."

service quality Meeting and/or exceeding customer service expectations.

More and more companies are turning to **service quality** as a strategy to acquire and maintain customers. A salesperson must be able to convince a customer that service is important, demonstrate service quality, and then maintain a high level of service over an extended time.

The problem is that every salesperson claims to provide outstanding service. The goal today is not to meet customer expectations but to exceed them. Salespeople will rarely be given a second chance to prove that they provide outstanding service if they do not get it right the first time. A sign in a small-town business reads,

> *Service is advertised . . .*
> *Service is talked about . . .*
> *But the only time service really counts . . .*
> *Is when it is delivered . . .*
> *And we promise your experience with us will be outstanding.*

Customers do not care about slogans and service claims until something happens to them. This is called a moment of truth. Each salesperson experiences daily moments of truth—brief moments that occur whenever a customer comes into contact with a salesperson, the training staff, installers, field engineers, or service personnel and has an opportunity to form an impression. These moments of truth are when the customer will determine if promises are being kept by the sales organization, and whether the salesperson truly cares about the customer or is simply an order getter!

Four benefits of service enthusiasm allow the sales organization to gain an advantage over its competitors. First, reputation is an important part of any organization's ability to attract and keep new customers. Reputation allows a salesperson to distinguish himself or herself from the competition. A solid reputation tells customers that you care and will help a salesperson build a loyal relationship in his or her market. Reputations take a long time to establish and only one negative event to destroy.

Second, by providing good customer service the first time, an organization makes the profit that it needs to stay in business. Whenever mistakes are made (e.g., wrong order, short order delivered), service personnel have to sort out the problem and fix it. The result could lead to a lost customer. In any event, it does not take long to go into the red when people have to be added to fix problems. Efficient operations, cost savings, and doing things right the first time increase the chances for increased profits.

The third benefit of service enthusiasm is convenience. It is critically important to put the customer's convenience first. For example, most customers are uncomfortable complaining. Thus, a salesperson must make it easy for his or her customers to discuss problems or complaints. Since customers can be reluctant to complain, the salesperson must be vigilant in asking customers to express their problems or concerns. Building a strong, trusting relationship with open communication will make it easier for customers to voice their concerns. To be convenient, salespeople must be readily accessible to customers. This involves using technology (e.g., cell phone, e-mail) to stay accessible, quickly acknowledging customer requests, and then responding in an appropriate and expedient manner.[21] When it comes to servicing customers, salespeople often must accommodate customers' schedules rather than their own. Naturally, this may pose some inconvenience to the salesperson, but customer needs must be considered first.

Salespeople must design user-friendly feedback systems. Periodically inquiring about customer satisfaction can greatly enhance a customer's feelings toward a salesperson and his or her organization. Ontario Systems (http://www.ontariosystems.com) provides a Client Resource Centre as one of its links on its website. Clients can easily get up-to-date information on product support, training, industry links, and discussion lists. Ontario Systems is always looking for ways to provide more services to its clients.

Finally, service enthusiasm goes hand in hand with spirit. A customer can be turned onto an organization by meeting many caring "can-do" people. The spirit must start with an enthusiastic, service-minded corporate culture. The salesperson, sales manager, field engineer, installer, and CSR (customer service representative) must all have the same service enthusiasm to generate the benefits of service enthusiasm. That is why the salesperson must monitor and coordinate all the people who have access to the account to ensure that good customer service is taking place.

The most difficult aspect of customer service is the potential for inconsistency. For instance, field engineer A, who has a great understanding of service enthusiasm, may be called into an account early in the week. The customer is very impressed. Three weeks later, the customer calls for help again. Field engineer A is out on another account, and field engineer B, who has few or no service skills, is sent out on the next call. Field engineer B is good at fixing the problem but has a hard time relating to customers; in fact, he is downright cold! As a result of this unevenness, the customer's level of satisfaction decreases.

The inconsistency of customer service is a problem for every sales organization. By understanding the benefits of service enthusiasm and the rewards of proper spirit, the sales organization can ensure consistency and exceed customer expectations.

MEET CUSTOMER EXPECTATIONS

A salesperson must meet the needs of his or her customer. At a minimum, customers expect a warm and friendly salesperson. Buyers have enough things going on during their day that it would not be a plus to have to deal with a surly salesperson. Warmth and friendliness are the building blocks of a successful relationship.

Reliability is another attribute that buyers look for in choosing a salesperson with whom to do business. Customers must have the confidence that the expected service will be delivered accurately, consistently, and dependably. Helpfulness and assistance are two more variables that buyers expect when working with a salesperson. Will the customer be able to find his or her salesperson when he or she needs to do so? Can the salesperson provide the speed and promptness needed by the customer? The salesperson can solve this issue by developing a regular call routine so that the customer knows when to expect the salesperson. Other customer expectations include follow-through as promised; empathy; and resolution of complaints, mistakes, or defects. The customer must know that if anything goes wrong, the salesperson will move in quickly and solve the problem. Ultimately, the customer is looking for someone who is personally accountable for their desired results.[22] Exhibit 9.6 summarizes what customers expect from their salesperson.

DEVELOP A SERVICE STRATEGY

Salespeople can calculate the lifetime value of their customers. For example, Hershey Foods Corporation knows exactly how much candy it has sold at the Walmart in Muncie, Indiana. It is easy for Hershey to calculate the loss if any customer decides to replace it. It is imperative for Hershey to provide the service level that each of its customers demands. Less than quality service can lead to the loss of a customer.

EXHIBIT 9.6
Customer Expectations of Salespeople

1. Warmth and friendliness
2. Reliability
3. Helpfulness/assistance
4. Speed or promptness
5. Assurance
6. Accuracy
7. Follow-through (as promised)
8. Empathy
9. Resolution of complaints, mistakes, or defects
10. Tangibles

Developing a **service strategy** allows a salesperson to plan his or her actions for each customer. A service strategy asks a salesperson to identify his or her business and customers and what the customers want and what is important to them. The salesperson also has to determine how his or her customers' needs and perceptions are changing. The salesperson cannot be afraid to ask how the customers rate him or her in terms of their expectations. What does the salesperson's company do best, and what can the organization do better? The salesperson, ultimately, must determine how to position his or her company in the market to differentiate its products and services. All this must be done while directing efforts against the competitors. Exhibit 9.7 is an example of a checklist for developing a service strategy.

service strategy A plan in which a salesperson identifies his or her business and customers and what the customers want and what is important to them.

communication A two-way flow of information between the salesperson and the customer.

resilience The ability of a salesperson to listen to a customer's complaint and always answer with a smile.

CUSTOMER SERVICE DIMENSIONS

There are three dimensions of customer service, with **communication** being the most important. Most problems arise because the customer was not informed of a change in plans (e.g., late delivery, price increase). Salespeople are extremely busy and many times do not have the time to communicate with all their customers. Communication tools such as e-mail can be used to quickly do mass communication to inform customers of these changes. Over time, the telephone and personal visits can be used to confirm that the customers are aware of the changes.

Another customer service dimension is **resilience**. Resilience is the ability of a salesperson to listen to a customer's complaint and always answer with a smile. A salesperson cannot lose his or her cool just because a customer does. A tired salesperson must

EXHIBIT 9.7
Checklist for Developing a Service Strategy

Questions a salesperson must ask when developing a service strategy:

- What is our business?
- Who are our customers?
- What do our customers want, and what is important to them?
- How are our customers' needs and perceptions changing?
- How are social, economic, and political factors affecting current and future customer needs and our ability to respond to them? How are competitors responding to these factors?
- How do customers rate us in terms of their expectations?
- For what are we best known?
- What do we do best?
- What can we do better?
- How can we position ourselves in the market to differentiate our services?

© iStock/Thinkstock

treat late-afternoon, difficult customers the same way that he or she would treat an early-morning dilemma while full of energy. They must both be treated well. Finally, **service motivation** is another important customer service dimension. Salespeople must be motivated to find time each day to deal with difficult customers and problems that exist. Ignoring these activities will not make them go away. Working diligently on behalf of the customer indicates to him or her that the salesperson truly cares about the partnership. If a salesperson has a complaint from a customer and gladly fixes it, the customer becomes a more committed customer.

service motivation The desire of a salesperson to service customers each day.

Salespeople who take great care of their customers are a little bit like superheroes.

Visit **www.nelson.com/student** to find the resources you need today!

Located at the back of the textbook are rip-out Chapter Review cards. Make sure you also go online to check out other tools that SELL offers to help you successfully pass your course.

- Flashcards
- Glossary
- PowerPoint Notes
- Role-Play Videos
- Games
- Interactive Quizzing

CHAPTER 9 CASE

NATURALLY BEAUTIFUL INC.

Background

Naturally Beautiful Inc. is a maker and marketer of organic cosmetics. Its cosmetics are formulated from all-natural organic ingredients. Although the company currently serves primarily the higher-end market, distributing through upscale department stores and boutiques, it would like to expand its distribution channels. It is currently developing an organic line to sell through outlets such as drug store chains and discount retailers. Long-term plans include expanding internationally, first to the US and Mexico, and eventually to Western Europe and beyond. Sales are strong and continue to rise. The company gives much of the credit for its success to its salesforce, which has done a great job expanding into new outlets while establishing and maintaining strong customer relationships. Heather Aunaturale, a nontraditional student, was hired as a sales representative by Naturally Beautiful out of college approximately ten months ago. Since being hired she has had a good deal of success, landing several new accounts. In fact, if she can land a few more accounts by the end of the rapidly approaching fiscal year, she will exceed her quota and achieve a hefty bonus. Heather is counting on this bonus because she has planned a big family trip and does not want to let her family down.

Current Situation

Lately, Heather has heard various concerns from several of her customers. For instance, the other day she received a voice mail from Rick at Beauty Boutique, a recently acquired customer whose order was missing a few items. Heather figured that shipping must have inadvertently omitted the items and that Rick could give them a call to get it fixed. She figured that it was not her fault; Rick still had product to sell and she certainly did not have time to mess with this. Similarly, she received a text from Kim at Devine's department store indicating that an expected delivery was late. Again, Heather figured she could not do anything about the delivery. She texted Kim to tell her to contact the shipping department at Naturally Beautiful about the matter. Heather also received a second e-mail from Sarah at Cosmetics Unlimited:

> *Dear Heather,*
>
> *A few weeks ago you promised you would return to train our beauty consultants on your newest product line. Our consultants need to fully understand the benefits of this new product and how it is to be applied so that they can best serve our customers. As you know, we take great pride in providing the highest quality products and services to our customer base. We discussed this when you offered me your line. Although we like your line, if we are unable to offer our customers top-shelf service with your brand then we may have to look elsewhere.*
>
> *Sincerely,*
>
> *Sarah*

Heather recalls telling Sarah that she would conduct training for her sales consultants but has been so busy working to get new accounts that she put it on the back burner. Heather was not sure that she could put Sarah off much longer, but felt it would be in her best interest to write her back and stall her for at least a couple more weeks. By then, she thought, she might have exceeded her quota.

To Heather, these incidents were minor customer issues, not even problems. In her opinion, they were nothing more than "needy" customers. As far as she was concerned, she was delivering a great product at a great price. Besides, she had more sales to make and nobody was going to help her if she came up short on providing that great family vacation she promised.

Questions

1. For each of the concerns expressed by Heather's customers in the case, explain an alternative means for handling the concern.
2. What are the potential long-run implications of how Heather is handling her current customers?
3. What types of activities can Heather do after acquiring an account to enhance customer value and ensure long-term customer relationships?

Role Play

Situation: Read the Naturally Beautiful Inc. case

Characters: Heather Aunaturale, sales representative for Naturally Beautiful; Rick, customer at Beauty Boutique; Kim, customer at Devine's department store; Sarah, customer at Cosmetics Unlimited

Scene: Employing a more personal touch, Heather contacts each customer and takes appropriate action to ensure customer satisfaction. Role play these conversations.

CHAPTER 9

Role Play: Expanding Customer Relationships: Midwest Live Bait & Tackle, LLC

Background

Midwest Live Bait & Tackle, LLC, located in Haliburton, Ontario, is a regional wholesaler of live bait and tackle to bait shops and service stations around Haliburton, Bracebridge, and Huntsville. Known for its high-quality live bait, reasonably priced tackle, and good customer service, the company has been able to maintain a steady market share over the years. Its five salespeople have been primarily responsible for selling and servicing the company's current accounts. This involves making sure that customers have bait and tackle when needed, assisting them with merchandising and pricing, and ensuring their complete satisfaction. Wanting to retire, the owner recently sold the business. The new owner was very ambitious and had big plans for expanding the company's market share. He felt that the quickest and most efficient way to move in that direction was to have his current salespeople actively pursue new accounts. Thus, he mandated new customer quotas, compensated salespeople for achieving targeted growth goals, and threatened their jobs if minimal new account requirements were not met.

Current Situation

Don Laton has been a sales representative for Midwest for over five years. Until the new ownership, he enjoyed his job very much and made a good living doing it. With his fourth child on the way, a poor economy, and a tight job market, Don did not want to jeopardize his position with the company and reluctantly went along with the new changes. However, he was very concerned with how much time prospecting for new business was taking. He felt it may be endangering his current customer relationships. What follows are excerpts from a recent conversation with Jeff Carp, a very significant customer, especially considering he sold bait and tackle out of his service station convenience store:

Jeff: Don, I've been having some problems recently with the minnows you've supplied for me. Some loss is typical, but lately the loss percentage has increased. What's going on here?

Don: I don't know Jeff. None of my other customers are having problems with their minnows. You're making sure that you don't add chlorinated water when replenishing your minnow holding tanks, aren't you?

Jeff: Of course! I recently refurbished my tanks and added a new oxygen system. Maybe that has something to do with the increasing loss. Could you check it out and see what you think?

Don: Just let me know how many minnows you think you lost and I'll see what I can do.

Jeff: Okay, but since this has been going on for the last couple of weeks I was just hoping you might be able to give me your thoughts on my new system. By the way, that new line of fishing poles doesn't seem to be moving very well. How are they moving for your other customers?

Don: I haven't heard much about those, so I guess they are moving okay.

Jeff: Do you have any ideas on how I might improve my merchandising so I can move more of them? Perhaps my price point is too high. What do you think?

Don: I'm really busy today Jeff. I have several stops yet to make and I need to call on a couple of new prospects in the area.

Jeff: You're not planning to supply my competition down the street, are you?

Don: I don't know Jeff. I've got to make a living, too, you know.

Jeff: Last week you promised to bring by some of those new plastic cricket containers you were telling me about. Did you bring any of those for me to examine?

Don: Oh no, those completely slipped my mind.

Jeff: Hmm. Well, certainly you brought me the crayfish you promised me last week. I've had customers coming in every day asking for them. Also, how about those waterdogs we talked about? I've been getting some requests for those.

Don: I should have told you sooner, but our usual crayfish supplier is having difficulty getting us as many crayfish as we need. I know you wanted 500 but I think I can give you 100. I thought we'd have the waterdogs by now, at least that is what I was told. We're still waiting.

Jeff: Don, I'm beginning to wonder how much you value my business. If you can't take care of me any longer, maybe I need to look for someone who can.

Don: I've been under a lot of pressure lately to get more done in the same amount of time. My new boss is driving me nuts! I definitely want your business.

Don needed to hurry off to meet with a new prospect. He didn't have time to preview some of the new spinner baits his company was now carrying.

Role-Play Activity

Characters: Don, sales rep; Jeff, service station owner

Action: Role play the meeting between Don and Jeff. This time have Don handle the situation (i.e., respond) as a sales rep who takes customer complaints seriously and cares about providing great customer service.

Not having sufficient time to get everything done is not the problem. We need to reprioritize the time we have so as to maximize that time and invest it where it accomplishes the most.

what do you think?

Most of the time, I set specific goals and objectives to be accomplished before making plans and taking action.

1 2 3 4 5 6 7

strongly disagree — strongly agree

10 Adding Value

Self-Leadership and Teamwork

After completing this chapter, you should be able to

10-1 Explain the five sequential stages of self-leadership.

10-2 Identify the four levels of sales goals and explain their interrelationships.

10-3 Describe two techniques for account classification.

10-4 Interpret the usefulness of different types of selling technology and automation.

10-5 Delineate six skills for building internal relationships and teams.

Introduction

Dennis Gallinat, sales management specialist for Quest Communications Business Markets Group, recounts a conversation with a highly successful salesperson in which the salesperson described how he initiates selling conversations with prospective buyers. The salesperson explained that he begins the selling conversation by stating that the most valuable thing they both had was their time, and he was not going to waste it. He would continue by saying ". . . if at any point during their conversations they became convinced taking the next step in the sales process was not in their mutual best interest, he would promptly end the dialogue." The idea was that rather than continuing a sales dialogue having minimal probability of being productive, he would stop the current sales process and then shift his focus to other prospects having greater sales potential.

Gallinat emphasizes that this salesperson "was one of the most productive, respected salespeople in the organization." Gallinat notes "the true value of a salesperson's time often rivals that of the highest paid executives in the company," which underscores the significance of understanding the value and importance of using time sensibly. Nevertheless, a recent study by the Industrial Performance Group Inc. points out that most salespeople fail in using their time productively. This study of 1,502 salespeople across 17 industries in North America found that salespeople spend an average of only 38 percent of their time in selling activities, with another 39 percent of their time spent on operations and management tasks, and the remaining 23 percent was spent on questionable and unproductive activities. "Their study also compared the time management of peak sales performers with non-peak performers and found the peak performers were spending 58 percent of their time on revenue generating sales activities, fully 20 percent more time selling than the average salesperson. Since all the salespeople have the same hours in a week, the peak performers clearly are managing their time better, more productively, and with greater sales results."

The Industrial Performance Group research study also investigated causes of the differences in sales productivity between the peak and average sales performers. Respondents indicated the gap was the result of inefficient, outdated work processes, lack of proper focus, insufficient information, and outdated training. Gallinat emphasizes that "the root cause linking each of these negative influences is a failure to manage available time wisely. By managing time wisely, salespeople create an opportunity to overcome other barriers and establish real value for their customers, higher sales volumes for their employers, and consistently greater economic rewards for themselves. While there may be many things salespeople can do to improve their sales performance, gaining control over the use of their own time may have the most lasting effect."

Dennis Gallinat, "How to Manage Time to Maximize Sales Results," *Sales and Marketing Management* (July 31, 2010), http://www.salesandmarketing.com/articles (accessed April 15, 2014).

hen observing the actions of a person who has truly mastered the skills of his or her profession, we think the person's actions come naturally. However, closer consideration will most often reveal that these seemingly innate and natural abilities are actually the result of years of fervent and purposeful planning, combined with many hours of practice. This is true for world-class surgeons, sports stars, leading educators, top attorneys—and yes, even high-performance salespeople. Good salespeople are consciously developed, not born. Toward the objective of *developing* strong salespeople, this chapter builds on the process of self-leadership to generate a framework for developing and enhancing selling skills and abilities.

First, setting effective selling goals and objectives is discussed and integrated with methods for territory analysis and account classification. This is followed by a discussion of how the objectives and information from the territory and account analysis become inputs for generating and implementing effective multilevel sales planning. The importance of assessing performance results and level of goal attainment is also reviewed. Wrapping up the chapter is an examination of teamwork as a vehicle for expanding the capabilities of an individual salesperson, increasing customer value, and creating sustainable competitive advantage for salespeople.

self-leadership The process of doing the right things and doing them well.

© peepo/Vetta/Getty

Like the skills and abilities of an athlete, the skills and abilities required for success in selling are the result of purposeful planning and many hours of practice.

10-1 Effective Self-Leadership

How often have you said or thought to yourself, "I just don't have enough time to get everything done?" In reality, most people do not need more time. Rather, they need to prioritize the time they have. There are only so many hours in a day, and highly effective salespeople know that they can never have enough quality selling time. To maximize their selling time, these high performers have developed strong self-leadership skills and treat time as a valuable, irreplaceable resource and invest it wisely where it will accomplish the most good.

Self-leadership—a critical requirement for success in any career—has been described as doing the right things and doing them well. It is not simply the amount of effort that determines an achievement, but rather how well that effort is honed and aligned with our goals. In selling, this is often restated as selling smarter rather than selling harder. That is, before expending valuable time and resources, salespeople must establish priorities in the form of objectives. Then, and only then, do they implement the strategic plan that has been specifically developed to achieve their objectives in the light of the available resources and market potential that exist within the territory. Self-leadership translates to a process of first deciding what is to be accomplished and then putting into motion the proper plan designed to achieve those objectives.

The process of self-leadership is composed of five sequential stages. First, goals and objectives must be set that properly reflect what is important and what is to be accomplished. This is followed by an analysis of the territory and classification of accounts. Next, with goals in place and accounts classified, strategic plans designed to achieve the objectives through proper allocation of resources and effort are implemented. The next stage maximizes the effectiveness of allocated resources through the process of tapping technology and automation to expand resource capabilities. Finally, assessment activities are conducted to evaluate performance and goal attainment and to assess possible changes in plans and strategies. The nature of the sequential interrelationships among these five stages is illustrated in Figure 10.1.

FIGURE 10.1

Five Sequential Stages of Self-Leadership

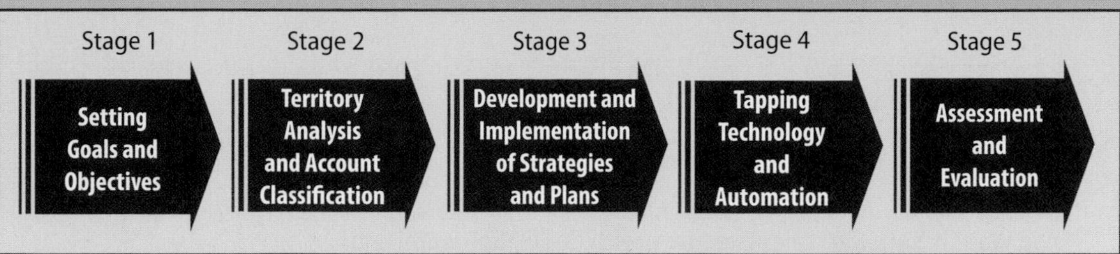

Self-leadership is a process of first deciding what is to be accomplished and then setting into motion the proper plan to achieve the desired objectives.

© traveler1116/iStockphoto

There are only so many hours in a day. Maximize your effective selling time by developing strong self-leadership skills.

10-2 STAGE ONE: SETTING GOALS AND OBJECTIVES

Establishing priorities by setting **goals and objectives** is the key to effective self-leadership. This first stage of self-leadership has been appropriately referred to as "beginning with the end in mind."[1] First of all, if a salesperson does not understand what is important, how does that salesperson know what to focus on? Further, if a salesperson does not understand what he or she is setting out to accomplish, how could that salesperson know where to begin, how to proceed, or even which plan is best for getting there? Finally, without clear goals, how could salespeople know when the objective has been achieved? Without clear goals and objectives, it is very natural to drift from task to task and typically focus on minor and less-productive tasks, as they are the easiest to complete. The end result of this natural drift is poor sales performance and frustration. The positive impact of planning ahead and establishing priorities is further evidenced by the experiences of David Waugh, a software sales executive for Confio Software, in "Professional Selling in the 21st Century: Develop Task-Driven Activity Plans to Drive Selling Success."

goals and objectives The things a salesperson sets out to accomplish.

What Makes a Good Goal?

Although goals and objectives might best be described as desired outcomes, these two words carry specific meaning. *Desired* implies that it is something worthy of working toward and expending resources to reach. *Outcome* connotes that it is a specific result or effect resulting from certain activities or behaviours—something that can be described and pointed out. As illustrated in Exhibit 10.1, properly developed goals share three key characteristics: They are (1) realistic, yet challenging, (2) specific and quantifiable, and (3) time specific.

PROFESSIONAL SELLING IN THE 21ST CENTURY

Develop Task-Driven Activity Plans to Drive Selling Success

© alexsl/iStockphoto

David Waugh, software sales executive with Confio Software, knows the value of self-leadership in a high-tech business environment. Waugh, a 14-year veteran of software and consulting sales, has seen many different sales environments. With experience spanning working for a Fortune 100 corporation to managing a salesforce for a start-up company, he has learned that having task-driven activity plans and utilizing automation technology are essential for success.

At Confio, Waugh ends each day by developing a task-driven activity plan for the following day. He uses software products integrated with his e-mail and online calendar to lay out upcoming tasks and appointments. Waugh starts each business day knowing exactly what he must complete in order to accomplish his daily goals. Tasks are broken down into categories including telephone calls, lead management activities, strategic planning sessions, and prospecting for new clients. "No matter how you lay out your daily activity plan," he is quick to point out, "it must be straightforward and easy to follow."

When he started his career in 1994, the norm for activity plans was paper day planners and note cards. Today, Waugh utilizes a Web-based salesforce automation tool to manage the hundreds of e-mails, telephone calls, and business contacts in his daily activity plan. By combining his daily regimen of task-driven activity plans with an automated system, he can quickly navigate through his day and follow a sales process with each prospect that can be tracked for effectiveness and efficiency.

EXHIBIT 10.1

Required Characteristics of Goals and Objectives

Effective Goals and Objectives Must Possess Three Fundamental Characteristics:

- Goals should be realistic, yet challenging.
- Goals should be specific and quantifiable.
- Goals should be time specific.

- *Realistic, Yet Challenging*—Goals should be realistic and reachable. When set beyond what is possible, goals cease to motivate and often become a disincentive to performance. At the same time, goals should be challenging. If goals are continually set at a level that is too easy to reach, performance tends to regress to the lower standard. Goals that are challenging tend to be more motivating than goals that are easily achieved.
- *Specific and Quantifiable*—Without specificity, goals become ambiguous and have no clear meaning. For instance, the goal of having the top territory in the district could be interpreted in many ways. Does top territory translate to having the largest increase in sales, having the fewest number of customer defections, having the highest customer satisfaction scores, having the smallest number of price discounts,

or possibly having the largest reduction in travel expenses? Without specificity, the goal becomes a moving target, and it is difficult to know where to apply effort. In a similar fashion, goals should be quantifiable—that is, they should be measurable. The goal of increasing sales is certainly commendable, but how might it be judged as having been accomplished? Is a 1 percent increase sufficient or is 12 percent more in line with expectations? If a 12 percent increase is the expectation, then the goal should be a 12 percent increase in sales—a quantifiable and measurable outcome that can be objectively measured and assessed.

- *Time Specific*—Stating a specific time line is the third requirement of goals and objectives. A goal of achieving a 12 percent increase in sales by December 31 is much more appealing than simply stating that the goal is to increase sales by 12 percent. Associating time lines with goals establishes a deadline for planning purposes and provides motivation by instilling a sense of urgency for taking action.

Working with Different Levels and Types of Goals

For maximum effectiveness, salespeople establish goals at four different levels: personal goals, territory goals, account goals, and sales call goals. Although each level requires different types of effort and produces different outcomes, each of the levels is interrelated and interdependent on the others. These interrelationships and dependencies are illustrated in Exhibit 10.2. A salesperson's **personal goals** might include achieving a $70,000 annual income during the current year ending December 31. If the salesperson receives a commission of 11 percent on sales, this personal goal is directly related to and dependent on achieving the **territory goal** of selling $636,364 in products across the territory in the same time period. Assuming 19 equally sized accounts compose the territory, the territory goal is dependent on achieving the **account goal** of an average of $33,493 in products sold to each account during the year. Considering that each account is called on twice every month, a **sales call goal** of $1,396 in sales per call is required to achieve the account goal. As illustrated in this example, each higher level goal is ultimately dependent on the salesperson setting and achieving lower level, specific goals for each and every sales call.

Although illustrative of the interdependence among different levels of goals, the previous example is admittedly simplistic in its exclusive use of goals based on sales volume. In reality, there are many different types of goals that a salesperson might effectively use. Exhibit 10.3 illustrates examples of common sales goals.

personal goals A salesperson's individual desired accomplishment, such as achieving a desired annual income over a specific period.

territory goal A salesperson's desire to sell a certain amount of product within an area or territory to achieve personal goals.

account goal A salesperson's desire to sell a certain amount of product to one customer or account to achieve territory and personal goals.

sales call goal A salesperson's desire to sell a certain amount of product per each sales call to achieve account, territory, and personal goals.

territory analysis The process of surveying an area to determine customers and prospects who are most likely to buy.

EXHIBIT 10.2

Four Interdependent Levels of Salesperson Objectives

Personal goal—desired annual income	$ 70,000
Is dependent on annual territory sales goal (11% commission on sales)	$636,364
Is dependent on annual account sales goal (19 equally sized accounts)	$ 33,493
Is dependent on sales call goal (each account is called on twice a month)	$ 1,396

10-3 STAGE TWO: TERRITORY ANALYSIS AND ACCOUNT CLASSIFICATION

Territory analysis and classification of accounts, the second stage of self-leadership, is all about finding the customers and prospects who are most likely to buy. Who are they, and where are they located? What and why do they buy? How much and how often do they purchase? Who has the authority to buy, and who can influence the purchase decision? What is the probability of selling to this account? What is the potential share of account that might be gained?

EXHIBIT 10.3
Common Types of Sales Goals

• Financial goals	Income, financial security
• Career advancement goals	Work in chosen field, advancement
• Personal development goals	Education, training, relationships outside work
• Sales volume goals	Dollar sales, unit sales, number of orders, aggregates or by groups
• Sales call activity goals	Calls made, calls/day, calls/account, presentations made
• Sales expense goals	Total expenses, by category, percentage of sales
• Profitability goals	Gross profits, contribution margin, returns and discounts
• Market share	Total share of potential market, peer group comparisons
• Share of account	Share of customer's purchases
• Ancillary activity goals	Required reports turned in, training conducted, service calls made
• Customer retention goals	Number of accounts lost, complaints received, lost account ratios
• New account goals	Number of new accounts
• Customer service goals	Customer goodwill generation, level of satisfaction, receivables collected
• Conversion goals	Ratio of number of sales to number of calls made

account classification
The process of placing existing customers and prospects into categories based on their sales potential.

Many sources offer intelligence that will assist the salesperson in answering these questions, and the information boom on the Internet makes accessing this information easier than ever before. In addition to numerous supplier directories available on the Web, commercial business information suppliers, such as *Canadian Trade Index*, Scott's Directories, *Standard & Poor's*, and *Canadian Key Business Directory*, offer easy-to-use databases that are fully searchable by company, industry, and geographic location. Salespeople can also access individual company websites, trade directories, professional association membership listings, and commercial mailing list providers. Personal observation, discussions with other selling professionals, and company sales records are also excellent sources for gaining valuable information.

Much of this information can be plotted to develop detailed territory maps and pinpoint pockets of existing and potential business. In addition, understanding the territory at the individual account level provides the input required for account classification.

Account Classification

Account classification places existing customers and prospects into categories based on their sales potential and assists salespeople in prioritizing accounts for call planning and time allocation purposes. During the process of account

© StockLite/Shutterstock

Territory analysis is all about finding the customers and prospects who are most likely to buy and identifying who has the purchasing authority.

classification, it is common for salespeople to find that 80 to 90 percent of their sales potential is generated by 10 to 20 percent of the total accounts. Consequently, the results of account classification can guide salespeople in more efficient allocation of time, effort, and resources while simultaneously enabling them to be more effective in achieving sales goals. Two commonly used methods for classifying accounts are single-factor analysis and portfolio analysis.

Single-Factor Analysis

Single-factor analysis, also referred to as ABC analysis, is the simplest and most often used method for classifying accounts. As the name suggests, accounts are analyzed on the basis of one single factor—typically the level of sales potential. On the basis of sales potential, the accounts are placed into three or four categories denoted by letters of the alphabet, A, B, C, and D. Accounts with the highest potential are traditionally sorted into category A, whereas those with medium potential go into B, and so on. All accounts in the same category receive equal selling effort. For example, A accounts may be called on every two weeks, B accounts every four to six weeks, and C accounts might receive a personal sales call once a year and be serviced by the seller's telemarketing team during the interim. Single-factor classification schemas used by three different sales organizations are summarized in Exhibit 10.4.

single-factor analysis
A method for analyzing accounts that is based on one single factor, typically the level of sales potential. Also called ABC analysis.

EXHIBIT 10.4

Different Single-Factor Account Analysis Schema Used by Different Companies

Class of Account	Schema One: InquisLogic Inc.	Schema Two: Web Resource Associates, LLC	Schema Three Federal Metal Products
A Accounts	Accounts with highest potential (the 20% that do or could account for 80% of sales) Annual number of calls = 24	Accounts with highest potential (the 20% that do or could account for 80% of sales) Annual number of calls = 52	High volume current customers (the 20% that currently account for 80% of sales volume) Annual number of calls = 48
B Accounts	Medium potential accounts (the 80% that account for 20% of sales volume) Annual number of calls = 12	Accounts with moderate sales potential but who are regular and reliable customers Annual number of calls = 24	Accounts with high potential but who are not current customers Annual number of calls = 12
C Accounts	Accounts with the least sales potential Annual number of calls = 4	Lower sales potential accounts Annual number of calls = 8	Medium potential accounts that are current customers Annual number of calls = 12
D Accounts	None. This schema only uses 3 classes of accounts	Accounts that cost more in time and energy than they produce in sales or profits Annual number of calls = 0	Accounts with medium potential but who are not current customers Annual number of calls = 6

The simplicity of single-factor analysis is a prime contributor to its popularity for use by field salespeople. It is straightforward and requires no statistical analysis or data manipulation. Although this lack of complexity is appealing, its ability to use only one factor for analyzing and classifying accounts is also a significant limitation. Sales potential is certainly an important input in allocating selling effort, but other factors should also be considered. Possible other factors of interest are the selling company's competitive strength in each account, the account's need for additional attention and effort, profitability of the account, and amount of competitive pressure on the account.

It is common for salespeople to find 80 to 90 percent of their sales potential generated by 10 to 20 percent of their accounts.

Portfolio Analysis

Also referred to as two-factor analysis, the **portfolio analysis** method attempts to overcome the weakness of single-factor analysis by allowing two factors to be considered simultaneously. Each account is examined on the basis of the two specified factors and sorted into the proper segment of a matrix. This matrix is typically divided into four cells, and accounts are placed into the proper classification cell on the basis of their individual ratings ("high" and "low" or "strong" and "weak") on each factor of interest. Cell location denotes the overall attractiveness of the different accounts and serves as a guide for the salesperson's allocation of resources and effort. Typically, each account in the same cell will receive the same amount of selling effort.

Exhibit 10.5 details the account characteristics and suggested selling effort allocations for a typical portfolio analysis incorporating the factors of (1) account opportunity and (2) seller's competitive position.[2] Account opportunity takes into consideration the buyer's level of need for and ability to purchase the seller's products, along with financial stability and growth prospects. Competitive position denotes the relationship between the account and the seller and includes such variables as the seller's share of account, competitive pressure, and the key decision maker's attitude toward the seller. Accounts sorted into Segment One are high on opportunity, exhibit strong competitive positions, and should receive the highest level of selling effort. Accounts falling into Segment Two are high on opportunity but weak on competitive position. These accounts should receive a high level of attention to strengthen the seller's competitive position. Segment Three contains the 80 to 90 percent of accounts doing 10 to 20 percent of the seller's volume. These accounts are loyal and regular customers (high on competitive position) but offer weak opportunity. Strategically, these accounts should receive a lower investment of selling effort designed to maintain the seller's current competitive position. Accounts sorted into Segment Four are considered unattractive and allocated minimal selling effort as they are characterized by low opportunity and weak competitive position. Within the past several years, many sellers have been successful in servicing Segment Three and Four accounts outside the personal selling channel by using alternatives, such as telemarketing, direct mail, and the Internet.

portfolio analysis A method for analyzing accounts that allows two factors to be considered simultaneously. Also called two-factor analysis.

Portfolio analysis offers the advantages of enhanced flexibility and ability to incorporate multiple variables for analyzing and sorting accounts. Reflecting these strong points, the use of portfolio analysis is gaining in popularity.

STAGE THREE: DEVELOPMENT AND IMPLEMENTATION OF STRATEGIES AND PLANS

Stage One provides the salesperson with the guidelines of what is important and the goals to be accomplished at the levels of individual sales calls, accounts, and the overall territory. Stage Two identifies and establishes the priority and potential of each account in the territory, along with the relative location of each account. Top salespeople do not stop there! They use this information to develop strategies and plans that will guide them toward achieving their goals by applying their available resources in a deliberate and organized fashion that effectively cultivates and harvests the potential sales available in the territory.

EXHIBIT 10.5

Portfolio/Two-Factor Account Analysis and Selling Strategies

Account Opportunity	Competitive Position: Strong	Competitive Position: Weak
High	**Segment One** **Level of Attractiveness** Accounts are very attractive because they offer high opportunity and the seller has a strong competitive position. **Selling Effort Strategy** Accounts should receive a heavy investment of effort and resources to take advantage of high opportunity and maintain/improve competitive position. **Exemplary Sales Call Strategy = 36 calls/yr.**	**Segment Two** **Level of Attractiveness** Accounts are potentially attractive because of high opportunity, but the seller currently has weak competitive position. **Selling Effort Strategy** Where it is possible to strengthen the seller's competitive position, a heavy investment of selling effort should be applied. **Exemplary Sales Call Strategy = 24 calls/yr.**
Low	**Segment Three** **Level of Attractiveness** Accounts are moderately attractive because of the seller having a fairly strong competitive position. However, future opportunity is low. **Selling Effort Strategy** Accounts should receive a moderately heavy level of selling effort that is sufficient to maintain current competitive position. **Exemplary Sales Call Strategy = 12 calls/yr.**	**Segment Four** **Level of Attractiveness** Accounts are very unattractive. They offer low opportunity and the seller has weak competitive position. **Selling Effort Strategy** Accounts should receive minimal personal selling effort. Alternatives such as telemarketing, direct mail, and Internet, should be explored. **Exemplary Sales Call Strategy = 6 calls/yr.**

Establishing and Implementing Selling Tasks and Activity Plans

When properly executed, **sales planning** results in a schedule of activities that can be used as a map for achieving objectives. First, start with the big picture—a long-term plan spanning the next 6 to 12 months. This big picture highlights commitments and deadlines and facilitates setting up the activities required to meet those commitments and deadlines. In turn, the longer range plans provide the basis for shorter time frame plans and selling activities. The salesperson planning program at Federal Metal Products (FMP) offers a good overview and prototype of effective salesperson planning.

FMP, a middle market supplier of metal production components, trains its salespeople to prepare and submit annual territory plans and budgets by November 15 each year. With that recurring deadline marked on their schedules, FMP salespeople work backward on their calendars to establish key checkpoints for their planning activities. This establishes a timeline to guide and assist salespeople in making the submission deadline.

If salespeople project that it will take four weeks to assemble and draft their territory sales plan, they work back four weeks from the November 15 date and establish October 15 as the date to begin assembling their data and building their plans. How long will it take

sales planning The process of scheduling activities that can be used as a map for achieving objectives.

© gerenme/iStockphoto

An effective plan works like a map, showing the way from where you are to where you want to go—your objective.

to collect the needed data properly? Six weeks? If so, their schedule should reflect beginning that activity by September 1.

Sales plans should take into consideration scheduled meetings and training sessions, holidays, trade shows, and vacation time. Plans should also contain periodic checkpoints for assessing progress toward goals. A salesperson's objective of $750,000 in sales for the year equates to a goal averaging $62,500 in sales every month. Accordingly, the long-term master plan should include monthly checkpoints to compare the schedule versus actual performance data. Is performance on course, ahead, or lagging behind? If not on schedule, the corresponding and more detailed weekly plans should be revised to reflect salespeople's strategies for getting back on course.

Salespeople at FMP develop weekly plans from their longer term annual plan. These shorter term plans detail the selling-related activities to be accomplished that week. To create a weekly plan, first identify the priorities that must be accomplished to stay on schedule. Then, for each of these priorities, detail the associated activities and schedule the time that it will take for completion. What areas of the territory will you focus on? What accounts will be called on, and what is the objective for each call? What are the best times to call for appointments? Are there account preferences as to what days and times they work with salespeople? How much time must be allowed for travel, waiting, and working with each account? What products will be featured? What information and materials will be needed?

In turn, the priorities and activities identified in the weekly plan should become the points of focus for the daily plan. Days that end on a successful note begin with a thorough and written schedule detailing tasks and priorities for that day and the activities that must be carried out to achieve them.

The optimum schedule emphasizes tasks and activities that will make the greatest sales impact—working with customers. As illustrated by the FMP's "Daily Sales Plan Worksheet" shown in Exhibit 10.6, daily plans should detail the amount of time projected for each scheduled task and activity. To maximize the effectiveness of daily sales plans, salespeople should adhere to two guiding principles.[3]

- *Do them, and do them in writing.* Written plans are better developed and provide more motivation and commitment for salespeople to carry them through to completion. Furthermore, written plans help to ensure that priority items do not fall through the cracks because something was forgotten.
- *Keep it current and flexible.* Make a new daily plan every day. Try as we might, things do not always go as planned. Consequently, changes may be needed, and uncompleted priorities or activities from one day may have to be carried over to the next.

Establishing Territory Routing Plans

Territory routing plans incorporate information developed in the territory analysis and account classification stage to minimize the encroachment of unproductive travel time on time that could be better spent working with customers. Good routing plans minimize the backtracking and crisscrossing that would otherwise occur and allow the salesperson to use time more efficiently.

Knowing how many calls can be made each day, the required call frequency for each account classification, and the relative geographic location of and distance between accounts, a salesperson can plot different routing strategies and decide on the optimal plan. Many sales professionals continue to use the traditional coloured map pins and felt-tip markers on a wall map. However, a variety of easy-to-use and affordable computer applications that

EXHIBIT 10.6

Example of a Typical Daily Sales Plan Worksheet

Federal Metal Products
Daily Sales Plan Worksheet
Salesperson: Shiv Manchanda Day: Friday Date: 8/29

Time	Task or Priority	Activity	People Involved	Time Needed	Goal/ Anticipated Results	Notes and Comments
8:30 a.m.	Set appointments	Phone calls	Jill Attaway Digital Systems	10 min	Appointment for next week	Requested that I come by
	"	"	Bart Waits Enterprise One	10 min	"	
	"	"	Kerri Williams Flo-Forms	10 min	"	Will be placing order in 3 weeks
9:00 a.m.	"	"	Marilyn Henry InQuisLogic	10 min	Clarify service problem	Send info to engineering
10:30 a.m.	Demonstrate new bearing line	Sales call	Mike Humphreys ICOM	60 min	Info gathering	Currently buying from Gem Rollers
12 noon	Get order commitment	Sales call— Lunch	Jack Kessler MDQG	120 min	$12,000 order	Gem submitted proposal 8/20
3:00 p.m.	Take sample of proposed line	Sales call	Aimee Williams MOCO, Inc	60 min	$15,200 order	Ready to buy, wants to see pdct. sample
4:30 p.m.	Check on delivery	Service call	Ron Meier Web Resources	50 min	Delight the customer	First time to buy from us!
6:00 p.m.	Complete paperwork	Submit call reports		45 min		
7:00 p.m.	Prepare daily schedule	Planning		45 min		

plot optimal routing plans are available and are growing in popularity.[4] Optimized routing plans correspond to one of five common patterns: straight line, cloverleaf, circular, leapfrog, and major city.

Straight-Line Routing Plans With a **straight-line routing plan**, salespeople start from their offices and make calls in one direction until they reach the end of the territory. As illustrated in Figure 10.2, at that point they change direction and continue to make calls on a straight line following the new vector. This continues until the salesperson

straight-line routing plan A territory routing plan in which salespeople start from their offices and make calls in one direction until they reach the end of the territory.

FIGURE 10.2

Territory Route Patterns

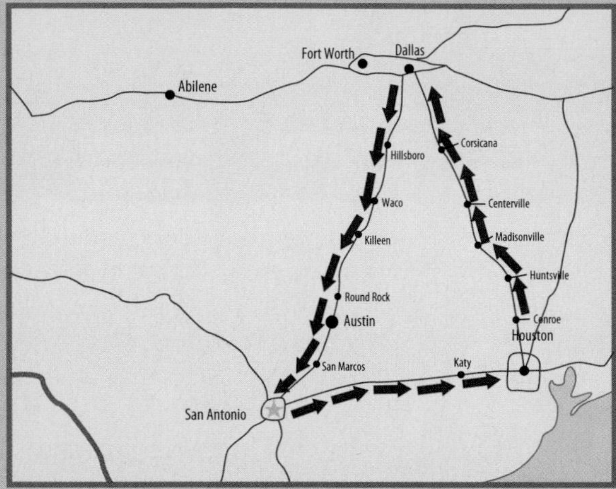

Straight-line territory routes make calls across the territory in one direction and then change direction to work back to the starting point.

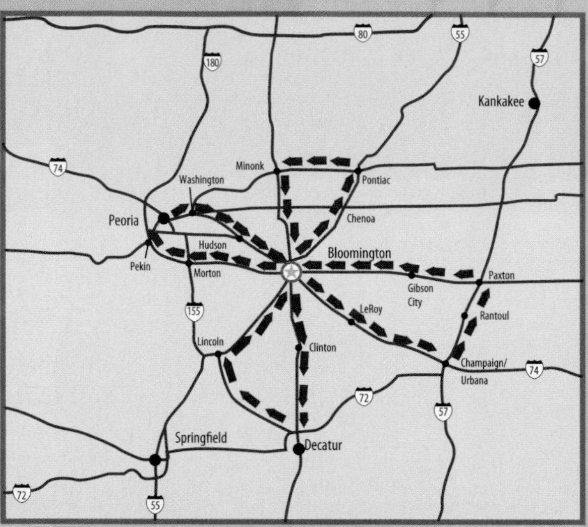

Cloverleaf territory routes work different parts of the territory in a series of circular loops.

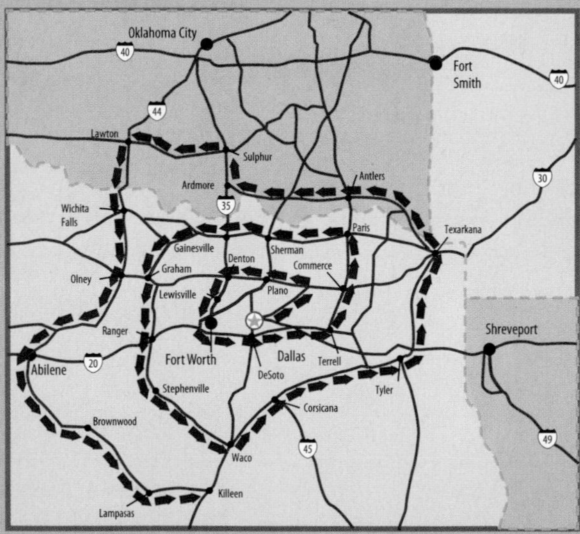

Circular territory routes cover the territory in a series of concentric circles spiralling across it.

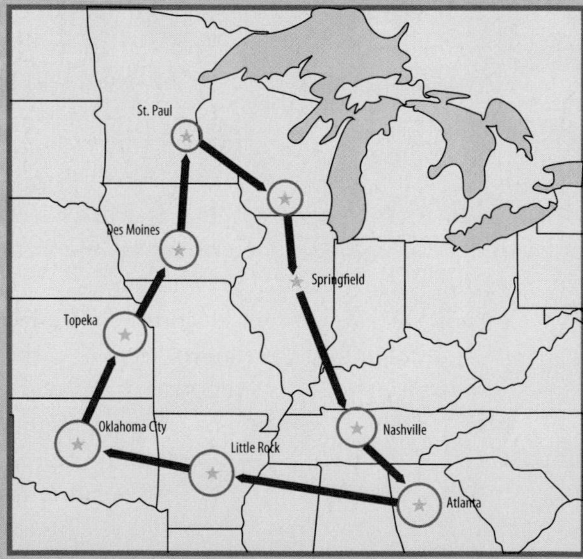

Leapfrog territory routes work accounts clustered in one location and then jump to a different cluster of accounts.

returns to the office location. The straight-line pattern works best when accounts are located in clusters that are some distance from one another.

Cloverleaf Routing Plans The **cloverleaf routing plan** pattern is best used when accounts are concentrated in different parts of the territory. On each trip, the salesperson works a different part of the territory and travels in a circular loop back to the starting point. An example of the cloverleaf routing plan is depicted in Figure 10.2. Each loop could take a day, a week, or longer to complete. A new loop is covered on each trip until the entire territory has been covered.

Circular Routing Plans Circular routing plans begin at the office and move in an expanding pattern of concentric circles that spiral across the territory. Figure 10.2 traces an exemplary circular routing plan working from an office in Dallas. This method works best when accounts are evenly dispersed throughout the territory.

Leapfrog Routing Plans The **leapfrog routing plan** is best applied when the territory is large and accounts are clustered into several widely dispersed groups. Beginning in one cluster, the salesperson works each of the accounts at that location and then jumps to the next cluster. As shown in Figure 10.2, this continues until the last cluster has been worked and the salesperson jumps back to the office or home. When the distance between clusters is great, the salesperson will typically make the jumps by flying.

Major City Routing Plans When the territory is composed of a major metropolitan area, the territory is split into a series of geometric shapes reflecting each one's concentration and pattern of accounts. Figure 10.3 depicts a typical **major city routing plan**. Downtown areas are typically highly concentrated with locations controlled by a grid of city blocks and streets. Consequently, the downtown segment is typically a small square or rectangular area allowing accounts to be worked in a straight-line fashion street by street. Outlying areas are placed in evenly balanced triangles or pie-shaped quadrants, with one quadrant being covered at a time in either a straight-line or cloverleaf pattern.

FIGURE 10.3

Major City Route Pattern

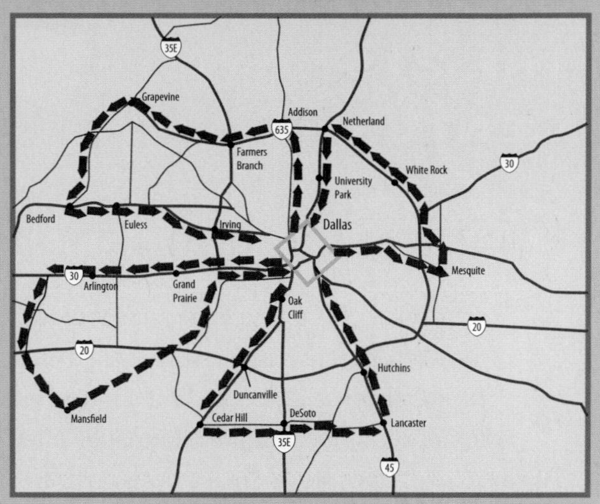

Major city territory routing patterns work downtown on a basis of street grids and work outlying areas by using a cloverleaf or straight-line pattern.

10-4 STAGE FOUR: TAPPING TECHNOLOGY AND AUTOMATION

Selling technology and automation tools are here to stay and are being transformed from neat toys to necessary tools. Properly applied, selling technology spurs and creates creativity and innovation, streamlines all aspects of the selling process, generates new and improved selling opportunities, facilitates cross-functional teaming and intraorganizational communication, and enhances communication and follow-up with customers.[5] In summary, tapping the proper selling technologies and salesforce automation tools allows salespeople to expand their available resources for enhanced selling performance and outcomes. Experiences with improved selling efficiency and customer satisfaction are illustrated in "Professional Selling in the 21st Century: Chatter: Facebook for Salespeople."

cloverleaf routing plan A territory routing plan in which the salesperson works a different part of the territory and travels in a circular loop back to the starting point.

circular routing plan A territory routing plan in which the salesperson begins at the office and moves in an expanding pattern of concentric circles that spiral across the territory.

leapfrog routing plan A territory routing plan in which, beginning in one cluster, the salesperson works each of the accounts at that location and then jumps to the next cluster.

major city routing plan A territory routing plan used when the territory is composed of a major metropolitan area and the territory is split into a series of geometric shapes reflecting each one's concentration and pattern of accounts.

© luchezar/iStockphoto

PROFESSIONAL SELLING IN THE 21ST CENTURY

Chatter: Facebook for Salespeople

Jim Steele, Salesforce.com president of worldwide sales, explains that their collaboration application, called Chatter, is designed to be a Facebook for salespeople. With Chatter, everyone involved with a customer account can share information affecting that account as it occurs. "As a result, salespeople can make decisions based on the most current information possible, just like the quarterback who can change a play at the line of scrimmage if he spots a weakness in the defense."

Using an example from his own experience, Steele explains: "I was going to meet with the CEO of a company in LA, so I went on Chatter and put in that I was on my way to call on this CEO, and within five minutes I received a message from the VP of marketing, who said, 'I just met with those guys last week. They have a really interesting scenario that I think we have a great solution for,' and he attached a link with more details. Within an hour, ten other people weighed in, which gave me a terrific, cross-functional view of what was going on at this particular account and a lot of great ideas for what I could talk to the CEO about."

Source: Malcolm Fleschner, "Collaboration Management," *Selling Power* (May/June 2010).

selling technology and automation Tools that streamline the selling process, generate improved selling opportunities, facilitate cross-functional teaming and intraorganizational communication, and enhance communication and follow-up with customers.

Salespeople, sales managers, and customers are unanimous in their agreement that the best salespeople are those who stay up with changes and developments in technologies with selling applications. With a multitude of rapidly changing and evolving technology choices, salespeople not only must master the technology itself but also must understand when and where it can be applied most effectively. Exemplary selling technologies being used by today's salespeople include the following tools.[6]

Mobile Sales Technologies

At the centre of virtually every selling technology is the computer. Choices include desktops, notebooks, laptops, netbooks, smartphones, and personal data assistants (PDAs). With the ever-expanding availability of broadband and wireless connectivity, today's salesperson is always in touch with customers, with sales support, and with sales data and information. For immediate immersion into the high-tech side of selling, simply walk through the waiting areas of any major airport. Salespeople can be seen entering customer orders, generating reports, and submitting proposals by using standard word-processing packages and even customized online electronic forms. Others are analyzing customer accounts by using spreadsheet applications and query-based database programs that access and analyze a database according to the questions the user wants to have answered. Several will be observed reviewing and updating customer files by using one of the many mobile and highly capable contact management/CRM software applications. These user-friendly programs provide salespeople with a convenient option to catalogue, search, and access comprehensive information regarding individual customers. Looking closer, numerous salespeople will be revising and polishing graphics and presentations with software, such as PowerPoint, Keynote, Flash, and Open Office Impress. Still others will be checking and responding to e-mail, submitting electronic reports, accessing online territory route maps, and using scheduling programs to set up the next day's call plans.

Salesperson Customer Relationship Management (CRM)

Effective customer relationships generate customer loyalty and the revenue increases critical for sustained performance. Toward meeting this challenge, companies of all sizes are deploying customer relationship management (CRM) applications and strategies that integrate multiple communication and customer contact channels—including the Web, e-mail, call centres, and salespeople—to maximize customer interactions. However, detailed customer information is of little use if a salesperson cannot access it when they need it—such as during a sales call in a customer's office. Sales professionals often work outside the office and need up-to-date information while in the field. Being able to access and offer the right information to customers at the right point in the sales cycle enables salespeople to increase sales dramatically while simultaneously increasing customer satisfaction and loyalty. **Mobile salesperson CRM solutions**, such as Siebel, Salesforce.com, Microsoft Dynamics, and SalesLogix, are the key to accessing this information from the field and provide remote access to data, such as contacts, customer information, leads, reports, price lists, inventory levels, and opportunity forecasting. Mobile CRM applications use wireless broadband access to enable users instantly to view, create, and modify data on any Internet-capable device, such as smartphones, tablets, and laptops. This hand-held access to valuable account information allows a salesperson to tap into the same sales, marketing, and customer service data they have access to in the office—without having to leave the field. Mobile CRM is rapidly becoming a critical requirement for effectively competing in today's fast-paced selling environment and increasing customer expectations in terms of customized levels of service.

Deal Analytics

Deal analytics is the descriptive name given to a new set of "smart" tools in the area of salesforce automation that are proving especially useful for salespeople. These analytical tools use mobile CRM systems to access and analyze data on past customer behaviour, cross-selling opportunities, and demographics to identify areas of opportunity and high interest to a customer. Salespeople also use deal analytics tools to access and compare competitive information, such as pricing and bundled offers, which can result in more effective proposals and negotiations.

The Internet, Intranets, and Extranets

Company networks have been used for many years; however, the advent of the Internet has made them much more affordable and easier to maintain.

Accessing the **Internet** instantly networks a salesperson with the world: customers, information sources, other salespeople, sales management, and others. More importantly, the Internet puts the salesperson into contact with his or her customer-community and support networks from anywhere in the world, 24 hours a day, seven days a week. Going beyond the convenience of e-mail, many sales organizations are setting up **intranets** and **extranets**—secure and proprietary organizational websites that are protected by passwords and security authorizations. Intranets are networks within the organization that use the Internet or commercial channels to provide direct links between company units and individuals. Extranets are a special form of intranet that is still for proprietary and restricted use but links to specific suppliers and customers to allow them controlled and secure access to the organization's network to facilitate communication and exchange.

These secure websites become instant organizational intranets used for communication, training, videoconferencing, Web-conferencing, and secure data interchange. Using such Web-enabled intranets, Diamond Equipment Corporation's salespeople can link to the latest product information and spec sheets, obtain updated inventory and production numbers, download company information, and print customized proposals for customer presentations from anywhere in the world. CDW provides each of their major accounts with a customized extranet that

mobile salesperson CRM solutions Wireless broadband applications that enable users to view, create, and modify data on any Internet-capable devices, such as smartphones, tablets, and laptops.

deal analytics "Smart" salesforce automation tools that analyze data on past customer behaviour, cross-selling opportunities, and demographics to identify areas of opportunity and high customer interest.

Internet A technology tool that instantly networks the salesperson with customers, information sources, other salespeople, sales management, and others.

intranets Secured networks within the organization that use the Internet or commercial channels to provide direct linkages between company units and individuals.

extranets A form of intranet that is still restricted but links to specific suppliers and customers to allow them controlled access to the organization's network and databases.

gives the customer access to CDW on a 24-hour-a-day, seven-day-a-week basis. Buyers can track orders online, download product and technical specifications, access customer support technicians, check prices and availability of products, and even place orders for next-day delivery. Rather than spending time travelling to customers' offices, Windy City Wire's salespeople deliver their sales presentations by combining teleconferences and Web presentations using WebEx. The use of Internet- and intranet-based technologies shortens the sales cycle by allowing sales meetings and presentations to be created and delivered in less time than traditional face-to-face processes would take. If a salesperson can save just 10 minutes a day by using Web-based presentation libraries and online product and pricing information, he or she will gain an additional week's worth of productivity over the course of a year. However, as illustrated by the situation described in "An Ethical Dilemma," the acceptance and adoption of advanced technologies are not always easy to accomplish.

An Ethical Dilemma

© pictafolio/iStockphoto

Janice is an account manager for Timaru Solutions and is responsible for selling the company's hardware and application-based technology solutions throughout the Greater Toronto Area. Embracing the collaborative selling approach, Timaru utilizes an extensive and highly interactive Internet-based extranet system to stay close to its customers and ahead of the competition. Timaru's extranet system allows customers to access product, service, and account information 24/7. Because the extranet allows customers to access proprietary information including order status, product availability, pricing, and even order entry and transactions, access is controlled through a secure password authentication process. Access is granted only to well-established, major customers. Janice has just learned that a technology buyer at Advanced Energy Partners, one of Janice's key accounts, has shared their extranet access codes with the salesperson for Timaru's main competitor. Apparently the competitor wanted access to Timaru's pricing structure so they could undercut the prices and acquire some of Timaru's major customers. What should Janice do?

a) Inform her sales manager so that Timaru can change their pricing as a result of the breach in security.
b) Deactivate the Advanced Energy Partners codes for accessing Timaru's extranet so the competitor can no longer access the information.
c) Provide the Advanced Energy Partners purchasing department with new access codes, remind them that the codes are proprietary, and use the breach of trust as an opportunity to enhance the Timaru–Advanced Energy Partners relationship.

High-Tech Sales Support Offices

Organizations that have salesforces widely dispersed geographically or travelling across multiple regions of the nation or world have found it advantageous to establish **high-tech sales support offices** at multiple locations. Both resident and nonresident salespeople use these offices to access a wider range of selling technology than could be easily carried on a tablet or laptop computer. These offices also provide points of access to the various networks, intranets, and extranets the organization maintains. IBM maintains such high-tech offices as these at its installations around the world. An IBM representative in Montreal might find himself working as part of a team on a project in Saint John. While in Saint John, the representative has access to the same technology and support as was available in Montreal. Full access is available to company networks, customer accounts, communication

high-tech sales support offices Offices set up at multiple locations where salespeople can access a wider range of selling technology than could be easily carried on a notebook or laptop computer.

links, and software applications. Consequently, convenience and productive time are maximized for the benefit of all parties.

STAGE FIVE: ASSESSMENT OF PERFORMANCE AND GOAL ATTAINMENT

A critical, and often overlooked, stage in the process of self-leadership is the periodic assessment of progress. Although certainly important, this stage should involve more than a simple check at the end of the period to determine whether goals were achieved. Assessment checkpoints should be built into plans at progressive points in time to encourage and facilitate the evaluation of a salesperson's progress. These frequent comparisons of actual performance with periodic checkpoints allow time to consider revisions or modifications before it is too late to make a difference. In addition to assessing progress, evaluation should also consider what is working well and what could be improved. This knowledge and understanding can be used to guide modifications in the various plans, tasks, and activities that populate the different stages of self-leadership to further enhance future success and performance.

© salesforce.com, inc. Used with permission.

Smartphones combined with mobile CRM applications enable salespeople instantly to view, create, and modify data from any location.

Increasing Customer Value Through Teamwork

Quality customer service is taking on a key role in competitive business strategy, and as customer expectations and needs continue to grow in complexity, selling organizations are finding that they can no longer depend solely on salespeople as the exclusive arbiter of customer satisfaction. Teamwork, both inside the organization and with customers, is being emphasized as the key to customer focus and sales performance.

INTERNAL PARTNERSHIPS AND TEAMS

The practices and experiences of top-ranked selling organizations, as well as considerable sales research, support the emphasis on teamwork as a key to long-term selling success. The results from three studies of more than 200 companies that employ some 25,000 salespeople supported the belief that cooperating as a team player was critical for success in selling.[7] Similar results have been found in other studies that examine what business-to-business buyers expect from suppliers. In two studies incorporating 6,708 customer evaluations of vendor performance and customer satisfaction in the financial services industry, the suppliers' performance in building internal and external partnerships was found to be the key driver of customer satisfaction.[8]

Building **external relationships** is the focal point of contemporary selling techniques and reflects the ongoing paradigm shift in today's salesforces. This emphasis on building *external* customer relationships could overshadow the critical role of building *internal,* close-working relationships with other individuals in their own company. The importance of these **internal relationships** would seem to be logical, as a salesperson's success depends on the degree of support he or

external relationships
Relationships salespeople build with customers outside the organization and working environment.

internal relationships
Relationships salespeople have with other individuals in their own company.

she receives from others in the various functional areas of the organization. Ultimately, the salesperson owns the responsibility for customer relationships, but the strength of those customer relationships depends on the joint efforts and resources contributed by multiple individuals across the selling organization.

Account managers at Contour Plastics Corporation have full responsibility for bringing together individuals from functional departments across the organization to work as a sales team dedicated to selling and providing presale and post-sale services to a specific account. As needed, team members will incorporate research chemists, application specialists, production engineers, and logistics specialists. Coordinated by the salesperson, each team member contributes his or her special expertise toward maximizing the understanding of the customer's situation and needs, and then working together to create a unique, value-added solution that few, if any, competitors can equal.

Teamwork results in a synergy that produces greater outcomes and results for all parties than would be possible with multiple individuals acting independently. Consequently, it is important that salespeople also develop the ability to sell internally as they represent their customers to the selling organization and give recognition to the important role others play in winning, keeping, and growing customer accounts.

James Champy, chairman of consulting for Perot Systems, notes that customers are expecting and receiving better service and product options than ever, and he characterizes the role of the salesperson as having been transformed to that of a trusted adviser.[9]

In this adviser role, the salesperson works with customers to develop a mutual understanding of the customer's situation, needs, possibilities, and expectations. On the basis of this information, the salesperson assembles a team of individuals, experts from across the selling organization, who work together to create a product response that will deliver more unique customer value than the competitors' offerings. In delivering this unique and added value for customers, salespeople often find themselves working with other individuals in sales, marketing, design and manufacturing, administrative support, shipping, and customer service.

© Nataliiap/Shutterstock

Periodic performance assessments should be built into plans so as to encourage evaluation of progress and identify where improvements might be needed in order to achieve goals.

Sales Partnerships

Within the sales department, salespeople often team with other salespeople to gain the strengths and expertise required for a specific selling situation or customer. Partnerships with sales managers and other sales executives are also important in winning support for developing innovative responses to customer needs. XL Capital is a global leader in alternative risk transfer products, financial risk management, and surplus lines of commercial property and casualty insurance. Selling to Fortune 500 and Fortune 1000 customers, XL Capital's salespeople (customer business unit managers) specialize along customer and industry lines. It is common for XL's salespeople to work together in teams to bring together the experience and expertise required to work with customers whose businesses span a large number of different industries.

Marketing Partnerships

Teaming with individuals in the marketing department is critical for salespeople in generating integrated solutions for customers over the long term. Marketing is responsible for developing organizational marketing strategies that serve as guidelines for the salesforce. Using information gathered in the field by the salesforce, marketing also assists in the generation of new market offerings in response to changing customer needs and requests. Marketing can also be a valuable partner for salespeople in accessing information and developing sales proposals.

At Pocahontas Foods, a top-10 institutional food broker with nationwide operations, account managers regularly work with members of the marketing department to communicate changes in customer needs and activities of competitors. This collaborative partnership allows Pocahontas to continue bringing innovative product offerings to the marketplace that are designed around the inputs from their salespeople.

Design and Manufacturing Partnerships

Salespeople often find themselves selling ideas for product designs and changes in manufacturing schedules to meet the needs of customers. When individuals from design, manufacturing, and sales work as a team, performance and delivery commitments are more likely to be met and customer satisfaction further enhanced. Wallace works to maintain its industry leadership in business forms and systems by aggressively nurturing a company-wide culture emphasizing customer orientation and support. As part of their training, salespeople actually work in production facilities to understand what has to be done to meet product design and delivery requirements that the salespeople might commit to in the field. By-products of this cross-training come about in the form of one-to-one personal relationships between salespeople and production staff. In the case of complex customer needs or special delivery needs, these relationships become invaluable.

Administrative Support Partnerships

Salespeople work with others from administrative support functions, such as management, finance and credit, billing, and information systems. Like sales, each of these functional units has certain goals and objectives that translate to policies and procedures that govern their own activities and affect operations throughout the organization—including sales. Customer needs are served best when salespeople have worked to establish effective relationships within these units and all parties work together for the mutual good of the organization and customer. Jim Gavic, account manager for Cross Canada Trucking, manages a territory stretching from the industrial sector of Calgary east to Halifax. Gavic credits his close relationships with individuals in the company's finance and credit department for making 20 percent of his annual sales. By working together, they were able to establish special billing terms for several of his larger accounts. If finance and credit had simply enforced Cross Canada's standard terms, these customers would have been lost to a competitor with more flexible credit policies.

Shipping and Transportation Partnerships

Salespeople periodically find themselves facing an urgent customer need that requires special handling of an order. Perhaps it is an expedited shipment for immediate delivery or the processing and shipping of an interim order of less than economical size. Whatever the need, it will affect other shipments getting out on time and could even increase the department's operating costs. Curtis James, territory manager for General Electric Appliances, found sales going better than usual at a new store opening in Winnipeg. To keep the customer from being caught short, he hand-carried a fill-in order to the GE district office, walked it through credit approval, hand-delivered the shipping order to the warehouse, and helped load the truck. Teamwork enabled Curtis to accomplish in less than a day what normally would have taken 8 to 10 days. It takes a team effort to work through exceptions such as these, and it is common to find the salesperson actually helping to make it happen by pulling orders, packing boxes, and even helping to load the truck.

> Salesperson effectiveness in building internal and external partnerships is a key driver of customer satisfaction.

Customer Service Partnerships

Teamwork between sales and customer service can create a synergy that has a broad-based impact that can translate

© Geber86/iStockphoto

Working as a team with individuals in the shipping department can provide critical relationships when a salesperson faces an urgent customer need for expedited shipment and delivery.

to higher customer satisfaction, higher rates of customer retention, and increased sales performance. On the one hand, customer service personnel, such as call centre operators and service technicians, often have more extensive contact with customers than the account representatives. As such, they can serve as an early warning system for salespeople and provide valuable information regarding customer complaints, problems, developing needs, and changes that they encounter through customer contacts. As a salesperson for Southwestern School Supply, Cap Williams regularly checks in and visits with the company's customer service personnel to keep abreast of contacts that they might have with any of his customers. The information he receives allows him to get ahead of any possible customer problems, provide an outstanding level of after-sale support that continues to mystify upper management, and helps to secure his receipt of Top Salesperson of the Year Award year after year. When salespeople such as Williams act on the information provided by customer service to further customer relationships and increase sales, customer service personnel will also be further inclined to work together to benefit the team. On the other hand, salespeople often assist customer service personnel by working directly with customers to address problems before they become complaints and provide instruction and training to assist customers in using the products sold.

10-5 BUILDING TEAMWORK SKILLS

As illustrated in "An Ethical Dilemma," effective teams do not form by default. Nor can a team be effective in producing synergistic benefits solely because it is called a team. Like customer relationships, internal relationships are built on reciprocal trust. The salesperson who arbitrarily and repeatedly asks for special production runs, extensions to customers' lines of

An Ethical Dilemma

© hillwoman2/iStockphoto

Michelle Moore is a senior account manager for DigiMD, a leader in medical imaging systems, and has been a consistent top producer for the last five years. Michelle leads a sales team of technical engineers who design, install, and maintain the company's digital imaging systems; sales system specialists who work with customers on a day-to-day basis responding to questions and operating problems; and dedicated, phone-based customer service representatives who serve as the 24/7 communications link between customers' staff and members of the DigiMD sales team. Michelle coordinates the team and personally interacts with customer staff. However, quality of the installation, customer satisfaction, and likelihood of future purchases depends on the commitment and level of service provided by the sales team. DigiMD has been experiencing rapid growth and adding personnel throughout the organization, especially sales system specialists and phone-based customer service representatives. As a result of adding all the new team members, the level of delivered quality has become unpredictable and consistently below the service levels promised by Michelle and other DigiMD account managers. Michelle has discussed these sales team support problems with her sales manager but nothing seems to change. Increasingly, Michelle finds herself working to patch over service failures caused by different members of her account sales teams and trying to win back customers who have left DigiMD. Not only is Michelle losing sales, but her reputation is also beginning to suffer due to actions and even inactions of various team members. Last week, one of DigiMD's major competitors contacted her about leaving DigiMD and coming to work for them. What would you do if you were Michelle?

a) Stay with DigiMD and hope that things will get better.
b) Take the job offer from the competitor.
c) Request a meeting with her sales manager and key sales team members to document service failures and collaborate toward developing solutions.

credit, expedited shipments, or special attention from customer service is simply asking for quick fixes. These quick fixes serve the objectives of the customer and salesperson but often work against the objectives of the functional unit and the organization as a whole.

Synergistic teamwork requires a commitment on the part of all parties to look for and work for win-win solutions. However, in the rush to take care of a customer, it is all too easy for salespeople to fall into a win-lose orientation. It is not that they want anyone to lose, but rather that they get what they want. This win orientation is most common in everyday negotiation—in which people think and act in terms of accomplishing their own goals and leave it to others to attain theirs. Optimum solutions develop from a team orientation based on the philosophy of win-win alternatives.[10] In turn, this can happen only when there are high levels of mutual trust and communication: "Not your way, not my way, but a better way."

In his bestselling book on personal development, Stephen Covey offers six keys to developing synergistic relationships and teams.[11] These are the six **teamwork skills** that salespeople must learn and sincerely apply in their process of building internal partnerships that translate to increased sales and organizational performance.

- *Understanding the Other Individuals*—Fully understanding and considering the other individuals in the partnership is necessary to know what is important to them. What is important to them must also be important to the salesperson if the partnership is to grow and be effective. This means that salespeople must take time to learn the objectives of other functional areas and consider how those needs and requests might affect the salesperson's goals and objectives.
- *Attending to the Little Things*—The little kindnesses and courtesies are often small in size and great in importance. In building relationships, the little things are the big things. Properly attended to and nurtured, they enhance the interrelationships. At the same time, if they are neglected or misused, they can destroy the relationship very quickly.
- *Keeping Commitments*—We all build our hopes and plans around the promises and commitments of others. When a commitment is not kept, disappointment and problems result. As a result, credibility and trust suffer major damage that is always difficult, and often impossible, to repair. However, consistency in keeping commitments builds and solidifies trust-based relationships.
- *Clarifying Expectations*—The root cause of most relational difficulties can be found in ambiguous expectations regarding roles and goals—exactly where are we going and who is responsible for what? Investing the time up front to clarify expectations regarding goals and roles can save even more time down the road when misunderstandings become compounded and turn into goal conflicts and breakdowns in communication.
- *Showing Personal Integrity*—Demonstrating personal integrity generates trust, whereas a lack of integrity can quickly undermine the best of teamwork orientations. People can seek to understand others, carry through on the little things, keep commitments, and clarify expectations, but still fail to build trust by being inwardly duplicitous and pursuing a personal agenda. Be honest, open, and treat everyone by the same set of principles.
- *Apologizing Sincerely When a Mistake Is Made*—It is one thing to make a mistake. It is another thing not to admit it. People forgive mistakes. What is harder to forgive are the ill intentions and motives justifying any attempt to cover up. "If you are going to bow, bow low." The apology must be perceived as sincere and not simply as automated lip-service response.

teamwork skills Skills salespeople must learn to build internal partnerships that translate into increased sales and organizational performance.

Visit **www.nelson.com/student** to find the resources you need today!

Located at the back of the textbook are rip-out Chapter Review cards. Make sure you also go online to check out other tools that SELL offers to help you successfully pass your course.

- Flashcards
- Glossary
- PowerPoint Notes
- Role-Play Videos
- Games
- Interactive Quizzing

CHAPTER 10 CASE

UNIVERSAL CONTROL CORP.

Background

Universal Control Corp. is a leading supplier for process control systems and equipment used in a wide variety of production and distribution applications. You have taken a sales representative job with Universal and, having just completed training, been given a territory of your own. Your district manager has provided you with a list of accounts as well as several boxes of notes and files that had been assembled and used by your predecessor. These are the accounts currently buying your products. You are expected to build these accounts and add new accounts to the list as you increase your territory's sales performance. You have summarized the account information into the summary set of account profiles, which follows on the next page.

Questions

1. Develop a portfolio classification of accounts and assess the allocation of sales calls your predecessor made over the past year.
2. What problems do you find with the previous allocation of calls on these accounts?
3. Based on your account classification analysis, suggest a new sales call allocation strategy that would make better use of your time in the territory.

Role Play

Situation: Read the case.

Characters: Zack Hanna, salesperson for Universal Control Corp.; Gage Waits, district sales manager and Hanna's immediate supervisor

Scene:

Location—Gage Waits's office at Universal Control Corp.

Action—Zack has just been assigned this territory and has completed an analysis of sales and customer files to profile the individual accounts and sales call allocation strategies used by the previous salesperson in the territory. Based on this information, Hanna has developed information responding to each of the three questions following the Universal Control Corp. case materials. This information includes a new sales call allocation strategy. Hanna is meeting with his sales manager to explain his new sales call allocation plan.

As Hanna, answer the three questions previously listed. Using this information, role play your interaction with your sales manager, Gage Waits, as you discuss and explain (1) your analysis of the previous salesperson's sales call allocation and (2) your new plans and how they will increase the effectiveness and efficiency of your selling efforts in this territory.

Account Name	Account Opportunity	Competitive Position	Annual Number of Sales Calls Last Year
Mueller Distribution	High	Low	30
Tri-State Specialties	Low	High	20
Birkey Paper Co.	Low	High	26
Normal Supply	Low	Low	12
Darnell Aggregate Products	Low	High	21
Reinhart Chemicals	High	High	26
ACCO Manufacturing	Low	High	23
Tri-State Manufacturing	High	Low	28
Ideal Engineering	Low	Low	11
Terracon	High	High	25
Lowry Foods	High	Low	26
SCS Industrial	High	High	27
Lowell Services	Low	High	18
Bowles and Sons	Low	High	21
American Foundry	High	Low	22
Hewitt & Associates	Low	Low	16
Bright Metals Inc.	High	High	22
Decatur Extrusions	Low	Low	14
King Chemicals	Low	High	22
Bear's Steel Corp.	Low	High	20
Hoffman Pharmaceuticals	High	Low	20
Barlow & Clark Systems	Low	High	18

After completing the role play, address the following questions:

1. How might Hanna's sales allocation plan be different if he had used single-factor analysis (ABC analysis) instead of portfolio analysis?
2. Develop a sales call allocation plan using single-factor analysis. Compare the results of Hanna's portfolio analysis with the results of your single-factor analysis. Where and how are they different?
3. How might those differences translate to increased selling effectiveness and efficiency?

CHAPTER 10

Role Play: Adding Value: Self-Leadership And Teamwork: Payroll Pro

Background

You are a business development specialist for Payroll Pro, an industry leader providing automated payroll processing and related record keeping for medium to large businesses having 15 or more employees. Your primary selling responsibility is new account development and working with existing accounts to increase share of account by selling them additional employment-related services. Account management and day-to-day servicing responsibilities are performed by a team of customer service representatives who work with customers through the phone and Internet. Due to a combination of rapid growth in the number of customers and several customer service representatives being new to the job, the resulting level of service provided by the customer service team has become inconsistent and all too often below the level you have promised to your customers. As a result, you are spending much of your time trying to patch over service shortcomings and working to win back accounts that have been lost to competitors due to the service problems. Not only are you losing business, but your own reputation is beginning to suffer along with that of Payroll Pro.

Role Play

In discussing these problems with your sales manager, it was decided that you would meet with the team of customer service representatives in order to discuss and find a workable solution to the problems.

Role play how you would approach and initiate a positive discussion with the members of the customer service team that would generate improved experiences and outcomes for your customers and Payroll Pro. Remember to employ Covey's six teamwork skills discussed in this chapter.

what do you think?

A sales manager's job is to motivate their salespeople.

1 2 3 4 5 6 7

strongly disagree — strongly agree

The most successful

sales managers develop effective sales strategies and lead salespeople to implement these strategies and achieve desired results.

11 Sales Management and Sales 2.0

After completing this chapter, you should be able to

11-1 Discuss the key considerations in developing and implementing effective sales strategies.

11-2 Understand the recruitment, selection, and training processes involved in developing the salesforce.

11-3 Identify key activities in directing the salesforce by leading, managing, supervising, motivating, and rewarding salespeople.

11-4 Explain the different methods for evaluating the performance and effectiveness of sales organizations and individual salespeople.

11-5 Describe how sales organizations are using Sales 2.0 to co-create value with customers.

Introduction

According to motivational speaker and super-coach Steve Chandler, your number one job as a sales leader is to increase the optimism of everyone on your team. "Managers who spend their whole sales meeting dispensing information are wasting everyone's time," says Chandler. "The only real purpose of bringing everyone together is to make sure that your salespeople leave more motivated, more encouraged, and more optimistic than they came in."

But don't get the idea that this is all about pumping 'em up and sending 'em out. Chandler, who has authored more than 20 CD courses and books, believes that external motivation is "like a drug. It's an adrenaline rush, a short-term stimulus that eventually fades, often leaving the person more down than ever. Lasting optimism is the result of changing how you think, and that happens through repetition."

Smart managers motivate not by creating wild enthusiasm at a yearly sales meeting, but rather by teaching their teams how to think optimistically on a day-to-day basis.

Most people have any number of self-limiting beliefs, many of them involving their business skills—or their perceived lack of them: "I'm not good on the phone. Cold calling scares me. I've never been able to remember names." Chandler calls these beliefs "our story."

"The funny thing about business is that it often doesn't matter what you're naturally good at," Chandler says. "You might tell yourself that you're not good at cold calling, but if you put that story aside and make the call anyway, the odds are that you'll achieve something. It's irrelevant whether or not you're good at something compared to what you can achieve if you just try."

Chandler suggests putting the brakes on your internal dialogue whenever you catch yourself telling a story, and managers should interrupt their salespeople when they begin storytelling. "You might say, 'This is hard,' This guy is tough to close,' or 'I'm not good at this or that,'" Chandler says, "but if you drop all these stories and wander in as an innocent, as someone who doesn't have a story, you may do a great job. And you'll certainly get a lot further than if you talked yourself out of trying at all."

Chandler says managers make a big mistake when they open a sales meeting by talking about what the sales team needs to improve. "When the first item on the docket is all about what's not working," he says, "you've opened the door to a meeting of wailing

sales management
Managing an organization's personal selling function to include planning, implementing, and controlling the sales management process.

and venting and excuses. Instead, start by acknowledging what is going well—people who have succeeded and opportunities that exist."

Of course, there are always problems that need to be addressed, but Chandler suggests you address them with the individual salespeople involved either before or after the meeting. "Bad news can be handled one-on-one," he says. "Spend your precious meeting time discussing where the opportunities are."

Source: Kim Wright Wiley, "Optimism Always Wins," *Selling Power*, http://www.sellingpower.com/magazine/article.php?i=1352&ia=9264.

Our focus to this point has been on personal selling. The purpose of this chapter is to examine sales management. We begin by providing an overview of sales management. Then, each stage in the sales management process is presented in more detail. The chapter concludes by discussing Sales 2.0, which is the use of new and emerging technologies throughout a sales organization.

Sales Management Overview

Sales management is the managing of an organization's personal selling function. This requires attention to strategic and leadership issues by developing and executing plans. Our sales management overview examines the sales management process, different sales management positions, and best practices in sales management.[1]

SALES MANAGEMENT PROCESS

The major stages in the sales management process are presented in Figure 11.1.[2] Sales managers must have a deep understanding of the personal selling function to manage it effectively. This understanding has been provided to you in the other chapters in this book. The remaining stages of the sales management process build on this personal selling knowledge.

Defining the strategic role of the sales function addresses the strategic aspects of sales management. The development of sales strategies for individual customers or customer segments and the integration of these sales strategies with a firm's corporate, business, and marketing strategies are especially important. Then, an effective sales organization must be created and the deployment of salespeople and selling effort is determined.

Developing the salesforce is concerned with getting the best sales talent and providing them with the knowledge and skills to be successful. Sales managers are involved in recruiting and selecting salespeople, as well as in designing and implementing sales training programs.

Directing the salesforce focuses on efforts to encourage and help salespeople achieve personal and organizational goals. This includes effective leadership and management activities by sales managers, as well as various types of reward programs. Some companies use an incentive-driven compensation plan to get salespeople motivated. But sales managers also spend a great deal of time coaching salespeople and working closely with them to develop and implement sales plans.

Determining salesforce effectiveness and performance emphasizes an assessment of how well the sales organization and units, such as areas and districts, as well as salespeople and sales managers, are performing.

These evaluations provide a basis for rewards, but they also generate feedback that can be used to improve all aspects of the sales management process. Companies

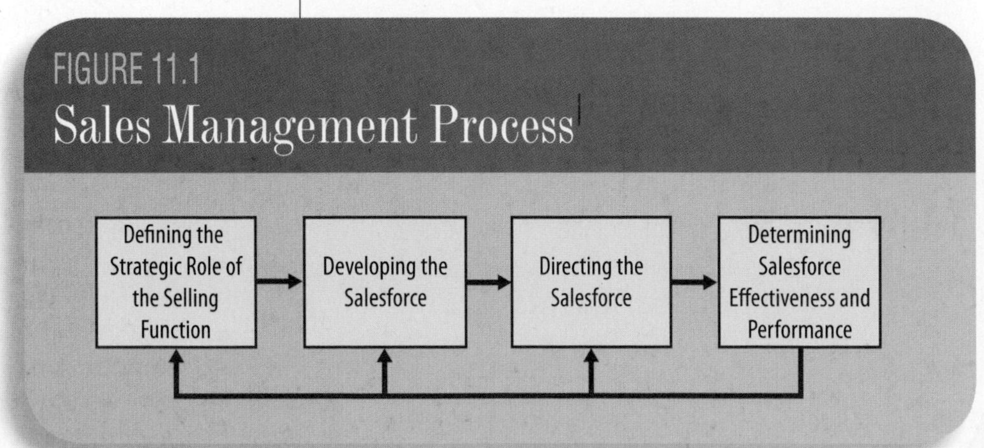

The sales management process consists of understanding the personal selling function and implementing the four major stages of sales management activities.

may assess the effectiveness of their sales organization through market share and sales growth determinations and the performance of their salespeople according to achieving sales and other goals. This provides a basis for rewarding salespeople, but it also leads to improvements that reduce turnover.

SALES MANAGEMENT POSITIONS

Although there are a variety of sales management positions with different titles at different firms, most of these positions fit into three categories. Many firms have a top-level sales executive usually called a chief sales officer (CSO) or vice president of sales. This position has responsibility for the entire sales organization. Then, there are often one or more levels of sales managers who report to the top level sales executive and are responsible for sales managers below them. Typical titles are regional sales manager or area sales manager. Finally, field sales managers have direct responsibility for salespeople and report to the sales manager directly above them in the sales organization structure. These sales managers work closely with salespeople in the field and usually have titles like district sales manager or sales manager. Each of these positions is involved in the sales management process, but each usually performs different activities depending on the level of the position and the specific structure of a sales organization.

SALES MANAGEMENT BEST PRACTICES

The complex, dynamic, and competitive environment facing sales organizations has prompted sales consulting firms, such as HR Chally and Forum, and academic researchers to identify the most effective sales management practices. This research suggests that the best sales organizations[3]

1. Create a customer-driven culture throughout the sales organization and firm.
2. Recruit, hire, and retain the best sales talent.
3. Train and coach the right skill set.
4. Focus on key strategic issues by segmenting accounts in meaningful ways and providing differentiated offerings to find, win, and retain customers.
5. Develop an appropriate and adaptable sales organization structure.
6. Implement formal sales and relationship-building processes.
7. Use information technology effectively to learn about customers and enable salesperson success.
8. Align sales operations with business and marketing strategies.

In essence, these research findings indicate that the best sales organizations perform all stages of the sales management process effectively.

Other research has examined the characteristics and activities of the best sales managers. Studies indicate that high-performing sales managers possess good communication and listening skills; human relations skills; organization and time management skills; industry, company, product, and general business knowledge; coaching, motivating, and leadership skills; and honest and ethical tendencies.[4] These sales managers use these skills to[5]

1. Prepare their sales team for constant change by being a role model and mentoring salespeople.
2. Earn the trust of salespeople by being dependable, competent, and exhibiting integrity.
3. Give salespeople continual feedback in a positive manner.
4. Build enthusiasm throughout the sales team.
5. Get involved by being accessible to salespeople and visible to customers.
6. Grow and develop salespeople by emphasizing continual job improvement and career development.

As you can see, sales managers occupy an important and demanding position. They need a variety of skills and must be engaged in many different activities to be successful.

Sales managers occupy different positions in many firms.

© Andres Rodriguez/Alamy

11-1 Developing and Implementing Effective Sales Strategies

ales managers should be aware of the key strategic decisions taking place at the corporate, business, marketing, and sales levels in their organizations. Corporate- and business-level strategic decisions typically provide guidelines within which sales managers and salespeople operate. This is typically true for firms focusing on a customer relationship management (CRM) strategy. Professional selling plays an important role in sales managers' strategic planning. Strategic decisions at the corporate, business, and marketing levels must be translated into strategies for individual accounts. Sales strategies are designed for individual accounts or groups of similar accounts. Therefore, sales managers must be continually working to identify and classify accounts into useful categories.

SALES STRATEGY

Sales managers and salespeople are generally responsible for strategic decisions at the account level. A sales strategy is designed to execute an organization's marketing strategy for individual accounts. The major purpose of a sales strategy is to develop a specific approach for selling to individual accounts within a target market. A sales strategy capitalizes on the important differences among individual accounts or groups of similar accounts. A firm's sales strategy is important for two reasons. First, it has a major impact on a firm's sales and profit performance. Second, it influences many other sales management decisions, such as recruitment, selection, training, compensation, and performance.

account targeting strategy The classification of accounts within a target market into categories for the purpose of developing strategic approaches for selling to each account or account group.

relationship strategy A determination of the type of relationship to be developed with different account groups.

selling strategy Involves the planning of sales messages and interactions with customers. Selling strategy can be defined at three levels: for a group of customers, that is, a sales territory; for individual customers; and for specific customer encounters, referred to as sales calls.

Sales managers must develop strategies for forming key elements of strategic decision making. A discussion on account targeting, relationship strategies, selling strategies, and channel strategies will follow.

Account Targeting Strategy

The first challenge a sales manager may face is deciding which accounts to pursue. All accounts within the target market are not created equally. Some accounts may not be good prospects because they have a solid relationship with a competitor. Even good prospects or current customers differ in how much they buy or how much they might buy in the future or how eager they are to do business with the sales organizations. Accounts may therefore require different servicing.

An **account targeting strategy** is the classification of accounts within a target market into categories for the purpose of developing strategic approaches for selling to each account or account group. The account targeting strategy provides the basis for all other elements of a sales strategy. Just as different marketing mixes are developed to serve different target markets, sales organizations need to use different relationships, selling, and sales channel strategies for different account groups.

Relationship Strategy

As discussed in previous chapters, there is a clear trend toward a relationship orientation between buyers and sellers. A **relationship strategy** is a determination of the type of relationship to develop with different account groups. The relationship strategies may range from a transaction relationship based on ease of acquisition and low price to a collaborative relationship where the buyer and seller work closely together for the benefit of both businesses. In between these extremes are intermediate types of relationships based on a lower commitment from the buyer and seller. Selling costs are increased to serve accounts with higher level relationships. Sales organizations must consider the costs associated with using different relationship strategies for different account groups. The critical task is balancing the customer's needs with the cost of serving the account.

Selling Strategy

Successfully executing a specific relationship strategy requires a unique selling approach. A **selling strategy** is the planned selling approach for each relationship strategy. Exhibit 11.1 matches the appropriate selling

EXHIBIT 11.1
Matching Selling and Relationship Strategies

Relationship Strategy			
Transactions	**Solutions**	**Partnership**	**Collaborative**
Stimulus response Mental states	Need satisfaction Problem solving	Consultative	Consultative Customized

strategy with the appropriate relationship strategy. As indicated, the stimulus-response and mental states approaches typically fit with transaction relationship strategy. The need satisfaction and problem-solving selling strategies are normally used with a solutions relationship strategy. The consultative approach is most effective with the partnership and collaborative relationship strategies. Sometimes, a collaborative relationship strategy requires a selling strategy that is completely customized to the specific buyer–seller situation. The important point is that achieving the desired type of relationship in a productive manner requires using different selling strategies. Matching selling strategies and relationship strategies is an important sales management task.

Sales Channel Strategy

Sales channel strategy ensures that accounts receive proper selling effort and coverage. Various methods are available to a selling organization to provide proper coverage to accounts, including a company salesforce, the Internet, distributors, independent representatives, team selling, telemarketing, and trade shows.

The Internet is quickly becoming a critical sales channel in selling to organizations. On the surface, it would appear the Internet is being used to reduce selling costs. Other applications include reordering, product information, and linkage to customer and support representatives. The Internet is being blended not only into other field selling efforts but also into other sales channels, such as industrial distributors, independent representatives, and telemarketers.

Distributors and other wholesalers provide another sales channel alternative. Distributors usually employ their own salesforce and may carry (1) the products of one manufacturer, (2) related but noncompeting products from different manufacturers, or (3) competing products from different manufacturers. Firms that employ distributors normally have a small company salesforce to serve and support the efforts of the distributors.

Companies using personal selling can choose to cover accounts with **independent representatives** or **manufacturer representatives** (sometimes referred to as reps). Reps are independent sales organizations that sell complementary, but noncompeting, products from different manufacturers. Independent representatives do not normally carry inventory or take title to the products they sell. These reps are typically compensated on a commission basis for products sold.

The use of **team selling** is increasing in many firms. This is especially true as a sales channel for a firm's most important prospects and customers. Generating the best new prospects into customers and expanding relationships with the most profitable existing customers often requires the participation of many individuals from both the buying and selling firms. This can be a very expensive sales channel approach, but prospects and customers seem to appreciate the attention they receive. The team selling strategy has helped Data Cert obtain top clients, such as UPS, Microsoft, and AT&T.[6]

Trade shows are typically industry-sponsored events in which companies use a booth to display products and services to potential and existing customers. Trade shows can be used to achieve both selling and nonselling objectives. Selling objectives might include testing new products and closing sales. Nonselling objectives include servicing current customers, gathering competitive information, identifying new prospects, and enhancing corporate image. Typically, trade shows are only once a year for a few days and should be viewed as a supplemental method for account coverage.

independent representatives or manufacturer representatives Independent sales organizations that sell complementary but noncompeting products from different manufacturers; also called manufacturer's representatives or reps.

team selling The use of multiple-person sales teams in dealing with multiple-person customer buying centres.

SALES STRUCTURE

Many different types of structures can be used successfully and many variations are possible within each type. Often, the resulting structure is complex and it considers specialization, centralization, span of control versus management levels, and line versus staff responsibilities.[7]

Specialization

In small organizations, each salesperson could perform all the selling tasks and the sales manager could perform all the management activities. Most organizations are too complex for this structure and require some degree of specialization. Salespeople may sell only part of the product line or call on existing accounts. Sales managers may work only with new hires or be solely involved with the training of the sales staff. Specialization allows individuals to become experts on those tasks and leads to better performance.

Centralization

A centralized structure is one in which authority and responsibility are placed at higher management levels. While no organization is totally centralized or totally decentralized, most typically centralize some activities and decentralize others. When building a sales team that encourages the development of or relationships with customers, a decentralized structure facilitates such decision making in the field.

Span of Control versus Management Levels

Span of control refers to the number of individuals who report to each sales manager. The larger the span of control, the more salespeople the sales manager must manage. Management levels determine the number of different hierarchical levels of sales management within the organization.

In effect, organizations can go one of two ways. In a flat sales organization structure, there will be relatively few sales management levels, with each manager having a relatively large span of control. In a tall structure, there will be more sales management levels and smaller spans of control.

span of control The number of individuals who report to each sales manager.

Line versus Staff Positions

Sales management positions can be differentiated as line or staff positions. Line sales managers have direct responsibility for a certain number of salespeople and report directly to management at the next highest level in the sales organization. Staff sales management positions are not in the direct chain of command in the sales organization structure. Staff managers do not directly manage people, but they are responsible for particular functions, such as training and recruiting. Staff managers are generally not responsible for sales-generating activities.

© Dmitriy Shironosov/Shutterstock

Managers must be prepared to manage more salespeople as organizations get flatter.

Designing the Sales Organization

A sales organization might be structured in a tremendous number of ways. There are several traditional types to choose from and each has its advantages and disadvantages. Typical structures include geographic sales organization, product sales organization, market sales organization, and functional sales organization. We will briefly look at each type of sales organization.

Geographic Sales Organization

Probably the most widely used system for dividing responsibility is to organize the salesforce on the basis of geographic territories. This is the least specialized and the most generalized type of salesforce. Salespeople are typically assigned a geographic area and are responsible for all the selling activities to all the customers and prospects within the assigned territory. There is no attempt to specialize by market, function, or product. The greatest advantage of this structure is the low cost and few management levels. There is also no geographic or customer duplication. The greatest disadvantage of a geographic sales organization is its limited specialization.

Product Sales Organization

The type of product sold is another basis for dividing the responsibilities and activities within a sales department.

Product specialization assigns a salesperson the selling responsibility for a specific product or typically a product line. The objective is for the salesperson to become an expert on the assigned product category. The major advantage of this form of organization is the specialized attention given to each product by the salesperson. There is a downside to the product sales organization: It is extremely costly. If a company carries many products, then it must hire a large salesforce to learn and sell the entire product line. It is costly to have 10–15 sales reps within a geographic territory when one or two will do.

Market Sales Organization

The focus of a market sales organization is to ensure that the salesforce understands how their customers use and purchase their products. Once this is understood, the salesforce should be able to direct their selling efforts to better satisfy customer needs. Market specialization has become an increasingly important type of specialization and is growing in use.[8] Market specialization includes selling to government, education, medical, wholesalers, retailers, military, manufacturers, and financial institutions, to name a few. The biggest advantage is getting to know the customer intimately. This in turn can help develop a better understanding of unique customer needs. Market organizational structure has disadvantages similar to a product organization in that it produces high costs and duplication of effort.

Functional Sales Organization

The final type of specialization is functional specialization. Many selling activities are required for a sales organization's success. Entry-level salespeople could be groomed to generate leads and qualify prospects, while the more experienced salespeople could concentrate on sales-generating activities. This is an example of a firm specializing by function. The major advantage of functional specialization is the efficiency in performing selling activities. Whether generating leads, qualifying prospects, or generating sales, if a salesperson has to concentrate only on one or two of these activities, he or she can progressively gain expertise. However, it has disadvantages: a great deal of geographic and customer duplication occur, requiring extensive coordination between salespeople. A review of the advantages and disadvantages of organizational structures can be found in Exhibit 11.2.

EXHIBIT 11.2
Sales Organization Alternatives

Organizational Structure	Advantages	Disadvantages
Geographic	• Low cost • No geographic duplication • No customer duplication • Fewer management levels	• Limited specialization • Lack of management control over product or customer emphasis
Product	• Salespeople become experts in product attributes and applications • Management control over selling effort allocated to products	• High cost • Geographic duplication • Customer duplication
Market	• Salespeople develop better understanding of unique customer needs • Management control over selling effort allocated to different markets	• High cost • Geographic duplication
Functional	• Efficiency in performing selling activities	• Geographic duplication • Customer duplication • Need for coordination

Thomas N. Ingram, Raymond W. LaForge, Ramon A. Avila, Charles H. Schwepker, Jr., and Michael Williams, *Sales Management: Analysis and Decision Making*, 7th ed. (Armonk, NY: M. E. Sharpe, 2009). Copyright © 2009 by M. E. Sharpe, Inc. Reproduced with permission of M.E. Sharpe in the format Republish in a book via Copyright Clearance Center.

In summary, designing a sales organization is a difficult and complex task. Trends do tend to be emerging. Organizations are moving toward more specialization as salespeople are concentrating on specific types of customers. Market specialization has become an increasingly important type of specialization. As companies are doing more downsizing and eliminating middle managers, companies are becoming flatter, with larger spans of control. Restructuring in some organizations has caused a move toward decentralization, which has resulted in elimination of staff positions. This in turn has moved companies to outsource their sales-training function to sales-training firms. Decisions like these should be based on the specifics of each selling organization; different companies may take on very different strategies.

11-2 Developing the Salesforce

Having determined the basic structure for personal selling efforts, sales managers must ensure the appropriate salespeople are available and have the necessary skills to function effectively and efficiently in the sales organization. This entails activities involved in planning and executing salesforce recruitment and selection activities. After the appropriate sales talent is hired, sales managers must oversee the training process, which may encompass both initial and ongoing training programs.

job analysis An examination of the tasks, duties, and responsibilities of the sales job.

job qualifications Indicate the aptitude, skills, knowledge, personal traits, and willingness to accept occupational conditions to perform the job.

THE RECRUITMENT AND SELECTION PROCESS

Typically, principal responsibility for recruitment and selection lies with sales managers who have direct supervisory responsibilities for salespeople. This is a critical task as poor implementation can lead to supervisory problems, increased training costs, inadequate sales coverage, lack of customer follow-up, difficulty in establishing relationships, and inadequate salesforce performance. Figure 11.2[9] illustrates the steps in the recruitment and selection process. We will briefly examine each step.

Planning for Recruitment and Selection

When planning for recruitment and selection, it is important to understand the position for which candidates are sought. This can be accomplished by conducting a **job analysis**, which involves examining the tasks, duties, and responsibilities of the sales job. Once we understand what the job involves, we need to determine the qualifications necessary to execute the job. Thus, **job qualifications** indicate the aptitude, skills, knowledge, personal traits, and willingness to accept occupational conditions to perform the job. Typical job qualifications address communication skills, relationship management skills, problem-solving skills,

FIGURE 11.2
Recruiting and Selecting Sales Talent

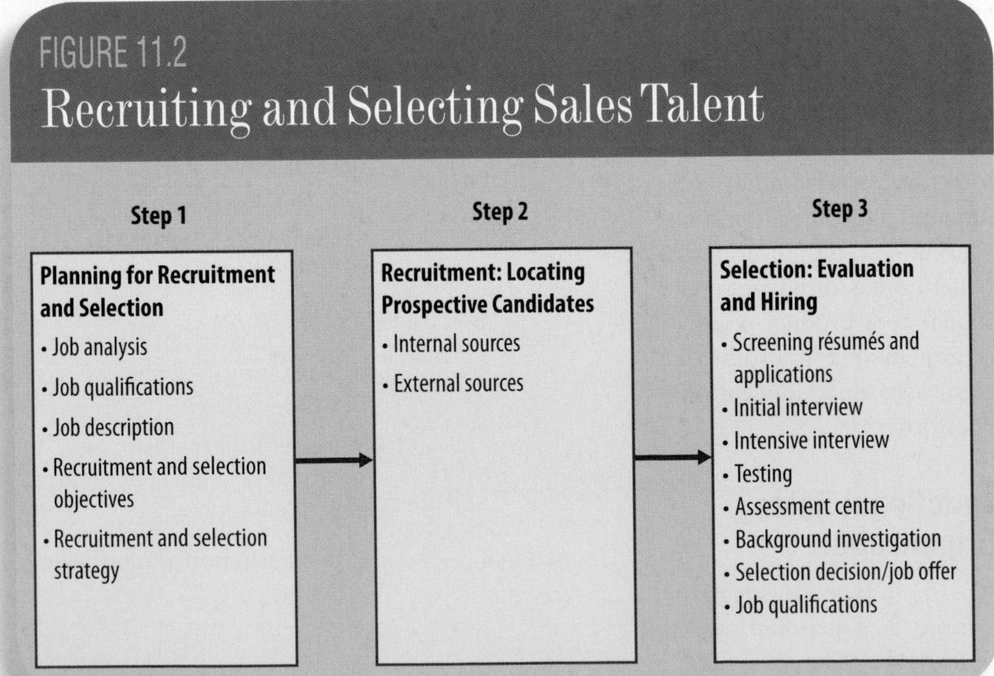

The recruitment and selection process involves planning, recruiting, and selecting sales talent.

education level, sales experience, willingness to travel and relocate, attitude, enthusiasm, empathy, integrity, and self-motivation, among others. The company's sales manager or human resource manager uses the job analysis and job qualifications to write a written summary of the job, the **job description**. This document provides candidates a picture of what the job involves and the characteristics they must possess to be successful. It is important that the planning stage lay out the recruitment and selection objectives (e.g., increasing the number of qualified applicants at a specified cost) and strategy. While the objectives determine what is to be achieved, the strategy includes the scope and timing of recruitment activities, such as how the job will be portrayed, when the process will occur, the best sources for qualified candidates, who will do the recruiting and selecting, and the amount of time given to a candidate to accept an offer.

Locating Prospective Candidates

The second major step in the recruitment and selection process is to locate prospective job candidates. Both internal and external sources can be helpful in locating sales talent. A very popular internal source is the employee referral program. Having employees refer sales candidates can be a very effective means of locating quality sales people. In one study, 47 percent of sales managers surveyed indicated they found their best salespeople through referrals.[10] Other internal sources include using company newsletters, the company intranet, bulletin boards, meetings, or memos to announce sales job openings. External sources are varied. For instance, companies may advertise job openings in newspapers (print or online), online through the company's website, or in job banks, such as Workopolis.com, Monster.com, CareerBuilder.com, SalesJobs.com, and TheLadders.com. Online recruiting and résumé-search services offered by companies such as Wonderlic.com and CIRSsearch.com are also useful. Increasingly, social networking sites such as LinkedIn (www.linkedin.com) and Facebook (www.facebook.com) are being used to recruit job candidates. Some companies are even acquiring talent through Twitter by "tweeting" (text broadcasting) position openings.

Private employment agencies will help locate candidates for a fee, typically 15–25 percent of the first year's earnings of the employee hired. Companies often recruit on college and university campuses or attend career fairs, in which employers are brought together in one location (even in the virtual world) for recruiting. Sales managers who belong to professional organizations, such as Sales & Marketing Executives International or the American Marketing Association, use these organizations to network and identify potential job candidates.

Evaluation and Hiring

The final step in the recruitment and selection process is evaluation and hiring. Various tools are used to evaluate job candidates' qualifications to find the best talent. Having gathered many potential candidates in the recruitment phase, the first step is to narrow the list by screening candidates' résumés and job applications. While résumés provide useful insight, a job application can ensure essential information and exclude unnecessary information. When the pool is large, screening software provided by companies such as Taleo.com or TalentFlow.com can help identify the candidates who best match the company's job qualifications. After narrowing the pool of candidates, it is important to get a more comprehensive look at the candidate. An initial interview that is typically an hour or less allows the recruiter to clarify any questions about the candidate's job qualifications and make an initial judgment. This is typically followed by a more intensive interview that may encompass several hours or days and may include meetings with several individuals from the employing firm. Candidates may also be subjected to tests designed to assess intelligence, aptitude, personality, or other interpersonal factors. Depending on the job, a physical exam and drug testing may be required. Some companies utilize an **assessment centre**, in which several assessment tools, such as presentations, role-playing exercises, group discussion, and business game simulations, are used to identify candidate strengths and weaknesses relative to job qualifications. Candidates who make it through these screening processes may be subjected to a **background investigation** in which references and others are contacted to verify information reported by the job candidate. Finally, the sales manager chooses the sales talent that best fits the job qualifications and makes the job offer, or decides to search further. When making the job offer, the sales manager should enthusiastically

job description A written summary of the job.

assessment centre Systematic use of several assessment tools, such as presentations, role-playing exercises, group discussion, and business game simulations, to identify candidate strengths and weaknesses relative to job qualifications or for employee development.

background investigation References and others are contacted to verify information reported by the job candidate.

The career fair hosted by the National Collegiate Sales Competition provides participating companies with an excellent source of sales candidates.

pursue the job candidate while being mindful to accurately portray the job. The job offer should be written but can initially be given orally.

SALES TRAINING

Having hired new talent, the next step in developing them is sales training. An extensive review of sales management research suggests that although who the company recruits is important, it is likely to be less important than what the sales manager does to and with the recruits that determines salesforce performance.[11] Research indicates that U.S. companies spend around $15 billion a year on sales training, averaging $2,000 per year in training expenditures per salesperson,[12] all in an attempt to maintain or improve the performance of the salesforce. Some research suggests that when well designed and executed, sales training has the fastest return on investment that a company can make.[13]

needs assessment
Activities undertaken to determine the extent to which the members of the salesforce possess the skills, attitudes, perceptions, and behaviours required to be successful.

Sales managers play an important role in both planning and implementing sales training. Figure 11.3[14] outlines the sales training process, which, if executed properly, should produce a more effective salesforce. We will now briefly look at each of these steps.

Assess Sales Training Needs

The first step is to conduct a **needs assessment** to determine the extent to which the salesforce possesses the skills, attitudes, perceptions, and behaviours required to be successful. A variety of methods can be used to determine training needs. In some cases, performance testing can determine the proficiency of salespeople in a particular area, such as product knowledge. In some cases, by simply observing the salesforce, sales managers can identify training needs. Some firms will poll their salesforce to determine where they believe they need training. Similarly, a customer survey might be conducted to ask customers where they believe salespeople are deficient in serving their needs. Finally, the job analysis discussed earlier can be used to provide insights regarding training needs. While any number of training needs might be identified, typical needs include sales techniques, time and territory management skills, and knowledge regarding products, customers, and competitors. To explore a scenario that suggests the need for additional training, read "An Ethical Dilemma."

FIGURE 11.3
Sales Training Process

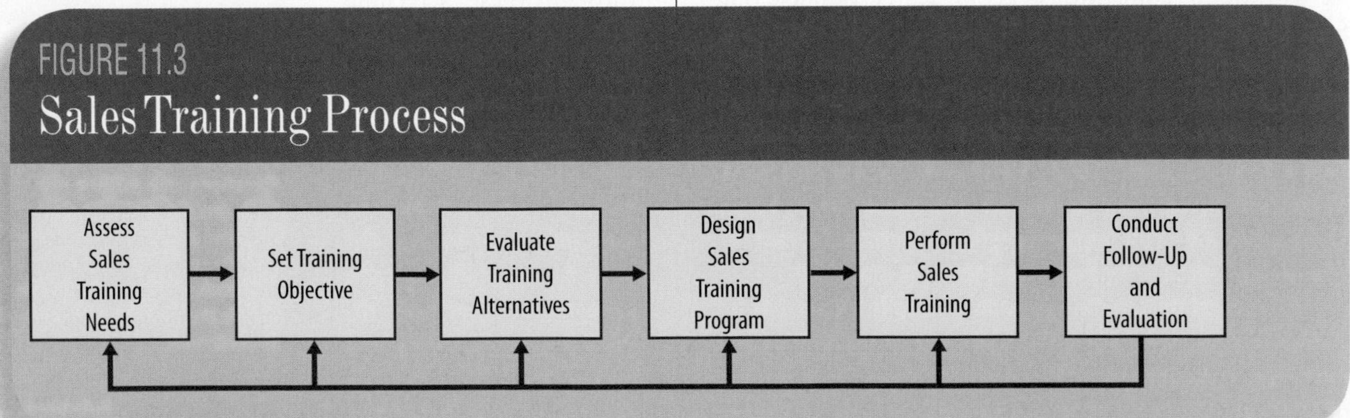

These are the steps involved in the training process. Future training may be altered as a result of feedback obtained during follow-up and evaluation.

An Ethical Dilemma

As the sales manager for UnderNorth Plastics, you have just been informed your region has not met its goals for the third quarter and if things continue you will miss your first President's Club trip in 12 years. This in turn will cost your boss her first President's Club trip since she became district manager. Your boss, ever the competitor, wants to know what you are going to do during the fourth quarter to turn things around so you each earn a President's Club trip. Given the ultimatum from your boss, coupled with your own desire to lead your sales team to new heights, you decide to ride along with several of your salespeople to observe their behaviours. To your surprise you notice many of your older salespeople are starting to slow down. They are not making as many calls as your younger salespeople. Your older reps are essentially taking care of their existing accounts but are bringing in very little new business. Having discovered these behaviours, what will you do?

a) Threaten your older reps with a new territory assignment. Tell them you may have to give their territory to a harder working younger sales rep.
b) Have a meeting with the full sales team and let them know the President's Club goal probably is not going to be met and if that happens, heads are going to roll.
c) Coach the older salespeople individually. Help them realize that balancing existing and new customers is the key to a successful territory and reaching the branch's goal of winning another President's Club trip.

Set Training Objectives

After determining the areas in which training is needed, training objectives should be set. The objectives will vary by training need, but all should be specific, measurable, and obtainable to maximize their effectiveness. General objectives might include, for example, increasing sales or profits by a certain amount, teaching salespeople relationship-building skills, or improving the ethical decision making of salespeople. Setting objectives helps sales managers to determine training expectations and avoids training simply for training's sake.

Evaluate Training Alternatives

In the third step of the sales training process, the sales manager evaluates various options for achieving the training objectives. Criteria including cost and time constraints, training location, flexibility of training materials, and opportunity for reinforcement training should be established for evaluating the alternatives. In this step of the process, the sales manager must decide who will do the training, where it will be conducted, and what methods and media will be used. Typically, sales training is done by company personnel, such as sales managers, senior salespeople, or company sales trainers. However, sometimes companies find it more effective and efficient to hire an outside sales training company. Although some organizations use central training facilities or off-site locations, the sales organization's home, regional, or field sales offices are typically where the training is conducted. When it comes to training methods, the variety from which to choose can be broken down into four categories. One method involves a trainer providing lectures, demonstrations, and class

Some companies use sales training software that allows salespeople to interact with a buyer in a simulated sales call.

© Klaus Tiedge/Photolibrary

discussion in a classroom or conference setting. This might be used for teaching product knowledge or legal and ethical issues, among other topics.

A second method, on-the-job training, involves salespeople learning while doing the job, often with the help of a supportive mentor or sales manager. Behavioural simulations, whereby learning occurs through a simulated experience through the use of business games, simulations, and role play, offer yet another training method. Games and simulations offer a means for salespeople to practise skills or decision making in a contrived but relevant environment by playing games or interacting with a computer to address simulated real-world selling scenarios. Role playing is extremely popular and generally involves one trainee playing the salesperson and the other the buyer as they interact in a simulated sales presentation. Finally, absorption training involves providing trainees or salespeople with materials that they can study on their own, such as product manuals or sales bulletins. The media used to deliver the training message must also be chosen. While personal or written media have been long used, advances in technology allow for providing training materials via the Internet or a company's intranet, desktop personal computer, video Web conferencing, online chat rooms, satellite television feeds, sales training software, and e-mail, among others.

Design the Sales Training Program

Step four in the sales training process involves committing resources to the training so that inputs from the first three steps can be used to design the actual training program. Budget approval may have to be obtained. The responses to *what, how, where,* and *when* are finalized as the ideas from the first three steps materialize.

sales leadership Activities that influence others to achieve shared goals to advance the organization.

sales management Managing an organization's personal selling function to include planning, implementing, and controlling the sales management process.

sales supervision Sales managers working with subordinates, including salespeople and sales staff, on an ongoing basis.

Perform Sales Training

The fifth step involves actually conducting the training as planned. During this stage, the sales manager should monitor the progress of trainees and ensure that training topics are being adequately covered. At the beginning of training, it is important to make sure that trainees understand how the training will benefit them as this is likely to improve their motivation to learn.

Conduct Follow-Up and Evaluation

The final step in the training process is to determine the effectiveness of the sales training. This can be done in a variety of ways, including trainee feedback, exams, sales manager observations of trainees back in the field, customer feedback, new business and sales volume growth, and return on investment, among others. It is also important to do training reinforcement that is integrated with the salesperson's current work to enhance behaviour change, as one study of more than 6,000 sales professionals found that training participants remember only half of what they learned within five weeks of the training.[15]

11-3 Directing the Salesforce

Directing the salesforce includes two broad dimensions: leadership, managerial, and supervisory functions; and motivation and reward system management. In more progressive sales organizations, the leadership, managerial, and supervisory functions are not entirely a collection of top-down processes in which higher-ups dictate what subordinates must do. Rather, these functions are shared responsibilities in which senior sales leaders, field sales managers, and salespeople play an active role in leadership, management, and supervision. **Sales leadership** includes activities that influence others to achieve shared goals to advance the organization. **Sales management** focuses on planning, implementation, and control of the sales management process. **Sales supervision** involves working with subordinates on an ongoing basis. As illustrated in Exhibit 11.3,[16] senior sales leaders, sales managers, and salespeople are frequently engaged in sales leadership, sales management, and sales supervision activities. Since this chapter deals with sales management, we will use the sales manager as the key person in our discussion of directing the salesforce. In this discussion, we are thinking primarily of sales managers who have salespeople reporting directly to them and who spend a considerable amount of time working with salespeople in their respective territories.

EXHIBIT 11.3

Multilevel Leadership, Management, and Supervision

	Leadership	Management	Supervision
Senior sales leadership	Influencing the entire sales organization or a large subunit by creating a vision, values, culture, direction, alignment, and change, and by energizing action	Planning, implementation, and control of sales management process for entire sales organization or large subunit	Working with sales administrative personnel on a day-to-day basis
Field sales managers	Influencing assigned salespeople by creating a climate that inspires salespeople	Planning, implementation, and control of sales management process within assigned sales unit	Working with salespeople on a day-to-day basis
Salespeople	Influencing customers, sales team members, others in the company, and channel partners	Planning, implementation, and control of sales activities within assigned territory	Working with sales assistants on a day-to-day basis

These types of sales managers are frequently referred to as **field sales managers**.

Directing the salesforce also includes motivating salespeople and managing the reward system. The most commonly used definitions of **motivation** have three dimensions: intensity, persistence, and direction.[17] Intensity is the amount of mental and physical effort salespeople expend. Persistence is the salesperson's ongoing choice to expend effort, especially when faced with adversity. Direction recognizes that salespeople may make choices about how they spend their time on the job. To be fully motivated, salespeople must expend enough effort on the right job activities and be capable of pursuing goals even when they do not have immediate success.

Reward system management involves the selection and administration of organizational rewards to encourage salespeople to achieve organizational objectives. Rewards include compensation such as salaries, bonuses, and commissions, and noncompensation rewards such as recognition and opportunities for growth and development.

SALES LEADERSHIP APPROACHES

One way to view sales leadership is in terms of **leadership style**, which is a general orientation applied to leadership activities. Among many alternative leadership styles, two have received the most attention in sales management. A transactional leadership style relies heavily on the use of rewards and punishment, which are administered according to subordinates' job performance.[18] A transformational leadership style is quite different in that it concentrates on inspiring employees to engage in certain behaviours and to perform at high levels. Important dimensions of transformational leadership include articulating a vision, leading as a role model, encouraging acceptance of group goals, giving individual support, and providing intellectual stimulation.[19] There are many variations of these two basic

field sales managers Sales managers who have salespeople reporting directly to them and who spend a considerable amount of time working with salespeople in their respective territories.

motivation Comprising three dimensions: intensity, persistence, and direction. Intensity is the amount of effort expended, persistence is the ongoing choice to expend effort, and direction refers to how salespeople spend their time on the job.

reward system management Selection and administration of organizational rewards to encourage salespeople to achieve organizational objectives.

leadership style A general orientation applied to leadership activities. Transactional and transformational leadership styles are two well-known leadership styles.

leadership styles, and current research indicates that the most effective leaders use multiple leadership styles, depending on the situation. Thus, in some cases, effective leadership could call for the use of rewards and punishment in a transactional mode, while other leadership challenges are best addressed through one or more dimensions of transformational leadership. The importance of different leadership approaches is presented in "Professional Selling in the 21st Century: Leading the Salesforce."

Another way to view sales leadership is to focus on the relationships between the sales manager and each salesperson within the work unit. This is referred to as the leader–member exchange (LMX) model. Studies of the LMX model indicate that when sales managers and salespeople establish mutual trust, it has positive effects on salespeople's job satisfaction, perceived job climate, willingness to change, goal commitment, and performance.[20]

Given the emphasis on establishing trust-based relationships with customers, it seems highly appropriate that sales organizations would embrace trust-building among sales leaders, sales managers, salespeople, and other key people within the organization. In the intensely competitive, ever-changing business environment facing many sales organizations, the need to move quickly is essential. In such situations, it is advantageous to have interpersonal trust between the key players. As is true in the sales process, trust between sales managers and salespeople can be built through demonstrated expertise, dependability, candour, compatibility and likability, and being responsive to the needs of the other party. With these thoughts in mind, we will now discuss several key areas that should be considered when directing a salesforce.

Professional Selling in the 21st Century

© Robert Daly/OJO Images/Getty

Leading the Salesforce

Janice Hunter, district sales manager in the pharmaceutical industry for over 25 years, discusses her leadership approach.

It's paramount on my part to find out what is important from a career goals and development standpoint from each of my sales reps. If I can accomplish this, I'll have a better chance of having a fully engaged employee. One management style does not fit everyone.

I'd say that my leadership style has to be one of flexibility. That is, I have to be able to change direction with my salespeople depending on the situation. I've managed through mergers and takeovers. Early in my career, transactional leadership was more readily accepted by management and my salespeople. Today my salespeople expect me to have a more transformational leadership style. I spend a couple of days each month with my reps and it is important that I offer each of them individual support. I spend time with each rep going over our company vision, sharing and encouraging company goals with my team, and providing each with the tools they need to be successful. It's critical that I use the leadership style that is best suited to the situation I am addressing with each of my sales reps.

THE ROLE OF POWER

As people work together, they routinely exercise various forms of power to influence the actions of others. According to the pioneering work of social psychologists French and Raven,[21] individuals in the workplace may establish power by virtue of their position, for example sales managers have the right of power to direct salespeople simply because they are higher up on the organizational chart. Sales managers also have the power to reward and punish salespeople based on job performance and job behaviour. Both salespeople and sales managers have power related to their job knowledge and expertise.

In some cases, highly knowledgeable, top-performing salespeople hold a great deal of power in their dealings with sales managers. Salespeople and sales managers also have power based on their interpersonal skills and their ability to work well with others.

The use of power in leadership, management, and supervision is essential, but it is wise to use it judiciously. For example, sales managers who overuse the power of their position in a "my way or the highway" approach will most likely have difficulty in motivating and retaining top salespeople. The same is true for sales managers who overrely on punishment as a coercive tool in directing salespeople. To use power effectively, sales managers should

- Not be reluctant to use any form of power if the situation warrants it. Punishment is sometimes necessary, such as terminating a poor performer who will not respond to corrective action.
- Be careful not to overuse the power of the position or punishment in directing the salesforce. The most talented salespeople are typically less tolerant of managers who are inflexible or lead by intimidation, and turnover can become a problem.
- Not fall into the trap of rewarding all desired job outcomes or behaviours. Some things just have to be done and cannot be immediately rewarded. Consistent good performance and desired job behaviours can and should be rewarded.
- Enhance their power and therefore effectiveness by increasing their knowledge and expertise and by establishing a good working relationship with subordinates.

SALESFORCE COMMUNICATIONS

Most sales organizations are spread across a large geographic area in which salespeople work in a fast-moving, ever-changing environment. Sales managers must communicate effectively not only with their salespeople but also with key customers and others within their companies. To maintain effective communications, sales managers should

- Use coaching as a primary communications and developmental tool.
- Seek feedback from salespeople, customers, and other important parties on a regular basis.
- Use persuasion and promises far more frequently than threats to influence others.

Successful sales managers rely heavily on **coaching**, which focuses on the continual development of salespeople by providing job feedback and serving as a role model to salespeople. When giving salespeople feedback, it is important to provide insights into job outcomes; that is, whether or not salespeople accomplish the desired result. It is also important to provide insights into why and how salespeople should pursue job outcomes. More talented employees appreciate the opportunity to learn on the job and become more effective at their work. To be effective coaches, sales managers should:

- Establish a team approach that focuses on collaboration and learning from other members of the salesforce and others in the organization.
- Encourage salespeople to evaluate themselves and take appropriate corrective action.
- Ensure that salespeople diagnose successes, not just failures, in an attempt to improve overall sales performance.
- Document corrective actions expected of salespeople, and have salespeople confirm that the corrective actions have been taken.
- Recognize that salespeople are individuals and attempt to communicate with each salesperson in a manner suited to that person.
- Follow up coaching sessions with structured training when necessary.
- Serve as a role model to demonstrate desired behaviours to salespeople.

Giving feedback is an important part of sales management, and it is also important that sales managers receive reliable feedback. One of the best ways for sales managers to seek feedback is to work with salespeople in the field. Customer feedback, when coupled with salespeople's opinions, provides sales managers with extremely valuable information. When calling on customers, sales managers can assess sales support and customer service, product performance, and customer satisfaction. In addition, as they accompany salespeople in the field, sales managers can solicit feedback from those salespeople about what is working and what is not. To supplement feedback gained in the field, sales managers can establish customer advisory boards and use feedback from proven salespeople to assist in decision making and strategy development. Another option is to have salespeople submit call reports and weekly summaries that identify major accomplishments,

coaching Sales managers focus on continual development of salespeople through provision of feedback and serving as a role model.

problems, competitive activity, and support needed from sales management.

In communicating with the salesforce, it is advisable to use persuasion and promises rather than threats to gain compliance. Certainly, there are times when a straightforward directive is appropriate and persuasion is unnecessary. When major changes are on the horizon, however, it is wise to get salesforce buy-in before implementing the changes. For example, if a company is changing its salesforce compensation plan to redirect salespeople's efforts to new strategic priorities, it is wise to gain the enthusiastic support of the salesforce in advance of the changes.

The most successful sales managers spend a lot of time on coaching activities to help their salespeople develop and improve.

MOTIVATION AND REWARD SYSTEMS

Salespeople may be motivated in part because they find their job to be interesting and challenging, and thus inherently rewarding. Salespeople are also typically motivated by rewards provided by the sales organization, such as pay and formal recognition programs. Sales managers may have the opportunity to completely develop a reward system, while in other cases they can modify reward systems to balance the needs of the sales organization, salespeople, and customers. The reward system should help attract and retain productive salespeople who want a competitive pay package, some stability of future earnings, and performance-based incentive pay. Salespeople also expect their pay levels to be equitable—that is, fair when compared with others in the sales organization who are achieving comparable job results. Reward systems should also be consistent with the employer's financial objectives and strategic priorities. For a challenging situation in managing the reward system, read "An Ethical Dilemma."

Some sales organizations pay their salespeople on a straight salary basis, and others choose commission-based plans in which sales commissions are paid on sales volume or a percentage of profit. Most sales organizations use combination pay plans with a salary component plus some form of commission and/or bonus. These combination plans are popular because they offer salespeople a component of earnings stability with the upside potential to earn more based on performance. Further, sales organizations can direct salespeople's efforts not only by virtue of the salary component but also through variable pay components, such as commissions, bonuses, and sales contests.

It takes more than a decent reward system to motivate salespeople fully. Sales managers should recruit salespeople whose personal motives match job requirements and rewards. It is important to ensure that salespeople understand how they should proceed on the job and that they are properly equipped through coaching and training. When possible, sales managers may be able to enrich the sales job by adding new duties and responsibilities for selected salespeople. It is important to build the confidence and job-related self-esteem of salespeople to maximize salesforce motivation. Finally, sales managers should actively seek out sources of motivational problems and take action as early as possible to maximize motivation and the overall morale of the salesforce.

11-4 Determining Salesforce Effectiveness and Performance

As depicted in the four-stage sales management process model shown earlier in Figure 11.1, effective sales management requires that sales managers continually monitor the salesforce to determine current performance. The information from this evaluation process provides critical inputs for future sales strategy and salesforce development decisions, as well as diagnosing problems and developing solutions to positively affect future sales performance. Determining salesforce effectiveness and performance is not an easy task, as it requires evaluations to be made at multiple levels: (1) evaluation of the effectiveness of sales units within the organization and (2) evaluation of the performance of individual salespeople.

© petesaloutos/iStockphoto

An Ethical Dilemma

As district sales manager for Western Engineering, you decided it would be a good idea to hold a sales contest to motivate your salespeople during the first quarter of the year. Western's board has taken an aggressive approach to the year to increase sales by 20 percent. As the district manager overseeing the northern half of the country, you feel it important to get off to a good start to reach the 20 percent goal. Your salesforce has had an impeccable reputation with your customers over the past several years. About halfway into the first quarter you started to get some hints that the contest has gone awry. Recently, several phone calls have come in that suggest the contest is causing your salesforce to do some things they'd normally not do. To your surprise, several of your reps have "stretched the truth" to make a sale. Others are overselling their customers. In other words, they are selling customers the more expensive product (more than meets their needs) when a similar less expensive version of the product is exactly what they need. All of this is being done to win a contest. What would you do?

a) Stop the contest immediately and hope your contest has not done too much damage.
b) Have a meeting with the full sales team and let them know of your findings.
c) Revamp the contest to incorporate complaints and lost customers into the reward system.

Sales organization effectiveness is an overall assessment of how well the sales organization achieved its goals and objectives. **Salesperson performance** evaluates how well salespeople perform the activities necessary to carry out their sales responsibilities, as well as their results and contributions to organizational objectives.[22] As illustrated by these definitions, salesperson performance contributes to, but it is not the sole determinant of, sales organization effectiveness. Additional factors, such as sales organization structure, selling strategies, deployment, sales management, and uncontrollable environmental influences, also affect sales organization effectiveness.[23]

The objective of evaluating sales organization effectiveness and salesperson performance is to improve the performance of individual salespeople and the overall operations of the sales organization.

EVALUATING SALES ORGANIZATION EFFECTIVENESS

Performance evaluation at the sales organization level focuses on evaluating the effectiveness of the various selling units that compose the overall sales organization. The focus is typically on results, such as total sales volume, market share, costs, profit contribution, return on assets, and other relevant outcomes. These indicators of effectiveness might refer to the entire sales organization or to subdivisions, such as regions, districts, territories, and even zones. The results from these organizational evaluations provide important managerial feedback regarding the effectiveness of plans and quality of execution, which serve as inputs for strategic decision making and corrective actions.

sales organization effectiveness An overall assessment of how well the sales organization achieved its goals and objectives.

salesperson performance How well salespeople perform the activities necessary to carry out their sales responsibilities, as well as their results and contributions to organizational objectives.

There is no one best method for evaluating sales organization effectiveness, and the preferred approach and methodologies used will vary from company to company. In practice, typical evaluation methods include the more comprehensive sales organization audit as well as a variety of more focused analyses designed to assess sales, costs, and profitability. Each of these methods is discussed in turn here.

Sales Organization Audit

The **sales organization audit** is a comprehensive, systematic approach for evaluating sales organization effectiveness and provides management with diagnostic and prescriptive information.[24] Accordingly, audits such as this are undertaken for the purpose of identifying existing or potential problems, determining their causes, and facilitating the needed corrective actions. Sales organization audits analyze four major areas: sales organization environment, sales management evaluation, sales organization planning system, and sales management functions. Important factors in the business environment include competition, technology, customer perceptions, the level of support and integration of sales and other functions within the company, and economic trends. Sales management is evaluated in terms of adequacy of sales managers and management practices. The sales organization planning system is examined in light of its objectives and strategies. Finally, sales management functions, such as recruiting, training, motivation, supervision, and budgeting are analyzed.

To better ensure objective and unbiased evaluations, audits are best conducted by individuals outside the sales organization with sales managers and salespeople serving an active role and providing most of the information for the audit. Reflecting the comprehensive nature of this approach, it can become an expensive and time intensive process. Nevertheless, this approach is widely used as the benefits realized from analysis significantly exceed the costs incurred. Exemplary benefits resulting from sales organization audits include increased productivity as well as enhanced sales and profits because of the improvements in sales operations and management.

sales organization audit A comprehensive, systematic approach for evaluating sales organization effectiveness, which provides management with diagnostic as well as prescriptive information.

sales analysis Examines the sales organization's past, current, and future sales performance in comparison with projections, competition, and industry sales.

Sales Analysis

With the basic function of a sales organization being the generation of sales, **sales analysis** is obviously an important element in evaluating sales organization effectiveness and examines the sales organization's past, current, and future sales performance in comparison with projections, competition, and industry sales. Figure 11.4 illustrates the many different types and combinations of sales analyses that can be performed across four key decision areas: (1) unit of analysis, (2) organizational level of analysis, (3) type of sales to be included, and (4) method of analysis to be used.

- *Unit of Analysis*—Sales can be analyzed in dollar or in unit terms. The decision as to which unit is appropriate is important and can affect the results of the analysis. For instance, in a period of rising prices, it is possible for dollar sales to increase even while unit sales decrease.
- *Organizational Level of Analysis*—Sales analysis should be performed at each level that is relevant to the subject organization. Managers at each level of the organization need the results from sales analysis at their level and the levels immediately under them if they are to carry out their managerial responsibilities effectively. For example, a district sales manager needs sales analysis for all districts as well as for all territories within his or her district. This makes it possible for the manager to assess the effectiveness of the region in comparison with other regions and also to determine the comparative sales contribution of each territory within his or her responsibility.
- *Type of Sales*—Examining sales at the aggregate level of total sales can obscure useful details that might be occurring within different areas or categories of sales, such as product or account type, distribution method used, or size of order placed. Disaggregating sales data for analyses by relevant types of sales can solve this problem. For example, Central Equipment Corporation (CEC) manufactures hydraulic control equipment and sells through its own company salesforce as well as independent distributors. A recent sales analysis documented that overall sales for the year had increased by 14 percent over the previous period. Further analysis by type of sale revealed that sales through the CEC salesforce had increased by 21 percent while sales through independent distributors were actually down by 16 percent. This led to changes in sales strategies and policies relevant to the independent distributors to address the problems identified from the sales analysis. Had aggregate sales analysis been the sole focus, the differences across types of distribution would not have been identified.

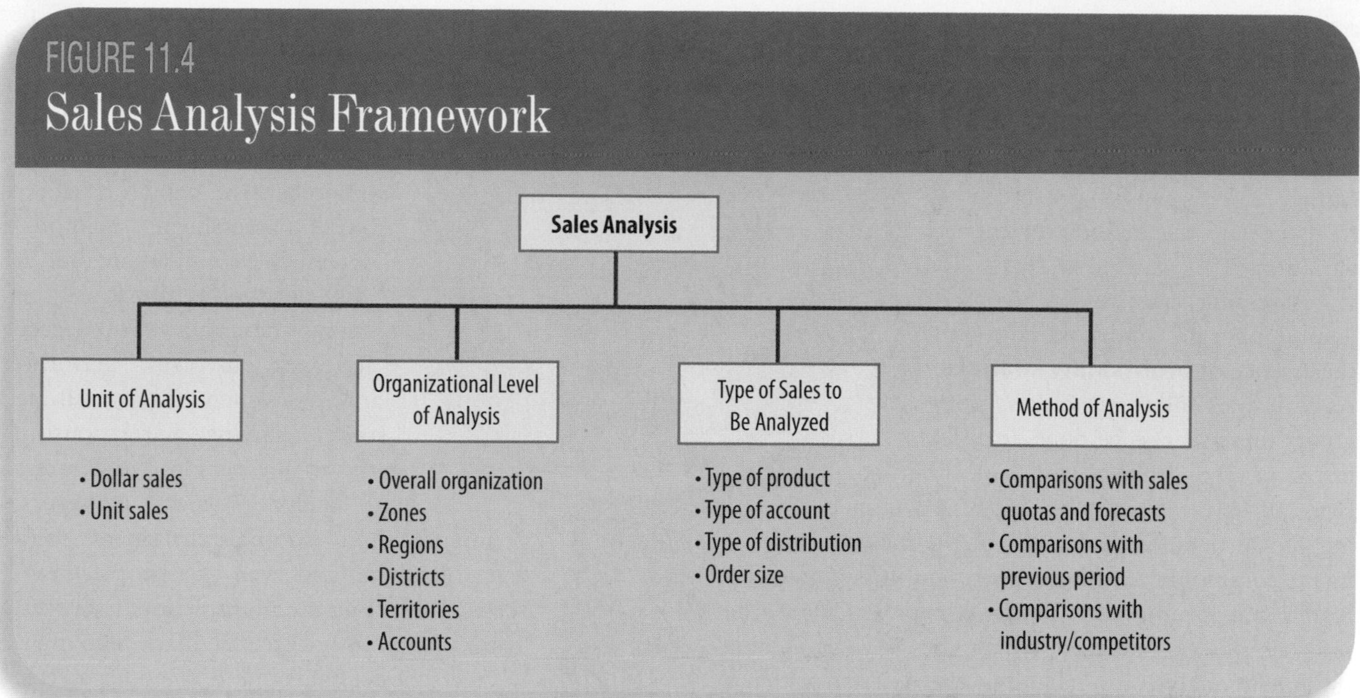

FIGURE 11.4
Sales Analysis Framework

Sales analysis can be conducted using different combinations of unit of analysis, level within the organization, type of sale, and analysis methods.

- *Method of Analysis*—Actual dollar and/or unit sales results for the different organizational levels and types of sales certainly provide important information for management. The information content resulting from these analyses can be further enhanced by methods of analysis allowing comparisons of actual sales with benchmarks, such as sales forecasts and quotas, previous periods, and industry or competitor sales. Continuing with the Central Equipment Corporation sales analysis example, their 14 percent increase in overall sales became more meaningful to management when it was compared against the industry's growth figure of only 6 percent for the same period.

Cost and Profitability Analysis

In **cost analysis**, the focus is on assessing costs the sales organization incurs in the process of generating sales. The more typical approach to cost analysis compares incurred costs with the planned costs as reflected in sales budgets. Cost analysis addresses controllable costs rather than uncontrollable costs. Controllable costs are those that are directly controlled by sales organization management, such as salaries and commissions, bonuses, travel expenses, recruiting, training and development, meetings, and sales administrative costs.

Are we counting apples or oranges? The decision to analyze sales in either dollar or unit terms can yield very different results.

© photos.com

The purpose of incurring selling costs within the sales organization is to generate sales. Consequently, it should be noted that the purpose of cost analysis is *not* to minimize selling cost. The purpose of cost analysis is to ensure that the selling plan's budgeted relationships between sales and selling costs are maintained. In accomplishing this objective,

cost analysis Assesses costs the sales organization incurs in the process of generating sales by comparing incurred costs with the planned costs in sales budgets.

costs analysis examines variances between actual costs and budgeted costs. For units or types of sales in which large variances are found, especially when actual costs exceed budgeted costs, further analysis can be undertaken to determine the reasons for the variations.

Assessing the results from combining sales and cost data is the essence of **profitability analysis**. As with sales and cost analyses, profitability analysis can be done at different levels of the organization and different types of sales. Profitability analysis routinely includes a detailed evaluation of the income statement, commonly called the profit-and-loss statement. Additional profitability analysis may calculate the return on assets managed, which goes beyond income statement analysis by including the asset investment that is required to produce sales outcomes.

© Rob Wilkinson/Alamy

EVALUATING SALESPERSON PERFORMANCE

This level of analysis focuses on the performance and effectiveness of salespeople relative to how well they perform the activities necessary to carry out their responsibilities and contribute to organizational objectives. Salesperson performance analysis pertains to individual salespeople, not the sales organization. While the analysis of sales organization effectiveness is most often focused on strategic issues and decisions, the results of salesperson performance evaluations tend to be more tactical in nature. That is, they provide information leading sales managers to take specific actions to improve the performance of an individual salesperson.

In practice, performance appraisal continues to be primarily a top-down approach in which each manager evaluates each of the people directly reporting to them. However, with the growing complexity and strategic importance of the selling function, the trend is toward more comprehensive and broader-based assessment methods. One such assessment method is **360-degree feedback**. As the name describes, 360-degree feedback involves performance assessments from multiple sources having a relationship with the salesperson. These raters might include sales managers, internal and external customers, sales team members, and even salespeople themselves. Reflecting the multiple input sources, results from 360-degree feedback help managers better understand customer needs, assess training and development needs, detect barriers to success, increase job involvement, reduce assessment bias, and improve salesperson performance.

Another evaluation approach gaining favour over the traditional top-down method is referred to as **performance management**. This approach involves sales managers and individual salespeople working together on setting goals, giving feedback, reviewing, and rewarding. Under this evaluation approach, salespeople participate in setting realistic quotas and budgets, create their own development plans, and assume responsibility for their careers. Rather than an autocratic supervisor, the sales manager is a partner in this process and provides timely feedback focused on what is within the salesperson's control to change.

Regardless of the specific approach used, performance evaluation typically incorporates four distinct stages. In stage one, the sales manager and salesperson discuss the salesperson's evaluation. This evaluation might come from the traditional manager's appraisal of the salesperson, a 360-degree feedback methodology, or the performance management approach. In stage two, the sales manager rates the salesperson according

360-degree feedback involves performance evaluations from the full circle of sources having relationships with the salesperson.

profitability analysis Evaluates the results from combining sales and cost data to identify and assess sales organization profitability.

360-degree feedback Performance assessments of a salesperson from multiple sources having a relationship with the salesperson.

performance management A performance evaluation approach that involves sales managers and individual salespeople working together on setting goals, giving feedback, reviewing, and rewarding.

to predetermined criteria or performance standards to determine whether the salesperson is above or below expectations. Stage three reviews the salesperson's performance relative to his or her previous performance evaluation to determine accomplishments in areas noted as needing improvement in the previous appraisal. Effective evaluations focus on both the good and the bad to assist the salesperson in identifying and understanding what he or she can do to further improve his or her performance. The final stage focuses on the future. In this stage, mutual agreements are reached regarding sales objectives, action plans for improvement, as well as the resources, structure, and training that are needed to support the objectives and plans. When properly integrated into a systemic evaluation, these four stages identify the salesperson's current level of activity and performance, develop relevant comparisons to expected performance standards and previous performance appraisals, and construct a thoughtful plan for performance improvement in the upcoming period.

Criteria for Evaluating Salesperson Performance

Sales jobs are multidimensional, involving numerous products sold to a diverse set of customers and requiring a variety of selling and nonselling activities. As a result, any valid and comprehensive evaluation of performance must include multiple criteria. These criteria are most often grouped into two types: the behavioural perspective and the results or outcome perspective. The behaviour-based perspective incorporates assessments—often subjective—of salesperson characteristics and behaviours with considerable monitoring and directing of salesperson behaviour by sales managers. In contrast, the outcome-based perspective focuses on objective measures of selling results with minimal monitoring or directing by sales managers.[25] The importance of using multiple criteria is presented in "Professional Selling in the 21st Century: Salesperson Performance Evaluation Criteria at Pfizer."

Considerable support from sales management practice and research supports the conclusion that sales organizations should use both outcome-based and behaviour-based evaluations when assessing salesperson performance. Hybrid approaches incorporating both types of measures place considerable emphasis on supervision, evaluation of attitude, effort,

PROFESSIONAL SELLING IN THE 21ST CENTURY

© Fry Design Ltd/Getty Images

Salesperson Performance Evaluation Criteria at Pfizer

Chris Aiken, certified medical representative and senior professional healthcare representative for Pfizer Pharmaceuticals, discusses how the criteria used to evaluate salesperson performance incorporate much more than just sales revenue outcomes.

Our salespeople are evaluated on several criteria: Sales and profitability, territory management, product knowledge, teamwork, innovation, leadership, and customer rapport. While sales performance is still the ultimate goal, it is also very important for our salespeople to develop rapport with their key customers AND staff. Good sales numbers are a direct result of having access to our key customers. Having access to those customers is the result of the rapport that has been established with them from each previous interaction. In addition, superb customer rapport helps sustain business during challenging times. Our most successful representatives are those who have positioned themselves as a resource that brings value to their customer through customer and patient education and other programs as opposed to being viewed as a sales representative looking for a short-sighted return.

outcome-based evaluations Evaluation of the actual sales results salespeople achieve.

behaviour-based evaluations Evaluation of the activities salespeople perform in the generation of sales and in completing nonselling responsibilities.

behaviourally anchored rating scales (BARS) A performance evaluation method with the ability to link salesperson behaviours with specific outcomes and allow managers to indicate the level of behaviour a specific salesperson has achieved.

and quantitative results, and complex, accurate paperwork. Regardless of the mix between the two types of sales management controls, research also documents that greater levels of control lead to higher levels of salesperson job satisfaction, organizational commitment, and job performance while reducing the level of job stress.[26]

Outcome-Based Evaluations

Outcome-based evaluations focus on actual results salespeople achieve. This immediate and direct connection to the purpose of the selling function has resulted in its attractiveness and logical choice as a component of the salesperson evaluation process. Sales outcomes frequently evaluated include total sales volume, current year sales compared with last year's sales, sales versus quota, percentage increase in sales volume, sales volume by product line, and sales volume per customer.

While sales outcomes are extremely important in evaluating salesperson performance, they present several challenges in use. One such challenge is that measures of sales outcomes by themselves do not reflect the differing territory situations faced by individual salespeople in the organization. The salesperson having the highest sales productivity may have the best territory and may not be the best performer in generating sales. When salespeople perceive performance criteria as arbitrary and without consideration for situational differences in accounts and territories, there can be a negative effect on performance and job satisfaction. Sales managers address this potential problem by comparing actual sales outcomes with standards designed to reflect unique territory situations faced by each salesperson. These territory standards are typically referred to as sales quotas—a sales objective for a specific sales unit, such as a territory, region, district, or zone.

Behaviour-Based Evaluations

Behaviour-based evaluations consist of criteria related to the activities salespeople perform. These criteria include activities directly related to the generation of sales, as well as nonselling activities necessary for assuring customer satisfaction, self-development, and providing accurate information to the sales organization. The most common sales behaviours considered in evaluations include number of sales calls, number of sales calls per day, and the completion of administrative requirements, such as submitting reports in a timely manner.

Performance Evaluation Methods

Sales managers have a number of different methods available for evaluating salesperson performance. For example, a graphic rating or checklist could be used or salespeople could be ranked against other salespeople on various performance dimensions. In some cases, salespeople are evaluated against written objectives. If behaviour is to be evaluated instead of or in addition to sales outcomes, a **behaviourally anchored rating scale (BARS)** could be used. BARS instruments are developed with input from sales managers and salespeople, and the idea is to define the desired behaviour, which will lead to desired sales outcomes. Whichever method, or combination of methods, is used, the evaluation methods should have these characteristics:

- *Reliability:* The measures should be stable over time and exhibit internal consistency.
- *Validity:* The measures should provide accurate assessments of the criteria they are intended to measure.
- *Standardization:* The measurement instruments and evaluation process should be similar throughout the sales organization.
- *Practicality:* Sales managers and salespeople should understand the entire performance appraisal process and should be able to implement it in a reasonable amount of time.
- *Comparability:* The results of the performance evaluation process should make it possible to compare the performance of individual salespeople directly.
- *Discriminability:* The evaluative methods must be capable of detecting differences in the performance of individual salespeople.
- *Usefulness:* The information provided by the performance evaluation must be valuable to sales managers in making various decisions.

Developing evaluation methods possessing all these characteristics is a complex, essential task. It is a crucial task, however, as evaluating sales performance and effectiveness provides important information to sales management. The critical sales management task is to use this information to improve the performance of individual salespeople and the overall operations of the sales organization. This requires that sales managers have a detailed understanding of the personal selling and sales management processes so they can determine the causes of performance problems and identify appropriate strategies, plans, and managerial actions to solve the problems.

11-5 Sales 2.0

A major focus of this chapter is on the need for sales organizations to develop and execute strategies and processes to guide personal selling and sales management activities. Our attention now turns to technology. The basic role of technology is to help salespeople and sales managers implement these strategies and processes effectively. Strategies and processes should drive sales organizations with the appropriate technologies employed to facilitate successful execution. LBMC Technologies provides an excellent example of integrating the sales process and technology. The company has a well-defined sales process and a customer relationship management (CRM) system that includes only information that will help reps sell and sales managers support salespeople throughout their sales process. Everyone in the company can access the CRM system on smartphones and laptops.[27]

The use of technology in sales has evolved in several phases.[28] Contact management software was used initially to organize basic information about prospects and customers. This was expanded into salesforce automation products to keep track of leads and the basic stages in the sales process for account planning and forecasting purposes. Then, customer relationship management (CRM) systems were introduced to collect and manage extensive information about customers and relationships with access available to individuals in different business functions. These technologies have been useful in providing information to help salespeople communicate more effectively to prospects and customers. However, the orientation has been internal with an emphasis on one-way communication.

Now, new Web-based technologies, often called Web 2.0, are being used to help sales organizations change to an external orientation based on two-way communication and collaboration with customers. **Sales 2.0** is the use of customer-driven processes enabled by the latest Web 2.0 technologies to co-create value with customers. The focus is on interaction between buyer and seller, and the alignment of strategy, people, process, and technology to enhance the art and science of sales.[29] These technologies engage customers in an ongoing dialogue and can be used throughout the sales and sales management processes presented in this book. We will discuss key trends in CRM systems and specific Web 2.0 products that salespeople and sales managers are using to implement a Sales 2.0 approach.

Sales 2.0 The use of customer-driven processes enabled by the latest Web technology to co-create value with customers.

© salesforce.com, inc. Used with permission.

Web-based CRM products with mobile versions are useful to salespeople.

CUSTOMER RELATIONSHIP MANAGEMENT (CRM)

Recent trends indicate that CRM systems are becoming more valuable to users. First, CRM product offerings have evolved from large software installations at individual firms to Web-based products that use a software-as-a-service model. NetSuite and Salesforce.com are examples. These firms maintain and update the software regularly, with companies paying a monthly fee for each user. The software-as-a-service model makes CRM systems available to sales organizations of all sizes. Another important trend is the commercial open-source model for CRM systems. For example, SugarCRM is based on a modular architecture and provides access to its source code so that users can customize the software to meet their specific needs by making changes, adding applications, or fixing problems and publishing these fixes online for others

social networking The ability to create, access, and interact with networks of contacts electronically.

cloud computing Combining applications, communications, and content into one digital cloud that can be easily accessed from many different devices.

to use. This lowers the operating costs for SugarCRM, which generates a lower price and a more adaptable product for users.[30] Third, more CRM vendors are providing wireless access for salespeople and sales managers from smartphones. This gives salespeople and sales managers access to "real time" CRM in the field. Finally, new Web 2.0 products are continually being introduced. A few years ago, there were fewer than 100 Sales 2.0 applications, now there are more than 1,000.[31] More and more of these products are designed to collaborate with or be integrated into CRM systems.

WEB 2.0 PRODUCTS

One increasingly important category of Web 2.0 products is social networking services. **Social networking** is the ability to create, access, and interact with networks of contacts electronically. The use of Facebook for personal social networking has exploded in recent years. And, business applications of Facebook are increasing. Web-based social networking is also growing rapidly in the B2C marketplace. Now, new social networking products, such as LinkedIn, Jigsaw, Orkut, Xeequa, and Twitter, are being used more by salespeople and sales managers in B2B situations.[32] IBM is using social media to identify leads and to increase collaborative communication between salespeople and customers. The company is giving all of its salespeople personal Web pages linked to Twitter and Facebook with live chat from Lotus Sametime and video cameras to show things to customers.[33]

Although each product has somewhat different features, all provide an opportunity to develop a profile and list of contacts, and to access the networks and profile information of those in an individual's contact list. LinkedIn is one of the most popular sites for salespeople and sales managers. Salespeople can use it to identify key decision makers at prospect companies, learn about them from their profiles, and get access to them through someone in their network. Sales managers find LinkedIn helpful in identifying, learning about, and accessing potential hires for various sales positions.

A list and brief application description of other Web 2.0 products useful to salespeople and sales managers is presented in Exhibit 11.4. The table provides a sample of the various ways that Web-based products can be used to improve different aspects of the sales and sales management process.

The rapid pace of Web-based technology development continues. An interesting trend is cloud computing. **Cloud computing** is combining applications,

EXHIBIT 11.4
Selected Web 2.0 Applications for Sales 2.0

Sales Process Applications

Genius increases collaboration between marketing and sales as e-mails from marketing are sent to salespeople when a prospect indicates interest in a firm's product.

Hoover's improves prospecting and sales dialogue planning by providing detailed information about a prospect's business.

Landslide guides salespeople through the best sales process for specific types of buyers.

Brainshark helps salespeople develop customized, multimedia sales presentations for specific buyers.

EchoSign assists salespeople in gaining commitment through an automated contract and approval management system.

Sales Management Process Applications

SAVO is a knowledge management system that facilitates the sharing of information and knowledge by everyone in a sales organization.

TerrAlign is an automated system that helps sales managers optimize sales territory design.

Synygy helps sales managers plan, implement, and manage sales compensation and incentive programs.

Lucidera provides analytics to help sales managers improve sales forecasts.

Sales ScoreBoard helps sales managers evaluate salesperson performance and identify problems that need to be addressed.

communications, and content into one digital cloud that can be easily accessed from many different devices. For example, Siri has introduced an artificial intelligence system that can be used as a virtual assistant. A salesperson could ask this virtual assistant to pull together all the needed information to make the best sales presentation to a specific customer. The virtual assistant draws from a variety of sources to assemble what the salesperson requests.[34] A recent survey found that 85 percent of the companies would be using cloud computing tools moderately and 14 percent minimally within the next three years. Currently, 75 percent indicated some form of cloud computing use.[35] The most successful sales organizations are likely to be those that create effective personal selling and sales management processes and use the emerging technologies to co-create value for their salespeople and customers.

Visit **www.nelson.com/student** to find the resources you need today!

Located at the back of the textbook are rip-out Chapter Review cards. Make sure you also go online to check out other tools that SELL offers to help you successfully pass your course.

- Flashcards
- Glossary
- PowerPoint Notes
- Role-Play Videos
- Games
- Interactive Quizzing

CHAPTER 11 CASE

ALLIANCE ADHESIVES & PLASTICS INC.

Background

As one of three regional sales managers for Alliance Adhesives and Plastics Inc., you have just received summary details from a study of the company's national field salesforce. The study was done at the request of the vice president for sales and marketing and used a variety of assessment tools to identify the strengths and weaknesses of the company's 97 salespeople located across Canada. Based on these results, the vice president for sales and marketing has assigned you and your three-person regional managers team the task of developing a step-by-step program that will move the company forward toward a revitalized and more effective salesforce.

In response to the company's new marketing strategy designed to "get close to the customer," the salesforce was completely reorganized a little over four years ago, moving from a strictly geographic-based territory system to a specialized selling force organized around the different served markets. As the result of the reorganization and transformation of the company's salespeople into a salesforce specialized around served markets, definite improvements were realized in account penetration and customer retention. Nevertheless, spot checks randomly made across various customers indicate that there is still much room for improvement. Customer satisfaction levels are still low, and the company has some difficulty keeping good accounts.

Current Situation

Customers give Alliance salespeople strong marks for product knowledge—probably a reflection of the existing training program, which has intensive initial and recurrent training on the wide variety of products offered. Surprisingly, while customers rate the salespeople high for their product knowledge, they also indicate that Alliance salespeople appear somewhat arrogant and self-centred. Many of the responses show that, overall, the salesforce does not care about the customer and does not attempt or even take the time to fully explore and understand problems or new applications requiring novel solutions. Instead, the salesforce always seems to have some fixed response and attempt to pressure and persuade buyers rather than offering creative or customized product solutions.

Questions

1. Based on the information given, what are the major problems facing the sales organization?
2. What changes in the recruiting and selection of salespeople would you suggest? Why?
3. What changes in sales training would you suggest? Why?
4. What changes in sales management leadership would you suggest? Why?

Role Play

Situation: Read the case.

Characters: The four regional sales managers

Scene: The four regional sales managers are meeting in a conference room to identify ideas to improve the company's sales organization. The ideas generated will be presented to the vice president of sales and marketing next week.

Role play the meeting among the four regional sales managers to determine the plan that will be presented to the vice president of sales and marketing next week.

After completing the role play, answer the following questions:

1. Discuss the advantages and disadvantages of the ideas discussed during this meeting.
2. Present the details of what was agreed to during this meeting.
3. Describe the process used to determine the plan that will be recommended.

Role Play: Sales Management and Sales 2.0: Improving Sales Training

Background

Daniel Roche, national sales manager at The Widget Company, is concerned about his company's sales training program. The Widget Company is based in Hamilton, but operates throughout Canada with 100 salespeople. Sales and profit growth has slowed in recent quarters. Some of this is due to the tough economic climate, but company studies indicate that customer satisfaction and retention rates have been declining. A sales organization audit identified potential problems with the current sales training program.

The audit indicated that current training costs are about 23 percent higher than those of other companies in the industry. The costs of bringing all salespeople to Hamilton for face-to-face, centralized training, conducted by members of the corporate Training and Development Division, was particularly high. However, the centralized training seemed to produce strong camaraderie and commitment among the members of the salesforce. In addition, most of the current training focused on the technical attributes of the products. So, it was also convenient to have training in Hamilton, where the main development and testing labs and technicians are located. There are clear benefits to centralized training, but the costs associated with this approach are increasing rapidly.

The results from the audit also suggested that The Widget Company was overemphasizing product and technical training, and short-changing business knowledge and consultative sales skills. There was not enough training emphasis on questioning and listening skills, presentation skills, and relationship-building skills. Many salespeople were dissatisfied with the sales training being offered and indicated that the lack of training in these areas put them at a disadvantage against salespeople from competing firms.

Current Situation

Daniel Roche has decided to bring a regional sales manager, field sales manager, and salesperson to meet with him in Hamilton to determine the best ways to improve the company's sales training program. Each stage in the sales training process will be discussed at this meeting. The objective of the meeting is to develop a basic sales training improvement plan.

Role Play

Situation: Read the role play

Characters: National sales manager, regional sales manager, field sales manager, and salesperson

Scene: The meeting takes place in the national sales manager's office in Hamilton

Role play this meeting by discussing each stage of the sales training process from the perspective of the national sales manager, regional sales manager, field sales manager, and salesperson.

After completing the role play, address the following questions:

1. What ideas were generated for each stage of the sales training process?
2. How did the perspectives of the national sales manager, regional sales manager, field sales manager, and salesperson differ during this meeting?
3. What ideas for improving the sales training program were agreed to during the meeting? Why?

ENDNOTES

Chapter 1

1 Marjorie J. Caballero, Roger A. Dickinson, and Dabney Townsend, "Aristotle and Personal Selling," *Journal of Personal Selling & Sales Management* 4 (May 1984): 13.

2 William T. Kelley, "The Development of Early Thought in Marketing," in *Salesmanship: Selected Readings*, ed. John M. Rathmell (Homewood, IL: Irwin, 1969): 3.

3 Thomas L. Powers, Warren S. Martin, Hugh Rushing, and Scott Daniels, "Selling Before 1900: A Historical Perspective," *Journal of Personal Selling & Sales Management* 7 (November 1987): 1–7.

4 Stanley Hollander, "Anti-Salesman Ordinances of the Mid-19th Century," in *Salesmanship: Selected Readings*, ed. John M. Rathmell (Homewood, IL: Irwin, 1969): 9.

5 Jon M. Hawes, "Leaders in Selling and Sales Management," *Journal of Personal Selling & Sales Management* 5 (November 1985): 60.

6 Thomas Wotruba, "The Evolution of Selling," *Journal of Personal Selling & Sales Management* (Summer 1991): 1–12; Jon M. Hawes, Anne K. Rich, and Scott Widmier, "Assessing the Development of the Sales Profession," *Journal of Personal Selling & Sales Management* 24 (Winter 2004): 27–38; synthesized from Eli Jones, Steven P. Brown, Andris A. Zoltners, and Barton A. Weitz, "The Changing Environment of Selling and Sales Management," *Journal of Personal Selling & Sales Management* 25 (Spring 2005): 105–111; William C. Moncrief and Greg W. Marshall, "The Evolution of the Seven Steps of Selling," *Industrial Marketing Management* 34 (January 2005): 13–22; Raymond W. LaForge, Thomas N. Ingram, and David W. Cravens, "Strategic Alignment for Sales Organization Transformation," *Journal of Strategic Marketing* (June–August 2009): 199–219; Jagdish N. Sheth and Arun Sharma, "The Impact of the Product to Service Shift in Industrial Markets and the Evolution of the Sales Organization," *Industrial Marketing Management* 37 (May 2008): 260–269.

7 "America's 500 Largest Sales Forces," *Selling Power* (October/November 2010): 40–56.

8 Robert A. Willett, "Transforming to a Customer Centric Enterprise," Presentation February 14, 2008, http://www.slideshare.net/nasscom/transforming-to-a-customer-centric-enterpriserobert-a-willett-chief-executive-officer-best-buy-international, accessed April 1, 2009; Laura Heller, "Customer-Centric Model Future Focus at Best Buy," *DSN Retailing Today* (April 25, 2005): 22.

9 To learn more about what customers expect from salespeople, see Tom Atkinson and Ron Koprowski, "Sales Reps' Biggest Mistakes," *Harvard Business Review* 84 (July–August 2006): 20; Philip Kreindler and Gopal Raj Guru, "What B2B Customers Really Expect," *Harvard Business Review* 84 (July–August 2006): 22–24.

10 Robert F. Gwinner, "Base Theory in the Formulation of Sales Strategy," *MSU Business Topics* (Autumn 1968): 37.

11 Adapted from D. Forbes Ley, *The Best Seller* (Newport Beach, CA: Sales Success Press, 1986).

12 Marji McClure, "What's the Problem?" *Selling Power* (May 2008): 64–67.

13 For more discussion of consultative selling, see Mack Hanan, *Consultative Selling*, 8th ed. (New York: American Management Association, 2011); Kevin J. Corcoran, Laura K. Petersen, Daniel B. Baitch, and Mark F. Barrett, *High Performance Sales Organizations* (Chicago: Irwin, 1995): 44; and Jonathan Farrington, "Strategic Selling—All Three Roles Defined," http://www.superperformance.com/strategicsell.php, accessed August 12, 2011.

14 Yellow Pages. *Yellow Pages Group, 2010*, http://www.ypg.com/en/, January 3, 2010; Mark Marone and Seleste Lunsford, *Strategies That Win Sales* (Chicago, IL: Dearborn Trade Publishing, 2005): 83.

15 E. Robert Dwyer, Paul Schurr, and Sejo Oh, "Developing Buyer–Seller Relationships," *Journal of Marketing* (April 1987): 11–27; Jon M. Hawes, Kenneth E. Mast, and John E. Swan, "Trust Earning Perceptions of Sellers and Buyers," *Journal of Personal Selling & Sales Management* 9 (Spring 1989): 1; Gary K. Hunter and William D. Perreault, "Making Sales Technology Effective," *Journal of Marketing* 71 (January 2007): 16–34.

16 Interview by the authors with Blake Conrad, sales representative with Centurion Specialty Care.

Appendix Chapter 1

1 Thomas N. Ingram and Charles H. Schwepker, Jr., "Perceptions of Salespeople: Implications for Sales Managers and Sales Trainers," *Journal of Marketing Management* 2 (Fall/Winter 1992–1993): 1–8.

2 Katherine B. Hartman, "Television and Movie Representations of Salespeople: Beyond Willie Loman," *Journal of Personal Selling & Sales Management* 26 (Summer 2006): 283–292.

3 Thomas N. Ingram, "Relationship Selling: Moving from Rhetoric to Reality," *Mid-American Journal of Business* 11 (Spring 1996): 5–12.

4 Emin Babakus, David W. Cravens, Ken Grant, Thomas N. Ingram, and Raymond W. LaForge, "Removing Salesforce Performance Hurdles," *Journal of Business and Industrial Marketing* 9, no. 3 (1994): 19–29.

5 See Herbert M. Greenberg and Jeanne Greenberg, *What It Takes to Succeed in Sales* (Homewood, IL: Dow-Jones Irwin, 1990).

6 James M. Comer and Alan J. Dubinsky, *Managing the Successful Sales Force* (Lexington, MA: D.C. Heath and Co., 1985): 5; Steven P. Brown, Thomas W. Leigh, and J. Martin Haygood, "Salesperson Performance and Job Attitudes," in *The Marketing Manager's Handbook*, 3rd ed., eds. Sidney J. Levy, George R. Frerichs, and Howard L. Gordon (Chicago: The Dartnell Corporation, 1994): 107.

7 Babakus et al., "Removing Salesforce Performance Hurdles," 19; Greg W. Marshall, Daniel J. Goebel, and William C. Moncrief, "Hiring for Success at the Buyer–Seller Interface," *Journal of Business Research* 56 (April 2003): 247–255.

8 Rosann L. Spiro and Barton A. Weitz, "Adaptive Selling: Conceptualization, Measurement, and Nomological Validity," *Journal of Marketing Research* 27 (February 1990): 61.

9 Marshall et al., "Hiring for Success," 251.

10 Kevin J. Corcoran, Laura K Petersen, Daniel B. Baitch, and Mark F. Barrett, *High Performance Sales Organizations* (Chicago: Irwin Professional Publishing, 1995): 77.

11 Marshall et al., "Hiring for Success," 251.

12 Arun Sharma and Rajnandini Pillai, "Customers' Decision-Making Styles and Their Preference for Sales Strategies: Conceptual Examination and an Empirical Study," *Journal of Personal Selling & Sales Management* 16 (Winter 1996): 21.

13 Victoria D. Bush, Gregory M. Rose, Faye Gilbert, and Thomas N. Ingram, "Managing Culturally Diverse Buyer–Seller Relationships: The Role of Intercultural Disposition and Adaptive Selling Behavior in Developing Intercultural Communication Competence," *Journal of the Academy of Marketing Science* 29, no. 4 (Fall 2001): 391–404.

14 Gabriel R. Gonzalez, K. Douglas Hoffman, and Thomas N. Ingram, "Improving Relationship Selling Through Failure Analysis and Recovery Efforts: A Framework and Call to Action," *Journal of Personal Selling & Sales Management* 25 (Winter 2005): 57–66.

Chapter 2

1 Sherry Kilgus, "Building Trust into High Level Alliances," *NAMA Journal* 34 (Winter 1998).

2 John Andy Wood, James S. Bales, Wesley Johnston, and Danny Bellinger, "Buyers' Trust of the Salesperson: An Item-Level Meta Analysis," *JPSSM* 28, no. 3 (Summer 2008): 263–283.

3 Michael Ahearne, Ron Jelinck, and Eli Jones, "Examining the Effect of Salesperson Service Behavior in a Competitive Context," *Journal of Academy of Marketing Science* 35 (2007): 603–616.

4 *Ibid.*

5 John E. Swan and Johannah Jones Nolan, "Gaining Customer Trust: A Conceptual Guide for the Salesperson," *Journal of Personal Selling & Sales Management* 5, no. 2 (November 1985): 39.
6 Robert F. Dwyer, Paul H. Schurr, and Sejo Oh, "Developing Buyer–Seller Relationships," *Journal of Marketing* 51 (April 1987): 11.
7 Lubomira Radoilska, "Trustfulness and Business," *Journal of Business Ethics* 79 (2008): 21–28.
8 This was the concluding point of the symposium on trust held by the National Account Management Association at Wake Forest University, September 24–26, 1997.
9 Kevin Bradford and Barton Weitz, "Salespersons' Management of Conflicts in Buyer–Seller Relationships," *JPSSM* 29, no. 1 (Winter 2009): 25–42.
10 Interview with Missy Rust, GlaxoSmithKline, February 13, 2000.
11 Robert Petersen, "Consultative Selling: A Qualitative Look at the Salesperson Credibility Requirements," *AMA Educator Proceeding Enhancing Knowledge Development in Marketing* 8 (1997): 224.
12 *Ibid.*
13 American Marketing Association's Code of Ethics. Reprinted by permission of American Marketing Association.
14 Gerhard Gschwandtner, "Lies and Deception in Selling: How to Tell When Customers or Prospects Are Lying to You," *Selling Power* 15, no. 9, 2010.
15 Sergio Roman and Salvador Ruiz, "Relationship Outcomes of Perceived Ethical Sales Behavior: The Customer's Perspective," *Journal of Business Research* 58 (2005): 439–445; Douglas B. Grisaffe and Fernando Jaramillo, "Toward Higher Levels of Ethics: Preliminary Evidence of Positive Outcomes," *Journal of Personal Selling & Sales Management* 27, no. 4 (2007): 355–371.
16 Reprinted by permission of Sales & Marketing Executives International, Inc. (http://www.smei. org). "SMEI Certified Professional Salesperson" and "SCPS" are registered trademarks of Sales & Marketing Executives International, Inc.
17 *Ibid.*
18 Thomas Ingram, Scott Inks, and Lee Mabie, *Sales and Marketing Executive Certification Study Guide* (Memphis, TN: Marketing Executive International, 1994).
19 Nigel F. Piercy and Nikala Lane, "Ethical and Moral Dilemmas Associated with Strategic Relationships between Business-to-Business Buyers and Sellers," *Journal of Business Ethics* 72 (2007): 87–102; Thomas N. Ingram, Raymond W. LaForge, and Charles H. Schwepker, Jr. "Salesperson Ethical Decision Making: The Impact of Sales Leadership and Sales Management Control Strategies," *Journal of Personal Selling & Sales Management* 27, no. 4 (2007): 301–324.
20 Interview with John Huff, Shering-Plough, November 15, 2004.

Chapter 3

1 Howard Stevens and Theodore Kinni, *Achieve Sales Excellence* (Avon, MA: Platinum Press, 2007).
2 Adapted from Jagdish N. Sheth, Bahwari Mittal, and Bruce I. Newman, *Customer Behavior: Consumer Behavior and Beyond* (Fort Worth, TX: The Dryden Press, 1999); Jagdish N. Sheth, Bruce I. Newman, and Barbara L. Gross, *Consumption Values and Market Choice: Theory and Application* (Cincinnati, OH: South-Western Publishing Co., 1991).
3 Bixby Cooper, Cornelia Drodge, and Patricia Daughtery, "How Buyers and Operations Personnel Evaluate Service," *Industrial Marketing Management* (February 1991): 81–85.
4 Adapted from Michael A. Humphreys and Michael R. Williams, "Exploring the Relative Effects of Salesperson Interpersonal Process Attributes and Technical Product Attributes on Customer Satisfaction," *Journal of Personal Selling & Sales Management* 16 (Summer 1996): 47–58; Michael A. Humphreys, Michael R. Williams, and Ronald L. Meier, "Leveraging the Total Market Offering in the Agile Enterprise," *ASQ Quality Management Journal* 5 (1997): 60–74.
5 D. W. Merrill and R. H. Reid, *Personal Styles and Effective Performance* (Radnor, PA: Chilton Book Company, 1981).
6 Reprinted by permission of Growmark, Inc.
7 Henry Canaday, "In Transition," *Selling Power* 31 (May/June, 2011): 38–41.
8 Wesley J. Johnston and Thomas V. Bonoma, "The Buying Center: Structure and Interaction Patterns," *Journal of Marketing* (Summer 1981): 143–156.
9 Geoffrey James, "How to Make Technology Productive," *Selling Power*, June 2007, 65–68.
10 Chris Koch, "ITSMA's Eight Big B2B Marketing Trends for 2011," ITMSA Web site, http://www.itsma.com/ezine/eight-b2b-marketing-trends-for-2011/, accessed May 11, 2011.
11 Ivana Taylor, "Business to Business Marketing Trends for 2011," DIY Marketers Web site, http://www.diymarketers.com/2011/01/20/business-to-business-marketing-trends-for-2011/, accessed May 11, 2011.
12 *Ibid.*
13 Robert McGarvey, "All About Us," *Selling Power* 30 (November/December, 2010): 48–52.
14 Jakki Mohr and John R. Nevin, "Communication Strategies in Marketing Channels: A Theoretical Perspective," *Journal of Marketing* (October 1990): 36–51.
15 Alan S. Khade and Nathan Lovaas, "Improving Supply Chain Performance: A Case of Wal-Mart's Logistics," *International Journal of Business Strategy* 9 (2009): 157–164.
16 Howard Stevens and Theodore Kinni, *Achieve Sales Excellence* (Avon, MA: Platinum Press, 2007).
17 Sander de Leeuw and Jan Fransoo, "Drivers of Close Supply Chain Collaboration: One Size Fits All? *International Journal of Operations and Production Management* 29 (2009): 720–739.
18 Roy Chitwood, "Keeping Your Customers by Offering Added Value," http://www .maxsacks.com/articles/article1105.html, accessed May 10, 2011.

Chapter 4

1 S. D. Morgan, *Selling with Integrity: Reinventing Sales Through Collaboration, Respect, and Serving* (San Francisco, CA: Berrett Koehler Publishers, Inc., 1997).
2 R. L. Jolles, *Customer Centered Selling* (New York: The Free Press, 1998).
3 Neil Rackham, *Spin Selling* (New York: McGraw Hill, 1998).
4 Thomas Ingram, Tubs Scott, and Lee Mabie, *Certification Study Guide* (New York: Sales and Marketing Executives International, 1994): 44–46.
5 Jerry Acuff and Wally Wood, *The Relationship Edge in Business* (Hoboken, NJ: John Wiley & Sons, Inc., 2004): 149–150; Geoffrey James, "How to Build Customer Relationships—An Interview with Jerry Acuff," *Selling Power* (March 2006): 43–46.
6 T. N. Ingram, C. Schwepker, Jr., and D. Huston, "Why Salespeople Fail," *Industrial Marketing Management* 21 (1992): 225–230.
7 R. P. Ramsey and R. S. Sohi, "Listening to Your Customers: The Impact of Perceived Salesperson Listening Behavior on Relationship Outcomes," *Journal of the Academy of Marketing Science* 25 (Spring 1997): 127–137.
8 L. Barker, *Listening Behavior* (Englewood Cliffs, NJ: Prentice Hall, 1971): 30–32.
9 Lucette Comer and Tanya Drollinger, "Active Empathetic Listening and Selling Success: A Conceptual Framework," *Journal of Personal Selling & Sales Management* 9 (Winter 1999): 15–29; Stephen B. Castleberry and C. David Shepherd, "Effective Interpersonal Listening and Personal Selling," *Journal of Marketing Theory and Practice* 7, no. 1 (Winter 1999): 30–39.
10 From *Effective Listening: Key to Your Success* by L. K. Steil, L. L. Barker, and K. W. Watson: 21. Reprinted by permission of The McGraw-Hill Companies.
11 Ibid.; Ramsey and Sohi, "Listening to Your Customers."
12 Ibid., 72–73.
13 J. C. Mowen and M. Minor, *Consumer Behavior* (New York: Macmillan Publishing Co., 1997).
14 Julia Chang, "Selling in Action," *Sales & Marketing Management* 156 (May 2004): 22; G. P. Thomas, "The Influence of Processing Conversational Information on Inference, Argument Elaboration, and Memory," *Journal of Consumer Research* 19 (June 1992): 83–92.
15 R. A. Avila, T. N. Ingram, R. W. LaForge, and M. R. Williams, *The Professional Selling Skills Workbook* (Fort Worth, TX: The Dryden Press, 1996): 83.
16 Joann Peck and Jennifer Wiggins, "It Just Feels Good: Customers' Affective Response to Touch and Its Influence on Persuasion," *Journal of Marketing* 70, no. 4 (October 2006): 56–69; R. A. Peterson, M. P. Cannito, and S. P. Brown, "An Exploratory Investigation of Voice Characteristics and Selling Effectiveness," *Journal of Personal Selling & Sales Management* 15 (Winter 1995): 1–15.
17 Adapted from R. M. Rozelle, D. Druckman, and J. C. Baxter, "Nonverbal Communication," in *A Handbook of*

Communication Skills, ed. O. Hargie (London: Croom and Helm, 1986): 59–94; T. Alessandra and R. Barrera, *Collaborative Selling* (New York: John Wiley & Sons, Inc., 1993): 121–122.

Chapter 5

1 "Many Salespeople Generate Their Own Leads," *Selling Power* (July/August 2008): 84.
2 G. Gschwandtner, "How Much Time Do Your Salespeople Spend Selling?" *Selling Power* (March/April 2011): 8.
3 Lain Chroust Ehmann, "Sales Up! Why Reports Selling Is a Dying Profession Are Widely Exaggerated," *Selling Power* (January/February 2011): 40–44.
4 *Ibid*.
5 J. B. Oldroyd, K. McElheran, and D. Elkington, "The Short Life of Sales Leads," *Harvard Business Review* (March 2011): 28.
6 E. A. Sullivan, "A Worthwhile Investment," *Marketing News* (12/30/09): 10–11.
7 H. Canaday, "In Transition," *Selling Power* (May/June 2011): 39–41.
8 H. Baldwin, "Big Change @ Big Pharma," *Selling Power* (May/June 2011): 29–32.

Chapter 6

1 Robert F. Kantin, "Customer-Driven Proposals Can Give You the Winning Edge," http://www.salesproposals.com/pdf/a_winning_edge.pdf, accessed August 26, 2011; Brad Douglas, "Write a Successful Sales Proposal," http://office.microsoft.com/en-us/word-help/write-a-successful-sales-proposal-HA001205411.aspx?CTT=1, accessed August 26, 2011; and Geoffrey James, "Tom Sant Demystifies the Mystery of Effective Proposals," *Selling Power* (June 2004): 27–30.
2 Bob Kantin, *Sales Professionals Guide to Writing Winning Proposals* (Minneapolis, MN: Bascom Hill Publishing Company, 2007): 31–38.
3 From "Quality Selling through Quality Proposals, A Guide to Writing Winning Sales Proposals," by R. F. Kantin and M. W. Hardwick. Copyright © 1994. Reprinted with permission of South-Western, a division of Thomson Learning: http://www.thomsonrights.com.
4 For more discussion of customer value propositions, see James C. Anderson, James A. Narus, and Wouter van Rossum, "Customer Value Propositions in Business Markets," *Harvard Business Review* (March 2006): 91–99.
5 Thomas N. Ingram, Michael D. Hartline, and Charles H. Schwepker Jr., "Gatekeeper Perceptions: Implications for Improving Sales Ethics and Professionalism," *Proceedings of the Academy of Marketing Science* (1992): 328.

Chapter 7

1 Adapted from Brian Tracy, *Advanced Selling Strategies* (New York: Simon & Schuster, 1995): 302.
2 Wright Wiley, "Eye-to-Eye Selling," *Selling Power* (May/June 2011): 27
3 Jeffrey Jacobi, "Voice Power," *Selling Power* (October 2000): 66.
4 Geoffrey James, "Lifesaving Sales," *Selling Power* (June 2009): 40–43
5 Heather Baldwin, "Big Change @ Big Pharma," *Selling Power* (May/June 2011): 29–32
6 Adapted from Mary Ann Oberhaus, Sharon Ratliffe, and Vernon Stauble, *Professional Selling: A Relationship Approach* (Fort Worth, TX: The Dryden Press, 1995): 410–412.

Chapter 8

1 Marc Diener, "Don't Know When to Cut Your Losses and Leave the Negotiating Table? Look for These Telltale Signs," *Entrepreneur Magazine*, August 2003, http://www.entrepreneur.com/magazine/entrepreneur/2003/august/63334.html, accessed July 26, 2011.
2 Brad Huisken, "Saving the Sale: Objections, Rejections and Getting to Yes," *JCK* (January 2003): 62–63.
3 Tom Reilly, "Why Do You Cut Prices?" *Industrial Distribution* (June 2003): 72.
4 Robert Menard, " 'Cost' Is About More Than the Price," *Selling* (July 2003): 9.
5 Kim Sydow Campbell and Lenita Davis, "The Sociolinguistic Basis of Managing Rapport When Overcoming Buying Objections," *Journal of Business Communication* (January 2006): 43–66.
6 Salespeople can forestall known concerns, but they should not bring up issues that are not even a problem with a particular prospect. Thus, the need for good precall information gathering becomes obvious. See "Think Like a Consumer to Make Buying from a Cinch," *Selling* (November 2004): 8.
7 Mark Borkowski, "How to Succeed in Closing Deals, without Closing," *Canadian Electronics* 19 (May 2004): 6.
8 Neil Rackham, *Spin Selling* (New York: McGraw-Hill, 1988): 19–51.
9 Joan Leotta, "Effortless Closing," *Selling Power* (October 2001): 28–31.
10 Susan Del Vecchio, James Zemanek, Roger McIntyre, and Reid Claxton, "Updating the Adaptive Selling Behaviors: Tactics to Keep and Tactics to Discard," *Journal of Marketing Management* 20 (2004): 859–875.

Chapter 9

1 Howard Stevens and Theodore Kinni, *Achieve Sales Excellence* (Avon, MA: Platinum Press, 2007).
2 Michael Ahearne, Ronald Jelinek, and Eli Jones, "Examining the Effects of Salesperson Service Behavior in a Competitive Context," *Journal of the Academy of Marketing Science* 35 (December 2007): 603–616.
3 Robert W. Palmatier, Srinath Gopalakrishna, and Mark B. Houston, "Returns on Business-to-Business Relationship Marketing Investments: Strategies for Leveraging Profits," *Marketing Science* 25 (September/October 2006): 477–493.
4 "2009 Customer Experience Management Benchmark Study," http://www.socialbusinessone.com/files2/2009_cem_study_exec_summary.pdf, accessed September 19, 2011.
5 John Tashek, "How to Avoid a CRM Failure," *eWeek* 18, no. 40 (October 15, 2001): 31.
6 Michael Ahearne, Ronald Jelinek, and Eli Jones, "Examining the Effect of Salesperson Service Behavior in a Competitive Context," *Journal of the Academy of Marketing Science* 35 (Winter 2007): 603–616.
7 Strativity Group, "Recent Customer Experience Management Benchmark Study," http://www.strativity.com/products/Experience-Management-Benchmark-Study.aspx, accessed January 12, 2011.
8 Interview with John Haack, Saint-Gobain Containers, April 19, 2000.
9 Interview with Darrell Beaty, Ontario Systems Corporation, February 29, 2000.
10 Christine Galea, "What Customers Really Want," *Sales & Marketing Management* 158 (May 2006):
11 Kelley Robertson, "Inadequate Salesmen," *Sales & Service Excellence* 9 (January 2009): 14.
12 "Advance CRM Solutions," *Personal Selling Power* (January/February 2007): 96–99.
13 Gabriel Gonzalez, Douglas Hoffman, Thomas Ingram, and Raymond LaForge, "Sales Organization Recovery Management and Relationship Selling: A Conceptual Model and Empirical Test," *Journal of Personal Selling & Sales Management* 30 (Summer 2010): 223–237.
14 Michael W. Michelson, "Fielding Customer Complaints," *American Salesman* 50 (December 2005): 22–25.
15 The Forum Corporation, "Why Do Customers Stop Buying?" *Sales & Marketing Management* (January 1998).
16 Chris Taylor, "The Art of the Winback," *Sales & Marketing Management* 157 (April 2005): 30–34.
17 Sandra Rothenberger, Dhruv Grewal, and Gopalkrishnan R. Iyer, "Understanding the Role of Complaint Handling on Customer Loyalty in Service Relationships," *Journal of Relationship Marketing* 7, no. 4 (2008): 359–376.
18 Chia-Chi Chang, "When Service Fails: The Role of the Salesperson and the Customer," *Psychology & Marketing* 23 (March 2006): 203–224.
19 "Consistent Success in an Inconsistent World: Solid Customer Relationships Are the Key," *Selling Power* (May 1996): 28; Robert D. Ramsey, "How to Handle Customer Complaints," *American Salesman* 55 (June 2010): 25–30.
20 "At Your Customer's Service: The True Test of a Salesperson's Value Comes after the Sale," *Selling Power* (May 1996): 58.
21 Howard Stevens and Theodore Kinni, *Achieve Sales Excellence* (Avon, MA: Platinum Press, 2007).
22 Stevens and Kinni, *Achieve Sales Excellence*.

Chapter 10

1 S. R. Covey, *The 7 Habits of Highly Effective People* (New York: Simon & Schuster, 2004).
2 T. Ingram, R. W. LaForge, R. Avila, C. H. Schwepker, Jr., and M. Williams, *Sales Management: Analysis and Decision Making*, 7th ed. (Armonk, NY: M.E. Sharpe, 2009).

3 B. Kimball, *AMA Handbook for Successful Selling* (Chicago: American Marketing Association, 1994).

4 W. Ferguson, "A New Method for Routing Salespersons," *Industrial Marketing Management* (April 1980): 171–178; "Planning a Road Trip?" *An Executive Guide to Sales and Marketing Technology,* a supplement to *Sales & Marketing Management* (June 1996): 39; E. Strout, "Charting a Course," *Sales & Marketing Management* (August, 1999): 46–53.

5 For a good discussion of selling technology, see D. Peppers and M. Rogers, "Marketing's New Direction: How Campaigns Are Becoming Faster and More Precise through Automation," *Sales & Marketing Management* (March 1999): 48–54; Peppers and Rogers Group and Microsoft Business Solutions, *Striking the CRM Balance: Greater Productivity, Lower Costs, Tight Integration,* http://www.knightent.com/Striking%20 the%20CRM%20Balance.pdf, 2003, accessed July 25, 2011; Sue Hildreth, "Six Smart CRM Strategies for Meeting Sales Quotas in a Down Economy," http:// searchcrm .techtarget.com/news/1353734/Six-smart-CRM-strategies-for-meeting-sales-quotas-in-a-down-economy, April 14, 2009, accessed July 26, 2011.

6 For a guide to sales and marketing automation systems, technology, and software, see http://www.salesandmarketing .com/article/implementing-integrated-sales-management-process.

7 E. Babakus, D. W. Cravens, K. Grant, T. N. Ingram, and R W. LaForge, "Removing Salesforce Performance Hurdles," *Journal of Business and Industrial Marketing* 9, no. 3 (1994): 19–29.

8 J. Attaway, M. Williams, and M. Griffin, *The Rims-QIC Quality Scorecard* (Nashville, TN: The Quality Insurance Congress, 1998, 1999).

9 James Champy, "Selling to Tomorrow's Customer," *Sales & Marketing Management* (March 1999): 28.

10 Excerpt from *The 7 Habits of Highly Effective People,* © 2004 Stephen R. Covey. The Time Management Matrix phrase and model are trademarks of Franklin Covey Co., http://www.franklincovey.com. Used with permission. All rights reserved.

11 Covey, *The 7 Habits of Highly Effective People.*

Chapter 11

1 The sales management portion of this chapter borrows heavily from Thomas N. Ingram, Raymond W. LaForge, Ramon A. Avila, Charles H. Schwepker, Jr., and Michael R. Williams, *Sales Management: Analysis and Decision Making* (Armonk, New York: M.E. Sharpe, 2009).

2 This figure is adapted from Ingram et al., *Sales Management: Analysis and Decision Making,* 5.

3 This section is synthesized from Forum Corporation, *How Sales Forces Sustain Competitive Advantage,* Sales Force Research Report, http://www.forum.com/_assets/ download/4f928d21-072a-485f-b757-90e7fb884d13.pdf, accessed October 5, 2011; Chally Group, "Building a World-Class Sales Team," http://www.industrialsupplymagazine .com/pages/Print-edition—NovDec10_ BuildingWorldClassSalesTeam.php, accessed October 5, 2011; "Driving Sales Results in Any Economy: Executive Summary of the 2010 Miller Heiman Sales Best Practices Study," http://store.millerheiman.com/kc/ abstract.aspx?itemid=0000000000000714, accessed October 5, 2011; and Nigel Piercy, "Evolution of Strategic Sales Organizations in Business-to-Business Marketing," *Journal of Business & Industrial Marketing* 5 (2010): 349–359.

4 Dawn R. Deeter-Schmelz, Karen Norman Kennedy, and Daniel J. Goebel, "Understanding Sales Manager Effectiveness: Linking Attributes to Sales Force Values," *Industrial Marketing Management* (2002): 617–626; Dawn Deeter-Schmelz, Daniel J. Goebel, and Karen Norman Kennedy, "What Are the Characteristics of an Effective Sales Manager? An Exploratory Study Comparing Salesperson and Sales Manager Perspectives," *Journal of Personal Selling and Sales Management* (Winter 2008): 7–20.

5 Maryann Hammers and Gerhard Gschwandtner, "Tap into the 7 Qualities of the Best Sales Managers," *Selling Power* (May 2004): 60–65; Deeter-Schmelz et al., "What Are the Characteristics of an Effective Sales Manager? An Exploratory Study Comparing Salesperson and Sales Manager Perspectives," 7–20.

6 Adapted from John F. Tanner, Jr., Michael Ahearne, Thomas W. Leigh, Charlotte H. Mason, and William C. Moncrief, "CRM in Sales-Intensive Organizations: A Review and Future Directions," *Journal of Personal Selling & Sales Management* (Spring 2005): 169–170.

7 See Robert W. Ruekert, Orville C. Walker, Jr., and Kenneth J. Roering, "The Organization of Marketing Activities: A Contingency Theory of Structure and Performance," *Journal of Marketing* (Winter 1985): 13, for a more complete presentation of structural characteristics and relationships. The discussion in this section borrows heavily from this article.

8 Christian Homburg, John P. Workman, Jr., and Ove Jensen, "Fundamental Changes in Marketing Organization: The Movement toward a Customer-Focused Organizational Structure," *Journal of the Academy of Marketing Science* (Fall 2000): 459–478.

9 Thomas N. Ingram, Raymond W. LaForge, Ramon Avila, Charles H. Schwepker, Jr., and Michael R. Williams, *Sales Management: Analysis and Decision Making,* 7th ed. (Armonk, NY: M.E. Sharpe, Inc., 2009).

10 James A Breaugh, Leslie A. Greising, James W. Taggart, and Helen Chen, "The Relationship of Recruiting Sources and Pre-Hire Outcomes: Examination of Yield Rations and Application Quality," *Journal of Applied Social Psychology* 33 (November 2003): 2257–2287.

11 Gilbert A. Churchill, Jr., Neil M. Ford, Steven W. Hartley, and Orville C. Walker, Jr., "The Determinants of Salesperson Performance: A Meta-Analysis," *Journal of Marketing Research* 22 (May 1985): 117.

12 Jennifer J. Salopek, "The Power of the Pyramid," *T & D* 63 (May 2009): 70–75.

13 Geoffrey James, "Budget Your Investment Wisely," *Selling Power* (March 2006): 86–89.

14 Thomas et al., *Sales Management: Analysis and Decision Making,* 7th ed.

15 Julia Chang, "What Worked," *Sales & Marketing Management* 155 (July 2003): 29.

16 This exhibit is adapted from Thomas N. Ingram, Raymond W. LaForge, William B. Locander, Scott B. MacKenzie, and Philip M. Podsakoff, "New Directions for Sales Leadership Research, *Journal of Personal Selling & Sales Management* (Spring 2005): 137–154.

17 Orville C. Walker, Jr., Gilbert A. Churchill, Jr., and Neil M. Ford, "Where Do We Go from Here? Selected Conceptual and Empirical Issues Concerning Motivation and Performance of the Industrial Salesforce," in *Critical Issues in Sales Management: State-of-the-Art and Future Research Needs,* eds. Gerald Albaum and Gilbert A. Churchill, Jr. (Eugene, OR: Division of Research, College of Business Administration, University of Oregon, 1979): 25.

18 Bernard M. Bass, *Leadership and Performance Beyond Expectations* (New York: Free Press, 1985).

19 Philip M. Podsakoff, Scott B. MacKenzie, Robert H. Moorman, and Richard Fetter, "Transformational Leader Behaviors and Their Effects on Follower's Trust in Leader, Satisfaction, and Organizational Citizenship Behaviors," *Leadership Quarterly* (1990): 107–142.

20 Karen E. Flaherty and James M. Pappas, "The Role of Trust in Sales Organizations," *Journal of Personal Selling & Sales Management* (Fall 2000): 271–278.

21 John French, Jr., and Bertram Raven, "The Bases of Social Power," in *Studies in Social Power,* ed. D. Cartwright (Ann Arbor, MI: The University of Michigan Press, 1959).

22 Artur Baldauf and David W. Cravens, "The Effect of Moderators on the Salesperson Behavior Performance and Salesperson Outcome Performance and Sales Organization Effectiveness Relationships," *European Journal of Marketing* 36, no. 11/12 (2002): 1367.

23 David W. Cravens, Thomas N. Ingram, Raymond W. LaForge, and Clifford E. Young, "Hallmarks of Effective Sales Organizations," *Marketing Management* 1 (March 1992): 56; Thomas et al., *Sales Management: Analysis and Decision Making,* 7th ed.

24 Thomas et al., *Sales Management: Analysis and Decision Making,* 7th ed.

25 Erin Anderson and Richard L. Oliver, "Perspectives on Behavior-based versus Outcome-based Salesforce Control Systems," *Journal of Marketing* 51 (October 1987): 76.

26 Artur Balauf, David W. Cravens, and Ken Grant, "Consequences of Sales Management Control in Field Sales Organizations: A Cross-National Perspective," *International Business Review* 11 (October 2002): 577–609; David W. Cravens, Greg W. Marshall, Felicia G. Lassk, and George S. Low, "The Control Factor," *Marketing Management* 13 (January/February 2004): 39–44.

27 Henry Canaday, "The Same Team," *Selling Power* (January/February 2011): 51–53.

28 Julia Chang, "Sales 2.0," *Sales & Marketing Management* (April 2007): 31–34.

29 "How Will Sales 2.0 Increase Your Sales?" *Selling Power* (May 2009): 19–25; Anneke Seley and Brent Holloway, *Sales 2.0: Improve Business Results Using Innovative Sales Practices and Technology* (Hoboken, NJ: John Wiley & Sons, 2009): 5–9.

30 Kim Wright Wiley, "How Sweet It Is," *Selling Power* (April 2009): 44–47.

31 "Sales 2.0 Innovation Leads to Sales Acceleration," *Selling Power* (March 2009): 73.

32 Marshall Lager, "Sales and Social Media: No One's Social (Yet)," *Customer Relationship Management* (June 2009): 29–33.

33. Henry Canaday, "The Pace of Change," *Selling Power* (July/August 2011): 46–48.

34 Steve Hamm, "Cloud Computing's Big Bang for Business," *BusinessWeek* (June 15, 2009): 42–48.

35. "How the Cloud Looks from the Top: Achieving Competitive Advantage in the Age of Cloud Computing," *A Report by Harvard Business Review Analytic Services* (2011): 1–8.

INDEX

E

F

G

H

I

J

K

L

M

N

O

P

Q

R

S

T

U

V

W

X

Y

CHAPTER 1 IN REVIEW

Overview of Personal Selling

Chapter Summary

1-1 Define personal selling and describe its unique characteristics as a marketing communications tool. Personal selling, an important part of marketing, relies heavily on interpersonal interactions between buyers and sellers to initiate, develop, and enhance customer relationships. The interpersonal communications dimension sets personal selling apart from other marketing communications, such as advertising and sales promotion. Personal selling is also distinguished from direct marketing and electronic marketing in that salespeople are talking with buyers before, during, and after the sale. This allows a high degree of immediate customer feedback, which becomes a strong advantage of personal selling over most other forms of marketing communications.

1-2 Distinguish between transaction-focused traditional selling and trust-based relationship selling, with the latter focusing on customer value and sales dialogue. As summarized in Exhibit 1.2, trust-based selling focuses more on the customer than does transaction-focused selling. The salesperson will act as a consultant to the customer in trust-based selling, whereas in transaction-based selling the salesperson concentrates more on making sales calls and on closing sales. There is far more emphasis on postsales follow-up with relationship selling than with transaction selling, and salespeople must have a broader range of skills to practise relationship selling. Rather than pitching products to customers, trust-based selling focuses on establishing sales dialogue with customers, and salespeople not only communicate customer value but also help create and deliver customer value.

1-3 Describe the evolution of personal selling from ancient times to the modern era. The history of personal selling can be traced as far back as ancient Greece. The Industrial Revolution enhanced the importance of salespeople, and personal selling as we know it today had its roots in the early twentieth century. The current era of sales professionalism represents a further evolution.

1-4 Explain the contributions of personal selling to society, business firms, and customers. Salespeople contribute to society by acting as stimuli in the economic process and by assisting in the diffusion of innovation. They contribute to their employers by producing revenue, performing research and feedback activities, and composing a pool of future managers. They contribute to customers by providing timely knowledge to assist in solving problems.

1-5 Discuss five alternative approaches to personal selling. Alternative approaches to personal selling include stimulus-response, mental states, need satisfaction, problem solving, and the consultative approach. Stimulus-response selling often uses the same sales presentation for all customers. The mental states approach prescribes that the salesperson leads the buyer through stages in the buying process. Need satisfaction selling focuses on relating benefits of the seller's products or services to the buyer's particular situation. Problem-solving selling extends need satisfaction by concentrating on various alternatives available to the buyer. Consultative selling focuses on helping customers achieve strategic goals, not just meeting needs or solving problems.

Glossary Terms

personal selling An important part of marketing that relies heavily on interpersonal interactions between buyers and sellers to initiate, develop, and enhance customer relationships.

trust-based relationship selling A form of personal selling that requires that salespeople earn customer trust and that their selling strategy meets customer needs and contributes to the creation, communication, and delivery of customer value.

customer value Customers' perception of what they get for what they have to give up; for example, benefits from buying a product in exchange for money paid.

sales dialogue Business conversations between buyers and sellers that occur as salespeople attempt to initiate, develop, and enhance customer relationships. Sales dialogue should be customer focused and have a clear purpose.

canned sales presentation Sales presentations that include scripted sales calls, memorized presentations, and automated presentations.

sales professionalism A customer-oriented approach that uses truthful, nonmanipulative tactics to satisfy the long-term needs of both the customer and the selling firm.

economic stimuli Something that stimulates or incites activity in the economy.

diffusion of innovation The process whereby new products, services, and ideas are distributed to the members of society.

revenue producers A role fulfilled by salespeople that brings in revenue or income to a firm or company.

adaptive selling The ability of salespeople to alter their sales messages and behaviours during a sales presentation or as they encounter different sales situations and different customers.

stimulus-response selling An approach to selling in which the key idea is that various stimuli can elicit predictable responses from customers. Salespeople furnish the stimuli from a repertoire of words and actions designed to produce the desired response.

continued affirmation An example of stimulus-response selling in which a series of questions or statements furnished by the salesperson is designed to condition the prospective buyer to answering "yes" time after time, until, it is hoped, he or she will be inclined to say "yes" to the entire sales proposition.

mental states selling An approach to personal selling that assumes that the buying process for most buyers is essentially identical and that buyers can be led through certain mental states, or steps, in the buying process; also called the formula approach.

AIDA An acronym for the various mental states salespeople must lead their customers through when using mental states selling: attention, interest, desire, and action.

need satisfaction selling An approach to selling based on the notion that the customer is buying to satisfy a particular need or set of needs.

problem-solving selling An extension of need satisfaction selling that goes beyond identifying needs to developing alternative solutions for satisfying these needs.

consultative selling The process of helping customers reach their strategic goals by using the products, services, and expertise of the sales organization.

strategic orchestrator A role the salesperson plays in consultative selling in which he or she arranges the use of the sales organization's resources in an effort to satisfy the customer.

business consultant A role the salesperson plays in consultative selling in which he or she uses internal and external (outside the sales organization) sources to become an expert on the customer's business. This role also involves educating customers on the sales firm's products and how these products compare with competitive offerings.

long-term ally A role the salesperson plays in consultative selling in which he or she supports the customer, even when an immediate sale is not expected.

sales process A series of interrelated steps beginning with locating qualified prospective customers. From there, the salesperson plans the sales presentation, makes an appointment to see the customer, completes the sale, and performs postsale activities.

sales support personnel A firm's personnel whose primary responsibility is dissemination of information and performance of other activities designed to stimulate sales.

missionary salespeople Salespeople who usually work for a manufacturer but may also be found working for brokers and manufacturing representatives. Sales missionaries are expected to "spread the word" to convert noncustomers to customers.

detailer A salesperson in the pharmaceutical industry working at the physician level to furnish valuable information regarding the capabilities and limitations of medications in an attempt to get the physician to prescribe their product.

technical support salespeople Technical specialists who may assist in design and specification processes, installation of equipment, training of the customer's employees, and follow-up service of a technical nature.

pioneers Salespeople who are constantly involved with either new products, new customers, or both. Their task requires creative selling and the ability to counter the resistance to change that will likely be present in prospective customers.

1-6 Understand the sales process as a series of interrelated steps.

As presented in the figure below, the sales process involves initiating, developing, and enhancing customer relationships. Salespeople must possess certain attributes to earn the trust of their customers and be able to adapt their selling strategies to different situations. Throughout the sales process, salespeople should focus on customer value, first by understanding what customer value is to the customer and then by working to create, communicate, and continually increase that value. Salespeople initiate customer relationships through strategic prospecting, assessing the prospect's situation, planning value-based sales dialogue, and activating the buying process. Relationships are then further developed through engaging prospects in a true dialogue to earn commitment from those prospects. Salespeople enhance customer relationships by following up after the sale, taking a leadership role, and sometimes working as part of a team to increase constantly the value received by the customer. The details of the sales process are covered in Chapters 5–10 in this book.

FIGURE 1.5

Problem-Solving Approach to Selling

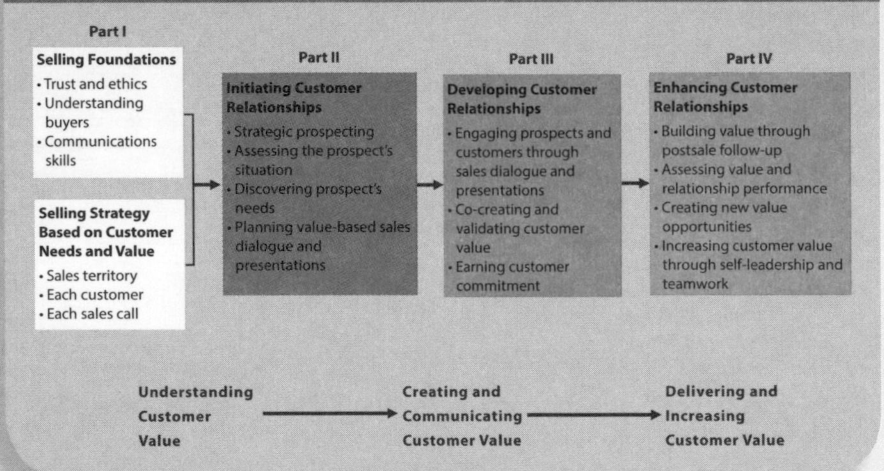

Part I

Selling Foundations
- Trust and ethics
- Understanding buyers
- Communications skills

Selling Strategy Based on Customer Needs and Value
- Sales territory
- Each customer
- Each sales call

Part II

Initiating Customer Relationships
- Strategic prospecting
- Assessing the prospect's situation
- Discovering prospect's needs
- Planning value-based sales dialogue and presentations

Part III

Developing Customer Relationships
- Engaging prospects and customers through sales dialogue and presentations
- Co-creating and validating customer value
- Earning customer commitment

Part IV

Enhancing Customer Relationships
- Building value through postsale follow-up
- Assessing value and relationship performance
- Creating new value opportunities
- Increasing customer value through self-leadership and teamwork

Understanding Customer Value → Creating and Communicating Customer Value → Delivering and Increasing Customer Value

order-getters (hunters) Salespeople who actively seek orders, usually in a highly competitive environment.

order-takers (farmers) Salespeople who specialize in maintaining existing business.

inside sales Nonretail salespeople who remain in their employer's place of business while dealing with customers.

combination sales job A sales job in which the salesperson performs multiple types of sales jobs within the framework of a single position.

empathy The ability to see things as others would see them; salespeople with empathy are better able to adapt to various sales situations and adjust to customer feedback.

ego drive An indication of the degree of determination a person has to achieve goals and overcome obstacles in striving for success.

ego strength The degree to which a person is able to achieve an approximation of inner drives.

self-efficacy The strong belief that success will occur on the job.

interpersonal communication skills Skills that include listening and questioning.

enthusiasm A strong feeling of excitement. Salespeople should have an enthusiastic attitude in a general sense and a specific enthusiasm for selling.

service motivation A strong desire to provide service to the customer. Service motivation comes from desiring the approval of others.

CHAPTER 2 IN REVIEW

Building Trust and Sales Ethics: Developing Trust and Mutual Respect with Clients

Chapter Summary

2-1 Explain what trust is, explain why it is important, and understand how to earn trust. Trust occurs when a buyer believes that he or she can rely on what the salesperson says or promises to do in a situation where the buyer is dependent on the salesperson's honesty and reliability. One of the keys to a long-term relationship with any client is to create a basis of trust between the sales representative and the client organization.

The *trust* described here goes beyond the typical transaction-oriented trust schema. Many issues—Will the product arrive as promised? Will the right product actually be in stock and be shipped on time? Will the invoice contain the agreed-on price? Can the salesperson be found if something goes wrong?—are only preliminary concerns. In relationship selling, trust is based on a larger set of factors because of the expanded intimacy and longer-term nature of the relationship. The intimacy of this relationship will result in both parties sharing information that could be damaging if leaked or used against the other partner.

In today's increasingly competitive marketplace, buyers typically find themselves inundated with choices regarding both products and suppliers. Buyers are demanding unique solutions to their problems, which are customized on the basis of their specific needs. This shift toward relationship selling has altered both the roles played by salespeople and the activities and skills they exercise in carrying out these roles—the selling process itself. Today's more contemporary selling process is embedded within the relationship marketing paradigm. As such, it emphasizes the initiation and nurturing of long-term buyer–seller relationships based on mutual trust and value-added benefits. The level of problem-solving activity common to relationship selling requires deliberate and purposeful collaboration between both parties. These joint efforts are directed at creating unique solutions based on an enhanced knowledge and understanding of the customer's needs and the supplier's capabilities so that both parties derive mutual benefits.

Buyers are constantly asking themselves whether the salesperson truly cares about them. Salespeople can answer this question for the buyer through trust-building activities. Trust can be earned by demonstrating expertise, dependability, candour, customer orientation, competence, and compatibility.

FIGURE 2.1
Trust Builders

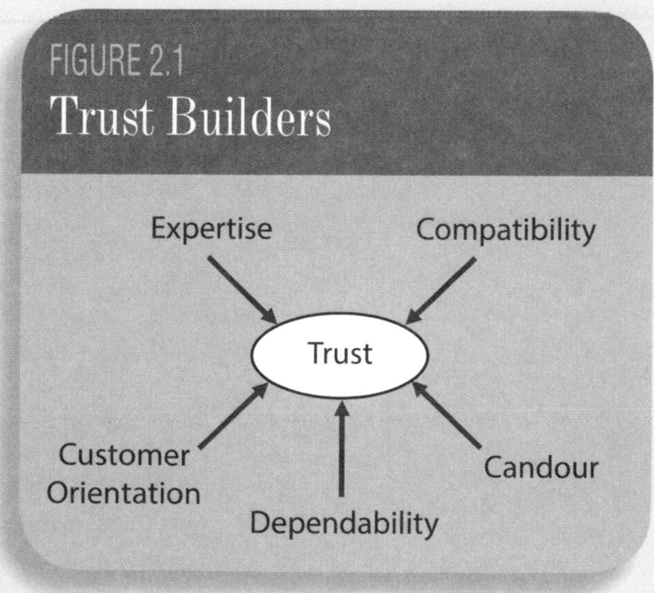

Glossary Terms

trust The extent of the buyer's confidence that he or she can rely on the salesperson's integrity.

openness Completely free from concealment; exposed to general view or knowledge.

honesty Fairness and straightforward conduct.

confidentiality The state of being entrusted with information from a buyer that cannot be shared.

security The quality of being free from danger.

reliability Consistency of a salesperson over time to do what is right.

fairness Impartiality and honesty.

expertise The ability, knowledge, and resources to meet customer expectations.

contributions Something given to improve a situation or state for a buyer.

dependability Predictability of a person's actions.

predictability A salesperson's behaviour that can be foretold on the basis of observation or experience by a buyer.

candour Honesty of the spoken word.

customer orientation The act of salespeople placing as much emphasis on the customer's interests as their own.

compatibility and likeability A salesperson's commonalities with other individuals.

competitor knowledge Knowledge of a competitor's strengths and weaknesses in the market.

product knowledge Detailed information on the manufacture of a product and knowing whether the company has up-to-date production methods.

promotion knowledge Knowledge tools salespeople must possess to explain their firms' promotional programs.

price knowledge Knowledge tools salespeople must have about pricing policies in order to quote prices and offer discounts on products.

market knowledge Information salespeople must have if larger companies break their customers into distinct markets; salespeople must be familiar with these markets to tailor their sales presentations.

customer knowledge Information about customers that is gathered over time and from very different sources that helps the salesperson determine customer needs to better serve them.

technology knowledge Information salespeople must have about the latest technology.

ethics The right and wrong conduct of individuals and institutions of which they are a part.

price fixing Agreements between sellers to prevent or unduly lessen competition or to unreasonably enhance the price of a product by selling at a fixed price.

bid rigging An agreement in which competitors agree in advance who will win a bid based on the tenders submitted.

price discrimination Knowingly and systematically selling the same goods or services at different prices to different buyers.

predatory pricing A firm or an individual deliberately sets prices to incur losses for a long time to eliminate a competitor or to inhibit competition in the expectation that the firm or individual will later be able to recoup its losses by charging prices above competitive levels.

bait and switch selling Firms or individuals advertise products at bargain prices that they do not have available in reasonable quantities and try to sell more expensive products instead.

pyramid selling Fees or commissions paid not on the basis of product sales but on the recruitment of others to make sales.

express warranty A way a salesperson can create product liabilities by giving a product warranty or guarantee that obligates the selling organization even if the salesperson does not intend to give the warranty.

misrepresentation False claim(s) made by a salesperson.

negligence False claim(s) made by a salesperson about the product or service he or she is trying to sell.

basis of the bargain When a buyer relies on the seller's statements in making a purchase decision.

2-2 Know how knowledge bases help build trust and relationships.

Salespeople do not have much time to make a first impression. If a salesperson can demonstrate competitive knowledge and expertise in the buyer's industry, company, marketplace, and so on, then the buyer will more likely be willing to listen. The salesperson must bring valued experience to the buyer.

2-3 Understand the importance of sales ethics and its legal implications.

Salespeople are constantly involved with ethical issues. A sales manager might encourage his or her salesforce to pad their expense account in lieu of a raise. A salesperson might sell a product or service to a customer that the buyer does not need. A salesperson might exaggerate the benefits of a product to get a sale. The list goes on and on. How a salesperson handles these situations will go a long way in determining the salesperson's credibility. One wrong decision can end a salesperson's career.

Three of the more popular areas of unethical behaviour are deceptive practices, illegal activities, and noncustomer-oriented behaviour.

- Deceptive practices: Salespeople giving answers they do not know to be right, exaggerating product benefits, and withholding information may appear only to shade the truth, but when it causes harm to the buyer, the salesperson has jeopardized future dealings with the buyer.
- Illegal activities: Misuse of company assets has been a longstanding problem for many sales organizations. Using the company car for personal use, charging expenses that did not occur, and selling samples for income are examples of misusing company assets. Some of these violations discovered by company probing also constitute violations of Canada Revenue Agency (CRA) law and are offences that could lead to jail time or heavy fines.
- Noncustomer-oriented behaviour: Most buyers will not buy from salespeople who are pushy and practise the hard sell. Too much is at stake to fall for the fast-talking, high-pressure salesperson.

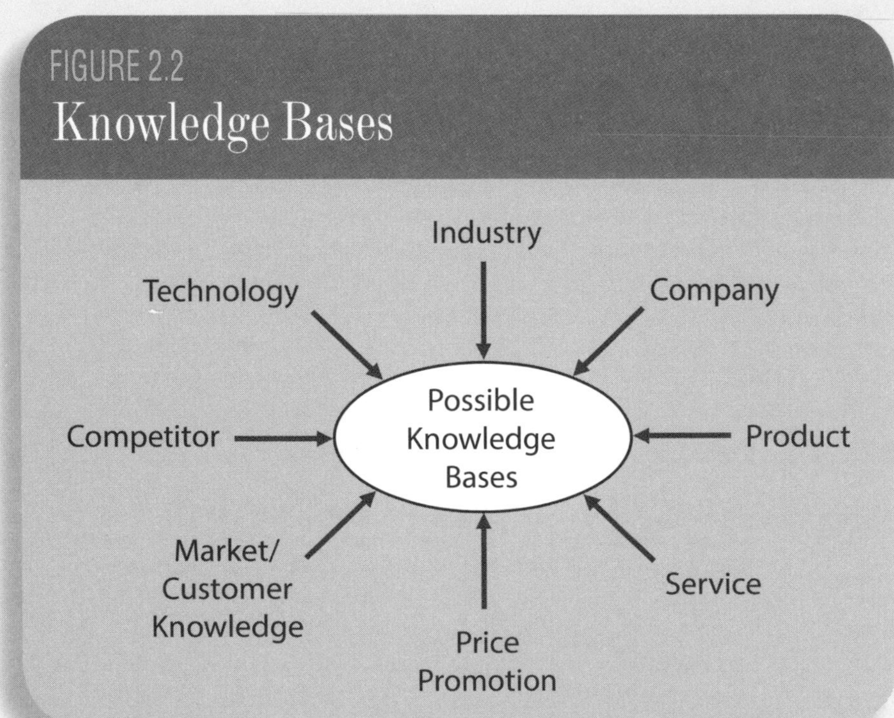

CHAPTER 3 IN REVIEW

Understanding Buyers

Chapter Summary

3-1 Categorize the primary types of buyers, and discuss the distinguishing characteristics of business markets. Buyers are classified according to the unique buying situations that influence their needs, motivations, and buying behaviour. The most common categorization splits buyers into either consumer markets or business markets. Consumers purchase goods and services for their own use or consumption, whereas members of the business market acquire goods and services to use as inputs into manufacturing, for use in doing business, or for resale. Business markets are further divided into firms, institutions, and governments.

Among the more common distinguishing characteristics of business markets are consolidation, which has resulted in buyers being fewer in number but larger in size; demand that is derived from the sale of consumer goods; more volatile demand levels; professional buyers; multiple buying influences from a team of buyers; and increased interdependence and relationships between buyers and sellers.

3-2 List the steps in the business-to-business buying process. This process involves (1) recognition of the problem or need, (2) determination of the characteristics of the item and the quantity needed, (3) description of the characteristics of the item and quantity needed, (4) search for and qualification of potential sources, (5) acquisition and analysis of proposals, (6) evaluation of proposals and selection of suppliers, (7) selection of an order routine, and (8) giving of performance feedback and evaluation.

3-3 Discuss the different types of buyer needs. Salespeople are better able to generate and demonstrate value-added solutions by understanding different types of buyer needs. The five general types of buyer needs are described as follows:

Situational needs: Needs that are related to, or possibly the result of, the buyer's specific environment, time, and place.

Functional needs: The need for a specific core task or function to be performed—the need for a sales offering to do what it is supposed to do.

Social needs: The need for acceptance from and association with others; a desire to belong to some reference group.

Psychological needs: The desire for feelings of assurance and risk reduction, as well as positive emotions and feelings, such as success, joy, excitement, and stimulation.

Knowledge needs: The desire for personal development and need for information and knowledge to increase thought and understanding as to how and why things happen.

3-4 Describe how buyers evaluate suppliers and alternative sales offerings by using the multiattribute model of evaluation. Using the multiattribute model, buyers establish the attributes they perceive as important and evaluate the degree to which each of the specified attributes is present (or how well each performs) in a proposed solution. Each evaluation is then multiplied by the attribute's relative level of importance to calculate a weighted average for each attribute. These weighted averages are then totalled to derive an overall score for each supplier or product being compared. The product or supplier having the highest score is favoured for the purchase.

3-5 Explain the two-factor model that buyers use to evaluate the performance of sales offerings and develop satisfaction. The two-factor model is a special type of multiattribute model in which further analysis of the multiple characteristics results

Glossary Terms

consumer markets A market in which consumers purchase goods and services for their use or consumption.

business markets A market composed of firms, institutions, and governments that acquire goods and services to use as inputs into their own manufacturing process, for use in their day-to-day operations, or for resale to their own customers.

derived demand Demand in business markets that is closely associated with the demand for consumer goods.

acceleration principle When demand increases (or decreases) in the consumer market, the business market reacts by accelerating the buildup (or reduction) of inventories and increasing (or decreasing) plant capacity.

desired states A state of being based on what the buyer desires.

actual states A buyer's actual state of being.

needs gap A perceived difference between a buyer's desired and actual state of being.

situational needs The needs that are contingent on, and often a result of, conditions related to the specific environment, time, and place.

functional needs The need for a specific core task or function to be performed.

social needs The need for acceptance from and association with others.

psychological needs The desire for feelings of assurance and risk reduction, as well as positive emotions and feelings, such as success, joy, excitement, and stimulation.

knowledge needs The desire for personal development, information, and knowledge to increase thought and understanding as to how and why things happen.

requests for proposals (RFPs) A form created by firms and distributed to qualified potential suppliers that helps suppliers develop and submit proposals to provide products as specified by the firm.

multiattribute model A procedure for evaluating suppliers and products that incorporates weighted averages across desired characteristics.

competitive depositioning Providing information to create a more accurate picture of a competitor's attributes or qualities.

two-factor model of evaluation A postpurchase evaluation process buyers use that evaluates a product purchase by using functional and psychological attributes.

functional attributes The features and characteristics that are related to what the product actually does or is expected to do.

must-have attributes Features of the core product that the customer takes for granted.

psychological attributes A category of product characteristics that refers to how things are carried out and done between the buyer and seller.

delighter attributes The augmented features included in the total market offering that go beyond the buyer's expectations and have a significant positive impact on customer satisfaction.

straight rebuy decision A purchase decision resulting from an ongoing purchasing relationship with a supplier.

electronic data interchange (EDI) Transfer of data electronically between two computer systems.

new task decision A purchase decision that occurs when a buyer is purchasing a product or service for the first time.

modified rebuy decision A purchase decision that occurs when a buyer has experience in purchasing a product in the past but is interested in acquiring additional information regarding alternative products and suppliers.

assertiveness The degree to which a person holds opinions about issues and attempts to dominate or control situations by directing the thoughts and actions of others.

responsiveness The level of feelings and sociability an individual openly displays.

amiables Individuals who are high on responsiveness, low on assertiveness, prefer to belong to groups, and are interested in others.

expressives Individuals who are high on both responsiveness and assertiveness, are animated and communicative, and value building close relationships with others.

drivers Individuals who are low on responsiveness, high on assertiveness, and detached from relationships.

analyticals Individuals who are low on responsiveness and assertiveness, and are analytical, meticulous, and disciplined in everything they do.

buying teams Teams of individuals in organizations that use the expertise and multiple buying influences of people from different departments throughout the organization.

initiators Individuals within an organization who identify a need.

influencers Individuals within an organization who guide the decision process by making recommendations and expressing preferences.

users Individuals within an organization who will actually use the product being purchased.

deciders Individuals within an organization who have the ultimate responsibility of determining which product or service will be purchased.

purchasers Organizational members who negotiate final terms of the purchase and execute the actual purchase.

gatekeepers Members of an organization who are in a position to control the flow of information to and between vendors and other buying centre members.

supply chain management The strategic coordination and integration of purchasing with other functions within the buying organization as well as external organizations.

outsourcing The process of giving to a supplier certain activities that the buying organization previously performed.

target price The price buyers determine for their final products through information gathered from researching the marketplace.

in two primary groupings of factors: functional attributes and psychological attributes. Functional attributes are the more tangible characteristics of a market offering whereas the psychological attributes are primarily composed of the interpersonal behaviours and activities between the buyer and seller. The psychological attributes have been repeatedly found to have higher levels of influence than functional attributes on customer satisfaction and repeat purchase.

3-6 **Explain the different types of purchasing decisions.** The three types of purchasing decisions are described as follows:

Straight Rebuy—Comparable with a routine repurchase in which nothing has changed, the straight rebuy is often the result of past experience and satisfaction, with buyers purchasing the same products from the same sources. Needs have been predetermined, with specifications already established. Buyers allocate little, if any, time or resources to this form of purchase decision, and the primary emphasis is on continued satisfactory performance.

Modified Rebuy—The buyer has some level of experience with the product but is interested in acquiring additional information regarding alternative products and suppliers. The modified rebuy typically occurs as the result of changing conditions or needs. Perhaps the buyer wants to consider new suppliers for current purchase needs or new products offered by existing suppliers.

New Task—New task decisions occur when a buyer is purchasing a product or service for the first time. With no experience or knowledge on which to rely, buyers undertake an extensive purchase decision and search for information designed to identify and compare alternative solutions. Reflecting the extensive nature of this type of purchase decision, multiple members of the buying centre or group are usually involved. As a result, the salesperson often works with several different individuals rather than a single buyer.

3-7 **Describe the four communication styles and how salespeople must adapt their own styles to maximize communication.** Based on high and low levels of two personal traits, assertiveness and responsiveness, communication styles can be categorized into four primary types:

- Amiables are high on responsiveness and low on assertiveness.
- Expressives are defined as high on both responsiveness and assertiveness.
- Drivers are low on responsiveness but high on assertiveness.
- Analyticals are characterized as low on assertiveness as well as responsiveness.

Mismatched styles between a seller and a buyer can be dysfunctional in terms of effective collaboration and present significant barriers for information exchange and relationship building. Differences in styles manifest themselves in the form of differences in preferred priorities (relationships versus task orientation) and favoured pace (fast versus slow) of information exchange, socialization, and decision making. To minimize potential communication difficulties stemming from mismatched styles, salespeople should adapt their personal styles to better fit the preferred priorities and pace of the buyer.

3-8 **Explain the concept of buying teams and specify the different member roles.** In the more complex modified rebuy and new task purchasing situations, purchase decisions typically involve the joint decisions of multiple participants working together as a buying team. Team members bring the expertise and knowledge from different functional departments within the buying organization. Team members may also change as the purchase decision changes. Team members are described by their roles within the team: initiators, influencers, users, deciders, purchasers, and gatekeepers.

3-9 **Identify current developments in purchasing.** There are several key developments shaping the face of purchasing today, including increasing use of information technology, emphasis on building cooperative and collaborative relationships, increasing use of supply chain management, expanded use of outsourcing by buying organizations, more emphasis on establishing target prices by buyers, and greater dependence on salespeople to provide buying organizations creative solutions to unique customer needs.

CHAPTER 4 IN REVIEW

Communication Skills

Chapter Summary

4-1 Explain the importance of collaborative, two-way communication in trust-based selling. The two-way exchange inherent in collaborative communication facilitates accurate and mutual understanding of the objectives, problems, needs, and capabilities of each of the parties. As a result, solutions can be generated that provide mutual benefits to all participants. This would not be possible without collaboration, and one party would benefit at the expense of the other. Although this might be good for the winning party, the disadvantaged party would be less inclined to continue doing business and would seek out other business partners.

4-2 Explain the primary types of questions and how they are applied in selling. Questions can be typed into two categories according to (1) the amount of information and specificity desired and (2) the strategic purpose of the question.

- Questions typed by the amount of information and specificity desired include open-end questions, closed-end questions, and dichotomous questions. *Open-end questions* encourage the customer to respond freely and provide more expansive information. They are used to probe for descriptive information. *Closed-end questions* limit responses to one or two words and are used to confirm or clarify information. *Dichotomous questions* request the buyer to choose between specified alternatives.
- Questions typed by their strategic purpose include questions for (1) probing, (2) evaluative, (3) tactical, and (4) reactive purposes. *Probing questions* penetrate beneath surface information to provide useful details. *Evaluative questions* uncover how the buyer feels about something. *Tactical questions* are used to shift the topic of discussion. *Reactive questions* respond to information provided by the other party and ask for additional details about that information.

4-3 Illustrate the diverse roles and uses of strategic questioning in trust-based selling. Questions are used to elicit detailed information about a buyer's situation, needs, and expectations while also providing a logical guide promoting sequential thought. Effective questioning facilitates both the buyer's and the seller's understanding of a problem and proposed solutions. Questioning can also test the buyer's interest and increase his or her cognitive involvement and participation in the selling process. Questions can also be used to redirect, regain, or hold the buyer's attention subtly and strategically.

4-4 Identify and describe the SPIN and ADAPT systems for effective questioning in a sales dialogue. The four steps of SPIN are situation questions, problem questions, implication questions, and need-payoff questions.

- *Situation questions* are used early in the sales call to provide salespeople with leads to develop the buyer's needs and expectations fully.
- *Problem questions* are used to further probe for specific difficulties, developing problems, and areas of dissatisfaction that might be positively addressed by the salesperson's proposed sales offering.
- *Implication questions* are used to assist the buyer in thinking about the potential consequences of the problem and to understand the urgency of resolving the problem in a way that motivates him or her to seek a solution.
- *Need-payoff* questions are based on the implications of a problem; they are used to propose a solution and develop commitment from the buyer.

Glossary Terms

trust-based sales communication Talking *with* rather than *at* the customer. A collaborative and two-way form of communication that allows buyers and sellers to develop a better understanding of the need situation and work together to co-create the best response for resolving the customer's needs.

open-end questions Questions designed to let the customer respond freely; the customer is not limited to one- or two-word answers but is encouraged to disclose personal or business information.

closed-end questions Questions designed to limit the customer's responses to one or two words.

dichotomous questions A directive form of questioning; these questions ask the customer to choose from two or more options.

probing questions Questions designed to penetrate below generalized or superficial information to elicit more articulate and precise details for use in needs discovery and solution identification.

evaluative questions Questions that use the open- and closed-end question formats to gain confirmation and to uncover attitudes, opinions, and preferences the prospect holds.

tactical questions Questions used to shift or redirect the topic of discussion when the discussion gets off course or when a line of questioning proves to be of little interest or value.

reactive questions Questions that refer to or directly result from information the other party previously provided.

SPIN A questioning system that sequences four types of questions designed to uncover a buyer's current situation and inherent problems, enhance the buyer's understanding of the consequences and implications of those problems, and lead to the proposed solution.

situation questions One of the four types of questions in the SPIN questioning system used early in the sales call that provides salespeople with leads to develop the buyer's needs and expectations fully.

problem questions One of the four types of questions in the SPIN questioning system that follows the more general situation questions to further probe for specific difficulties, developing problems, and areas of dissatisfaction that might be positively addressed by the salesperson's proposed sales offering.

implication questions One of the four types of questions in the SPIN questioning system that follows and is related to the information flowing from problem questions; they are used to assist the buyer in thinking about the potential consequences of the problem and understanding the urgency of resolving the problem in a way that motivates him or her to seek a solution.

need-payoff questions One of the four types of questions in the SPIN questioning system that is based on the implications of a problem; they are used to propose a solution and develop commitment from the buyer.

ADAPT A questioning system that uses a logic-based funnelling sequence of questions, beginning with broad and generalized inquiries designed to identify and assess the buyer's situation.

assessment questions One of the five stages of questions in the ADAPT questioning system that do not seek conclusions but rather should address the buyer's company and operations, goals and objectives, market trends and customers, current suppliers, and even the buyer as an individual.

discovery questions One of the five stages of questions in the ADAPT questioning system that follows up on the assessment questions; they should drill down and probe for further details needed to develop, clarify, and understand the nature of the buyer's problems fully.

activation questions One of the five stages of questions in the ADAPT questioning system used to activate the customer's interest in solving discovered problems by helping him or her gain insight into the true ramifications of the problem and to realize that what may initially seem to be of little consequence is, in fact, of significant consequence.

projection questions One of the five stages of questions in the ADAPT questioning system used to encourage and help the buyer project what it would be like without the problems that have been previously discovered and activated.

transition questions One of the five stages of questions in the ADAPT questioning system used to smooth the transition from needs discovery into the presentation and demonstration of the proposed solution's features, advantages, and benefits.

social listening An informal mode of listening that can be associated with day-to-day conversation and entertainment.

serious listening A form of listening that is associated with events or topics in which it is important to sort through, interpret, understand, and respond to received messages

active listening The cognitive process of actively sensing, interpreting, evaluating, and responding to the verbal and nonverbal messages of present or potential customers.

SIER A model that depicts active listening as a hierarchical, four-step sequence of sensing, interpreting, evaluating, and responding.

The five steps of ADAPT are assessment questions, discovery questions, activation questions, projection questions, and transition questions.

- *Assessment questions* are broad, general, nonthreatening questions designed to spark conversation. Assessment questions elicit factual information about the customer's current situation that can provide a basis for further exploration and probing.
- *Discovery questions* probe for details needed to identify and understand a buyer's problems and needs. The buyer's interpretations, perceptions, feelings, and opinions are sought in regard to his or her needs, wants, dissatisfactions, and expectations.
- *Activation questions* help the customer evaluate the negative impact of an implied need. The objective is to activate interest in solving discovered problems by helping the customer gain insight into the true consequences of the problem.
- *Projection questions* encourage the buyer's decision making by projecting what it would be like if the problems or needs did not exist. They switch the focus from problems to benefits—the payoff for taking action and investing in a solution—and allow the buyer to establish the perceived value of solving the problem or need.
- *Transition questions* smooth the transition to a subsequent phase in the selling process. They are typically closed-end and evaluative in format and strive to confirm the buyer's desire to seek a solution and move forward with the buying/selling process.

4-5 Discuss the four sequential steps for effective active listening.

- *Sensing* is the first activity in active listening and involves receiving the message. Sensing is more than just hearing the message and requires concentration and practice.
- *Interpreting.* After sensing the message, it must be interpreted in terms of what the sender actually meant. In addition to meanings of words and symbols, the experiences, knowledge, and attitudes of the sender should also be considered.
- *Evaluating.* Effective communication requires the receiver to decide whether or not he or she agrees with the sender's message. This requires evaluating the results from the interpretation stage to sort fact from opinion and emotion.
- *Responding.* Collaborative communication requires listeners to provide feedback to the other party. Responses take the form of paraphrasing the sender's message, answering questions, or asking questions to gain additional details and clarification.

4-6 Describe and interpret the different forms of verbal and nonverbal communication. Verbal communication refers to statements of fact, opinion, and attitude that are encoded in the form of words, pictures, and numbers in such a way that they convey meaning to a receiver. However, many words and symbols mean different things to different people. Different industries, different cultures, and different types of training or work experience can result in the same word or phrase having multiple interpretations. Nonverbal behaviours are made up of the various movements and utterances that people use. These can be conscious or unconscious and include eye movement and facial expressions; placement and movements of hands, arms, head, and legs, as well as body orientation; the amount of space maintained between individuals; and variations in vocal characteristics. Sensing and interpreting groups or clusters of nonverbal cues can provide a reliable indicator of the underlying message and intent. Evidence shows that nonverbal behaviours carry 50 percent or more of the meaning conveyed in the process of interpersonal communication.

nonverbal communication The conscious and unconscious reactions, movements, and utterances that people use in addition to the words and symbols associated with language.

proxemics The personal distance that individuals prefer to keep between themselves and other individuals; an important element of nonverbal communication.

nonverbal clusters Groups of related nonverbal expressions, gestures, and movements that can be interpreted to better understand the true message being communicated.

CHAPTER 5 IN REVIEW

Strategic Prospecting and Preparing for Sales Dialogue

Chapter Summary

5-1 Discuss why prospecting is an important and challenging task for salespeople. Prospecting is important because market changes could cause current customers to buy less, customers could go out of business or be acquired by other firms, or business could be lost to competitors. Salespeople often fear rejection, and prospective buyers may be difficult to contact because they have never heard of a salesperson's firm, do not have the time with all potential new suppliers, and are somewhat shielded by gatekeepers trained to limit access.

5-2 Explain strategic prospecting and each stage in the strategic prospecting process. Strategic prospecting is a process for identifying the best sales opportunities. The strategic prospecting process consists of generating sales leads, determining sales prospects, prioritizing sales prospects, and preparing for sales dialogue.

FIGURE 5.1
Sales Funnel

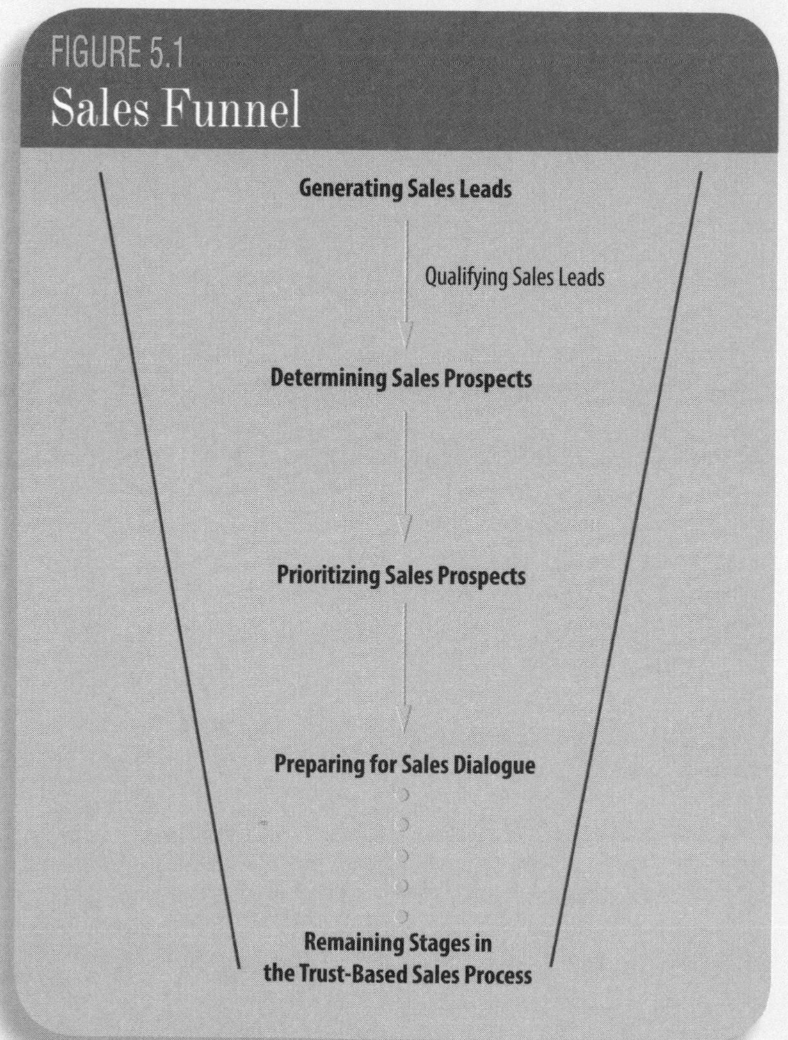

Glossary Terms

strategic prospecting A process designed to identify, qualify, and prioritize sales opportunities, whether they represent potential new customers or opportunities to generate additional business from existing customers.

sales funnel or **pipeline** A representation of the trust-based sales process and strategic sales prospecting process in the form of a funnel.

sales leads or **suspects** Organizations or individuals who might possibly purchase the product or service a salesperson offers.

qualifying sales leads The salesperson's act of searching out, collecting, and analyzing information to determine the likelihood of the lead being a good candidate for making a sale.

sales prospect An individual or organization that has a need for the product or service, has the budget or financial resources to purchase the product or service, and has the authority to make the purchase decision.

ideal customer profile The characteristics of a firm's best customers or the perfect customer.

cold calling Contacting a sales lead unannounced and with little or no information about the lead.

referral A name of a company or person given to the salesperson as a lead by a customer or even a prospect who did not buy at this time.

introduction A variation of a referral in which, in addition to requesting the names of prospects, the salesperson asks the prospect or customer to prepare a note or letter of introduction that can be sent to the potential customer.

centres of influence Well-known and influential people who can help a salesperson prospect and gain leads.

noncompeting salespeople Salespeople selling noncompeting products.

electronic networking Using Web sites designed to help salespeople identify and gather information about prospects.

company records Information about customers in a company database.

advertising inquiries Sales leads generated from company advertising efforts.

inbound telemarketing A way to locate prospects in which the prospect calls the company to get information.

outbound telemarketing A way to locate prospects in which the salesperson contacts the prospect by telephone.

trade shows Events at which companies purchase space and set up booths that clearly identify each company and its offerings and that are staffed with salespeople who demonstrate the products and answer questions.

seminars A presentation salespeople give to generate leads and provide information to prospective customers who are invited to the seminar by direct mail, word of mouth, or advertising on local television or radio.

directories Electronic or print sources that provide contact and other information about many different companies or individuals.

commercial lead lists Lists that focus on virtually any type of business or individual; they range from simple listings of names, addresses, and phone numbers to more detailed listings with a full profile of the different entries included in the list.

strategic prospecting plan A salesperson's plan for gathering qualified prospects.

tracking system Part of the strategic prospecting plan that records comprehensive information about the prospect, traces the prospecting methods used, and chronologically archives outcomes from any contacts with the prospect.

5-3 Describe the major prospecting methods and give examples of each method. Salespeople should use different prospecting methods. The major prospecting methods are cold canvassing (cold calling, referrals, and introductions), networking (centres of influence, noncompeting salespeople, and electronic networking), company sources (company records, advertising inquiries, telephone inquiries, trade shows, and seminars), and published sources (directories and commercial lead lists).

5-4 Explain the important components of a strategic prospecting plan. A strategic prospecting plan consists of setting specific goals for the numbers of prospects to be identified, a regular schedule for prospecting activities, a tracking system to keep records of prospecting activities, an evaluation system to assess prospecting progress, and a positive and confident attitude.

5-5 Discuss the types of information salespeople need to prepare for sales dialogue. Salespeople must gather information about the prospect that will be used to help formulate the sales presentation. Buyer's needs, buyer's motives, and details about the buyer's situation should be determined. The more a salesperson knows about the buyer, the better chance he or she will have to meet the buyer's needs and eventually earn the commitment.

FIGURE 5.2
Prospecting Plans Are the Foundation for Effective Prospecting

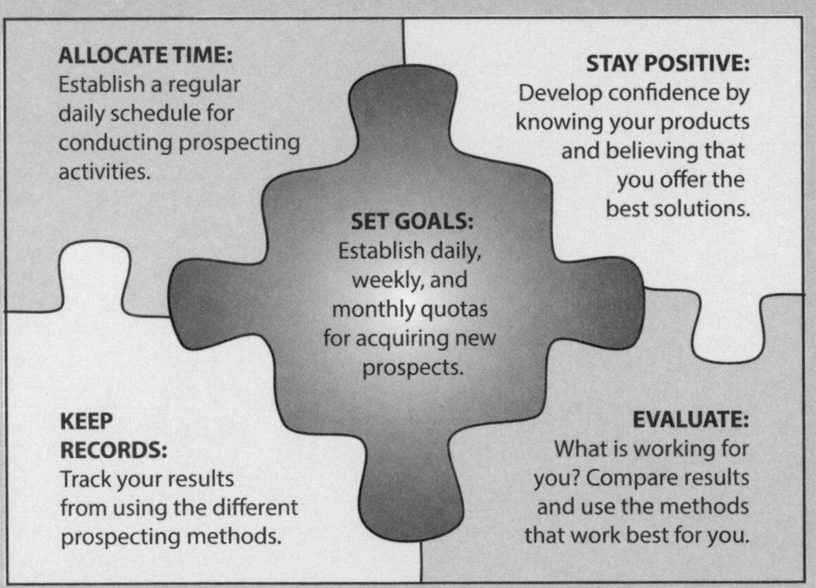

CHAPTER 6 IN REVIEW

Planning Sales Dialogues and Presentations

Chapter Summary

6-1 Explain why it is essential to focus on the customer when planning sales calls. Buyers are well informed and have little time to waste on unproductive conversations with salespeople. To optimize the time spent on sale calls, salespeople should focus on customer needs and how the customer defines value. Customers differ in how they define value, and salespeople must understand each customer's concept of value so that they can establish sales dialogues that are clear, credible, and interesting.

6-2 Understand alternative ways of communicating with prospects and customers through canned sales presentations, written sales proposals, and organized sales dialogues and presentations. Canned sales presentations include scripted sales calls, memorized presentations, and automated presentations. Effective canned presentations have usually been tested with real customers before an entire salesforce uses them. Canned sales presentations can be complete and logically structured. Objections are anticipated in advance, and appropriate responses can be formulated as part of the presentation. A written sales proposal is a complete, self-contained sales presentation. A sales proposal should be prepared after the salesperson has made a thorough assessment of the buyer's situation as it relates to the seller's offering. An organized sales dialogue, which could include a comprehensive sales presentation, is tailored to the prospect's particular situation and needs. It is a flexible format that allows for maximum input and feedback from the prospect. Sales dialogues and organized sales presentations (sometimes referred to as sales conversations) can take place over multiple sales calls before a purchase decision is made.

6-3 Discuss the nine components of the sales dialogue template that can be used for planning an organized sales dialogue or an organized sales presentation. The sales dialogue template consists of nine sections: (1) prospect information; (2) customer value proposition; (3) sales call objective; (4) situation and needs analysis—linking buying motives, benefits, support information, and other reinforcement methods; (5) competitive situation; (6) beginning the sales dialogue; (7) anticipating questions and objections; (8) earning prospect commitment; and (9) building value through follow-up action. This template should not be used to develop a rigid script for a sales call. It is properly used to help the salespeople ensure that they are prepared to discuss all pertinent content with the customer.

Glossary Terms

sales call An in-person meeting between a salesperson or sales team and one or more buyers to discuss business.

sales dialogue Business conversations between buyers and sellers that occur as salespeople attempt to initiate, develop, and enhance customer relationships. Sales dialogue should be customer focused and have a clear purpose.

sales presentations Comprehensive communications that convey multiple points designed to persuade the customer to make a purchase.

canned sales presentation Sales presentations that include scripted sales calls, memorized presentations, and automated presentations.

written sales proposal A complete self-contained sales presentation on paper, often accompanied by other verbal sales presentations before or after the proposal is delivered.

organized sales dialogue Also known as the organized sales presentation. Unlike a canned sales presentation, an organized sales dialogue has a high level of customer involvement.

organized sales presentation A sales presentation that allows a salesperson to implement appropriate sales strategies and tactics based on customer research or information gathered during previous sales calls. Organized sales presentations feature a high-level two-way dialogue with the customer.

sales dialogue template A flexible planning tool that assists the salesperson in assembling pertinent information to be covered with the prospect.

customer value proposition A statement of how the sales offering will add value to the prospect's business by meeting a need or providing an opportunity.

buying motives A need-activated drive to search for and acquire a solution to resolve a need or problem; the most important factors from the customer's perspective in making a purchase decision.

rational buying motives Typically relate to the economics of the situation, including cost, profitability, quality, services offered, and the total value of the seller's offering as perceived by the customer.

emotional buying motives Include such motives as security, status, and the need to be liked; sometimes difficult for salespeople to uncover these motives.

features Qualities or characteristics of a product or service that are designed to provide value to a buyer.

benefits The added value or favourable outcome derived from features of the product or service the seller offers.

FIGURE 6.1

The Trust-Based Selling Process: A Need-Satisfaction Consultative Mode

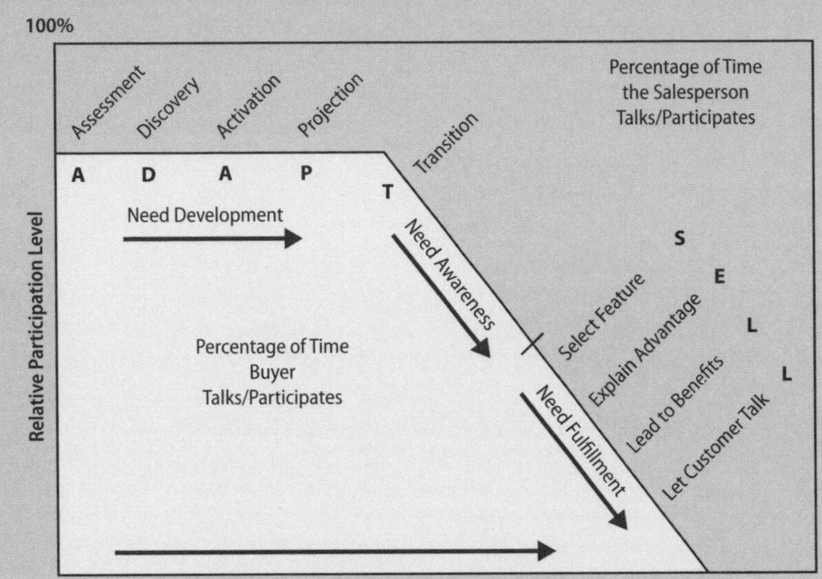

6-4 Explain how to write a customer value proposition statement. A customer value statement should be simple so that it provides a clear direction for upcoming sales dialogues. Salespeople should not attempt to include all their benefits in a value proposition statement—rather, they should choose the key benefits that are likely to be most important to the specific customer. The value proposition should be as specific as possible, on listing tangible outcomes, such as revenue improvement, cost containment or reduction gain in market share, process speed and efficiency, or the enhancement of a customer's strategic priority. Value proposition statements should promise only what can be consistently delivered. Strictly speaking, a customer value proposition in the planning stage is not a guarantee; it is a belief based on the salesperson's knowledge and best judgment. As the sales process moves along, appropriate guarantees can be made.

6-5 Link buying motives to benefits of the seller's offering, support claims made for benefits, and reinforce verbal claims made. Organized sales dialogues and organized sales presentations should focus on the most important motives for a given buyer. Benefits must be linked to both rational and emotional motives, and supporting information must be given for each claim made about a benefit. In some cases, the claim needs support beyond the spoken word (e.g., through audio-visual content, printed collateral material, third-party research studies, or testimonials from satisfied customers).

6-6 Engage the customer by setting appointments. Salespeople customarily set an appointment, at least for their initial sales calls on new prospects. Appointments may be arranged by telephone, email, or a combination of phone and mail and should include a request for a specific time and date, as well as the amount of time being requested for the sales call. Salespeople have a better chance of securing an appointment if they are prepared to give the customer a good reason for spending time with them.

CHAPTER 7 IN REVIEW

Sales Dialogue: Creating and Communicating Value

Chapter Summary

7-1 **Describe the key characteristics of effective sales dialogue.** The most effective sales dialogues are planned and practised by salespeople, encourage buyer feedback, focus on creating value for the buyer, present value in an interesting and understandable manner, engage and involve the buyer, and support customer value through objective claims.

7-2 **Describe the differences among features, potential benefits, and confirmed benefits, and describe the role they play in benefits selling.** Salespeople can generate feedback from buyers by paying attention to nonverbal cues from the buyer and using check-backs or response checks to get the buyer to respond to what the salesperson has said throughout the sales dialogue.

7-3 **Describe how verbal support can be used to communicate value in an interesting and understandable manner.** Salespeople need to communicate value in an interesting and understandable manner. This can be accomplished by varying the pitch and speed of speech, using examples and anecdotes, and including comparisons and analogies.

EXHIBIT 7.1

Keys to Effective Sales Dialogue

The most effective sales dialogues

1. Are planned and practised by salespeople.
2. Encourage buyer feedback.
3. Focus on creating value for the buyer.
4. Present value in an interesting and understandable way.
5. Engage and involve the buyer.
6. Support customer value through objective claims.

7-4 **Discuss how sales aids can engage and involve buyers.** Sales aids are various tools salespeople can use to engage and involve buyers, generate interest and attention, and be more persuasive. Visual materials, electronic materials, and product demonstrations are the major categories of sales aids. It is important for salespeople to select the appropriate sales aids, but also to use them effectively. The SPES sequence of stating the selling point and introducing the sales aid, presenting the sales aid, explaining the sales aid, and summarizing can help salespeople use sales aids successfully.

7-5 **Explain how salespeople can support product claims.** Salespeople need to be able to support the claims they make concerning their products. Proof providers, such as statistics, testimonials, and case histories, represent the major approaches for supporting product claims.

Glossary Terms

FAB A form of selling that focuses on the features, advantages, and benefits of a product.

features Qualities or characteristics of a product or service that are designed to provide value to a buyer.

potential benefits A general form of value that is assumed by the salesperson to be of importance but is not yet acknowledged as such by the buyer.

confirmed benefits The benefits the buyer indicates are important and represent value.

check-backs or response checks Questions salespeople use throughout a sales dialogue to generate feedback from the buyer.

verbal support The use of voice characteristics, examples and anecdotes, and comparisons and analogies to make sales dialogue interesting and understandable.

voice characteristics The pitch and speed of speech, which salespeople should vary to emphasize key points.

example A brief description of a specific instance used to illustrate features and benefits of a product or service.

anecdote A type of example that is provided in the form of a story describing a specific incident or occurrence.

comparison A statement that points out and illustrates the similarities between two points.

analogy A special and useful form of comparison that explains one thing in terms of another.

sales aids The use of printed materials, electronic materials, and product demonstrations to engage and involve buyers.

visual materials Printed materials, photographs and illustrations, and charts and graphs used as sales aids.

electronic materials Sales aids in electronic format, such as slides, videos, or multimedia presentations.

proof providers The use of statistics, testimonials, or case histories to support product claims.

statistics Facts that lend believability to product claims and are used as proof providers.

testimonials Proof providers that are in the form of statements from satisfied users of the selling organization's products and services.

case histories A testimonial in story or anecdotal form used as a proof provider.

preselling Salespeople present their product or service to individual buyers before a major sales dialogue with a group of buyers.

7-6 Discuss the special considerations involved in sales dialogue with groups. Sales dialogues with individual buyers and with groups have many similarities and several important differences. Salespeople interacting with a group of buyers need to address their arrival tactics, how to handle questions, the proper use of eye contact, and how to communicate most effectively to the group and to individuals within the group.

© Fuse/Jupiter Images

Salespeople are increasingly involved in group sales dialogue.

Addressing Concerns and Earning Commitment

Chapter Summary

8-1 Explain why it is important to anticipate and overcome buyer concerns and resistance. During the early years of selling, salespeople looked at sales resistance as a negative that was a likely indication their buyer was not going to buy. This notion has changed over the years, and now objections are viewed as opportunities to sell. Salespeople should be grateful for objections and always treat them as indications that the prospect needs more information; if the salesperson provides the correct information, he or she is moving closer to gaining the sale.

8-2 Understand why prospects raise objections. Some prospects are happy with their present suppliers and want to avoid the sales interview. In other instances, the salesperson has failed to qualify the prospect properly. A prospect who has recently purchased a product is probably not in the market for another. Sometimes, prospects simply lack information on the salesperson's product category, and they are uncomfortable making a decision.

8-3 Describe the five major types of sales resistance. Typically, objections include the following: "I don't need your product," "Your product is not a good fit," "I don't know your company," "Your price is too high," and "This is a bad time to buy."

EXHIBIT 8.2 Types of Objections

No need	Buyer has recently purchased or does not see a need for the product category. "I am not interested at this time."
Product or service objection	Buyer may be afraid of product reliability. "I am not sure the quality of your product meets our needs." Buyer may be afraid of late deliveries, slow repairs, etc. "I am happy with my present supplier's service."
Company objection	Buyer is intensely loyal to the present supplier. "I am happy with my present supplier."
Price is too high	Buyer has a limited budget. "We have been buying from another supplier that meets our budget constraints."
Time or delay	Buyer needs time to think it over. "Get back with me in a couple of weeks."

Glossary Terms

sales resistance A buyer's objections to a product or service during a sales presentation.

need objection Resistance to a product or service in which a buyer says that he or she does not need the product or service.

product or service objection Resistance to a product or service in which a buyer does not like the way the product or service looks or feels.

company or source objection Resistance to a product or service that results when a buyer has never heard of or is not familiar with the product's company.

price objection Resistance to a product or service based on the price of the product being too high for the buyer.

time objection Resistance to a product or service in which a buyer puts off the decision to buy until a later date.

LAARC An acronym for listen, acknowledge, assess, respond, and confirm that describes an effective process for salespeople to follow to overcome sales resistance.

forestalling A response to buyer objections in which the salesperson answers the objection during the presentation before the buyer has a chance to ask it.

direct denial A response to buyer objections in which the salesperson tells the customer that he or she is wrong.

indirect denial A response to buyer objections in which the salesperson takes a softer, more tactful approach when correcting a prospect or customer's information.

translation or **boomerang** A response to buyer objections in which the salesperson converts the objection into a reason the prospect should buy.

compensation A response to buyer objections in which the salesperson counterbalances the objection with an offsetting benefit.

questioning or **assessing** A response to buyer objections in which the salesperson asks the buyer assessment questions to gain a better understanding of what the buyer is objecting to.

third-party reinforcement A response to buyer objections in which the salesperson uses the opinion or data from a third-party source to help overcome the objection and reinforce the salesperson's points.

commitment signals Favourable statements a buyer makes during a sales presentation that signal buyer commitment.

direct commitment A selling technique in which the salesperson asks the customer directly to buy.

alternative or legitimate choice A selling technique in which the salesperson asks the prospect to select from two or more choices during a sales presentation.

summary commitment A selling technique in which the salesperson summarizes all the major benefits the buyer has confirmed during the sales calls.

T-account or **balance sheet commitment** A selling technique in which a salesperson asks the prospect to brainstorm reasons on paper of why to buy and why not to buy.

success story commitment A selling technique in which a salesperson relates how one of his or her customers had a problem similar to the prospect's and solved it by using the salesperson's product.

standing-room-only close A sales closing technique in which the salesperson puts a time limit on the client in an attempt to hurry the decision to close.

assumptive close A sales closing technique in which the salesperson assumes that an agreement has been reached, places the order form in front of the buyer, and hands him or her a pen.

fear or emotional close A sales closing technique in which the salesperson tells a story of something bad happening if the purchase is not made.

continuous yes close A sales closing technique that uses the principle that saying yes gets to be a habit; the salesperson asks a number of questions formulated so that the prospect answers yes.

minor-points close A sales closing technique in which the salesperson seeks agreement on relatively minor issues associated with the full order.

8-4 Explain how the LAARC method can be used to overcome buyer resistance. LAARC allows the salesperson to listen carefully to what the buyer is saying. It allows the salesperson to better understand the buyer's objections. After this careful analysis, the salesperson can then respond. The buyer feels that the salesperson is responding to his or her specific concern rather than giving a prepared answer.

8-5 Describe the recommended approaches for responding to buyer objections. Salespeople have a number of traditional techniques at their disposal for handling resistance. Some of the more popular techniques include forestalling, or answering the objection before the prospect brings it up; direct denial; indirect denial, which softens the answer; translation or boomerang, which means to turn a reason not to buy into a reason to buy; compensation, or offsetting the objection with superior benefits; questions, which are used to uncover the buyer's concerns; and third-party reinforcements, which use the opinion or research of others to substantiate claims.

8-6 List and explain the techniques for earning commitment that secure commitment and closing. Many techniques can be used to earn commitment. Most are gimmicky in nature and reinforce the notion of traditional selling. Successful relationship-building techniques include the summary commitment, the success story commitment, and the direct commitment or ask for the order.

EXHIBIT 8.12

Techniques to Earn Commitment

1. Direct commitment—Simply ask for the order.
2. Legitimate choice/alternative choice—Give the prospect a limited number of choices.
3. Summary commitment—Summarize all the confirmed benefits to which there has been agreement.
4. T-account/balance sheet commitment—Summary close on paper.
5. Success story commitment—Salesperson tells a story of a business that successfully solved a problem by buying his or her products.

CHAPTER 9 IN REVIEW

Expanding Customer Relationships

Chapter Summary

9-1 Explain how to follow up to assess and take action to ensure customer satisfaction by using the latest technology. When assessing customer satisfaction, salespeople cannot be afraid to ask their customers, "How are we doing?" Periodic follow-up is critical to long-term sales success. New customers generally feel special because they have received a lot of attention from the salesperson. Longstanding customers may feel neglected because the sales rep has many new customers and cannot be as attentive as he or she was previously. Routine follow-up to assess "How are we doing?" can go a long way in letting a customer know that the salesperson cares and is willing to make sure that he or she is satisfied.

To ensure customer satisfaction, salespeople must follow up by performing specific relationship-enhancement activities, such as the following:

- Providing useful information to their customers
- Expediting orders and monitoring an installation for success
- Training customer personnel
- Correcting billing errors
- Remembering the customer after the sale
- Resolving complaints in a timely manner

Salespeople can use technology to enhance follow-up and buyer–seller relationships. Effective follow-up should include specific components designed to help salespeople interact, connect, know, and relate with their customers:

- *Interact*: The salesperson maximizes the number of critical encounters with buyers to encourage effective dialogue and involvement between the salesperson and the buyer.
- *Connect*: The salesperson maintains contact with multiple individuals in the buying organization who influence purchase decisions and manages the various touch points the customer has in the selling organization to ensure consistency in communication.
- *Know*: The salesperson coordinates and interprets the information gathered through buyer–seller contact and collaboration to develop insight regarding the buyer's changing situation, needs, and expectations.
- *Relate*: The salesperson applies relevant understanding and insight to create value-added interactions and develop relationships between the salesperson and buyer.

Salespeople can use a variety of technology-based salesforce automation tools to better track increasingly complex buyer–seller interactions and to manage the exchange, interpretation, and storage of diverse types of information. Among the more popular salesforce automation tools are the many competing versions of PC- and Internet-based software applications designed to record and manage customer contact information. PC-based software applications, such as Maximizer, Goldmine, and ACT!, and Internet-based applications, such as Netsuite and Salesforce.com, enable salespeople to collect, file, and access comprehensive databases detailing information about individual buyers and buying organizations.

Glossary Terms

building goodwill The process of converting new customers into lifetime customers by continually adding value to the product.

adding value The process of improving a product or service for the customer.

interact The salesperson acts to maximize the number of critical encounters with buyers to encourage effective dialogue and involvement between the salesperson and buyer.

connect The salesperson maintains contact with the multiple individuals in the buying organization who influence purchase decisions and manages the various touch points the customer has in the selling organization to ensure consistency in communication.

know The salesperson coordinates and interprets the information gathered through buyer–seller contact and collaboration to develop insight regarding the buyer's changing situation, needs, and expectations.

relate The salesperson applies relevant understanding and insight to create value-added interactions and generate relationships between the salesperson and buyer.

intranet An organization's dedicated and proprietary computer network that offers password-controlled access to people within and outside the organization (e.g., customers and suppliers).

extranet Proprietary computer networks created by an organization for use by the organization's customers or suppliers and linked to the organization's internal systems, informational databases, and intranet.

customer relationship management (CRM) system A system that dynamically links buyers and sellers into a rich communication network to establish and reinforce long-term, profitable relationships.

critical encounters Meetings in which the salesperson encourages the buyer to discuss tough issues, especially in areas in which the salesperson's organization is providing less than satisfactory performance.

collaborative involvement A way to build on buyer–salesperson relationships in which the buyer's organization and the salesperson's organization join together to improve an offering.

service quality Meeting and/or exceeding customer service expectations.

service strategy A plan in which a salesperson identifies his or her business and customers and what the customers want and what is important to them.

communication A two-way flow of information between the salesperson and the customer.

resilience The ability of a salesperson to listen to a customer's complaint and always answer with a smile.

service motivation The desire of a salesperson to service customers each day.

EXHIBIT 9.1

Relationship Enhancers and Detractors

Enhancers	Detractors
Focus on long term	Focus on short term
Deliver more than promised	Overpromise and/or underdeliver
Call regularly	Call sporadically
Add value	Show up only for another order
Keep communication lines open	Be unavailable to the customer
Take responsibility for problems	Lie, exaggerate, blame someone else

9-2 **Discuss how to expand collaborative involvement.** The easiest way to expand collaborative involvement is to get more people involved in the relationship from both the buyer's and the seller's firms.

9-3 **Explain how to add value and enhance mutual opportunities.** The salesperson can enhance mutual opportunities by reducing risk for the buyer through repeated displays of outstanding customer service. The salesperson can also demonstrate a willingness to serve the customer over extended periods of time. The buyer needs to experience a readiness on the seller's part to go to bat for the buyer when things get tough.

© photovideostock/iStockphoto

Great salespeople work hard to provide quality customer service.

Adding Value: Self-Leadership and Teamwork

Chapter Summary

© alexsl/iStockphoto

10-1 Explain the five sequential stages of self-leadership. As a process, self-leadership is composed of five sequential stages. First, goals and objectives must be set that properly reflect what is important and what is to be accomplished. In turn, an analysis of the territory and classification of accounts is conducted to better understand the territory potential and prioritize accounts according to revenue-producing possibilities. With goals in place and accounts prioritized, the third stage develops corresponding strategic plans designed to achieve sales goals through proper allocation of resources and effort. The next stage maximizes the effectiveness of allocated resources by incorporating technology and salesforce automation to expand salesperson resource capabilities. Finally, assessment activities are conducted to evaluate performance and goal attainment and to assess possible changes in plans and strategies.

10-2 Identify the four levels of sales goals and explain their interrelationships. There are four different levels of goals that salespeople must establish to maximize sales effectiveness:

(a) Personal goals: what the seller wants to accomplish for himself or herself

(b) Sales call goals: the priorities to be accomplished during a specific call

(c) Account goals: the objectives for each individual account

(d) Territory goals: what is to be accomplished for the overall territory

Each level requires different types of effort and produces different outcomes, and each of the levels is interrelated with and interdependent on the others. Ultimately, each higher level goal is dependent on the salesperson setting and achieving the specific goals for each lower level.

10-3 Describe two techniques for account classification. There are two basic methods of classifying accounts. In ascending order of complexity, these methods are single-factor analysis and portfolio analysis (also referred to as two-factor analysis).

- *Single-factor analysis:* Also referred to as ABC analysis, this is the simplest and most often-used method for classifying accounts. Accounts are analyzed on the basis of one single factor—typically the level of sales potential—and placed into either three or four categories denoted by letters of the alphabet: A, B, C, and D. All accounts in the same category receive equal selling effort.
- *Portfolio analysis (two-factor analysis):* This classification method allows two factors to be considered simultaneously. Each account is examined on the basis of the two factors selected for analysis and sorted into the proper segment of a matrix. This matrix is typically divided into four cells, with accounts placed into the proper classification cell on the basis of their individual ratings (high and low or strong and weak) on each of the two factors. Accounts in the same cell share a common level of attractiveness as a customer and will receive the same amount of selling effort.

Glossary Terms

self-leadership The process of doing the right things and doing them well.

goals and objectives The things a salesperson sets out to accomplish.

personal goals A salesperson's individual desired accomplishment, such as achieving a desired annual income over a specific period.

territory goal A salesperson's desire to sell a certain amount of product within an area or territory to achieve personal goals.

account goal A salesperson's desire to sell a certain amount of product to one customer or account to achieve territory and personal goals.

sales call goal A salesperson's desire to sell a certain amount of product per each sales call to achieve account, territory, and personal goals.

territory analysis The process of surveying an area to determine customers and prospects who are most likely to buy.

account classification The process of placing existing customers and prospects into categories based on their sales potential.

single-factor analysis A method for analyzing accounts that is based on one single factor, typically the level of sales potential. Also called ABC analysis.

portfolio analysis A method for analyzing accounts that allows two factors to be considered simultaneously. Also called two-factor analysis.

sales planning The process of scheduling activities that can be used as a map for achieving objectives.

straight-line routing plan A territory routing plan in which salespeople start from their offices and make calls in one direction until they reach the end of the territory.

cloverleaf routing plan A territory routing plan in which the salesperson works a different part of the territory and travels in a circular loop back to the starting point.

circular routing plan A territory routing plan in which the salesperson begins at the office and moves in an expanding pattern of concentric circles that spiral across the territory.

leapfrog routing plan A territory routing plan in which, beginning in one cluster, the salesperson works each of the accounts at that location and then jumps to the next cluster.

major city routing plan A territory routing plan used when the territory is composed of a major metropolitan area and the territory is split into a series of geometric shapes reflecting each one's concentration and pattern of accounts.

selling technology and automation Tools that streamline the selling process, generate improved selling opportunities, facilitate cross-functional teaming and intra-organizational communication, and enhance communication and follow-up with customers.

mobile salesperson CRM solutions Wireless broadband applications that enable users to view, create, and modify data on any Internet-capable devices, such as smartphones, tablets, and laptops.

deal analytics "Smart" salesforce automation tools that analyze data on past customer behaviour, cross-selling opportunities, and demographics to identify areas of opportunity and high customer interest.

Internet A technology tool that instantly networks the salesperson with customers, information sources, other salespeople, sales management, and others.

intranets Secured networks within the organization that use the Internet or commercial channels to provide direct linkages between company units and individuals.

extranets A form of intranet that is still restricted but links to specific suppliers and customers to allow them controlled access to the organization's network and databases.

high-tech sales support offices Offices set up at multiple locations where salespeople can access a wider range of selling technology than could be easily carried on a notebook or laptop computer.

external relationships Relationships salespeople build with customers outside the organization and working environment.

internal relationships Relationships salespeople have with other individuals in their own company.

teamwork skills Skills salespeople must learn to build internal partnerships that translate into increased sales and organizational performance.

10-4 Interpret the usefulness of different types of selling technology and automation. Properly applied, selling technology spurs creativity and innovation, streamlines the selling process, generates new selling opportunities, facilitates communication, and enhances customer follow-up. Salespeople not only must master the technology itself but also must understand when and where it can be applied most effectively. A wide selection of different-sized computers is at the centre of most selling technologies. They provide the production tools for generating reports, proposals, and graphic-enhanced presentations. Spreadsheet applications and database applications facilitate the analysis of customer accounts and searching for information needed by customers. Contact management software enables the salesperson to gather and organize account information and schedule calls. Access to the Internet and World Wide Web provide salespeople with access to an assortment of public and corporate networks that enable them to communicate, research, and access company information and training from anywhere in the world. Using pagers and cell phones puts salespeople in touch with customers, the home office, and even family while travelling cross-country or just walking across the parking lot to make a customer call. Voice mail voids the previous restrictions of time and place that accompanied the requirement to make personal contact. Messages can now be left and received 24 hours a day and seven days a week. High-tech sales support offices provide geographically dispersed salespeople with a common standard of computing technology, access to software applications, and portals to organizational networks at offices around the world. Wherever they may be working, salespeople have the tools and capabilities identical to those available to them in their home offices.

10-5 Delineate six skills for building internal relationships and teams.

(a) *Understanding other individuals:* Fully understanding and considering the other individuals in the partnership is necessary for knowing what is important to them. What is important to them must also be important to the salesperson if the partnership is to grow and be effective.

(b) *Attending to the little things:* Little kindnesses and courtesies are small in size but great in importance. Properly attended to and nurtured, they enhance the interrelationships. However, when neglected or misused, they can destroy the relationship very quickly.

(c) *Keeping commitments:* We build hopes and plans around the promises and commitments made to us by others. When a commitment is not kept, disappointment and problems result and credibility and trust suffer major damage that will be difficult or impossible to repair.

(d) *Clarifying expectations:* The root cause of most relational difficulties can be found in ambiguous expectations regarding roles and goals. By clarifying goals and priorities, as well as who is responsible for different activities up front, the hurt feelings, disappointments, and lost time resulting from misunderstandings and conflict can be prevented.

(e) *Showing personal integrity:* Demonstrating personal integrity generates trust. Be honest, open, and treat everyone by the same set of principles.

(f) *Apologizing sincerely when a mistake is made:* It is one thing to make a mistake. It is another thing not to admit it. People forgive mistakes, but ill intentions and cover-ups can destroy trust.

Sales Management and Sales 2.0

Chapter Summary

11-1 Discuss the key considerations in developing and implementing effective sales strategies. A sales organization must look closely at blending the following basic concepts in designing an effective sales organization structure: specialization, centralization, span of control versus management levels, and line versus staff positions. Different decisions in any of these areas produce different sales organization structures. There is no one right sales structure. A good sales manager will look at the specific characteristics of a given selling situation to determine the appropriate structure. Sales managers and salespeople are generally responsible for strategic decisions at the account level. A sales strategy is designed to execute an organization's marketing strategy for individual accounts. The major purpose of a sales strategy is to develop a specific approach for selling to individual accounts within a target market. A sales strategy capitalizes on the important differences among individual accounts or groups of similar accounts. A firm's sales strategy is important for two reasons. First, it has a major impact on a firm's sales and profit performance. Second, it influences many other sales management decisions, such as recruitment, selection, training, compensation, and performance.

11-2 Understand the recruitment, selection, and training processes involved in developing the salesforce. Developing the salesforce involves recruiting and selecting sales talent, as well as training both new hires and those already on the salesforce. Recruitment and selection is a three-step process that involves planning for recruitment and selection, locating prospective candidates, and evaluating and hiring. After talent has been acquired, they must be properly trained. The training process involves six interrelated steps: (1) assessing sales training needs, (2) setting training objectives, (3) evaluating training alternatives, (4) designing the sales training program, (5) performing sales training, and (6) conducting follow-up and evaluation.

11-3 Identify key activities in directing the salesforce by leading, managing, supervising, motivating, and rewarding salespeople. Sales leadership includes activities that influence others to achieve shared goals to advance the organization. As shown in Exhibit 11.3, sales executives, sales managers, and salespeople can all be involved in sales leadership. Sales management focuses on planning, implementation, and control of the sales management process. Sales supervision involves working with subordinates on an ongoing basis. Sales managers may use one or more leadership styles, including transactional, transformational, and leader-member exchange (LMX) to direct the salesforce. In directing the salesforce, sales leaders should use power judiciously and rely on coaching as a primary communications and development tool.

11-4 Explain the different methods for evaluating the performance and effectiveness of sales organizations and individual salespeople. Sales organization effectiveness is a summary evaluation of the overall sales organization's success in meeting its performance goals and objectives in total and at different organizational levels. In contrast, salesperson performance is an evaluation of individual salesperson performance in individual situations. Evaluations of sales organization effectiveness provide important information for managers to use in strategic decision making and policy development. At the sales organization level, the most comprehensive type of performance evaluation is a sales organization audit, which is a systematic assessment of all aspects of a sales organization: the sales organization environment, sales management, planning system, and sales management functions. The performance and effectiveness of sales organizations are also assessed through more

Glossary Terms

sales management Managing an organization's personal selling function to include planning, implementing, and controlling the sales management process.

account targeting strategy The classification of accounts within a target market into categories for the purpose of developing strategic approaches for selling to each account or account group.

relationship strategy A determination of the type of relationship to be developed with different account groups.

selling strategy Involves the planning of sales messages and interactions with customers. Selling strategy can be defined at three levels: for a group of customers, that is, a sales territory; for individual customers; and for specific customer encounters, referred to as sales calls.

independent representatives or manufacturer representatives Independent sales organizations that sell complementary but noncompeting products from different manufacturers; also called manufacturer's representatives or reps.

team selling The use of multiple-person sales teams in dealing with multiple-person customer buying centres.

span of control The number of individuals who report to each sales manager.

job analysis An examination of the tasks, duties, and responsibilities of the sales job.

job qualifications Indicate the aptitude, skills, knowledge, personal traits, and willingness to accept occupational conditions to perform the job.

job description A written summary of the job.

assessment centre Systematic use of several assessment tools, such as presentations, role-playing exercises, group discussion, and business game simulations, to identify candidate strengths and weaknesses relative to job qualifications or for employee development.

background investigation References and others are contacted to verify information reported by the job candidate.

needs assessment Activities undertaken to determine the extent to which the members of the salesforce possess the skills, attitudes, perceptions, and behaviours required to be successful.

sales leadership Activities that influence others to achieve shared goals to advance the organization.

sales management Managing an organization's personal selling function to include planning, implementing, and controlling the sales management process.

sales supervision Sales managers working with subordinates, including salespeople and sales staff, on an ongoing basis.

field sales managers Sales managers who have salespeople reporting directly to them and who spend a considerable amount of time working with salespeople in their respective territories.

motivation Comprising three dimensions: intensity, persistence, and direction. Intensity is the amount of effort expended, persistence is the ongoing choice to expend effort, and direction refers to how salespeople spend their time on the job.

reward system management Selection and administration of organizational rewards to encourage salespeople to achieve organizational objectives.

leadership style A general orientation applied to leadership activities. Transactional and transformational leadership styles are two well-known leadership styles.

coaching Sales managers focus on continual development of salespeople through provision of feedback and serving as a role model.

sales organization effectiveness An overall assessment of how well the sales organization achieved its goals and objectives.

salesperson performance How well salespeople perform the activities necessary to carry out their sales responsibilities, as well as their results and contributions to organizational objectives.

sales organization audit A comprehensive, systematic approach for evaluating sales organization effectiveness, which provides management with diagnostic as well as prescriptive information.

sales analysis Examines the sales organization's past, current, and future sales performance in comparison with projections, competition, and industry sales.

cost analysis Assesses costs the sales organization incurs in the process of generating sales by comparing incurred costs with the planned costs in sales budgets.

profitability analysis Evaluates the results from combining sales and cost data to identify and assess sales organization profitability.

360-degree feedback Performance assessments of a salesperson from multiple sources having a relationship with the salesperson.

performance management A performance evaluation approach that involves sales managers and individual salespeople working together on setting goals, giving feedback, reviewing, and rewarding.

outcome-based evaluations Evaluation of the actual sales results salespeople achieve.

behaviour-based evaluations Evaluation of the activities salespeople perform in the generation of sales and in completing nonselling responsibilities.

behaviourally anchored rating scales (BARS) A performance evaluation method with the ability to link salesperson behaviours with specific outcomes and allow managers to indicate the level of behaviour a specific salesperson has achieved.

Sales 2.0 The use of customer-driven processes enabled by the latest Web technology to co-create value with customers.

social networking The ability to create, access, and interact with networks of contacts electronically.

cloud computing Combining applications, communications, and content into one digital cloud that can be easily accessed from many different devices.

FIGURE 11.1

Sales Management Process

Defining the Strategic Role of the Selling Function → Developing the Salesforce → Directing the Salesforce → Determining Salesforce Effectiveness and Performance

focused analysis methods, such as sales analysis, cost analysis, and profitability analysis, where comparisons are made to forecasts, quotas, previous time periods, and competitors. Salesperson evaluations are more tactical in nature and provide inputs in compensation, promotion, training, and motivation decisions designed to support and improve performance. Salesperson performance is commonly evaluated in terms of both outcome-based and behaviour-based assessments. Outcome-based appraisals examine the actual results achieved by a salesperson. Behaviour-based evaluations focus on the activities salespeople use in generating the sales outcomes. Sales managers use different methods to evaluate salesperson performance, including graphic ratings/checklists, rankings, objective-based methods, and behaviourally anchored rating scales (BARS). These methods allow for reliable and valid comparisons of salespeople across territories, selling units, and product types for the purpose of identifying problems, determining their causes, and suggesting sales management actions to solve them.

11-5 Describe how sales organizations are using Sales 2.0 to co-create value with customers. Sales 2.0 is the use of customer-driven processes enabled by the latest Web 2.0 technologies to co-create value with customers. The focus is on two-way, interactive communication between buyer and seller and the alignment of strategy, people, process, and technology. New Web 2.0 technologies are being introduced and employed by sales organizations to improve personal selling and sales management processes. Customer relationship management (CRM) and social networking technologies are being integrated and used in a variety of ways by sales organizations. The Sales 2.0 trend is growing and likely to expand in the future as new technologies are developed and applied by sales organizations.

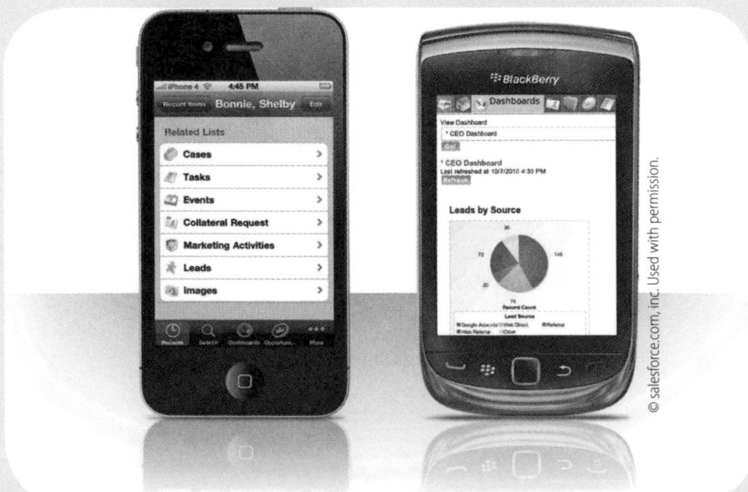

Web-based CRM products with mobile versions are useful to salespeople.

CHAPTER 1 CONTINUING CASE

Overview of Personal Selling

Introduction

The National Copier Company (NCC) sells a variety of copiers to small and medium-sized businesses. NCC has been in business for five years and has been growing at a steady pace. NCC differentiates itself from other copier companies by customizing its products to meet the specific needs of each customer and by providing excellent customer service. The company's salesforce plays a key role in creating value and managing customer relationships.

Brenda Smith has been an NCC salesperson for the past three years. She has steadily improved her sales performance during her time with NCC, and now she is in the top 25 percent of all NCC sales representatives as measured by two key metrics: overall sales volume and customer satisfaction. Brenda has been especially successful with small professional firms, such as attorneys, architects, accountants, and medical professionals. She is excited to begin her fourth year with NCC and has established challenging goals to increase sales from existing customers and to generate new customers.

Brenda recently met with Jin Tan, her sales manager, and was quite excited about the upcoming year. Jin had told Brenda that she was progressing toward a possible promotion into sales training if she had another good year in her sales position. In addition, Jin gave Brenda this feedback: "Brenda, I think you are doing a fine job with your customers, but I would like to see you become more of a consultative salesperson in the coming year. I would also like for you to sharpen your group communications skills, as that will be important if you are promoted into sales training. We will talk about the specifics more as the year goes along. Meanwhile, thanks for your results to date and good luck with the upcoming year."

Questions

1. Brenda had been thinking about Jin Tan's feedback that directed her to become more of a consultative salesperson. In thinking about her own selling approaches, she knew that she had been concentrating on the needs satisfaction and problem-solving approaches. What must Brenda do to become a more consultative salesperson?
2. Three months later, Brenda was having mixed results with the consultative selling approach. She was finding that some of her customers just wanted the convenience of having a copier in their offices and did not seem eager to discuss their strategic goals. She was beginning to wonder about the consultative selling model, thinking it was not such a good idea after all. What recommendations do you have for Brenda?
3. A month before the annual meeting for all NCC sales representatives, Jin Tan told Brenda, "For the upcoming meeting, I want you to prepare a 10-minute presentation about the pros and cons of the basic selling approaches that we use at NCC compared with our competitors." NCC's sales training program advocated the use of needs satisfaction, problem-solving, and consultative selling. Many of NCC's key competitors used the same approaches. However some of the toughest competitors used stimulus-response and mental states (AIDA) approaches. This latter category of competitors often stressed lower prices and used telemarketing instead of field sales representatives in selling their products. Put yourself in Brenda's role and prepare the presentation requested by Jin Tan.
4. Early in the year, Jin Tan told Brenda that her efforts were needed to gain more exposure for NCC's university recruiting program: "Brenda, I want you to be part of a two-person team to help with recruiting on two university campuses in your territory. The other team member will be an experienced recruiter who had sales experience before moving into recruiting. The two of you should seek out opportunities as guest speakers for classes and student organizations. Your role will be to talk about how sales can be a great place to start a career and for some, a great career path. Think about the future of selling and what it takes to be

successful and share your thoughts with students." Acting as Brenda, make note of ten key points you would like to make about the future of professional selling and what it takes to be successful. (*Hint:* Be sure you read the Appendix to Chapter 1 along with Chapter 1 before you undertake this task.)

Notes

CHAPTER 2 CONTINUING CASE

Building Trust and Sales Ethics: Developing Trust and Mutual Respect with Clients

Building Trust

Because the National Copier Company (NCC) has been in business for only five years, Brenda Smith is concerned that most of her competitors are older than she is. The prospective customers she has been calling on state they know they can count on her competitors, because they have a long track record. As NCC expands into new markets some of her prospects are not familiar with her company. One prospective customer, who works for one of the most prestigious and largest medical offices (30 doctors) in the area, told her he has been buying copiers from the same company for more than 25 years. He also told her his sales representative for the company has been calling on him for more than seven years, and he knows that when he calls on his copier supplier for advice, he can count on him for a solid recommendation. Brenda realizes these are going to be tough accounts to crack.

Brenda does have an advantage because of the high quality of NCC products. In a recent trade publication, NCC's copiers tied for first in the industry on ratings of copier quality and dependability. NCC was also given a high rating for service. Brenda has had this information for two weeks now and has brought it up in conversations with her prospective customers without much success. To make matters worse, one of her competitors must have started rumours about NCC. In the past month, she has heard the following rumours:

> "NCC is going out of business because of financial troubles."
>
> "NCC has missed several delivery deadlines with customers."
>
> "NCC's copiers have a software glitch that cannot be corrected."
>
> "NCC has cut its service staff."

Brenda knows these rumours are not true, but prospects might believe them. At a recent sales meeting, Brenda's manager suggested that their competitors must be getting nervous about NCC's success, causing them to tell those lies.

Brenda is sitting at her desk trying to figure out what to do next and she is not exactly sure how to proceed.

Questions

1. What would you recommend Brenda do to handle the challenges she faces?
2. Brenda appears to have an advantage with her products and services. Develop a plan for Brenda to build trust in NCC with prospective customers.
3. What do you recommend Brenda do to compete effectively against competitors that have a long and successful track record?
4. How should Brenda go about handling the rumour mill?

CHAPTER 3 CONTINUING CASE

Understanding Buyers

Understanding Tom Penders

It was Monday afternoon and Brenda Smith was very excited. She had just got off the phone with Tom Penders, the administrator in charge of a large medical office in her territory. After an introductory letter and several follow-up phone calls, Tom Penders had finally agreed to meet with Brenda next Friday to discuss the possibility of replacing his organization's old copiers, as well as adding new copiers to keep pace with his organization's rapid growth. The primary purpose of the meeting was for Tom to learn more about the National Copier Company (NCC) and its products and for Brenda to learn more about Tom's company and its specific needs.

When Brenda arrived about 10 minutes early for her meeting with Tom Penders at the medical offices on Friday, she was greeted by a receptionist who asked her to be seated. Ten minutes passed and Brenda was promptly shown to Tom's office. Brenda couldn't help but notice how organized Tom's office was. It appeared to Brenda that Tom was a man of detail. First, Tom explained that the medical offices housed more than 30 doctors specializing in a variety of fields. They occupied two floors and were planning to expand to the vacant third floor in the near future. Currently, they were organized into five divisions with an office professional assigned to approximately six doctors for each division. Each division ran its own office with a separate copier and administrative facilities. Tom also had an assistant and a copier. After giving his overview, Tom provided Brenda with an opportunity to ask questions. After that, Tom systematically went down a list of questions he had about NCC, its products, and Brenda herself. Following this, Tom had his assistant take Brenda on a tour of the facility so she could overview their processes. Before leaving, Tom agreed to meet with Brenda in two weeks.

Based on her conversation with Tom, Brenda did not find Tom to be a particularly personable individual. In fact, she found him to be somewhat cool and aloof, deliberate both in his communication and his actions. Yet Tom was willing to learn how NCC could help his medical office. Although Brenda preferred communicating with someone more personable and open, such as herself, she was determined to find a way to win Tom's business.

Questions

1. What type of communication style do you believe that Tom exhibits? What are the characteristics of this communication style?
2. Based on your understanding of Tom's communication style, outline a plan for selling to Tom Penders.
3. Identify other members of Tom Penders' organization that may play a role in the buying decision and explain the role they might play. How should Brenda handle these individuals?
4. Explain the types of buyer needs that will be most important in this selling situation.

CHAPTER 4 CONTINUING CASE

Communication Skills

Sharpening the Selling Tools

Brenda Smith is working in the office this morning preparing for tomorrow's sales call with Gage Waits, managing partner, and Tanisha Autry, operations manager, at Energy-Based Funds LLC. Energy-Based Funds is a major investment banking organization specializing in managing and marketing a variety of energy-based mutual funds. The company operates throughout Canada and employs 175 people, with offices occupying the top three floors of a major office building in the heart of the financial district. For the past several years, Energy-Based Funds has been leasing and purchasing office equipment from Altima Systems, one of Brenda's biggest competitors. Brenda has been working her network to get a chance to begin a sales dialogue with Energy-Based Funds and she finally has an appointment with the main players on the purchasing team: Gage and Tanisha.

Brenda knows that planning is a key part of success in selling and is diligently working on her strategy and plans in preparation for tomorrow's sales call with Gage and Tanisha at Energy-Based Funds. According to the sales call plan that Brenda is developing, the purpose of this initial meeting is twofold: (1) to discover more about Energy-Based Funds' current operations, their future plans, and the nature of their use of and needs for copiers; (2) to begin acquainting Gage and Tanisha with NCC and the value they can provide Energy-Based Funds. At this point in her sales call plan, Brenda is considering the different pieces of information she needs to get from the dialogue and what questions she might use to elicit that information from Gage and Tanisha.

Questions

1. Based on the purpose of probing questions explained in your text, explain how Brenda should use probing types of questions in her initial sales dialogue with Gage and Tanisha at Energy-Based Funds. Consider the types of information Brenda needs and develop several illustrative examples of probing questions Brenda might use.
2. Evaluative questions are also effective in sales conversations. Explain the purpose of evaluative questions and how Brenda might effectively use them in this initial sales call. Provide several illustrative examples of evaluative questions Brenda could use.
3. The ADAPT questioning system is a logic-based sequence of questions designed for effective fact-finding and gaining information about a buyer's situation. Develop a series of ADAPT questions that Brenda might use in her sales call to develop the information she needs regarding Energy-Based Funds, their operations, and their needs for copiers.
4. What recommendations would you give Brenda regarding nonverbal communication and how she might use it for more effective communication in this sales call?

CHAPTER 5 CONTINUING CASE

Strategic Prospecting and Preparing for Sales Dialogue

Fishing for New Customers

Brenda Smith has been very successful at getting existing customers to upgrade or purchase new copiers during the past two months. She is, however, disappointed in her efforts to get new customers. To add more new customers, Brenda has been spending a great deal of time prospecting. These efforts have produced a large number of leads. Once she generates a lead, she contacts the firm and tries to set up an appointment. Unfortunately, most of these leads are not interested in talking about copiers and are not willing to schedule a meeting with her. This has been so frustrating that she decided to make several cold calls this week to see if this would be a good way to get to meet with prospective customers. The cold calls were also not very successful and were extremely time consuming. Brenda did finally get a few leads to agree to meet with her, but these appointments were not very productive. The leads were typically satisfied with the copiers they were using and were not interested in learning about NCC copiers.

Jin Tan, her sales manager, accompanied her on a recent sales call to a lead. After the sales call, Jin expressed his disappointment that they had really wasted their time with this meeting. Jin then asked Brenda about her prospecting process, because it was clear that she was not identifying and spending her time with the best sales opportunities. Her approach was not working well and was taking a lot of time. If she continued doing the same things, Brenda was not likely to generate many new customers and might lose some existing customers, because she was spending too much of her time prospecting.

Brenda realizes that she must improve her prospecting process, but she is not sure exactly how to proceed.

Questions

1. What is Brenda doing wrong? What would you recommend Brenda do to improve her prospecting efforts?
2. Explain the strategic prospecting process to Brenda and discuss how she can implement it.
3. What secondary lead sources would you recommend Brenda use to identify the best attorneys, architects, accountants, and medical professionals as prospects?
4. What specific types of information should Brenda obtain before contacting a qualified prospect?

CHAPTER 6 CONTINUING CASE

Planning Sales Dialogues and Presentations

Custom Product, Custom Presentation

During the past three months, Brenda has improved her prospecting process. She is identifying more prospects that represent better sales opportunities. Brenda knows that it is important to plan her sales calls in advance to maximize the time she spends in face-to-face selling. In this selling environment, most customers are not interested in all the features of Brenda's products. Brenda has to determine what is important to each customer and customize her presentations accordingly. Further, she has to clearly communicate the benefits of her products and not overwhelm potential buyers with too much technical language. Assume that Brenda has an appointment with EFP, a nonprofit organization that raises money to promote environmentally friendly practices such as recycling. The organization uses e-mail, Web-based communications, and direct mail campaigns to reach potential donors. EFP currently uses an older-generation analogue copier. Brenda hopes to sell EFP a modern digital copier that offers several advantages over the analogue copier currently in use.

Questions

1. Using an Internet search engine, such as Google, find the general benefits of digital copiers over analogue copiers. You might enter "benefits of digital copiers" in the search engine, or examine data from copier providers, such as Ricoh, Canon, or Xerox, to find these benefits. List six to eight potential benefits of a digital copier to EFP.
2. From the listing developed in question 1, select four benefits. For each benefit, write a sentence or two that Brenda might use to communicate these benefits during her sales call with EFP.
3. For the four benefits identified in question 2, describe what information Brenda should have on hand when she makes the sales call on the EFP buyer. Also describe how this information would be best communicated—that is, what support materials will Brenda need to enhance her verbal communications?
4. Assume that the buyer acknowledges interest in at least two of benefits identified in question 2. Write a realistic buyer–seller dialogue of Brenda's interaction with the EFP buyer concerning these benefits.

CHAPTER 7 CONTINUING CASE

Sales Dialogue: Creating and Communicating Value

Up for the Challenge

Brenda has a meeting today with the office manager at the law firm Arseneau and Wilson (A&L). A&L is a local law firm with five attorneys and one main office. During her initial telephone conversation, the office manager indicated that the firm was reasonably satisfied with their current copiers but that he was always looking for ways to increase office productivity. He also mentioned that he was a little concerned that the firm was paying for many copier features that were not really used. The law firm needed to make a lot of legal-sized copies and be able to collate and staple them. There was little need for other "bells and whistles." It was also important that a copier was dependable, because the law firm made many copies each day. When the copier did break down, fast service was needed to get it repaired as soon as possible.

The office manager had some familiarity with NCC products and was eager to talk to Brenda. However, he made it clear that any decision to switch to NCC copiers would require that Brenda also meet with the attorneys and office personnel to get their approval. If Brenda convinced him that NCC copiers would increase office productivity at the law firm, he would be glad to set up a meeting for her with the attorneys and office personnel.

Brenda is excited about this opportunity. She knows that NCC copiers are very dependable and that NCC provides exceptional service. She can also offer the law firm a copier with the specific features A&L needs.

Questions

1. Prepare the sales dialogue Brenda might employ and use an anecdote to communicate the dependability of NCC copiers to the office manager.
2. Brenda will not be able to demonstrate a copier during this sales call. Describe the types of sales aids she should use to show the buyer an NCC copier with the exact features they need.
3. How can Brenda best use statistics and testimonials to support the excellent service provided by NCC?
4. Brenda did a terrific job in her sales call with the office manager. He is interested in NCC copiers and has scheduled a meeting for Brenda with the five attorneys and the office personnel. Discuss the major things Brenda should do during her sales call to this group.

CHAPTER 8 CONTINUING CASE

Addressing Concerns and Earning Commitment

Handling Sales Resistance

Brenda recently returned from a two-week training session that focused on how to handle sales resistance and how to earn commitment. Brenda has become quite familiar with the ADAPT questioning system and knows she must use assessment questions to allow the buyer to describe their present situation. She has also developed a pretty good set of discovery questions that helps her identify the buyer's needs and problems. Her challenge has been what to do with this information. Whenever Brenda attempts to use features and benefits to make her case, she encounters myriad objections. Brenda knows she has great products and service, but she has not been able to communicate this effectively to her prospects.

The objection she hears most often is, "I've never heard of your company. How long have you been in business?" If that is not bad enough, she heard the following objections in just one morning:

> "I'm not sure I am ready to buy at this time. I'll need to think it over."
>
> "Your company is pretty new. How do I know you'll be around to take care of me in the future?"
>
> "Your price is a little higher than I thought it would be."
>
> "Your company was recently in the news. Are you having problems?"
>
> "I think your company is too small to meet our needs."

Brenda hears most of these objections right after she attempts to earn a commitment. She is now getting a little reluctant about asking her prospects for the order.

Brenda is sitting at her desk trying to figure out what to do next. She is not sure how to proceed.

Questions

1. What would you recommend Brenda do to handle the challenges she faces?
2. Brenda appears to have an advantage with her products and services. Develop a plan for Brenda to overcome the sales resistance she is receiving.
3. Use the LAARC process to develop a suggested dialogue Brenda can use to address one of the major types of resistance she is receiving.
4. What can Brenda do in the future to encounter less sales resistance when she asks for the order?

CHAPTER 9 CONTINUING CASE

Expanding Customer Relationships

The Disgruntled Customer

It was 8:30 a.m. Friday morning when Brenda received the voice mail. It was Susan Swanson, owner of a small architecture firm, who Brenda had acquired as a customer nearly three months ago. "I'm finished with you all," she barked. "Come get my copier. I want my money back! This blasted machine you sold me keeps jamming. I was billed for extra toner that I never received. You promised me training, and I have yet to see any. And this machine is much slower than I thought it would be. I don't see how your company stays in business. I knew I should have gone with Xerox!"

It's true, Brenda had told Susan that she would provide training on how to use some of the advanced features of the copier. She had neglected to get back to Susan and since she had not heard from Susan she assumed Susan no longer desired the training. As for the paper jams, Brenda found this to be unusual. NCC carried high-quality copiers and she could not imagine what might be wrong. She was sure she had told Susan the specific type of paper to use for her application. However, using the wrong paper could lead to more frequent paper jams. But why hadn't Susan said anything to her about this sooner? As for the extra toner, Brenda recalls that Susan did order it and later contacted her to let her know that she had not received it. Brenda then contacted NCC's shipping department who said they would ship Susan the product. Brenda just assumed that it had been shipped. As for the speed of the machine, Brenda was certain its output was per specifications as equipment at NCC must pass strict quality control measures. Perhaps Susan simply misunderstood the machine's capabilities. *Wow*, Brenda thought, *now what am I going to do?*

Questions

1. How should Brenda handle this complaint?
2. What could Brenda have done to avoid this incident?
3. What steps can Brenda take to do a better job of maintaining open, two-way communication with Susan?
4. Assuming that Brenda can retain Susan as a customer, how can she add value to her relationship with Susan's firm?

CHAPTER 10 CONTINUING CASE

Adding Value: Self-Leadership and Teamwork

Managing and Classifying Accounts

Brenda's planning and extra effort in servicing and developing her accounts continue to produce increasing levels of profitable business for NCC. Her methodical approach to identifying new prospects and building repeat business within her existing accounts has been observed by her sales manager as well as the regional vice president of sales. As a result of Brenda's consistent performance, she has been given the opportunity to expand her current list of accounts by taking over part of the account list of a retiring salesperson and integrating them into an expanded territory. Brenda is working through the account information files for each of these added accounts and has summarized the information into the following table.

Account Name	Account Opportunity	Competitive Position	Annual Number of Sales Calls (Last Year)
Maggie Mae Foods	Low	High	23
C^3 Industries	High	Low	28
Trinity Engineering	High	High	28
Britecon Animations	High	High	22
Lost Lake Foods	High	Low	26
Attaway Global Consulting	High	High	24
Waits and Sons	Low	High	21
Reidell Business Services	High	High	26
Ferrell & Associates	Low	Low	16
Biale Beverage Corp	High	High	18
Captain Charlie's Travel	High	Low	23
Cole Pharmaceuticals	High	Low	20
PuddleJumper Aviation	Low	High	18
Tri-Power Investment Services	Low	Low	18
Ballou Resin & Plastics	Low	Low	14
Tri-Chem Customer Products	Low	High	20
Guardian Products	High	High	25
Bartlesville Specialties	Low	High	26

Questions

1. Develop a portfolio classification of Brenda's 18 new accounts. What is your assessment of the allocation of sales calls made by Brenda's predecessor over the previous year?
2. What specific suggestions would you make in terms of sales call allocation strategy for Brenda to make better use of available selling time in calling on these new accounts?
3. Develop a classification of these 18 accounts by using the single-factor analysis method. How do these results differ from the results from the portfolio analysis?
4. How might the differences between the single-factor analysis and the portfolio classification translate to increased selling effectiveness and efficiency for Brenda?

CHAPTER 11 CONTINUING CASE

Sales Management and Sales 2.0

The Finish Line

It is two weeks before the end of the fiscal year for NCC. Brenda has already achieved her annual sales quota and is pleased with her performance this year. She knows that she has improved her sales skills and is doing a good job in each stage of the sales process. Her sales manager, Jin Tan, will be working with her in the field this week and then will be conducting her annual performance review and discussing it with her within the next month.

Jin Tan and Brenda have just completed a sales call together. Although Brenda did not get the sale, she thought she did a good job and thinks the prospect might contact her in the future about NCC copiers. Jin Tan, however, is disappointed that Brenda did not move the sales process forward. Although the prospect was not necessarily expected to buy during this presentation, Jin thought Brenda missed an opportunity to get the prospect to visit the NCC office for a copier demonstration. This would have moved the sales process forward.

Jin was also thinking about the annual performance reviews next month. This is always a tense time. Jin is generally satisfied with Brenda's performance last year and with her development as a salesperson. But, as indicated in the recent sales call, she needs to improve her skills in gaining commitment. Brenda could also be more productive if she became more proficient in using some of the new sales 2.0 technologies, especially LinkedIn. These are two areas Jin will address during the annual performance review meeting with Brenda.

Questions

1. Jin and Brenda have just finished the joint sales call and are meeting for a coaching session. Present an example of the dialogue that should take place during this meeting.
2. Develop a sales training program Jin might use to improve Brenda's skills in gaining commitment from prospects.
3. Explain to Brenda how she might use LinkedIn to increase her sales productivity.
4. Jin and Brenda are getting ready to have their annual performance meeting. How should Jin conduct this meeting to motivate Brenda to increase her performance next year?

Notes

Notes

Notes

Notes